The Piano Handbook

Carl Humphries

Preface

Welcome to *The Piano Handbook*, a new kind of book that aims to introduce you to all aspects of the piano, and piano playing, in a single volume. The piano has emerged as the most exciting and important medium for creative music-making in our culture. As a result, it has a uniquely rich musical heritage. I've tried to reflect that richness in this book, on several levels.

Firstly, although *The Piano Handbook* is primarily a tutor, to be used either for self-study or with a teacher, it gives you the world of the piano as a whole. It guides you through the process of learning to play in a wide range of traditional and modern styles. It introduces the piano's enormous repertoire, and the vast choice of recordings available by great players. And it directs you to the many books written on more specialised aspects of the subject. It also tells the story of the evolution of the piano and its impact on western musical culture. In short, it aims to give you the broadest possible foundations for your own personal exploration of this wonderful instrument.

Secondly, *The Piano Handbook* takes a completely new approach to learning the piano, intended to reflect its special characteristics. The amazing versatility of the instrument – its ability to bring complex music within the grasp of the individual player – has made it central, not just for performers but for composers. That's why playing and composing have repeatedly come together on the piano to produce exciting approaches that treat playing itself as creative, in live performance as improvisation and in the privacy of the composer's studio. In this book, you'll learn to play, compose and improvise side by side, and you'll see how closely related these aspects really are.

Thirdly, this approach means you'll be able to compare and contrast techniques used by classical masters like Bach and Mozart with those of jazz and rock greats like Bill Evans or Jerry Lee Lewis. You'll also discover that those techniques are there for you to use in your own way, to help you unlock your own creative and musical potential. In other words, you'll learn about each different style in a way that take it on its own terms, giving it the respect it deserves as a culture or genre. That leaves you free to choose the elements you wish to take further, as you discover more about your own strengths and interests.

The approach I've taken in this book reflects my experience over many years as a player, composer and teacher. I've found that the best way to learn is generally to begin with things you *want* to learn. Too many modern teachers force young people to struggle with music they can't relate to, and which offers few obvious opportunities for self-expression and realising one's creative potential. It's one reason young people reject active involvement with their own musical heritage, in favour of Walkmans and computer games. Teachers are left trying to lure them back with watered-down imitations of popular musical styles that are actually less creative than the classical music that drove them away in the first place. Perhaps you have experienced something like this.

By contrast, *The Piano Handbook* encourages you to approach each and every style of music seriously: that is, in its own way. In other words, if you're going to play jazz, you've got to learn about scales, voicings, and soloing, so you can improvise alongside real jazz musicians. If you're going to play classical, you need to master classical technique and phrasing and understand the culture in which great masterpieces of the past were created. If 20th century music interests you, there's no substitute for learning to analyse and play challenging composers such as Schoenberg or

Bartok. Meanwhile, experimental free improvisation will require that you think about new ways of connecting up musical gesture and performance with other disciplines like physical theatre and performance and movement studies. And if you're interested in the latest dance-house groove, you'll want to see how sequenced drum-machine break-beats or Afro-American drumming techniques can be transformed into exciting piano textures. It's all here between the covers of *The Piano Handbook*.

That doesn't mean that the book is just a pick'n'mix of different styles, crammed into a single volume. It's not. It has become fashionable to assume that different cultures have nothing substantial in common: that the best they can hope for is to exist alongside one another in the isolated ghettos of our multicultural society, with only chaotic and random interactions. This view has dominated music education in the western world over the last few decades, but its limitations have become increasingly apparent to those who work in the field.

I've decided to challenge that approach, not just by looking at concrete historical connections between different musical cultures and languages, but also by focusing on the deeper organic and structural similarities between different kinds of music. All music reflects basic human resources and concerns: not just how we think and feel, but also how we hear, how our bodies get involved in playing and responding, and how our own playing and the music we relate to unfold in time itself.

One consequence of this is that in *The Piano Handbook* you're encouraged to develop musical *awareness* by thinking about issues critically for yourself. The aim is not just to see how different styles of music reflect the same deeper forces, but to grasp what that might mean for your own involvement as a player and creative individual. To help, I've recommended a wide range of books in the reference section, designed to deepen your critical understanding of music.

There's a full-length tutorial section, intended for older children and adults who want to move rapidly through the earlier stages of learning the piano to a level where they can take advantage of the rich repertoire of the instrument. Focusing on laying the foundations of a sound technique, the book combines established methods with the latest thinking about instrumental learning. You'll find quite a few of the best-loved classics of the piano repertoire, alongside newly composed study-pieces and exercises designed to illustrate and tackle the major points of technique and interpretation. There are often pointers to additional related pieces for learning, and exercises to practise, if you want to proceed at a more relaxed pace. As you progress, you'll come across sections dealing with improvisation, jazz and other non-classical styles, and the fundamentals of music theory and composition. These explain how and why melody, harmony and form work differently in various types of music. The outcome is a graded course that I hope will be enjoyable and challenging in new and exciting ways.

The piano as an instrument has always been about individuals finding uniquely rich ways to realise their potential as musicians. You could even say that's why the instrument was invented and developed in the first place. It's certainly what I've designed *The Piano Handbook* to prepare you for. But it also means that the really important things in your experience of piano playing aren't going to come from this or any book. They will come directly from you.

CARL HUMPHRIES 2002

Contents

The Piano Handbook

Carl Humphries

A BACKBEAT BOOK

First edition 2002

Published by Backbeat Books

600 Harrison Street,

San Francisco, CA 94107, US

www.backbeatbooks.com

An imprint of The Music Player Network United
Entertainment Media Inc.

Published for Backbeat Books by Outline Press Ltd,
115j Cleveland Street, London W1T 6PU, England

ISBN 0-87930-727-7

Art Director: Nigel Osborne

Design: Paul Cooper

Editorial Director: Tony Bacon

Editor: John Morrish

Photography: Miki Slingsby

Production: Phil Richardson

Origination by Global Graphics (Czech Republic)

Print by Colorprint Offset Ltd (Hong Kong)

08 09 8 7 6

The Story
of the
Piano

THE ORIGINS OF THE INSTRUMENT

The piano could be said to stand at the centre of the traditions of western music that have flourished in the last few centuries. As an instrument, it epitomises the role that technological sophistication has played in western music's attempt to develop a rich language without sacrificing expressive control or creative freedom.

Like other keyboard instruments (such as harpsichords and organs), the piano allows an individual player to create melody, harmony and texture all at once, unfolding the complex structures of western music in the process. At the same time, the piano retains a large element of the physically expressive control over sound that is natural to singing and playing but missing from other keyboard instruments.

This combination of factors has enabled the piano to become the central instrument of western music, both for virtuoso performers, composers, and improvisers, and for ordinary people making music in their own homes, where it remains easily the most mechanically complex piece of equipment to be found.

The piano uses small hammers that strike the strings inside and bounce off, leaving the strings to vibrate freely. This mechanism has its origins in early forms of zither – an instrument that dates back to the Bronze Age – in which strings stretched between sticks or over a wooden board are struck or plucked. Later the zither developed considerably, thanks to the addition of a resonating chamber and moveable bridges that could alter the pitch of the note, as on the monochords used by ancient Greeks in their early experiments with the mathematics of musical tuning and harmony. Sophisticated examples of zither still in use include the Japanese koto and Hungarian cimbalom.

The first zithers arrived in Europe from the Middle East in the 11th century as portable instruments (psalteries). From these the dulcimer evolved – the first such instrument with metal strings specifically designed to be struck by small hammers. The dulcimer became an important precursor of the expressive control over volume offered by the modern piano. Taken up and developed in the late 17th

Playing the spinet

Christina Antonio Somis playing a small octave spinet in the mid-18th century. Other members of Somis's family play violin and cello.

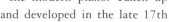

Bentside spinet

The spinet (above), the virginal and the harpsichord (right) produce their distinctive sounds by means of mechanically plucked strings. The spinet pictured is a wing-shaped model known as a "bentside" type, with strings running obliquely to the keyboard. The instrument was made in London in 1742 by Joseph Mahoon.

Virginal
The virginal was an early keyboard instrument. This one was produced in Italy in the 1660s and, given its lavish decoration, was probably made for a wealthy customer.

century by Pantaleon Hebenstreit, a virtuosic German player, the dulcimer showed the exciting possibilities of having a struck stringed instrument where volume could be freely and dramatically varied.

Although the Greeks are thought to have used a primitive form of water-organ that operated rather like a keyboard, the hurdy-gurdy (or organistrum) was probably the first stringed instrument to use a keyboard, appearing around the 10th century. This used a wheel that was turned by hand to stroke the strings, making a continuous sound, while simple levers (keys) caused small anvils to press against the string at different points along its length, altering the pitch.

Over the next few centuries, primitive pipe organs were also developed, with the pipes activated by sliders in turn controlled from identical handles (which had to be marked with identifying letters). These eventually became the pivoted keys that remain a feature of modern keyboards: black keys were gradually added in the 13th and 14th centuries. A fusion of this type of keyboard arrangement with the string-based sustaining mechanism of the hurdy-gurdy appeared in the 17th century. Known as the geigenwerck, it looked rather like a harpsichord.

By the 15th century, the keyed monochord and polychord had appeared, and it was from the latter that the clavichord most probably evolved. The compass of the keyboard on this and other keyboard instruments was significantly expanded during the 16th century, from two octaves to four-and-a-half. This process continued with the development of harpsichords, and then pianos, through to six-octave instruments at the end of the 18th century. The modern piano keyboard has a compass of 88 notes, covering a little over seven octaves.

Alongside the clavichord, whose existence was first reported in 1404, there

Clavichord
Clavichords were important early keyboard instruments; the one pictured below is German and dates from the early 1800s. Pictured above is its action, or playing mechanism. It employed a metal "tangent" at the end of each key to strike the string and make it vibrate.

emerged a family of keyboard instruments with mechanically plucked strings: the harpsichord, virginals and spinet. These used a sophisticated mechanism (the 'jack') to pluck the strings and then damp them when the key was released. They differ from one another in shape, size and arrangement of strings.

The clavichord, spinet and virginals, though extremely popular, were too quiet to be effective outside of small domestic gatherings. By contrast the harpsichord was expanded to produce a bigger sound, with the strings running perpendicular to the keyboard (in the same direction as the keys) and with several strings for each note, sometimes tuned to different octaves. Stops were introduced to create a crude sense of dynamic contrast, either by lifting all the dampers away from the strings at once (producing more resonance through sympathetic vibration of strings) or by keeping them partially in contact with the strings as the notes sounded.

In spite of its popularity and suitability for concert use throughout the 17th and 18th centuries, the harpsichord could not provide the dynamic control of individual notes offered by the dulcimer or even the clavichord. That meant demand for a concert keyboard instrument with real dynamic control remained unsatisfied, paving the way for the introduction of the piano.

Double-manual harpsichord

For greater musical versatility, extra keyboards ("manuals") were added to some harpsichords from the 17th century. This two-manual model replicates a 1638 Ruckers original.

CHRISTOFORI'S BRILLIANT INVENTION

By the end of the 17th century, three types of keyboard instrument were in use: organs, the harpsichord family, and clavichords. None offered the sort of dynamic response that would allow keyboard players to achieve the subtle expressive contrasts of volume being demonstrated by other performers, such as violinists and string orchestras.

The first instruments recognisable today as pianos were built by Bartolomeo Cristofori, the keeper of instruments at the Florentine court, at the turn of the 18th century. He built only a small number of pianos, but brilliantly solved the technical problems posed by an instrument in which strings have to be struck by hammers. But his results were practically ignored by the musicians of his own time in Italy.

A visitor to Cristofori described the resulting instrument as a "gravicembalo col piano e forte" (a harpsichord with soft and loud), and it is from this that the modern piano takes its name. (Piano is short for pianoforte: some early instruments are known as fortepianos.) In spite of the lack of interest, Cristofori continued to refine his piano action, even developing the una corda mechanism that corresponds to the left-hand pedal on modern pianos. He used a hand stop to direct the hammer at just one of the two strings used for each note. He also discovered that longer, thicker strings would produce more tone, providing that the strings could be securely maintained under a greater tension. That meant strengthening the case and altering the way the tuning pins were mounted in the wooden block that supported them.

Cristofori's greatest stroke of genius was his development of the escapement mechanism, whereby the single downward movement of the key is converted into

Playing the harpsichord

A musical scene painted by Edith Hipkins in 1885 shows a woman playing a harpsichord. (The instrument at the back of her chair is a cittern.)

Cristofori piano
This instrument was made by the man who virtually invented the piano, Bartolomeo Cristofori. He made this grand piano in Florence, Italy, in 1722.

Cristofori action
This sequence (below) illustrates the action of a 1726 Cristofori piano. The design is remarkably sophisticated considering it was the first of its type, though Cristofori went on to improve it.

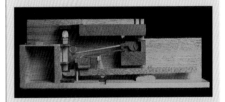

two distinct movements of the hammer: upwards to hit the string, then immediately back down again so that the string is left free to vibrate. The trick was to let the hammer (and its shank) 'escape' from the rest of the mechanism, so that it was free to rebound and fall back down (with gravity) on hitting the string, even if the piano key remained depressed. It was no longer connected to the part of the piano mechanism controlled by the keys.

In terms of tonal character, the pianos of Cristofori bear little resemblance to the instruments of today. The sound is much more delicate and projects less than that of the harpsichord, and the touch is extremely light, owing to the small size of the hammers. Nevertheless, they do achieve a real dynamic range while being considerably more powerful than the clavichord.

ACCLAIM FOR THE NEW INSTRUMENT
In the early decades of the 18th century a number of instrument manufacturers in France and Germany, inspired by the success of Hebenstreit and working independently of Cristofori, experimented with actions that used hammers to strike strings. None of these really took off until Gottfried Silbermann came across a description of Cristofori's instruments and attempted to recreate their design, developing his own version of the piano action, known as Prellmechanik.

In 1736 Silbermann showed his instruments to the greatest German composer of the time, Johann Sebastian Bach, who was impressed but stated that the action was heavy and the upper register weak. After many years of refinement Silbermann once again presented one of his pianos, this time in Potsdam at the court of Frederick the

Great (King Frederick II of Prussia), a keen music enthusiast and amateur composer. This time the instrument was acclaimed.

It is probably no coincidence that the court composer in Potsdam for many years was Carl Phillip Emmanuel Bach, the most original composer amongst the elder Bach's numerous sons, and the one who did more than anyone else to found the modern school of keyboard playing. C.P.E. Bach's intensely dramatic, emotionally involved, and highly adventurous approach to keyboard composing and extemporising reflected the new penchant for emotionalism (Empfindsamkeit) in German culture. Although his music was probably principally conceived for the harpsichord, it laid the foundations for the pianistic styles of Mozart, Haydn and Beethoven, as well as for the subsequent role of the piano as the instrument on which composing and improvising most fully overlap and interact. It retained this role throughout the 19th century and, through jazz, into the 20th century.

Silbermann's Prellmechanik action was taken up and developed by Johann Andreas Stein, who added his own escapement (zunge) to produce the Prellzungenmechanik or 'German action'. This became popular with German manufacturers and was later modified (with the addition of a check mechanism) to become the Viennese action in pianos used by many of the great composers of the classical period, such as Mozart and Haydn. By contrast, Cristofori's later action (which came to be known as Stosszungemechanik) influenced the 'English action' (known in its earliest pre-escapement forms simply as Stossmechanik) to form the basis of subsequent developments in English piano design.

The Seven Years War, which broke out in Germany in 1756, drove many piano manufacturers to England, including Americus Backers and Johannes Zumpe, who both sought to develop the possibilities of Cristofori's action. Zumpe developed a square piano with a simplified action (without an escapement) that could be built

Music by Carl Philip Emmanuel Bach.

Zumpe square piano

Probably invented in Germany in the early 1740s, the square piano rose to fame some 20 years later in England. It was smaller and more practical than the grand piano, with strings at right angles to the keys, and sold in large numbers, paving the way for the piano's coming popularity. The square piano shown here was made in London in 1769 by Johannes Zumpe and Gabriel Buntebart.

Beyer square piano
Almost contemporary with the example pictured opposite, this square piano was made in London by Adam Beyer in 1777. The footpedal raised and lowered part of the lid to provide some control over the instrument's volume and tone. The brass hand-stops (left) allowed various damping effects.

English single action
This system, shown in the sequence of two steps below, was developed from Cristofori's original action by Johannes Zumpe around 1760. It featured a jack, or pilot, that linked the key with the hammer.

English double action
Zumpe also pioneered this system, which was patented by Geib in 1786. The action, shown in sequence below, introduced an intermediate lever for escapement, allowing rapid repetition of notes.

easily at a lower cost than harpsichords. It was soon in huge demand in London, especially after J.C. Bach gave the first acclaimed public recital on the instrument in London, featuring his own works, probably the first to be composed specifically for the instrument. Zumpe marketed his instrument effectively, aiming it at the middle classes rather than the aristocracy, and keeping the casework simple with this in mind. Later models of square piano tended to be more ornate, however.

John Broadwood also began to build square pianos around the 1770s, and quickly produced an enhanced version, featuring underdamping (dampers below rather than above the strings) and a sustaining pedal: two important distinguishing features of the modern piano. However, as the demand grew for more tonal power and projection, it became necessary to increase the length and tension of the strings. This eventually forced Broadwood to develop an iron hitch pin plate that could be installed above the soundboard. By 1821 his firm had managed to build the first square piano with such a feature.

However, it was the grand piano that emerged as the principal concert instrument as the 19th century progressed. At the same time, the increasing size of the square piano eventually led to its replacement as a domestic instrument by the upright, since people wanted smaller instruments for their homes.

SUBTLETY OR POWER?

Vienna dominated the musical life of Europe from the late 18th century through to the early decades of the 19th century. The ruling Habsburgs were enthusiastic patrons of the arts, including music, and so artists and those with related skills were drawn to the city. Vienna became another focus for the piano industry, like London, but the sort of instruments that emerged in the two cities were quite different, as they rested on contrasting types of action: on one hand the 'Viennese' action, on the other the 'English' action.

Like London, Vienna attracted a number of German piano makers, and many of these adopted Stein's improved escapement action (Prellzungenmechanik), in which hammers are prevented from bouncing back up and restriking strings by the introduction of checks. This type of action continued to be used by numerous German makers right up to the start of the 20th century.

The sound of these Viennese grand pianos is much lighter and more delicate than that of modern instruments, and this can sometimes shed light on the musical intentions of the great Viennese composers such as Mozart, Haydn and Beethoven.

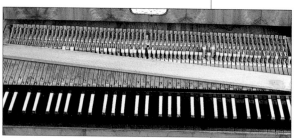

By the 1780s, the English and Viennese grand pianos had become quite distinct as instruments. The former has a lighter construction and is normally double-strung. The latter is usually triple-strung and has a heavier construction. The Viennese action is also lighter, while the English action is more complex, with the hammers mounted on a separate hammer rail.

White and black
Removed from the Rosenberger piano below, this keyboard and action shows black and white keys reversed, typical of many luxury Viennese pianos of the time.

English grand action
Devised by Americus Backers and others at Broadwood in London in the 1770s, this action helped in the development of a more powerful piano with superior tone and dynamic response.

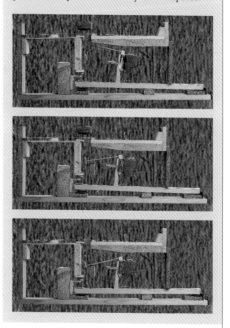

Viennese grand piano
Michael Rosenberger made this impressive instrument in Vienna in the early years of the 1800s. By this time the musically flourishing city was established as a leading centre of piano production.

Clementi's design

The exploded view below reveals the keyboard and action removed from the Clementi piano. Clementi's instruments often featured an unusual "harmonic swell" system, where an extra length of string was brought into play to create reverberation effects.

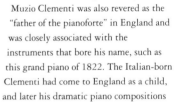

Clementi grand piano

Best known as a composer and pianist, Muzio Clementi was also revered as the "father of the pianoforte" in England and was closely associated with the instruments that bore his name, such as this grand piano of 1822. The Italian-born Clementi had come to England as a child, and later his dramatic piano compositions would influence the way Beethoven wrote for the instrument.

Unlike the more powerful English instruments, whose hammers strike the strings in a direct manner, the hammers of the Viennese instruments tend almost to caress the strings as they hit them, producing a gentler and sweeter sound. But unlike the English pianos, these instruments were constructed in such a way that it was impossible to adapt them to satisfy the ever-increasing demand for more volume, without sacrificing the responsiveness of the action. This eventually led them to fall out of favour as increasing numbers of players preferred to use the English and French models.

At the same time as this shift occurred, the centre of attention of musical culture in Europe was moving from Vienna to Paris.

In England the success of the square piano during the late 1760s had led to an especially strong demand for an instrument with a richer tone and greater dynamic response. The new action that was to facilitate this was developed by Backus, in conjunction with Broadwood and Stodart, on the basis of the designs of Cristofori and Silbermann. Here, pianos were already big business, causing Clementi, the leading piano composer and pianist of the day in London, to go into business as a manufacturer as well. The manufacturing process became geared to factory mass-production much more rapidly in Britain than elsewhere.

John Broadwood went further and engaged the assistance of scientific experts to help him improve the technical consistency of his designs. As a result he altered the

Muzio Clementi (1752-1832).

point at which the string is struck, to improve the quality of tone. He also divided the bridge into two sections. These modifications enabled him to add half an octave at the top and bottom of his grand pianos.

Such was the success of these improvements that the ageing and deaf Beethoven expressed his delight on being presented with a Broadwood grand. He believed it to be the only instrument remotely capable of fulfilling the taxing demands of his increasingly dramatic and extreme compositions.

THE ROMANTIC PIANO

The French Revolution led to several major piano makers in France leaving to set up factories in England. One of the most important to do this was Sébastien Erard, who spotted that the market was shifting away from the square piano and so focused on the grand piano.

Erard's most important innovation was the double escapement mechanism, which allows a note to be replayed without the key having to be fully released, permitting much speedier note repetition. English makers doubted the durability of this complex mechanism, and made the mistake of ignoring it for several decades.

The 19th century was the period in which the Romantic movement emerged in European classical music, leading to an emphasis on emotional intensity and drama in both works and performances. Audiences liked to see musicians transported into states of

Beethoven's piano

This contemporary illustration, dated 1820, shows the Broadwood grand piano that was owned by Beethoven.

Kirkman grand piano

A very grand piano indeed – this one was allegedly owned by King George IV and was kept for him at Brighton Pavilion in England. Made in London in 1820, the piano features Jacob Kirkman's "octave stop" feature that added extra harmonic colour by adopting some higher-pitched strings.

The Beethoven Broadwood Fortepiano
Melvyn Tan

Beethoven's Broadwood piano, still in use.

poetic and emotional rapture, and many concerts ended with wrecked pianos. In fact it was usually the strings, rather than the action, that presented the problem: their thickness (and thus their strength) was constrained by the limited tension that the framework of the instrument could support without warping. Thicker, stronger strings could be used, but to reach the same pitches as thinner strings they had to be put under higher tension, and that meant building a stronger framework.

Manufacturers began to use iron spacers between the pin block and the belly rail to which the hitch-pin plate is itself fixed, but even these could bend under pressure. The solution was to attach iron braces running above the soundboard, on the same plane as the strings, and fixed to the hitch-pin plate. Broadwood and Erard both lay claim to this development. Eventually the number of braces was reduced, owing to the advent of more efficient fixings capable of withstanding greater forces. With the increase in string tension, larger hammers and more robust actions became feasible. Steinway would achieve the other important advances paving the way for the modern grand piano in the mid-19th century, with the introduction of the full-iron frame (originally patented by Chickering) and the development of overstringing.

The musical consequences of these developments were enormous. The increased dynamic range over a much wider compass, along with the sustaining pedal, allowed romantic composer-performers such as Chopin, Schumann and Liszt to explore an unprecedented variety of new moods and textures, as well as performing technical fireworks that would previously have been unthinkable. The piano became the centrepiece of Romantic soirées, in which the great names of the day would entrance audiences with their displays of emotion and dazzling virtuosity.

Like the lean and other-worldly Paganini, a violinist whom many believed to be the devil in disguise, Liszt encouraged the public to see him as a demonically talented individual. He would often improvise extravagantly on his own and other people's compositions. Like Schumann, he exploited the piano's unique ability to evoke the complex and sensual images of Romantic literature through its rich variety of textures.

Meanwhile, the exiled Polish composer-virtuoso Chopin captured the hearts of audiences with the soulful melancholy and haunting sensuality of his piano compositions, still felt by many to encapsulate the innermost soul of the instrument. It is interesting to note that Chopin, together with some other performers of the day, preferred the tonal subtlety of Pleyel instruments to the

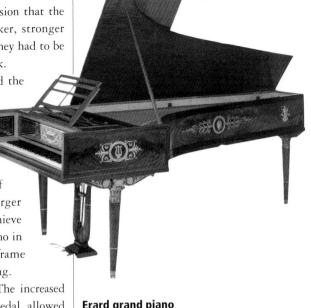

Erard grand piano
Another opulent instrument, this grand piano (above) was made by the Erard Brothers in Paris in 1808 for Louis, King of the Netherlands, who was Napoleon Bonaparte's brother. Today it is still owned by the Dutch royal family.

Erard's agraffe
An important innovation made by the Parisian Erard company was the agraffe, pictured above in early, simple form on a piano of 1818. Strings are threaded through the device, which prevents them moving when struck. It improved the piano's tuning stability and enhanced its tone.

Erard endorsements
Erard made the most technically advanced pianos of the time and had factories in London as well as Paris. The company's instruments attracted leading composers and musicians; this particular piano (left) was played by Mendelssohn and Liszt.

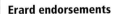

mechanical sophistication of Erards, but also played Broadwoods in England. As late as the end of the 19th century, a few late-Romantic composers, notably Mahler, still preferred the Viennese-style piano with its associations of old Vienna and the great classical masters.

This period also saw the foundation of the first great European school of piano playing. The brilliant composer Robert Schumann married the leading female virtuoso of the day, Clara Wieck. Her father was a leading piano teacher who had groomed her from birth for an international career. Clara Schumann, as she became known, taught many of great pianists, whose influence continued to be felt through into the 20th century, and her own performances of works by others were often proceeded by improvised preludes of her own invention. Her own compositional talents were sadly eclipsed by her husband's career, but she encouraged her students to improvise around the pieces of music they were learning in order to gain a better understanding of them – a method recently revived by some of the most progressive classical teachers of the present day.

Clara Schumann
Pictured above left, Clara Schumann (1819-96) was the leading female virtuoso pianist of her day, and taught many great players. (The violinist pictured is Wilma Neruda.)

THE EVOLUTION OF THE UPRIGHT

The upright we know today first appeared around 1800, following previous attempts to design vertical grand pianos (known as upright grands). It was developed to be a smaller, more economical and portable instrument. However, manufacturers also wanted an instrument whose sound retained as many as possible of the qualities of the grand piano.

More than one designer had independently realised that the legs of the upright grand were redundant, so the bass strings could go right to the floor. Shortly after that, Thomas Loud of London proposed running the strings diagonally, so that either longer strings could be incorporated or the size of the case could be reduced. Loud went to America, where he produced small pianos, while in Europe obliquely strung pianos of this kind became known as pianinos.

Another Londoner, William Southwell, had introduced the 'sticker' action in 1798, which allowed the hammer to be positioned at the optimum point on the strings, adding an escapement and a check, but it was Robert Wornum who

Jules Massenet
French composer Massenet is seen here playing an upright piano for a few admiring onlookers. The upright was perfect for entertaining in smaller homes at the turn of the century.

Mahler's Graf piano
Gustav Mahler was renowned as a composer and conductor. The instrument pictured was Mahler's first grand piano, made by Conrad Graf in Vienna around 1830. Seventy years later, Mahler still preferred to use this instrument when composing.

transformed the upright piano into the instrument we know today. Early on, Wornum built an upright that combined diagonal stringing with the English double action, and in the 1830s he went on to develop the tape-check action that remains the basis for the system used in uprights today. It employs a piece of tape to check the hammer so that it cannot strike more than once. In 1842 he patented his most advanced version of this action, and his innovation was further developed in Paris by Playel and Pape, so that it became known, wrongly, as the 'French' action. The French manufacturers of uprights were commercially successful, but in mass production to meet demand artistic standards may have suffered.

The upright piano was a product that could be sold to the middle classes, but it also had the prestige of having evolved from the grand pianos of the wealthier and more aristocratic parts of society. Size was an extremely important issue, since the typical middle class home in the mid-19th century had smallish rooms. The upright piano was often adapted or disguised to function as something else when not in use. Pianos could resemble tables and desks, or even chests of drawers. English and French manufacturers were especially inventive in enhancing the domestic appeal of the instrument, and the designs of Pape, though expensive, inspired other makers to experiment.

Wornum upright piano

The London-based maker Robert Wornum contributed a great deal to the development of the upright piano, including advances in actions. His "tape check" system prevented a hammer bouncing back and hitting a string, and is still in modified use today. This example of Wornum's craft (above) was produced in about 1835.

Sticker action

This sequence of three steps, pictured above, illustrates the mechanics of the so-called "sticker" action, named for the sticker that propels the hammer towards the string. Building on Geib's action, it was pioneered by John Landreth during the 1780s and then by William Southwell in the early 1800s.

THE EVOLUTION OF THE MODERN GRAND

The great exhibitions and world fairs of the 19th century offered excellent opportunities for the major piano manufacturers to present their new designs to the public. As a result, American piano makers, led by Steinway and Chickering, made a huge impact in the European market in the second half of the century. They won many awards at major exhibitions with their advanced production techniques and new ideas for design and marketing.

The Steinway family (originally called Steinweg) had emigrated to America after the 1848 revolution in Germany, where they had already been producing pianos. They produced a series of innovations in the production and design process: these represent the last major developments in the evolution of the modern grand piano.

In the 1850s they introduced overstringing to square pianos, and developed a cast-iron frame that could support far greater levels of tension in the strings, making it possible to produce instruments with a much bigger and richer sound. By 1860, they had produced the overstrung grand – the real forerunner of the modern concert grand – and had began to make use of a process for machine-felting their hammers to achieve a more consistent tonal quality.

Theodor Steinway, the only member of the family to have remained behind in Germany in the 1850s, worked closely with the great 19th century German scientist

Erard grand piano

European makers such as Erard were shocked by the influx of American-made instruments in the second half of the 19th century, primarily from Steinway, and the technical innovations they introduced, such as the overstrung grand. Instruments like this Erard grand made in 1866 would soon seem old fashioned.

Steinway celebration

A Steinway trade banquet in Berlin in 1926 (left) underlines the company's booming worldwide success. Guests of honour included eminent musicians, conductors and their families, as well as luminaries from Steinway itself.

and acoustician Hermann Helmholtz, who had investigated the acoustic foundations of musical instruments and musical harmony. After moving to America in the 1860s, Theodor Steinway introduced a whole series of technical refinements that were eventually taken up by other manufacturers around the world, notably the single-piece laminated piano rim.

During World War II the American factory of Steinway & Sons was used to make aircraft parts, while the German factory was taken over by the Nazis to produce dummy aeroplanes and rifle butts. The Steinway firm acquired the reputation as the world's premiere piano maker, partly through developing close relationships with international concert artists, many of whom were inclined to refuse to perform on any other kind of piano.

Apart from Broadwood & Sons and Steinway & Sons, the 19th century saw the emergence of a number of other great piano firms, three of which stand out for the quality of their instruments. Bösendorfer of Vienna and Bechstein of Berlin both prided themselves on creating instruments capable of surviving the ferocious onslaught of Liszt's piano playing. Bösendorfer supplied instruments to the Austrian Imperial Court, and remains the leading Austrian piano firm, also creating an instrument with additional notes at the very bottom that extended the range down to low C below the A that is normally the lowest note on modern pianos. Bechstein skilfully integrated the best of the many other developments in piano manufacture into their grand pianos.

The Leipzig-based firm of Julius Blüthner was admired for the tonal beauty of its instruments, particularly in the late 19th century and early 20th century, and production was revived after World War II under the auspices of the East German government. Blüthner made an important innovation in the form of the aliquot system, in which an extra string is added for each note in the higher register for sympathetic vibration, to enhance the singing quality of the tone.

Empress Eugénie Bösendorfer

One of the most famous pianos in the world, this ornate instrument was designed by Viennese craftsman Hans Makart and built by Bösendorfer in 1867. A number of stories surround its origins, but it was certainly owned by the Empress Eugénie, wife of Louis Phillipe Napoleon III.

PIANOS FOR THE MACHINE AGE

The popularity of the piano prompted manufacturers to try to think of ways to bring the instrument into homes where no one could actually play it. The obvious solution was to mechanise the instrument.

Mechanical instruments such as music boxes had been popular in Europe since the 14th century, and Mozart even wrote music specifically for them. The earliest system was the barrel mechanism; a cylinder turned, and nails inserted into it would trigger a lever that then caused a note to sound (or the nails would themselves pluck notes on strings). The circular shape of the cylinder meant that the music automatically returned to the beginning and then started again. In the 19th century, some manufacturers began to fit barrel mechanisms to their pianos, but with the exception of the street piano, barrel pianos had little commercial success.

This sort of solid barrel had many limitations. For an automatic instrument to gain wide appeal a more sophisticated way of storing music was required. The solution was to use a cylinder with punched holes instead of raised nails, and the first successful automatic piano based on this idea was produced by Giovanni Racca. In the 1880s he patented a Piano Melodico that used folded cardboard for storage.

In the 1860s a Frenchman, Fourneaux, developed a 'piano player' or 'Pianista' – a freestanding machine that could be wheeled up to the piano so that its mechanical 'fingers' played the keys. By contrast the term 'player piano' refers to an instrument with an automatic player mechanism already fitted inside it. The advent of the piano roll in the 1870s made both types of automatic piano viable, since it offered a compact and efficient way of storing information about the pieces of music to be played.

Most early piano rolls were lacking in expression or dynamics, but tempo, volume and pedalling could sometimes be adjusted in a crude way by an operator. Consequently, piano players and player pianos couldn't really reproduce an actual performance by a performer. This possibility became available with the development of 'reproducing pianos' in the early 20th century. Moreover, in 1904 Edwin Welte of Freiburg in Germany invented a system for encoding every nuance of a pianist's performance, including tempo changes, dynamics, and pedalling. He also introduced an electric motor to drive the mechanism instead of pedalled bellows.

The automated piano was the jukebox of its day. But the arrival of the gramophone, and eventually the jukebox itself, led to its inevitable and swift decline. Nevertheless, its creative use later, by individuals such as the American composer Conlon Nancarrow, can be regarded as anticipating the use of modern computer sequencing techniques.

Automated pianos were popular in cinemas, and this was part of a broader drive to exploit

Minx Miniature piano

Around the time of World War II the Minx Minature piano was a great success in Britain. Manufactured by Kemble from 1935, it was aimed at the domestic market by virtue of its small size – although as the picture above shows, it was also successful in ensembles. Remarkably, the Minx continued in production until 1966.

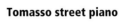

Tomasso street piano

Italian immigrants to England in the late 19th century brought with them the idea of "barrel" pianos. These were often wheeled around the streets on carts, like the one shown here. Each "pinned" barrel contained ten tunes and each tune lasted about 45 seconds. This street piano was made in London in about 1885.

Steck reproducing piano

Aeolian took over the New York-based George Steck company in 1904, putting its Duo-Art piano roll reproducing system of 1912 into Steck uprights (below). Piano rolls (above), invented by Edwin Welte in Germany in 1887, quickly became popular, with many great pianists making rolls for sale by Aeolian and other companies.

Racca Piano Melodico

This "melody piano" was patented in 1866 by Giovanni Racca and made in Bologna, Italy, around 1900. An improvement over the barrel piano, it allowed longer tunes to be played by using folded cardboard sheets and a crank-operated mechanism.

the popularity of the instrument by adapting it to as many social purposes and situations as possible. Pianos were adapted for use on yachts, and even in the ill-fated airships.

The development of electric pianos, in which the sound is electrically altered, and then of electronic pianos, in which the sound is electronically generated, produced alternative sound characteristics that were readily exploited by popular musicians. Of the former, the Fender-Rhodes achieved success and significance in popular culture thanks to its distinctive sound.

In recent decades, the musical instrument industry has seized upon computer technology and digital circuitry to develop increasingly sophisticated electronic keyboards, capable of exploring a wide range of synthetic sounds or simulating the sound of an acoustic piano. The advent of MIDI means that sound can now be processed entirely in the digital domain, as just another kind of numerical data. Acoustic pianos have also been fitted with MIDI technology, allowing them to store information about an actual performance on the instrument and then replay it 'for real' in the absence of the player.

Ironically, even the most sophisticated 'touch-sensitive' electronic keyboard technology has not yet succeeded in matching the extraordinary sensitivity to human touch of an ordinary piano action – one of the features whose expressive importance prompted the invention of the piano in the first place.

Modern grand action: 1: At rest

A modern grand piano action is shown in this sequence, featuring Steinway's Accelerated Action. As the key is pressed, the capstan screw rises, causing the jack to push up on the roller through a slot in the repetitive lever.

2: Hammer strikes string

The jack continues to move upwards until its toe encounters the set-off button. The jack flicks off the roller, leaving the hammer moving in free flight towards the string. Meanwhile the damper has been lifted off the string by the damper wire.

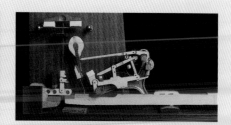

3: Hammer in check

With the key still held, the hammer bounces off the string and is grabbed by the check. The process of the downward movement of the hammer has caused the repetition lever to compress the repetition spring.

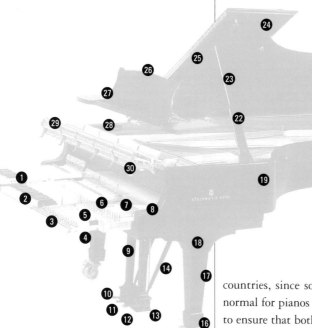

THE MODERN GRAND

The Steinway Model D concert grand piano (shown here) is the instrument used by most modern concert pianists for performance purposes. The first version of this model appeared in 1857, although it was only after another ten years that Steinway developed its unique technique for manufacturing the entire rim from a single piece of wood – a feature that contributes to the instrument's unique sound.

Steinway traditionally produced about 150 Model Ds each year in Hamburg (Germany) and New York (USA), with slight differences between the instruments originating in the two countries, since some raw materials have a different source. At the same time, it is normal for pianos of this calibre to be adjusted to suit the individual player, in order to ensure that both the tone and the responsiveness of the action are optimally suited to the individual user's musical preferences and way of playing.

Some players like to express a preference for Steinways made in the inter-war period (the 1920s and 1930s), which are felt to have a slightly darker, more introverted expressive tonal character. This may well be a reaction to the tendency to brighten the tone of modern grand pianos generally, to bring them into line with the preferences of the recording industry and of a modern concert-going public whose expectations are often influenced by what they hear on modern recordings. This characteristic is most pronounced in Far Eastern pianos (eg, Yamaha, Kawai). In other respects, however, such as the responsiveness of the piano action, these have now started to rival the subtlety that was once the sole province of the great European firms.

Tonal purists may even go out of their way to obtain one of old 'patent action' Blüthner grands – instruments known for their exceptionally subtlety and beauty of tone – possibly with a view to having it reconditioned. These pianos were built at a time when the manufacturer was using a more primitive type of action, now considered inadequate and rather unreliable. However, for those who value tonal beauty above all else, or who make only modest technical demands of the instrument, this can represent an interesting choice.

Key

1 balance weights/key leads	16 moulded toe
2 keys	17 leg
3 front baize/key bottom	18 leg cap
4 front rail	19 bent side
5 balance rail	20 heel
6 balance pin	21 rim or case
7 back rail	22 short stick
8 cheek	23 prop stick
9 lyre post	24 front half, front top
10 una corda pedal	25 top hinge
11 sostenuto pedal	26 music rest
12 damper pedal	27 music desk
13 lyre	28 straight side
14 lyre brace	29 action
15 castor	30 action standard/ hanger

4: Hammer freed

As the key is partly released, the hammer is freed from the check and rises slightly, caused by the repetition spring. This allows the jack back under the roller. If the key is played again, the hammer hits the string, though less forcefully this time.

5: Back to rest

When the key is fully released the hammer falls back so that it is just clear of the hammer rest. The toe of the jack leaves the set-off button and the jack is fully repositioned under the roller and the damper is lowered on to the string.

6: At rest, dampers raised

When the damper pedal is pressed, a series of levers raises the underlever, lifting the dampers. Once a string has been played and the pedal pressed, a tab prevents the damper wire of any note being held from falling back.

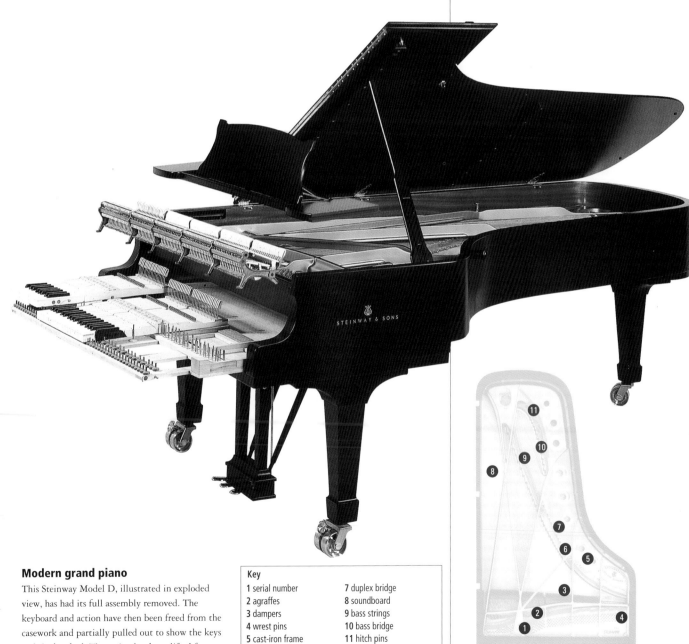

Modern grand piano

This Steinway Model D, illustrated in exploded view, has had its full assembly removed. The keyboard and action have then been freed from the casework and partially pulled out to show the keys and the key bed. The action has been lifted from the key assembly.

Key	
1 serial number	7 duplex bridge
2 agraffes	8 soundboard
3 dampers	9 bass strings
4 wrest pins	10 bass bridge
5 cast-iron frame	11 hitch pins
6 treble bridge	

Modern upright action

This sequence illustrates the action of a Bösendorfer Model 130, which is similar to most modern upright actions. This first photo (above) shows the parts of the action at rest.

Hammer strikes string

Just before the hammer strikes the string, the toe of the jack moves to the set-off button. The hammer then strikes the string and bounces back, aided by the bridle strap.

Hammer in check

The hammer is caught by the check, which prevents the hammer from bouncing back and re-striking the strings. The key is still held and so the damper remains off the string.

Key released

Now the wippen lowers, freeing the jack from the check. Then the jack, aided by the repetition spring, relocates in its notch. The note can be played again, though with less power.

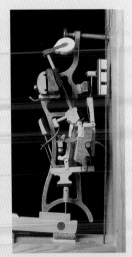

Half blow

When the half blow (soft) pedal is depressed, without a key being played, the half blow rail tilts forward, the hammer moves closer to the string, and the note sounds more quietly.

Art-case piano

This unusual "Ivory Spirit" Steinway upright was designed by New York artist and craftsman Wendell Castle in 1989.

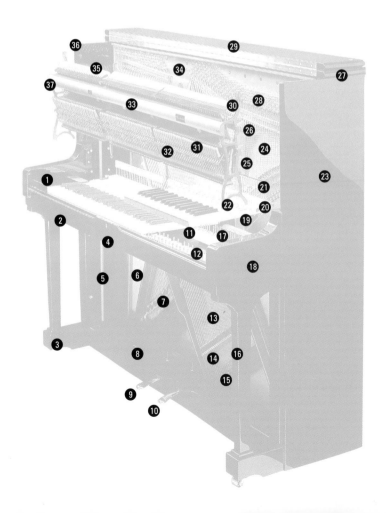

Modern upright piano

This Bösendorfer Model 130 is illustrated in exploded view, revealing its frame, action, keyboard and strings. Few companies produce their own actions today, and Bösendorfer is no exception, contracting the work to Louis Renner GmbH, one of the world's largest manufacturers of piano parts. Renner and Schwänder actions are both considered to be of the highest quality.

Key

1 key block	**20** pilot wire
2 lock rail	**21** pilot (capstan screw)
3 toe(s)	**22** action standard
4 lock	**23** treble end
5 side stick	**24** treble strings
6 soundboard (part)	**25** action rail
7 long bridge	**26** agraffes
8 pedal rocker	**27** back half
9 half-blow (soft) pedal	**28** wrest pins
10 damper pedal	**29** half top
11 key	**30** half-blow rail
12 bat (front) pin	**31** hammer checks
13 bass strings	**32** bridle wire
14 short (bass) bridge	**33** hammer rest rail
15 hitch pins	**34** frame
16 columns	**35** hammers
17 balance pin	**36** bass end
18 cheek	**37** half-blow crank
19 key weights	

THE MODERN UPRIGHT

Modern-day teachers and performers who require a top-quality instrument at a price that does not preclude home use have often favoured Bösendorfer pianos. Their Model 130 Studio (shown here) is one of the most highly regarded of modern upright pianos. Most of this instrument is hand-crafted, and it takes almost a year to produce. The challenge for a manufacturer of uprights is to compensate for the effect of the inevitably shorter string lengths on tonal range and projection. Another problem is that the action requires a shorter key, which consequently offers a diminished level of responsiveness.

The height of the Model 130 Studio is typical of modern full-size uprights: about 51″ (1300m). However, smaller sizes are available, known in America by different names depending on their height. A 'spinet' piano usually measures about 36-38″ (910-965mm) high, while a 'console' piano is about 38-43″ (965-1100mm). Above this are 'standard' uprights – known in Britain as 'full-size' uprights. Some Americans also like to refer to instruments of 43-47″ (1100-1200mm) as 'studio' pianos. The smaller types may incorporate some alterations to the action – notably the use of a 'drop' action.

The king of ragtime was Scott Joplin (top, left and right). Art Tatum (above) brought a virtuosic dimension to jazz piano, following the innovations of Jelly Roll Morton (below).

A NEW SOUND AND NEW VOICES

By the end of the 19th century, the piano had effectively completed its evolution. After that, there would continue to be subtle improvements in engineering, finish and manufacturing technique, but there would be no innovations with real musical consequences. Instead, composers and performers concentrated on exploiting the instrument as it was – and still is today.

At that point, however, the musical culture of the western world received a new stimulus by the incorporation of influences from Africa. For the most part, these did not come directly to Europe itself. Instead they came via America, where the music of former slaves and their descendants was beginning to be widely heard. And almost from the beginning, the piano played an important part.

In the last decade of the 19th century, two African-American musical styles began to develop a popular following: ragtime and blues. Ragtime was a syncopated solo piano style that evolved from minstrel songs and marches into something of a national obsession for Americans. It is most strongly associated with the rags composed by Scott Joplin (1868-1917). Subsequently it became fashionable to hear the music played at breakneck speed on piano rolls. Although ragtime incorporates Afro-American musical elements into an essentially European musical language, it did establish the typical 'stride' left-hand patterns whose rhythmic alternation of bass note and chord later served as a foundation for right-hand improvisation in early jazz piano. One can hear the transition from ragtime to early jazz piano in some of 'Jelly Roll' Morton's ragtime recordings.

By contrast, blues was an idiom that displayed the legacy of African-Americans in an immediately compelling manner, since it originated as a folk-song genre rooted in black slave songs in the American South. It used a distinctive scale in which notes were flattened or 'bent' from the normal major scale of European music, to reflect the African feeling for melodies and to produce an out-of-tune feel, expressive of raw suffering: these were known as 'blue' notes.

The form of the blues consisted of a repeated 12-bar harmonic sequence, which itself corresponds to a distinctive AAB form. This can be repeated and elaborated ad infinitum, often with a declamatory style of singing that has a rhythmically loose relationship to the underlying metre (which is always in 2 or 4 time) and therefore also a close connection with the rhythms and inflections of speech. Blues was sometimes performed with piano accompaniment, sometimes with guitar. However, its real influence on popular styles of piano playing emerged through its influence on other styles: initially boogie-woogie and barrelhouse, but also much of jazz, rock and country as these developed throughout the 20th century.

Barrelhouse acquired its name from the primitive huts that functioned as bars in the lumber camps of the Deep South of the US. There the piano and alcohol formed a close association in a rough and dangerous environment, where a saying like "Don't shoot the pianist, he's doing his best" may well have been used literally.

Boogie-woogie was also synonymous with the rough and licentious lifestyle associated with drinking establishments in urban America in the first few decades of the 20th century. In this respect, its pounding rhythms and rhythmically marked bass lines – echoing blues and banjo styles – contributed to its significance. Jimmy Yancey and Pinetop Smith were perhaps the most infamous early exponents, and other masters who can be heard on record include Pete Johnson, Meade Lux Lewis and Albert Ammons.

The slower, more bluesy feel of barrelhouse was taken up by many of the early jazz pianists, who fused it with the other musical idioms that contributed to the roots of jazz. Jazz emerged in the 1920s, characterised by an emphasis upon a solo performer improvising around a tune and/or a chord progression, while other musicians maintain the beat and the harmony in the background. The pianist and bandleader 'Jelly Roll' Morton is often credited with inventing jazz, which reflects the mix of Negro, Creole, Latin and European (especially French) cultural and musical influences in late 19th century New Orleans, where he lived and worked. In the 1910s and 1920s black musicians began to export the music to other cities, especially Chicago, where white musicians also took it up.

Great 'stride' pianists such as James P. Johnson began to emerge, and then, in the 1930s, Swing developed. It was characterised by big bands with written arrangements used as backing for solos, led by pianist-bandleaders such as Duke Ellington, Earl Hines, Nat 'King' Cole and Count Basie, or, on a smaller scale, Fats Waller. The 1940s saw the appearance of some phenomenally gifted virtuous solo pianists, notably Art Tatum, Erroll Garner and Oscar Peterson. It also saw the beginnings of a radically new conception of jazz with the emergence of bebop.

CLASSICAL IN THE 20TH CENTURY

Meanwhile, the world of classical music continued to change. The great pianist-composers of the mid-19th century like Mendelssohn, Schumann, Chopin, and Liszt had provided a glamorous model of fame and success and a brilliant repertoire, encouraging subsequent generations of virtuoso players to tour Europe and America,

Artur Schnabel was one of the greatest interpreters of Beethoven's piano works during the early 20th century.

Leading pianists at work: Ferruccio Busoni at the keyboard (below); Edwin Fischer and Walter Geiskeing on record (sleeves, bottom left); and Emil Gilels in concert (bottom right).

exploiting the mass popularity of the piano as an instrument. Other great pianists of the time, known for their dazzling technique and intensity, included Thalberg, Alkan, Gottschalk, Tausig, von Bulow and Anton Rubinstein.

By the start of the 20th century, a number of personalities had begun to dominate the world of piano performance. Their legacy would last into the age of piano rolls and early gramophone recordings. Their style of playing remains steeped in the intensity and drama of 19th century Romanticism, although the degree of rubato and expressive intensity can sound exaggerated to modern ears.

Ignace Paderewski (1860-1941), who also became Prime Minister of Poland, was probably the most famous of these, epitomizing the Romantic style with his loose tempi and desyncronisation of melody and accompaniment. Another Pole, Leopold Godowsky (1870-1938), was revered amongst pianists and considered to surpass even Liszt in his astounding technical brilliance and tone. Josef Hofmann (1876-1957) was famous for his spontaneity and risk-taking, while recordings testify to the subtlety and depth of insight that the Russian pianist and composer Sergei Rachmaninov (1873-1943)

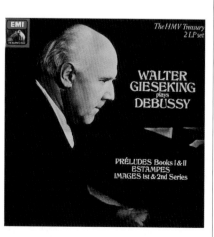

brought to his playing. By contrast, the Russian Josef Lhevinne (1874-1944) brought an element of classical restraint to the Romantic approach.

The Italian composer-pianist Ferruccio Busoni (1866-1924) is best known for his transcriptions of Bach's instrumental works in a Romantic pianistic idiom, resulting in music with a Gothic intensity and Art-Nouveau decadence. Valued at the time for achieving a distinctive aesthetic of its own, it is now disdained by advocates of authentic performance practice. Quite apart from his phenomenal technique and far-reaching intellectual engagement, Busoni was one of the era's most original composers for piano. His own works had to wait until the last decades of the 20th century to be appreciated.

The French pianist Alfred Cortot (1877-1962) became known as perhaps the greatest exponent of Schumann, Chopin, and Debussy of his day, thanks to his poetic feeling for tone, texture and mood, as well as his rigorous intellect.

Meanwhile the works of Beethoven, standing like a colossus at the very centre of the classical repertoire, found their authoritative exponent in the Austrian pianist Artur Schnabel (1882-1951). Schnabel captured the intellectual and emotional drama of Beethoven's sonatas in a way that remains unique, but he also pioneered Schubert's piano works, which were previously little known. Another great exponent of the classics was Edwin Fischer (1886-1960), whose Bach and Beethoven are imbued with a deep sense of humanity.

Walter Gieseking (1895-1956), born in France to German parents, achieved an unrivalled reputation for the interpretation of French music, especially Debussy. This was thanks to his exceptional subtlety of tonal detail and his pedalling, which make the instrument sing expressively, apparently transcending the physical limitations imposed by the piano action itself. The English pianist Solomon (1902-88) fused classicism and romanticism in his playing in a way that has stood the test of time. Solomon, who studied with a pupil of Clara Schumann, inherited the distrust of virtuosity for its own sake that was part of the legacy of this great teacher.

One of the most spiritual of pianist artists was the Rumanian Dinu Lipatti (1917-50), whose emotional refinement and sense of proportion, combined with a rich romantic palette of tonal colours, bridged the gap between those early 20th century pianists seeking to continue the perceived excesses of the 19th century Romantic style and those who sought to reintroduce classical values. Like Lipatti, the American pianist Julius Katchen (1926-69) saw his career cut short by illness, depriving the world of a great Brahms interpreter.

The inimitable Glenn Gould, one of the most distinctive modern players of Bach's music, pictured here with Leonard Bernstein.

The legendary final recital by Rumanian pianist Dinu Lipatti (far left), recorded days before his death. Glenn Gould's exciting debut recording of Bach (left) from 1955 is considered by many to be the most distinctive piano recording of the century.

Jerry Lee Lewis, the explosive showman of rock'n'roll, pictured (below) in relatively relaxed mood. His 1950s records for Sun (above) define rock'n'roll piano.

Another great Rumanian was Clara Haskil (1895-1960), who brought a subtlety, intimacy and purity to her interpretations of a range of composers (most notably Mozart) but is still not as widely appreciated as she deserves. Haskil was not the only great female pianist working at this time: Myra Hess (1890-1965) achieved iconic status in Britain for the expressive immediacy and religious conviction that her playing displayed.

The mid-20th century saw the emergence of both great romantic players such as Horovitz (described as a 'tornado') and Artur Rubinstein (whose Chopin is considered authoritative), and classicists such as the Argentine-born Claudio Arrau (1903-91), whose performances convey analytical insights that reveal his exceptional depth of musical understanding.

By contrast, Rudolf Serkin (1903-91) approached the works of Beethoven and others with a sense of struggle that could make each performance a unique and unpredictable event, while at other times achieving playing of wondrous lyrical subtlety. Emil Gilels (1916-1985) and Sviatoslav Richter (b.1915), both Russians, also emerged as supreme pianists whose combination of technical, intellectual and emotional mastery defies categorisation as classicist or Romantic. Their recorded legacies have increasingly revealed them to be giants of the instrument.

One of the most striking pianistic personalities of the century was the Canadian Glenn Gould (1932-82), whose performances of J.S.Bach combined a remarkably individual approach with unique insights and superlative technical competence.

Gould was also a superb interpreter of difficult 20th century composers such as Schoenberg, and a highly original thinker about music generally.

ROCK'N'ROLL AND ITS OFFSHOOTS

In the mid-1950s a new popular style emerged dramatically from a fusion of white American country music and African-American rhythm & blues. Rock'n'roll became identified with the emergence of mass youth culture in post-war America.

In its purest form it combined a catchy melody with a simple three-chord structure and a rebellious, driving backbeat. It catapulted the piano back into the foreground of popular culture, thanks to colourful personalities such as Little Richard and Jerry Lee Lewis, who exploited the physicality and showmanship of percussive, pounding playing to great effect.

A wide range of musical offshoots of rock'n'roll led to a range of distinctive rock piano styles, many of which involve imaginative transformations of emerging guitar playing techniques and drum grooves into keyboard equivalents. Country rock featured fingerpicking and strumming effects, as in the slip-note style of Floyd Cramer, while gospel and blues piano playing came to reflect the more extrovert approach of rock. Ramsey Lewis took gospel piano in the direction of soul, and the halftime funk feel which came out of blues and soul fed back into the rock piano of characters such as Elton John.

Blues piano playing has remained an active force throughout the 20th century, not just through its influence upon other popular styles, but also in its own right.

Jump blues developed on the West Coast of the United States as a synthesis of jazz and blues that offered interesting improvisational possibilities in addition to its influence on the likes of Little Richard. Meanwhile traditional blues piano continued to be played in places like Louisiana with little change, well into the second half of the 20th century.

A dominant influence among the younger bebop pianists was Bud Powell (above).

BEBOP AND THE RISE OF MODERN JAZZ

In the 1940s a new kind of jazz began to appear, in which the embellishment of familiar tunes was replaced by a fast and freer style of melodic soloing using scales derived from changes made to the chords of those tunes. This was accompanied by punchy and irregular rhythms, creating a whole new feel. Bebop had arrived, along with charismatic and virtuosic players such as Charlie Parker, Miles Davis and John Coltraine, and pianists like Bud Powell, Wynton Kelly, or the individualistic Thelonious Monk.

Bebop dominated jazz through the 1950s, but in the 1960s pianists like Bill Evans and McCoy Tyner appeared on the scene, developing this language even further, especially with their subtle techniques for laying out left-hand chords. This ushered in a period of post-bebop experimentation, including the use of electric keyboard instruments in jazz by the likes of Herbie Hancock, as well as west coast jazz and thirdstream jazz, in which players like Dave Brubeck introduced elements of modern classical music.

The legacy of bebop and post-bebop, from the 1970s through to the present day, has been a modern jazz scene that continues to include a wide range of experimental approaches, as shown by players such as Chick Corea, Keith Jarrett and Kenny Barron, not to mention advocates of free jazz and avant-garde jazz such as Anthony Braxton or Cecil Taylor.

Bill Evans (right) was perhaps the greatest of all jazz pianists, although Thelonious Monk has to be a close contender. Recordings are all that we have left of both Monk and Evans.

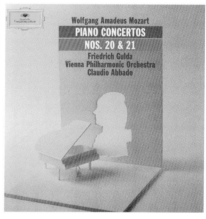

Alongside these developments, various traditional styles have persisted, although the general trend has been towards a more technically polished and less spontaneous style of playing, in which the interesting contrasts with classical ways of using the instrument have been watered down.

CLASSICAL PERFORMANCE TODAY

The playing of the majority of the great classical pianists of today reflects the ways in which technique and awareness of style have developed over the course of the 20th century. The general trend has been away from what have come to be perceived as the excesses of the Romantic approach that dominated the 19th century. This tendency has been reinforced by two important factors.

Firstly, the influence of the growth of the record industry and of improvements in recording technology has been felt throughout classical music. Listeners now expect to hear live performances with the same technical perfection they have come to expect on CDs at home, and artists feel they have to satisfy those expectations. At the same time, the role of musical showman has increasingly been taken over by performers of popular music. The downside of this tends to be a lack of awareness among all but the greatest performers that a live musical performance should still be a special event. It should be something that can never be fully planned, rehearsed, or prepared, that must leave room for spontaneity, risk-taking, and the intensity, inspiration and insight of the moment.

The second major factor has been the emergence of 'authentic' performance practices, in which musicians are encouraged to interpret music in a manner that reflects what researchers know of the performance practice at the time it was written. This is controversial. Some people argue that we simply cannot know how the music of the distant past was actually performed, since there are no recordings.

In the case of the piano, the matter is complicated further by the substantial changes that have occurred as keyboard instruments have evolved from harpsichord-type instruments, through early fortepianos to the modern concert grand. Should we play Bach on the harpsichord when playing it on the piano allows so much more

More piano greats: in jazz, Herbie Hancock (top left); in classical, Sviatoslav Richter (top right), Friedrich Gulda (above), and Krystian Zimerman (below).

in the way of possibilities for expressive shaping using dynamics and articulation? How much of the flavour of the harpsichord should we try to recreate on the piano? Would Beethoven have preferred to hear his sonatas on a modern concert grand, where even the most extreme textures retain clarity and projection, or on a piano of his own time, strained to its own limits and beyond in the attempt to deliver the music?

This is the complex and demanding world of choices for the modern pianist. In addition, they must negotiate the pressures of the international concert circuit, juggling record contracts with jet-set tours, concert managers and agents with record producers, and international competitions with prestigious arts festivals. What distinguishes the great players of the modern world is their ability to preserve a sense of artistic integrity, individuality and involvement through all these distractions.

The repertoire for the piano is vast – far larger than for any other instrument. (To get a rough idea how vast, cast a glance over the repertoire guide at the back of this book.) Many players have therefore achieved particular distinction in certain areas. Andras Schiff in J.S.Bach, Mitsuko Uchida and Murray Perahia in Mozart, Mikhail Pletnev in C.P.E.Bach and Russian music, Alfred Brendel in Haydn and Schubert, Richard Goode in Beethoven, Krystian Zimerman in Chopin, Radu Lupu in Brahms, and Maurizio Pollini in early and mid-20th century music are just some of the finest examples of this. At the same time, all of these performers could also lay claim to being masterly exponents of many other parts of the repertoire as well.

THE PIANO IN CONTEMPORARY MUSIC

Contemporary classical music has evolved in the last 50 years or so into something approaching a subculture of its own. The European avant-garde of the 1950s and 1960s produced important heavyweight works for piano, such as the sonatas of Barraqué and Boulez and the piano pieces of Stockhausen. For these composers, the piano was the ideal medium for an intellectually severe and uncompromising style, whose abstract and fragmented textures often typified the nihilistic intensity of mid-20th century musical modernism.

Meanwhile, American composers such as Cage and Nancarrow stretched our understanding of the piano as an instrument: Cage's prepared piano introduced foreign objects into the mechanism and strings to alter its sound, while Nancarrow's works for player-piano turn the instrument into a vehicle for multi-layered textures

Some players have become noted for their skills in specific areas or with the work of particular composers. Maurizio Pollini (above) excels in performances of 20th century music (not to mention Beethoven), while Alfred Brendel (right) is known for his penetrating interpretations of Haydn and Schubert.

of superhuman complexity, anticipating the results of more recent computer sequencing techniques.

The 1970s onward saw a retreat from radical experiment, in favour of a more positive engagement with the European musical past and with other cultures. World musics and popular musical idioms have both exerted a substantial influence on the 'postmodern' styles and attitudes of those now working in contemporary music. Modern composers such as Ligeti have attempted to fuse the intellectual rigour of classical composition with the new resources offered by an engagement with the subtleties of musical cultures previously dismissed as primitive. The piano has proved an ideal medium for this, thanks to its capacity for multi-layered rhythmic, harmonic and melodic textures.

Other composers, such as Ferneyhough, have pushed the complexity of which the piano is capable to its utmost extremes, producing expressionistic commentaries on the pressures of modern living. At the same time, younger classical pianists such as Joanna MacGregor have been successful in overcoming the barriers and prejudices that previously separated different musical subcultures, resulting in stimulating crossover experiences.

What is clear beyond doubt is that the piano, with its combination of technological sophistication and expressive subtlety, remains the most versatile, interesting and challenging instrument on the contemporary musical stage.

Murray Perahia (above) is a pianist revered for his musicality and understanding.

Joanna MacGregor (below) is pictured in rehearsal with Pierre Boulez and Harrison Birtwistle in France in the early 1990s. Today, she is helping to redefine the image of the piano as we move into the 21st century.

UNIT 1

SECTION 1

THE KEYBOARD

Open the lid of your piano and you'll find a neat arrangement of black and white keys: the **keyboard**. Don't worry, it's not so different from the keyboard on a computer, which was named after this one. In fact, it's a lot simpler. There are only two types of key, black and white.

Look at the pattern they form. Mostly, white keys alternate with black keys: white, black, white and so on. But sometimes two whites sit next to each other with no black key between them. That means some of the black keys have a larger gap between them than others. Look at the whole keyboard and you will see that the black keys are in a group of two, then a group of three, then another two and so on.

Those five black keys (a group of two and a group of three), with the seven white keys around them, form a pattern of 12 keys that repeats itself along the length of the keyboard. To understand the keyboard, you need to be able to pick one of the keys in that pattern, note its position, then find the equivalent key where the pattern repeats itself, then again and again. Each of the keys that makes up the pattern is a different **note**, with a name taken from the letters of the alphabet.

At the beginning, concentrate on getting to know the positions of the white notes in the pattern: the black keys are the signposts that help you find them. Each white note has a different letter-name until, after seven notes, we return to the start of the pattern. Then the letter-names start again from the beginning.

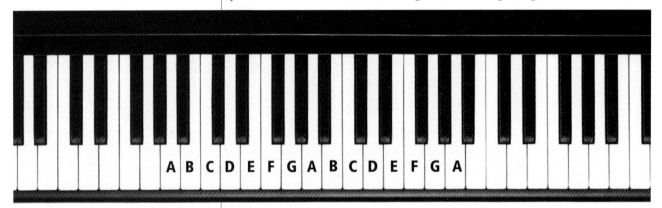

Press down the keys, one at a time, near the right-hand end of the keyboard: then again at the left-hand end. What's the difference? Notes further to the right sound higher, and those further to the left sound lower. This is their **pitch**. When you move along the keyboard to the right, the pitch goes up and the note name moves forward through the alphabet. When you move left you go down, and backwards through the alphabet. Try saying your alphabet backwards from G to A.

Exercise 1.1

Look at the picture of the keyboard. Middle C is close to the middle of the keyboard, immediately to the left of a group of two black notes. Now find it on the piano. Close the book and find every other C. Then find every D, E, F, G, A and B.

The distance from one note to the next one with the same letter-name is called an **octave**. So we say that the pattern repeats itself at every octave (every eighth step).

POSTURE AND TECHNIQUE

Apart from the drums, the piano may be the most physical instrument there is. Good pianists don't just play with fingers and hands, they're constantly aware of how every inch of their body contributes to the music.

That means your **posture** – how you position yourself at the piano – is really

The right height
Adjusting the height at which you sit every time you practise is a hugely boring waste of time. That's why you should have an adjustable piano stool, which you can set permanently at the right height for you. Don't settle for cushions on a chair, or for one of those old-looking stools with a place for the music inside: you can't adjust them. Later you may find it necessary to change the height slightly to play different kinds of music.

important. Correct posture means sitting upright with a straight back, keeping your shoulders loose, low and relaxed, and sitting at the right height and distance from the piano. Sit too low or close, and you'll restrict your freedom of movement across the keyboard. Sit too high or far away, and you lose intimacy and the ability to engage the weight of your body.

Everyone has a different body shape and size, so there's no simple rule for height and distance, but generally in classical music your forearms should be roughly horizontal or sloping slightly downwards towards the hands. Try crossing your hands while sitting at the keyboard, so the right hand is some way towards the bottom and the left towards the top. If you have to lean backwards away from the instrument to do this, you're sitting too close.

The general term for the physical aspects of playing an instrument is **technique**. An important aspect of this is **hand shape**. Look at your hands. All the fingers are a different size and shape, but somehow they've all got to work equally well when playing music. We need to position the hands on the keys to minimise the differences between fingers.

Place one hand on the white keys near the middle. Notice how the knuckles slope down, away from the thumb, in the direction of the smaller fingers. This means that the smaller, weaker fingers have no room to play. Twist the hand round slightly from the wrist (towards the thumb) until you have level knuckles; note how the fingers themselves have to be less flat to continue resting on the keys, as though the hand was cupped to hold an object in the palm of the hand. You need both level knuckles and rounded fingers. Observe how the thumb has to curve in towards the hand slightly to sit squarely on the key: don't let it stick out, or rest on the wood in front of the keys.

Now take a look at your wrist. It should be slightly lower than the rest of the hand, and should feel relaxed, but not so much that it causes the hand to collapse on to the keys. It must support the hand but not constrain it. If the hand tenses up, the knuckles may push downwards, forcing the wrist to rise. Most adult learners have this problem, at least with their weaker hand. As soon as this happens, stop playing and give your hand a good shake so the wrist goes floppy. Best to take a coffee break before starting again.

Now check your shoulders again. Are they still relaxed, or have they quietly tensed up and risen since you stopped thinking about them? Check your elbows too: don't let them stick out sideways when the hands are on the keyboard, feel your arms hanging loosely off the shoulders, and let the elbows find their natural place fairly close to the sides of your body.

Remember to keep checking for signs of tension, and never force yourself to keep on playing when it occurs. Of course, some tension is necessary for your body to operate at all, and for you to control it.

The golden rule of piano technique is: maximum relaxation + maximum control.

Hand shapes

Top: a good hand position means level knuckles and rounded fingers. Centre: letting your knuckles slope to the right leaves no room for your shorter fingers to play. Bottom: the high wrist is a sign of a tense hand. Time to take a break.

READING MUSIC: PITCH

With classical music, we normally learn to play from written music. Until recently, that was not the case with jazz and other non-classical styles. But these days even people who only want to play non-classical music are learning to read music notation because it really helps.

This should not diminish the importance of learning by ear in jazz, for example, where players tend to study recordings and live performances rather than written music. What's more, classical musicians also learn 'by ear', through seeing and hearing performances by other musicians.

At its simplest, music is written down using a group of five horizontal lines, known as a **stave** or **staff**:

Notes are written as circles, either on the lines, or in the spaces between them:

The higher or lower the note appears on the stave, the higher or lower it sounds. But there are more notes on the piano than can fit on a single stave, so the piano uses two staves. Each of the staves has a sign, called a **clef**, to indicate which part of the piano's range it relates to. It is written at the beginning of each line of music. These are the two clefs:

- **Treble clef** means the stave corresponds to the region above (right of) Middle C.
- **Bass clef** means the stave corresponds to the region below (left of) Middle C.

Treble clef: Bass clef:

The upper stave is normally played by the right hand, and uses the treble clef. The lower stave, normally played by the left, uses the bass clef. (Occasionally, in very advanced piano music, you'll see a third stave, but this is exceptional.) The two sets of notes represented by the staves meet at Middle C, which is indicated by a little line, known as a **leger line**, drawn through it. It only appears when it is actually required. The combination of treble and bass staves is sometimes called the **great stave**, because it amounts to a single large stave of eleven lines.

Middle C

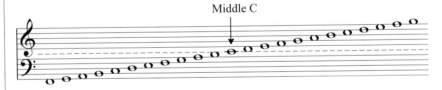

Note that the two clefs have to be read differently. A note on the middle line of the treble clef is B; but a note in the middle line of the bass clef is D. We need an easy way to remember the notes for each clef. Here it is:

Treble clef (right hand):
These are the notes in the spaces:

F   A   C   E

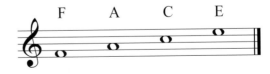

And these are the notes on the lines:

Classical music

Classical music means music written by composers for the mainly European tradition of music played in concert halls, at the opera, or in churches. Some people call this 'serious music', but this is misleading: not all 'classical' music takes itself seriously, while a good deal of other music has serious intentions. In this book we'll use the neutral term 'non-classical' to include jazz, blues, rock, folk, and mainstream 'popular' styles.

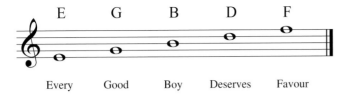

	Every	Good	Boy	Deserves	Favour
	E	G	B	D	F

Bass clef (left hand):

The spaces:

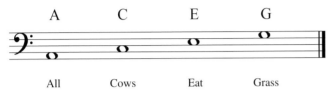

All	Cows	Eat	Grass
A	C	E	G

The lines:

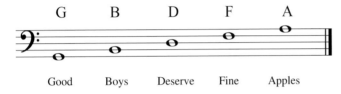

Good	Boys	Deserve	Fine	Apples
G	B	D	F	A

Of course, any fool can remember these phrases. What matters is whether you can remember which phrase or word refers to which clef (or hand). If it has five words you know it's got to be lines; if it has four words or letters, it's got be spaces. Try to learn them.

When notes go below the bass stave, or above the treble stave, we use more leger lines, like with Middle C. Note that the high C is the same distance above the treble stave as the low C is below the bass clef. (It's the only note that comes out symmetrically in this way.)

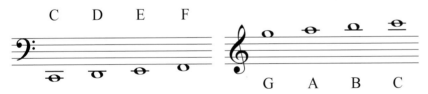

Because the hands often cross the middle of the piano, we sometimes need to write notes for the right hand below Middle C, and for the left hand above Middle C. Each hand tends to keep to its own stave and clef, so we use leger lines again:

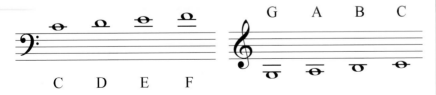

READING MUSIC: RHYTHM

Playing music isn't just about knowing what notes to play, it's about knowing when to play them. Music takes place in time. We read each line of music from left to right, like a book, but we don't just play the notes when we feel like it: the music tells us exactly when to move from one note to the next.

Timing in music has several aspects. Firstly, there's the pattern of longer (slower) and shorter (faster) notes in a musical phrase or tune: the **rhythm**. Just like in dancing, we feel how rhythms should go by relating them to a basic underlying **pulse** or **beat**. Usually, those individual beats are grouped, providing what is called the **metre** of the music (like metre in poetry).

Music is written down in sections, each several beats in length, called **bars** or **measures**. Each bar is separated from the next by a vertical line across the stave, called a **barline**. The metre is the number of beats per bar, which usually remains the same throughout a piece.

The end of a piece is indicated by two lines, one thin and one thick, close together. This is called a **double barline** (or 'double bar' for short). Two dots before a double barline tell you to go back to the beginning and repeat the piece.

Sometimes you'll see a double bar in the middle of a piece, indicating that you should stop there and go back to the beginning. The second time round, though, you must ignore the repeat sign and continue to the end. If you're supposed to start your repeat somewhere other than the beginning, you'll see a double barline followed by two dots.

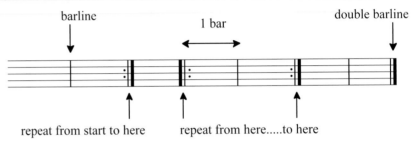

Rhythms are written using different kinds of note, each with a different length. The starting point is the longest commonly-used note, the semibreve. Shorter notes are created by dividing that long note, firstly into two notes of half its length, and then by subdividing those notes, and so on.

In northern Europe and America, the names of the notes reflect that process of division in a rational way. But the British use names that come directly from French and Latin.

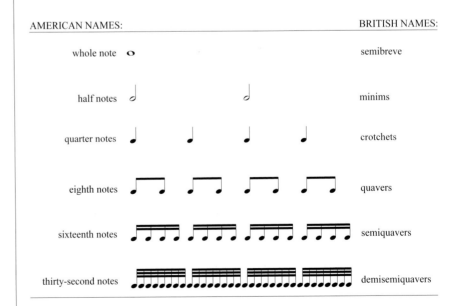

AMERICAN NAMES:		BRITISH NAMES:
whole note	𝅝	semibreve
half notes	𝅗𝅥 𝅗𝅥	minims
quarter notes	♩ ♩ ♩ ♩	crotchets
eighth notes	♫ ♫ ♫ ♫	quavers
sixteenth notes		semiquavers
thirty-second notes		demisemiquavers

Placing a dot after a time-value adds half as much again to the value of the note:

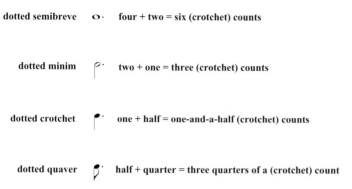

dotted semibreve 𝅝· **four + two = six (crotchet) counts**

dotted minim 𝅗𝅥· **two + one = three (crotchet) counts**

dotted crotchet ♩· **one + half = one-and-a-half (crotchet) counts**

dotted quaver ♪· **half + quarter = three quarters of a (crotchet) count**

Another way to think about different note lengths is as divisions or multiples of whatever note length represents the underlying pulse or beat of the music. This pulse is expressed at the start of the first line of music (in each stave) in what is called the **time signature**. The time signature looks like a fraction. The lower figure says which type of note provides the basic unit of the pulse. If the basic unit is a crotchet, that's a quarter of a whole note, so the figure in the lower part of the time signature is a 4. The upper figure in the time signature, meanwhile, indicates how many of those notes go to make up a bar: the piece's metre, in other words.

Here are the most common time signatures. (Note the alternative signs for some of them.)

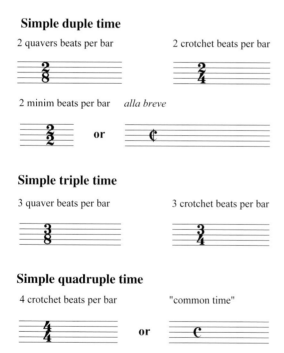

Simple duple time

2 quavers beats per bar

2 crotchet beats per bar

2 minim beats per bar   *alla breve*

or

Simple triple time

3 quaver beats per bar

3 crotchet beats per bar

Simple quadruple time

4 crotchet beats per bar

"common time"

or

RESTS

Music doesn't just consist of sounds arranged in time. The silences between sounds are often just as important. Each note has an equivalent **rest**, indicating a silence that lasts the same length of time. The rests have the same names as the notes they match: 'crotchet rest', 'eighth note rest' and so on. Dots may also be placed after rests, just as they are with notes, and they work the same way. (One difference: a whole bar of silence is indicated by the sign for a semibreve or whole note rest, even when the bar lasts for more or less time than this.)

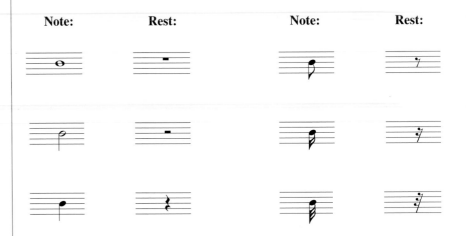

Note:	Rest:	Note:	Rest:

Exercise 1.2

Let's practise a few rhythms by themselves first. Remember, always feel how the rhythm relates to the underlying pulse or beat. In each of the following, clap the rhythm while counting the beats. Note that we start counting afresh with each new bar. We say the numbers for each main beat of the bar, 'and' to mark half beats, '-er' on quarter divisions and '-a' on three-quarter divisions. (This way of counting is very important in rhythmic music and modern popular styles, and is used by drummers.) Notice the relative strength and importance of the different beats of the bar, as indicated below: the first beat of each bar is always strong.

BASIC HAND POSITIONS AND FINGERING

In piano music, fingering is written just above or below the notes, using small numerals. Each hand is numbered outwards from the thumb (=1), through the index (=2), middle (=3) and ring (=4) fingers, to the little finger (=5). So fingering is symmetrical between the hands.

The basic hand position on the piano lets you play five notes side by side, one finger on each. For example, placing your right hand with the thumb on Middle C enables you to cover all the white notes from C to G. Placing your left hand with the thumb on Middle C means you cover all the white notes from C down to F. Try this one hand at a time, keeping in mind what was said earlier about **hand shape**. You can also position the left hand exactly one octave below the right hand, so the bottom (5th) finger sits on the C below middle C, as in the next exercise.

Exercise 1.3

When your hand is in position, play the notes under your fingers, one at a time, up and then down. Now shift the hand to a similar position on G (ie, with G at the bottom and D at the top), and do the same thing. Then move down a step to F, and then back to C. Then try the other hand.

> ### Correct fingering
> Whenever you're learning to play a piece, always make sure you practise it with the correct fingering. When fingering isn't given, it's up to you to work it out and write it in. Always have a pencil to hand. Using the same fingering every time you play a passage speeds up learning.

Right hand

Left hand

WARMING-UP.

Okay, it's time to get playing. Let's start with a couple of basic exercises to develop control of the fingers.

Exercise 1.4

'Five-finger running exercise.' Try playing the fingers of each hand, running up and down in the basic position, starting on Middle C. Make all notes the same length and volume, except for making the first of each group of four slightly stronger. Keep the hand relaxed, and make sure each finger (and especially the thumb) lifts by itself before playing. Gradually increase speed.

EXERCISE 1.4

Right hand

Left hand

How you move from one note to the next is very important. Connecting up notes creates the feeling of a musical line unfolding, which is what we mean when we talk about 'tunes' or melodies in music. Unless otherwise indicated, always join notes smoothly by holding each note on until the next one actually begins to sound. It's natural to want to let go of each note in order to begin playing the next, but this creates gaps between notes, breaking the sense of line. You should begin releasing the note just as you finish pressing down the next note. That means that (for a fraction of a second) the first note is still actually held as you play the next one.

Exercise 1.5

Basic trill exercise. A 'trill' is a regular alternation between two adjacent notes. Practise this exercise very slowly at first. There should be no gaps or audible overlaps between one note and the next. Check that each finger lifts by itself before playing, and let it fall with its own weight, sinking into the key to hold it down. Are your wrist and forearm relaxed? When you feel them aching, stop and give the hand a shake, or take a coffee break.

Right hand

Left hand

Whenever you practise, start by 'warming up' for a couple of minutes with these two exercises.

Artur Rubinstein at the keyboard.

HANDS SEPARATE PLAYING

With all of these pieces, try clapping the rhythms first: remember how they sound, then aim for the same sense of timing as you play the notes.

Exercise 1.6

CD: **TRACK 1**

'Frere Jacques', an old French song. Notice how the right hand moves up a step in bar 5 by changing to 4th on G, so you have a stretch from E back to thumb on C. The left hand is one step higher than in Middle C position, so thumb plays D instead of Middle C.

46

Exercise 1.7

'Oranges and Lemons': a great English tune to get you going. Here the left hand thumb also starts on D instead of C, but shifts down at the end so that it's playing an octave below the right hand, with thumb on G instead of 5th finger.

CD: **TRACK 2**

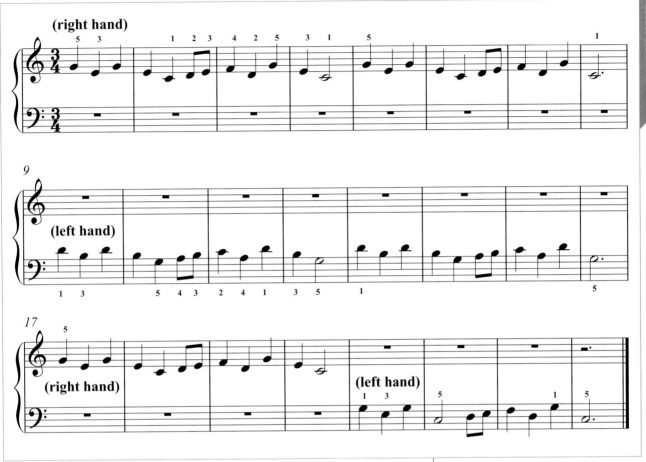

Exercise 1.8

CD: **TRACK 3**

In 'Fairy Dance' the basic hand position is slightly extended for both hands, and the melody swaps around between them. The right hand thumb has to shift from D to C in bar 4. Pass the left hand thumb under the 2ⁿᵈ finger to play F in bar 7, and don't forget to count rests as well as notes. Keep both hands in position over the keys, even when they're not in use.

EXERCISE 1.8

Exercise 1.9

CD: **TRACK 4**

For 'Bugle Call', set the hand to keep the gap between fingers the same, but at the same time keep everything loose and relaxed.

EXERCISE 1.9

Exercise 1.10

In 'Victory March', watch that the weak 4th and 5th fingers lift and play for themselves without disturbing the rest of the hand. Is the weaker side of each hand properly supported? Keep thumbs over the keys and pointing slightly in towards the hand, even when not playing.

CD: **TRACK 5**

Exercise 1.11

'Soldier's Song' requires good thumb mobility. The thumb should lift freely without pushing the hand over onto the weaker fingers. Relate dotted rhythms to the underlying pulse.

CD: **TRACK 6**

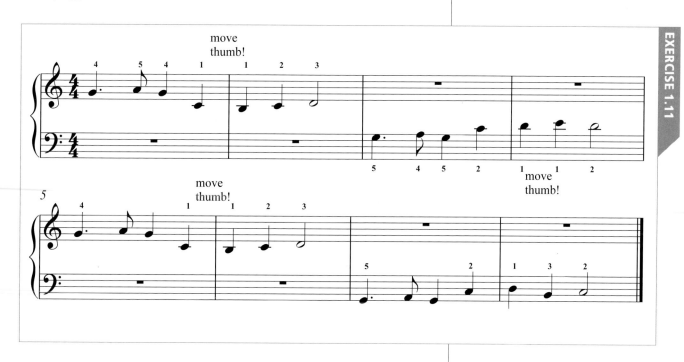

PLAYING WITH HANDS TOGETHER

Now it's time to start playing 'hands together'. This is one of the biggest challenges of the piano, so it's important to approach it in the right way. Generally, you should first practise each hand separately until fairly fluent, then combine the hands at a much slower speed. Take one short passage at a time and gradually bring it up to speed, paying equal attention to both hands and listening carefully to how they both sound.

Exercise 1.12

CD: **TRACK 7** *In 'Roundabouts', the hands mostly play the same notes an octave apart, with different fingers, but at the end they move in opposite directions, with the same finger in each hand. Notice how the left hand is also written in treble clef.*

Exercise 1.13

CD: **TRACK 8** *In 'Wedding Bells', each hand takes turns to move at a faster or slower speed than the other. Look out for the stretch between left hand thumb and 2nd finger in bar 7.*

50

Sometimes you'll see a curved line joining successive notes on the same line or space. This is a **tie**: it means you hold the first note for the combined length of both notes. This is most often used when a note carries on over the barline. In other words, when two notes are tied together, don't sound the second.

Exercise 1.14

'Morning Hymn' has many dotted rhythms, which you should practise by clapping first: feel the missing beat corresponding to the dot. Notice the tied note at the end, in the left hand.

CD: **TRACK 9**

THE PASSING THUMB (SCALE OF C)

If we play up and down an octave, we get a **scale**. When the first note is a C, we say it's a scale of C. Because we only have five fingers, we have to use a special technique to go beyond the fifth note: it's called the **passing thumb**. After we play the first three notes with thumb and first two fingers, we pass the thumb under after the 3rd finger and place it on the fourth note. Then we use the fingers to play the rest of the scale. Playing a downward scale with the left hand, the process is the same. The left thumb passes under the second and third finger and lands on the fourth note.

But when the right hand is playing a descending scale, or the left hand is going up, they do something different. In each case, we start with the 5th finger, but when we reach the thumb and run out of fingers, we cross our third finger *over* the thumb to play the next note. When passing over or under like this, be careful not to let your elbows stick out: make the wrist and fingers/thumb do the work.

Similar and contrary motion

When hands move in the same direction we call it *similar motion*; when hands move in opposite directions we call it *contrary motion*.

Exercise 1.15

First practise this scale of C major hands separately, then together. Combining hands is harder in the same direction than in opposite directions, because different fingers are playing at the same time.

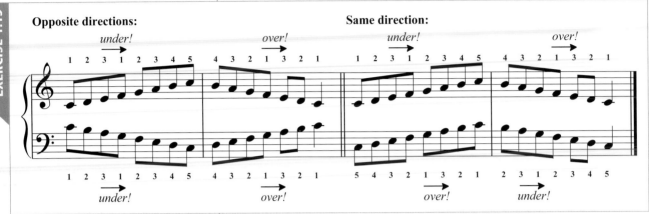

TRIADS

If we play the 1st, 3rd and 5th notes of the scale all at once we get a rich and satisfying sound, called a **triad**.

Pythagoras on musical theory

Triads provide the basis for harmony in European music. They were discovered by the Greek mathematician Pythagoras, who worked out that scales could be constructed by dividing a vibrating string at different points. He concluded that the ratios used to work out those points were fundamental to the construction of the universe. His cosmology was wrong, but his experiments with strings still form the basis of musical theory.

Exercise 1.16

First play the triad of C major, letting the hand (and the weight of the arm) sink into the keys. Can you make all three notes sound exactly together, and equally clearly? A good trick is to close your eyes and feel those fingers touching the keys, then depress them all as a single movement. Try to 'set' the hand in this shape, so that when you move the hand around the keyboard it still plays triads wherever it lands. Keep the wrist loose. Then try the same with the the other hand.

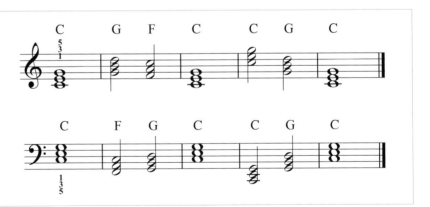

UNIT 2

SECTION 1

THE BLACK NOTES

Any two notes next to each other on the piano, whether two whites or a white and a black, are said to be a half step (semitone) apart. So if you tried playing every single note on the piano (black and white) from one end to the other you'd be moving all the time in identical semitone half steps.

Think of black notes in the first instance as **alterations** of neighbouring white notes: each black note can be an alteration of the white note to the left, or of the white note to the right.

In the first case, the white note has been altered upwards, raising or sharpening it by a semitone. In the second case, the white note has been altered downwards, lowering or flattening it by a semitone. The name of the black note reflects this idea. It carries the letter name of the white note below or above.

When it raises the note on the left it's a **sharp**; when it lowers the note on the right it's a **flat**. This means that the same black *key* can be a different *note,* with a different name, in different contexts. Two different note-names that share the same key are said to be **enharmonically equivalent**.

Here's how we write *sharps* and *flats* in music:

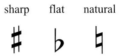

These signs are placed just in front of the notehead, on the same line or space. A **natural** sign is used to cancel a sharp or flat, telling you to play the normal white note.

Exercise 2.1

Close the book. Choose one black note at a time and find it in every octave. Where does it lie in the pattern of groups of two or three black keys? What two names can it have?

When you are playing music with a lot of black notes, don't be afraid to move your fingers further into the keyboard. That way they will they sit more comfortably on top of the black keys and in between them.

Altered pitch

Names for black notes treat them as alterations of white notes. This reflects the origins of our musical system in Ancient Greek, Byzantine and Arabic cultures. They used instruments tuned to a basic seven-note scale, but it is thought that they also allowed singers to *alter* the pitch of some notes slightly for expressive effect – just as modern folk singers do.

KEYS & KEY SIGNATURES

Music is usually based on the notes of a scale. The scale we have already seen is called the scale of C major.

It starts on C, and is called **major** because of the particular sequence of larger and smaller steps from one note to the next – which is what gives it its character. C major consists only of white notes, so the pattern of steps reflects the fact that some of the white notes have black notes between them (making them a tone apart) while others don't (making them a semitone apart) :

C	D	E	F	G	A	B	C
tone☐	tone☐	semitone☐	tone☐	tone☐	tone☐	semitone☐

We can create a major scale starting on any note, as long as we use the same pattern of larger and smaller steps. Here's the same pattern, starting on G.

G	A	B	C	D	E	F#	G
tone☐	tone☐	semitone☐	tone☐	tone☐	tone☐	semitone☐

To keep the pattern the same we have to introduce a black note – in this case *F-sharp*. If the music consistently uses notes from the scale of G, we say it's in the **key** of G, and that G is the **keynote**. This means it'll have F-sharps appearing regularly, rather than F naturals. Here it is as written music:

To make it easier to read, we write the necessary sharp just once, on the F line of the stave, at the beginning of each line of music. It appears after the clef but before any time signature:

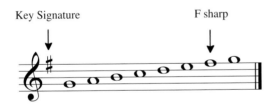

This tells you to play every F as F-sharp unless instructed otherwise. That tells you what key the piece is in and tells you what black notes to expect. It's called the **key signature**. Key signatures can include between one and seven sharps or flats. (Outside of some modern music, if a piece has no sharps or flats at all in the key signature, that *is* its key signature.)

If a sharp, flat or natural sign appears in front of a particular note, rather than in the key signature, we call it an **accidental**. You should note carefully the following differences between how a key signature works and how an accidental works:

- a key signature affects any note (in any octave) with the same letter name as that specified by the position of the sharp/flat sign at the beginning of the stave, and does so for the rest of the piece, or until the key signature is changed
- an accidental affects the note in front of which it is placed, and any other note with the same letter name *in the same octave* that follows afterwards *in the same bar*, or until cancelled by another accidental later in that bar.

Exercise 2.2

CD: **TRACK 10**

'Greensleeves' is an old English tune, traditionally said to have been composed in the early 16th century by King Henry VIII, though its existence was not recorded in print until 1580. Shakespeare mentions it in his comedy The Merry Wives of Windsor. Notice the key signature and accidentals. What key do you think it's in? Join the notes smoothly, especially in the right hand, so that it sounds like a song.

EXERCISE 2.2

The reign of Henry VIII (1491-1547) had important consequences for music. When the Pope refused him a divorce, he made himself head of the Church of England, separating it from the Catholic Church in Rome. The new church was influenced by Protestantism, which emphasised the role of the individual. Protestant countries like England, Germany and the Netherlands favoured straightforward homophonic music, often using their own languages rather than Latin. Musical styles were less decorative and more structured, with an emphasis on inwardness, later mirrored in Romanticism.

MAJOR & MINOR

If we change the sequence of larger and smaller steps between notes of a scale, we produce a different type of scale, with a different character. The main alternative to the **major** scale is the **minor** scale, which tends to feel sad, whereas major key music tends to feel happy. The minor scale differs from the major in having the 3rd and 6th notes flattened by one semitone. Here's A major, with three sharps, followed by A minor:

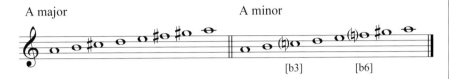

Sharps or flats are shown in a set sequence in a key s   Flat   r   Natural   how many of them there are. Each major key adds one more sharp or flat to those already in other major keys. For example, here are the key signatures for C, G, D and A majors:

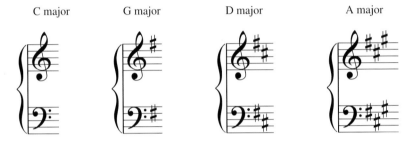

However, *minor* keys are also indicated by using the key signatures for *major* keys. Unfortunately, they don't quite do the job. The major key signature that gives you the necessary flattened 3rd and 6th of a minor scale also flattens the 7th, because it has to keep to the order of sharps or flats (which is fixed for all key signatures). But in the minor the 7th should not be flattened, so we have to sharpen the 7th in the music as an **accidental**.

Now look at the last example again. Can you see that the G-sharp in A minor is the sharpened 7th of the scale? The key signature here is the same as C major (ie, no sharps or flats). When the 7th is consistently sharpened in the music like this, it almost certainly means that it is in a minor key.

Now try playing the minor scale with just the notes of the key signature, and no raised 7th (in A minor, that means with G natural instead of G sharp: so just white notes). This is what non-classical musicians call the **natural minor** scale: it's important in rock music. However, in classical music this belongs to a family of scales used in early church music, known as **modes**, which were replaced by the major-minor system. (We'll learn about modes later anyway, since they came back into use in modern music and especially in jazz improvisation.)

The next two pieces are both minuets, a type of dance, from the late 17th century. In case you've forgotten your history, that's a period famous for scientists and philosophers such as Newton or Leibnitz. It was both the 'Age of Reason' and of men trying to look serious wearing huge wigs. Even their music unfolds with the logic of a perfect piece of machinery.

Which of the following pieces is major, and which is minor? In each case, try clapping just the rhythm first, then practise each hand separately before combining them.

Mind games

Leibnitz said that music was the mind doing mathematics without realising it. What do you think he meant?

Exercise 2.3

CD: **TRACK 11**

This short piece is by Henry Purcell, a great English composer of the 17th century. Watch out for the left hand from bar 5 onwards: the division into notes with stems going up and stems going down means your left hand is really playing two separate melodies at the same time! Join notes smoothly where possible.

EXERCISE 2.3

Henry Purcell (1659-1695) was born in London and brought up as a choirboy in Westminster Abbey, before becoming organist there. He was the most important English composer of the baroque period. Unlike his successors over the next two centuries, he created music that reflected the influence of Continental styles while still managing to preserve many of the distinctive features of the English musical tradition. He wrote excellent chamber music and theatre music, and his opera *Dido and Aeneas* is considered a miniature operatic masterpiece. Purcell was the last in a long line of great English composers, including Byrd, Dowland, Tallis and Wilbye. His death at the age of only 36 was a severe blow for English music. France, Germany and Italy flourished musically in the 18th and 19th centuries, but it wasn't until the 20th century that the English again began producing composers with truly individual voices. Historians have many theories about why this was, but no-one really knows.

Exercise 2.4

Johann Sebastian Bach was one of the greatest composers who ever lived. (He also found time to have twenty-one children.) In this piece by him, look out for changes of position in the right hand, and notice how the left hand returns differently when the tune is repeated. You'll find that the repeated G notes in the tune are more easily played as short notes with gaps in between – but this should not affect the rhythm.

CD: **TRACK 12**

INTERVALS

The different sizes of step between notes in a scale, such as tones and semitones, are examples of different **intervals**. The difference in pitch between any two notes in a scale can be named as an interval, by counting the number of steps in the major or minor scale needed to get from the lower note to the higher note. Take the lower note and build a scale on that, counting the steps, until you reach the higher note. If you start on C and want to get to F, that's C D E F, or four steps up the major scale. So the interval is a 4th. If you start on B and want to get to D, that's B C-sharp D, three steps up the minor scale, so the interval is a minor 3rd.

Intervals that fit the intervals in major or minor scales are called **diatonic** intervals. But sometimes that doesn't work. In these cases we treat the interval as an alteration of one of the normal intervals: as a **chromatic** interval:

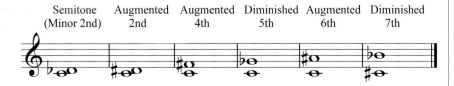

Augmented intervals enlarge a major or perfect interval by one semitone, whereas

Important intervals

Remember when you play music that the intervals between notes are often more important than the notes themselves. It's the intervals that make melodies interesting and expressive.

diminished intervals contract a minor or perfect interval by one semitone. (In the last example, note how raising the *lower* note also makes the interval smaller; conversely, lowering the lower note makes it larger.)

Note that the intervals of a minor 2nd and minor 7th from the keynote do not appear in the minor scale. The minor 7th is specified by the key signature, but the scale itself uses the raised 7th. (Later we'll learn another kind of minor scale in which the minor 7th appears.) The minor 2nd functions more like a chromatic interval: that's why it's more common to refer to it as a semitone. The naming of intervals also reflects the rules for interval inversion, but this is more advanced, so we'll deal with it later on.

Exercise 2.5

Find a G, D, or F on the piano. Work out the notes of the major and minor scales that start from these notes. Can you find all the diatonic and chromatic intervals mentioned so far, on each of these notes?

Exercise 2.6

CD: **TRACK 13**

'Song of the Lonely Beetle' has plenty of accidentals and chromatic intervals, so don't be afraid to move into the black keys, especially if the thumb plays them. Notice how the G-sharp and A-flat both refer to the same note on the keyboard. Join notes smoothly and keep the left hand quieter than the right. Don't rush.

EXERCISE 2.6

MAJOR & MINOR SCALES

The **passing thumb** technique, which allows us to cover an octave in the scale of C major without a break, also lets us extend the scale to two octaves.

Going up the scale in the right hand, we reach B with our 4th finger. Then we put the thumb under: it is quite a stretch. The thumb lands on C instead of the 5th finger, so it is now in the same place as it is at the start of a C scale. Now you can carry on with the ordinary one-octave fingering (passing thumb under after 3rd) to take you to the top of the second octave.

When you get there, you come back down (your 5th finger is on the top C) exactly as you do in the single-octave C scale. When your thumb arrives on C in the middle octave, you must stretch your fourth finger over your thumb and bring it down on to the B. Now you're in a position to carry on to the bottom using the one-octave fingering again. This is known as '3-4-3 fingering'.

The left hand does the same, but the other way round: after your thumb has played the C at the top of the first octave, your 4th finger stretches over to D and then you carry on as if you were playing the first octave again.

On the way down, when you have reached D with your 4th finger, your thumb passes under and lands on C. Then you carry on as before. Remember to make the wrist do the work of helping to stretch under or over, instead of allowing the elbows to swing out.

Almost all the two-octave scales below follow this pattern. The exception is the right hand of F major, which puts 4th on B-flat (in order to avoid passing the thumb under to a black note). This makes for '4-3-4 fingering', ending on the 4th rather than 5th finger at the top of the scale. The left hand of F major, however, uses the normal fingering.

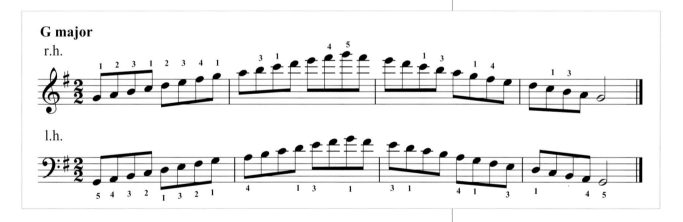

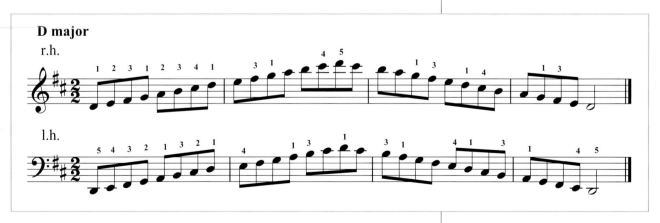

61

A major

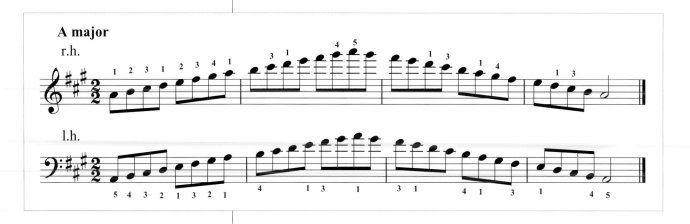

F major

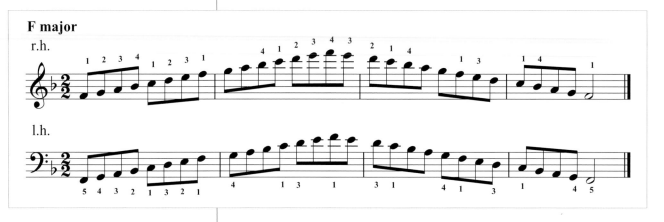

A minor

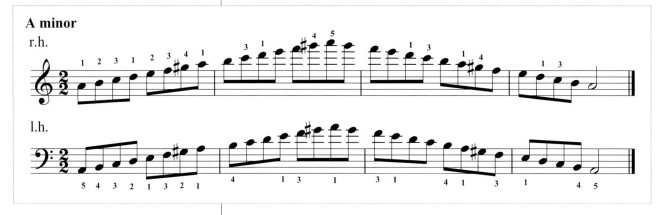

D minor

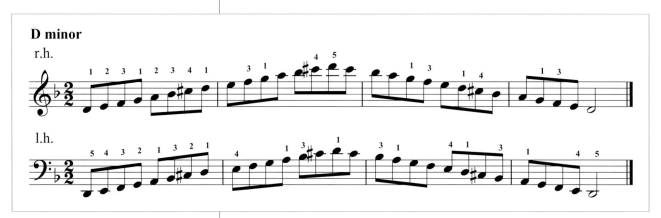

E minor

r.h.

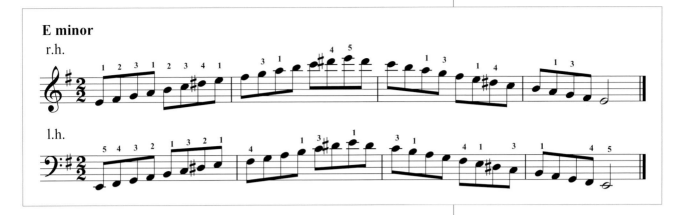

l.h.

Look out for the accidentals in the minor scales, and move your hand into the black keys, even for white notes next to black notes. Because the upper octave contains the same notes as the lower octave, this is a chance to get to know notes on leger lines.

When you can play each of these hands separately from memory, try playing them 'hands together' in the same direction, first one octave, then two. Two octaves is quite a bit harder: it's easy to lose the fingering on the way down. However this is the 'standard fingering' for scales starting on white notes (except F major), so maybe we should analyze it:

	Up		Down	
R.H.	1 2 3 1 2 3 4 1 2 3 1 2 3 4		5 4 3 2 1 3 2 1 4 3 2 1 3 2 1	
L.H.	5 4 3 2 1 3 2 1 4 3 2 1 3 2		1 2 3 1 2 3 4 1 2 3 1 2 3 4 5	

◍ *Thumb and 5th come together at the bottom and top of the scale.*
◍ *Thumbs come together on the keynote in the middle of scale.*
◍ *3rd fingers come together every time.*

The best way to memorize this combined pattern is to play it on the piano lid. When you can do this, apply it to C major, and then to the above scales. Be careful with F major though: the right hand fingering is irregular, because of the 4th on the B-flat, so the combined pattern of the two hands will be different as well. (In this case, thumbs coincide on C each time and on the F in the middle.) You can also try starting from the top of the scale and coming down first.

BROKEN CHORDS (1)

You will recall the triads, made up of the 1st, 3rd and 5th notes in a scale. Each triad can be played in three positions, each with a different note at the bottom. To prepare for playing chords, it's important to practise moving between these positions.

Exercise 2.7

Here are the three positions of a C major triad, with fingerings. Your 2nd finger replaces your 3rd in the right-hand middle position, and in the left-hand top position. Move to each new position in advance and play all three notes exactly together. As you play them, feel your hand sinking into the keys.

EX 2.7

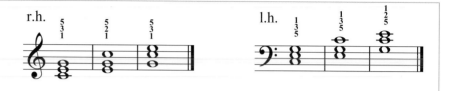

Play through the notes of all three positions one after another and you have a **broken chord** of C major. Make sure you join the notes smoothly, especially as you move between positions:

C major

Here are the other broken chords you should know right now. First play through each one in block chords, as with C major (Ex.2.7), then as written. Also practise them from memory.

G major

F major

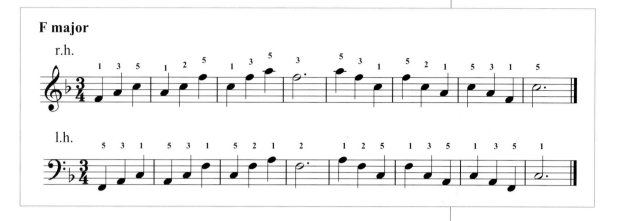

A minor

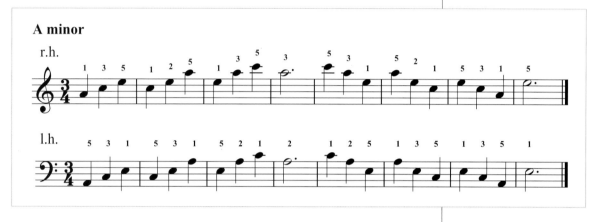

D minor

E minor

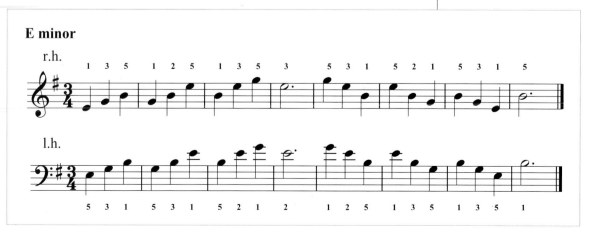

UNIT 3

SECTION 1

DYNAMICS, ARTICULATION AND EXPRESSION

Playing music isn't just about playing the right notes at the right time. It's also about playing them in the right way. How loudly or softly you play at different times can make an enormous difference to the character of the music: that's called **dynamics**. You should always listen carefully to check whether you're playing at the right level, and avoid playing too loudly when the music is awkward or fast.

Dynamic markings are placed in the music (usually between the staves) to indicate the appropriate degree of loudness. Each lasts until it is contradicted by the next. Italians were the first to use dynamic markings, so we still use Italian terms (or their abbreviations). Classical musicians from different countries can communicate, using these terms as a kind of international language.

Here are the main levels:

Italian	Abbreviation	Explanation
pianissimo	*pp*	very soft
piano	*p*	soft
mezzo piano	*mp*	fairly soft
mezzo forte	*mf*	fairly loud
forte	*f*	loud
fortissimo	*ff*	very loud

Other terms indicate gradual changes of volume. Dotted lines after the word show exactly how long these changes should take, or these "hairpin" signs are used:

Italian	Sign	Explanation
crescendo	⊂	getting gradually louder
diminuendo	⊃	getting gradually softer

Remember, these are gradual changes, so you shouldn't suddenly get louder or softer at the point marked. Instead, begin changing level just after that point. Other terms modify these basic terms:

Italian	Explanation
molto	very, much
poco	slightly, a little
poco a poco	gradually
subito	suddenly
sempre	always
piu	more
meno	less

Articulation markings refer to particular ways of playing and connecting notes:

A **slur** (a curved line, similar to a **tie**) between two or more notes of different pitch means that those notes should be joined smoothly (legato – see below) to form a **phrase**. Just as you find natural places to breathe when speaking or singing, so instrumental music is divided up into phrases.

These give structure to the music and make it more expressive. To reflect this in your playing you need to master the art of **phrasing**, one of the most important skills of the classical musician.

Loud and soft

There are no dynamic markings in early keyboard music. That's because early instruments like the **harpsichord** could only play at a single volume level (a bit like an electric keyboard that isn't touch sensitive). The piano was the first keyboard instrument to offer a real range of dynamic levels, which is why they called it the **fortepiano** ('loud and soft'). Later this was changed round to 'pianoforte', or 'piano' for short.

Here are four more articulation signs:

 = release immediately after playing; (staccato – see below)

 = very short and sharp (molto staccato)

 = accent this note for special emphasis

 = make the note sound clearly for its full length (marcato)

You should also know this sign, which concerns timing rather than articulation:

 = pause on this note, holding it beyond its written value (fermata)

Tempo is Italian for time, but in music it refers to speed. Many of the terms used to indicate speed also express something of the music's character. Eventually you should know all those in the glossary at the end of the book, but learn these first:

Italian:	Explanation:
Prestissimo	very fast
Presto	quick
Vivace	lively
Allegro	fast
Allegretto	quite fast
Moderato	moderate
Andantino	slightly faster (or slower) than Andante
Andante	leisurely, at a walking pace
Largo	fairly slow
Adagio	slow
Lento	very slow
accelerando (accel.)	gradually getting faster
ritardando (ritard.)	gradually getting slower
rallentando (rall.)	gradually getting slower
ritenuto (rit.)	hold back
a tempo	return to the original speed

THE EXTENDED HAND POSITION

The most common extension from the five-finger position comes when you have to stretch to play two notes an octave apart. You must learn to *feel* this, because when your hands are playing in different parts of the keyboard there's no way to watch them both at once – and anyway, you should generally be looking at the music, not at your hands.

Exercise 3.1

An Air was originally a slowish song, often accompanied by another instrument. In this example Henry Purcell (1659-1695) makes the right hand the soloist, while the left accompanies. Watch out for accidentals and octave stretches, especially when the hands are far apart. Try not to look down at the keys unless you really have to, and pay attention to phrasing. You can lift off a little at the end of each phrase in the right hand.

CD: **TRACK 14**

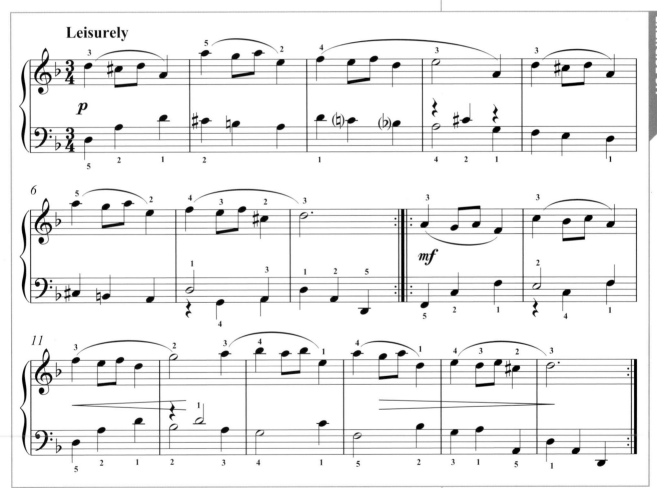

LEGATO AND STACCATO

On the piano it's normal to join notes smoothly, making a good **legato**, even when there are no specific instructions to do so.

In contrast, when **staccato** is required it is usually indicated. Remember, though, that early keyboard music, from before the invention of the piano, will have no articulation markings (unless added by an editor). It's up to you to figure out how the music should be played.

A good legato should contain neither audible gaps between notes nor obvious overlaps: release each note just after playing the next one. Avoid overlapping when moving from a black to a white note.

Staccato generally involves releasing the note just after playing it, but how you do this and how quickly depend on context. It's a complex effect involving musical character as well as note length. (Later we'll look at different kinds of staccato.) For now, keep the wrist loose and try not to pull away from the keys unnecessarily.

Exercise 3.2.

CD: **TRACK 15**

'Gnome Dance' requires a crisp staccato. Accenting the first beat of each bar makes for a more rhythmic feel. Watch out for sudden changes of position, and. use the left hand rests to get the hand into position in advance. Include dynamics and articulation from the start. Move into the black keys when playing black and white notes together.

TRIPLETS

Occasionally, we want to subdivide a beat of music into three equal parts instead of two, so we use a **triplet**. This means the notes are just a little faster than the normal subdivisions, as we're playing 'three notes in the time of two'. We write these like ordinary divisions into two, but with one extra note, and a figure 3 placed above or below the notes.

70

MORE CHANGES OF HAND POSITION

The next two pieces require even more changes of hand position. They should be practised one hand at a time, then without looking down at the keys unless you have to. They're both dances with a relaxed, light-hearted character, so stress the first beat of the bar while keeping a light feel.

Exercise 3.3.

Wolfgang Amadeus Mozart (1756-91) was an Austrian child prodigy, who was already performing and composing at the age of five. He wrote this Minuet when he was only six. If he could play it, so can you. Note the triplet in bar 7 and the pause in bar 20.

CD: **TRACK 16**

EXERCISE 3.3

Wolfgang Amadeus Mozart was a child prodigy. Born in Salzburg, Austria, his astonishing gifts as a composer and pianist were displayed at an early age on tours of France, England, Holland and Italy, as well as to the main cities of Germany and Austria. As a result, he absorbed many musical influences, and these bore fruit later as he developed into a creative genius of unrivalled spontaneity and imagination. Mozart met J.C. Bach in London, and was influenced by his incorporation of aspects of Italian operatic style into instrumental compositions, including works for piano. Mozart's piano sonatas and chamber music show wonderful musicality, melodiousness, and inventiveness, but his greatest achievements are almost certainly his piano concertos and operas, as well as his later symphonies and quintets, which date from the later part of his life in Vienna, then the cultural capital of Europe. Although they now celebrate him, the Viennese public of the time quickly deserted Mozart, and as a result he died in miserable poverty at an early age. Beethoven and Schubert later suffered similar treatment at their hands.

Exercise 3.4

CD: **TRACK 17**

This Dance by Joseph Haydn (1732-1809), who lived in Austria at the same time as Mozart, has lots of left hand octave jumps, and needs a clear contrast between staccato and legato. Watch the unusual fingering in bars 8-9, where the right hand has to play two notes at once.

Exercise 3.5

'Somersaults' has rapid shifts of position, and is made up of 'broken' chords, played a note at a time. First practise each group of three notes as a block, with all the notes played at once.

CD: **TRACK 18**

CHROMATIC SCALE ON D

A chromatic scale uses all the black and white notes available in an octave, and requires a special fingering. The 3rd finger is used on all the black keys in both hands, while the 2nd is only used when we come to play white notes with no black key between them. The fingers should be slightly more rounded than usual, well in towards the black keys, and close to the keys all the time.

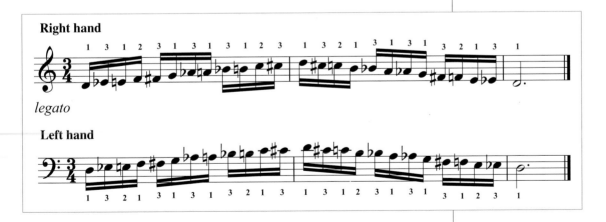

UNIT 4

SECTION 2

SHAPING A RHYTHM

Dotted rhythms, especially, can be difficult to get exactly right. Try clapping these rhythms, feeling the individual subdivisions first, then concentrating on the rhythm itself. The exercise below is based around dotted rhythms.

Exercise 4.1

This tune by Clementi sounds lovely when you get the rhythm just right. The right hand dotted rhythm should be relaxed at the beginning, but crisper when the time-values are halved in the second and fourth lines.

Sing – produce more sound – on long notes, and beware of changes between treble and bass clef in the left hand.

CD: **TRACK 19**

RAPID CHANGES OF HAND POSITION

Exercise 4.2

CD: **TRACK 20**

This Musette by Bach calls for some rapid changes of hand position, which must not be allowed to hold up timing or cause unwanted accents. The left hand octaves provide the repetitive 'drone' that is a feature of this baroque dance form: they should be kept light and staccato: especially the thumb. (Keeping the thumb in contact with the key even when it doesn't play helps to stop it banging.) Left hand octaves can strain the wrist, so practise keeping relaxed while you play them, and stop if you feel any forearm pain.

The hands cover the same notes in bars 3-4 as in bars 1-2, only an octave closer in. Practise jumping between the two positions, and back again, without looking at your hands. Always aim to arrive in position just before you need to play, so the hands settle and can play the next notes in a controlled way.

Watch out for places where the right hand plays legato, but the left hand staccato: keep them distinct. Learning the notes gets easier once you've spotted places where the hands play the same thing an octave apart, or where the left just repeats itself so you can focus on the right hand melody. The right hand notes tied over barlines (bar 13 onwards) need slow practise not to upset overall coordination and rhythm – aim to hold the tied D while changing the finger holding it.

EXERCISE 4.2

CANTABILE

Cantabile is Italian for playing in a 'singing' style.

It's a really important concept, because the ideal with a classical instrument is to make it sound like a singing voice (which is naturally expressive). This can be especially challenging on the piano, since its mechanical playing action (ie, the hammer and damper mechanisms) offers less direct physical control over the sound than is the case with wind or stringed instruments.

So we learn how to *recreate* the principal features of a sung melody by other means.

The two most important techniques are:

- Relating **tone and contour**: as in speaking, if the melody goes up, then it's becoming more intense, so you get louder; if it comes down, it's more relaxed, so get quieter.
- Relating **tone and time**: longer notes need more volume to last through until the next note, which they must do to sound like a melody sung smoothly in a single breath. (Equally, a note coming after a long note may need to be softened to follow on smoothly.)

Schumann's 'Humming Song' is a great opportunity to practise cantabile shaping. Look at the left hand first. Notice how it alternates between a line and a repeated note. This kind of alternating movement requires a technique called **rotation**.

Exercise 4.3

First position the left hand on the lid of the piano, with rounded fingers. Move 5th finger and thumb alternately, as though playing, and speed up gradually until your hand gets tired.

Now try the same thing again, but rock the whole hand to and fro from one side to the other, so that you cause the 5th finger and thumb to play as before, even though they themselves do nothing. This is rotation, which helps to keep the hand relaxed. It's a wrist movement – like turning a door handle. (Shut your eyes and imagine grasping a door handle; then turn it. How does it feel? Rotation should feel like that.) Repeat with the right hand.

Now play the left hand for the first section of 'Humming Song' (overleaf), using this technique. Keep the wrist relaxed, with the thumb loose and over the keys. The top joint of the thumb should point slightly inwards towards the hand to align it with the keys. Soften the thumb's impact by directing the rotation more towards the lower notes, and notice how rotation helps to keep the quavers rhythmically even.

Exercise 4.4

Still working with 'Humming Song' (overleaf), compare the opening left hand with the right hand in the middle section. It has similar alternations, but with melody notes as crotchets, to be joined.

First play the right hand rotations without joining the crotchets, then again but joining them up so they flow smoothly as a melody, keeping a gentle rocking movement going at the same time.

Correct thumb position

If the thumb is allowed to stick out (top), it will not be aligned with the note, preventing it from striking cleanly from above. The top joint needs to be angled slightly inwards (bottom) so the thumb is aligned with the keys.

Exercise 4.5

CD: **TRACK 21**

Now let's turn to the piece as a whole. Pay close attention to the position of each note in the right hand melody: where is it in relation to the high-point of the line? Listen for how the long notes connect up with succeeding notes, and keep your fingers close to the keys for legato. The left hand is the accompaniment, so it stays quietly in the background, even though it's more demanding to play. At the same time, notice how closely the left-hand line follows the shape of the right hand and make sure they sound exactly together.

EXERCISE 4.5

SCALES

E major has the same black notes as A major, plus D-sharp, which was in E minor.

B major adds an A-sharp, meaning that it has all five black notes. You can remember it by which *white* notes it has: B and E. Each hand uses the 3rd finger on groups of two black notes, and the 4th on groups of three, which is a feature of scales with all five black notes. Keep the hands further in over the black keys. The left starts on 4th and then passes 4th over onto F-sharp as well, which might feel strange.

B minor keeps the same fingering as B major, but because the minor scale flattens the 3rd and 6th degrees of the major we lose two of the black notes. This makes it more awkward to play. Keep well into the black keys when you reach the G natural.

Notice the rhythmic grouping of the notes in fours. Accenting the first note of each group can help achieve evenness of tone and time. Playing with dotted rhythms can help to build up fluency in tricky scales like this one.

Playing an arpeggio

The pictures show the lateral, left-to-right movement of the wrist in playing a right-hand arpeggio. Once the thumb has played (top), the wrist swings right to support the central fingers (middle) and then the little finger (bottom).

ONE-OCTAVE ARPEGGIOS

An **arpeggio** means playing the notes of a chord, one at a time, up and down, over one or more octaves. Arpeggiating or 'spreading' a chord means playing the notes one after another rather than exactly together, to sound like a harp (arpa in Italian).

C major

Right hand   Left hand

legato

Now try playing the same pattern with the same fingering, starting on F and G. This gives arpeggios of F major (FAC) and G major (GBD).

Then try D minor (DFA) and E minor (EGB) arpeggios, with the same fingering as A minor.

A minor

Right hand   Left hand

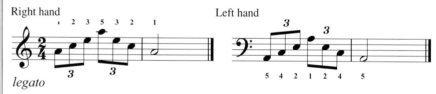

legato

Notice the extended fingering for 4-note chords, especially the use of the 4th finger in the left hand. You don't need to cover all the notes at once: as you move through the chord, the wrist swings round sideways to help the hand cover the notes it needs to play. This **lateral movement** is executed with the elbows kept fairly close in to the body.

UNIT 5

SECTION 2

COMPOUND TIME

Normal time values work by subdividing the beat into halves, but we've already seen how triplets divide the beat into thirds instead. We can also group beats into threes for the duration of a piece, using the time signature.

Compound time is different again. It gives each beat the value of a dotted note, so it has three, not two, subdivisions. Note lengths are normally expressed as fractions of a semibreve (a crotchet is a 'quarter-note', for instance) but there is no simple way of expressing dotted notes like that. Instead, we use the value of the individual subdivisions making up the dotted note, placing that at the bottom of the time signature. Above it we use the total number of those subdivisions in the bar. We know each beat has three of those subdivisions, so to find the number of beats in the bar we simply divide the top number by three.

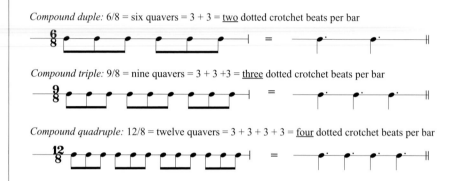

Compound duple: 6/8 = six quavers = 3 + 3 = <u>two</u> dotted crotchet beats per bar

Compound triple: 9/8 = nine quavers = 3 + 3 +3 = <u>three</u> dotted crotchet beats per bar

Compound quadruple: 12/8 = twelve quavers = 3 + 3 + 3 + 3 = <u>four</u> dotted crotchet beats per bar

In compound time, the subdivisions are 'beamed' together (written with their tails joined at the top) in threes rather than twos. However, notice that subdivisions of the subdivisions are still divided in half in the normal way. For example, in 6/8, quavers are grouped in threes to make up dotted crotchet beats, but semiquavers are still grouped in twos, because they are dividing up straight quavers, not dotted quavers.

If we start grouping semiquavers in threes, we create a dotted quaver beat. These are the same as dotted crotchet beats, but with all time values halved (they are written as 6/16 or 9/16 or 12/16, and are pretty unusual). The music will sound the same, whether it's written in 6/8 with dotted crotchet beats and quaver divisions, or in 6/16 with dotted quaver beats and semiquaver divisions. In **early music** you're more likely to come across compound time signatures such as 6/4, 9/4, or 12/4, with all time values doubled, so each beat is worth a dotted minim and divides into three crotchets. Again, the music will sound the same.

Note that 3/8 is not compound time, but is like 3/4 time, with time values halved. So in 'Für Elise' the quaver beats divide into groups of two semiquavers.

THUMB CONTROL

Developing flexibility and control of the thumbs is vital to good playing technique. We've already mentioned the positioning of the thumbs, which are more awkward than other fingers because their angle of movement is at odds with the natural movement of the thumb joint. Thumbs need to be trained to move independently of the hand without causing tension in the hand. Countless pianists are let down by poor thumb control, which results in an uneven tone and muscular tension in the hands and fingers.

Exercise 5.1

This is an important exercise, so be prepared to take your time to get it just right. First close the lid of the instrument. Position the left hand on the lid, just as you would on the keys, with rounded fingers and level knuckles. Take a moment to feel that your wrist and forearm really are relaxed and properly supported. Then lift the thumb up as far as is comfortable, without altering the angle of the hand. Try not to shift the hand over towards the weaker fingers. Hold the thumb in the air for five seconds; then let it fall and feel it resting on the lid. Relax the hand for five seconds, keeping the position, then do it again. Try the right hand, then open the lid and repeat the exercise (each hand in a five finger position in the middle of the keyboard), with the thumb holding down the note it plays. Try to control the dynamic level, and keep the other fingers sitting on the keys, while the thumb moves by itself. (A good trick for this is to close your eyes first and just feel the contact of the fingertips with the surface of the keys.)

Exercise 5.2

Now you've got the vertical movement of the thumbs sorted out, it's time to work on sideways movements and staccato. Try this exercise slowly, but with the staccato crisp and short. Then speed up.

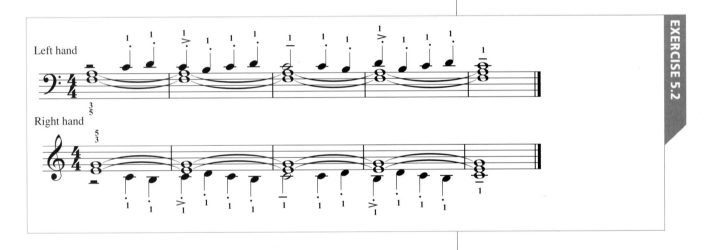

EXERCISE 5.3

Exercise 5.3

CD: **TRACK 22**

The next piece, 'Wheelbarrow Man', develops thumb control with lots of slight changes of hand position. Be careful when thumbs play off the beat. Keep them relaxed and controlled to avoid unwanted accents. The hands move together between different octave registers, as though joined by an invisible cord.

PEDALS

By now you've surely tried out the pedals for yourself to see what they do, but let's be clear about exactly what their function is.

The **left pedal, or 'soft pedal',** makes the sound softer and duller. We call this 'una corda' (literally 'one string'), because on a grand piano it shifts the hammers sideways so they don't strike all the strings for that note (or for bass register notes, the centre of the string). On an upright the same effect is created through the pedal moving all hammers closer to the strings so they gather less momentum and strike with less force. Notice how depressing the left pedal changes the quality of sound, not just the volume. Pianists often use the soft pedal to control the volume of piano textures, in order to keep in the background when accompanying a soloist, but when you play solo piano yourself you should avoid using it as a substitute for achieving genuine soft playing through the hands and fingers.

But when pianists talk about 'pedalling', they generally mean the **right pedal,** or **sustaining pedal,** which is the more important of the two. Depressing the pedal de-activates the dampers for the entire keyboard simultaneously. Normally these dampers cut off the note as soon as the key is released, so suspending their action means notes carry on sounding until you let go of the pedal, even after the keys have been released.

This frees up the fingers to play other notes while the previous ones are still sounding, but it also produces a kind of echoing ambience within the instrument – the result of the sympatheric resonance of other strings, which are also no longer damped. The result is that pedalling also changes the quality of sound, and often results in the accumulation of sound, texture, and volume.

Some pianos have a **third pedal.** On most uprights this is a **practice pedal** that mutes the sound so you don't drive the neighbours crazy; but on Steinways (whose manufacturer patented this device) and a few other instruments this is a **sostenuto pedal,** which is a more complicated kind of sustaining pedal, mainly used in specialised contemporary piano music.

DIRECT PEDALLING AND TONAL BALANCE

In direct pedalling, we put the pedal down just as we begin to play a note, chord, phrase or texture, and release it just as we finish playing that same material. This makes the note or notes in question more sonorous. In the case of a sequence of notes or chords, it also causes them to overlap with one another, producing a smoother and richer texture. (This is especially important for creating the atmospheric textures and dramatic effects common in Romantic piano music written in the 19th and early 20th centuries.)

The correct way to use the right pedal is for it to be covered by just the front portion of the foot, up to and including the 'ball' of the foot (ie, not just the toes) but no more, and with the heel rested firmly on the ground as support. This ensures that pressing the foot does not affect the poise and balance of the rest of your body.

When the pedal is not required for a significant length of time, the right foot may be withdrawn and returned to its normal position resting entirely on the ground. When the pedal is continuously in use, some pianists withdraw the left foot under the stool (see photo) as a counterbalance to the position of the right foot. (This is useful in advanced playing of a dramatic nature, but you shouldn't worry about it for the time being.)

Sometimes pedalling is indicated in the score, sometimes not. So you may have to decide whether it is appropriate to the music you're learning to play. Once you've done this, the main challenge is to prevent the act of depressing the pedal from interfering with your control of the volume produced by your fingers. In the next piece, this can happen with the left hand if you're not careful. Try to avoid an uncontrolled increase in sound every time you put the pedal down.

Correct use of the pedal

Top: the foot is not far enough on to the pedal. Middle: too far forward, and not secure on the ground. Bottom: the correct foot position. Always practise a piece without pedal first. Add pedal when you have the notes 'under your fingers'. Never use it to cover up your difficulties.

CD: **TRACK 23**

Exercise 5.4

'Für Elise' (opposite) is one of Beethoven's most atmospheric compositions for piano, so you must match your interpretation to the mood of the piece, which is hushed, mournful and reflective. Make the right hand as smooth and singing as you can, and pay careful attention to dynamics. Practise without pedal first. (This is especially important when practising the left hand figure in bar 4: you should be able to pass the 2nd finger over the thumb smoothly and easily before you add pedal.) Position the right hand slightly further into the black keys (the fingertips kept close to the keys) for the opening E/D-sharp alternation; then the hand can move out of the black keys as it completes the phrase. The arpeggio figures (bars 3-4) will sound more flowing when assisted with lateral movement of the kind introduced at the end of the last section (see One-Octave Arpeggios, p80). Connect the hands up smoothly here. Watch out for the left hand octaves in bars 13-14: the pedal allows the left hand to glide freely across the keyboard until it reaches the E above middle C; then each hand must prepare by moving into position just before it actually plays, keeping an even flow of semiquavers.

> **Preparation**
>
> In piano playing, preparation means positioning the hand or finger so that it's ready to play in advance of the actual moment of playing, so positioning does not interfere with playing. This is important for controlling dynamics during sudden changes of hand position.

ESPRESSIVO

When playing 'Für Elise', do you find yourself making small adjustments to the dynamic level of the melody line as you go along? If so, you've naturally begun to master expressive playing. This extends the idea of **cantabile** (see Unit 4) by bringing out subtle characteristics of the melody such as chromatic notes, changes of melodic direction, and expressive intervals. The aim is to create a sense of tension, climax, or repose at different points within the phrase, so that the music is played with feeling. Sometimes you'll see terms such as espressivo or molto espressivo (ie, 'very expressive') written in the music. More often, you'll have to judge for yourself whether this sort of playing is appropriate to the mood, character and style of a piece or musical passage.

Let's have another quick look at the start of 'Für Elise'. In the opening right hand alternation, the D-sharp is foreign to the key of A minor, so we could treat it as slightly more important than the E, even though it's off the beat. At the same time, the repeating alternation of the two notes is an expressive, tension-building device, so why not let it crescendo a little? Then we can drop back down again in volume as the line resolves downwards onto the tonic at the start of the next bar, but not before bringing out that lovely expressive twist when Beethoven delays the descent for a moment.

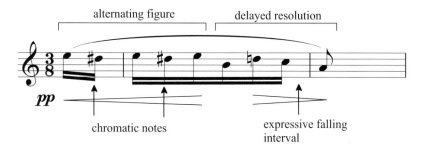

The next example shows how Beethoven creates that twist. You can see how moving up to D delays the C, which itself delays the underlying resolution from B down to A, interposing the more expressive interval of a minor third.

Song and dance

For music to sound more song-like, make smooth adjustments (within the overall dynamic levels) to reflect the importance of notes as they unfold as part of the line. For music to sound more dance-like, accent individual notes to show their importance in the underlying rhythmic or metrical pattern.

So by figuring out how Beethoven actually composed the opening phrase of his famous tune – as a series of decorations of a more basic line – we see how to perform it. (In the next section, Unit 6, you'll learn how to develop your own musical ideas by using techniques like those Beethoven is using here.)

Now look at the next two melodic phrases. Both ascend, the second reaching higher than the first; but it would be wrong to crescendo right through both of them, because the second completes itself over a resolution of the harmony, which means that a slight diminuendo at the end is also called for.

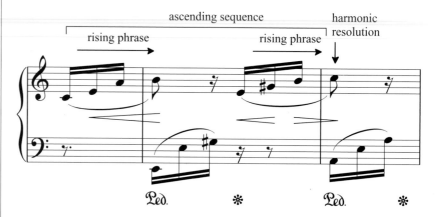

This shows the importance of considering all aspects of the music when developing your interpretation, including the underlying harmonic structure, so that you become sensitive to the unfolding of feelings of tension and repose, of expectation and arrival, which the music can evoke. Now try playing through the whole piece again, making all of it expressive.

4-NOTE BROKEN CHORDS

These require sideways ('lateral') swinging round of the wrist, just like the arpeggios in the last unit, but they also move through different positions, like 3-note broken chords.

Exercise 5.5

Start with this preparatory exercise in C major, which gives more time to move between positions. Focus on achieving good lateral freedom, with elbows kept close in to the body.

Now here's the same broken chord, as it should really be playe

C major

Here's the same thing on G.

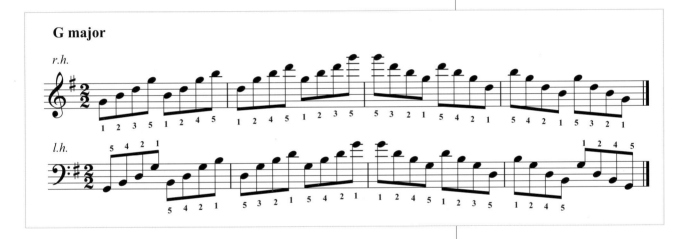

G major

Notice how G major (GBD) has exactly the same spacing of notes, and therefore the same fingering, as C major. The same goes for F major (FAC), A minor (ACE), D minor (DFA) and E minor (EGB). All of these broken chords share the same pattern because they have just white notes. You should practise all of them, beginning with the same kind of preparatory exercise shown above for C major.

CHROMATIC SCALE ON D: TWO OCTAVES

This would be a good time to learn the two-octave chromatic scale, starting on D. It works with exactly the same fingering as the one octave version. Just continue passing the 3rd over, or thumb under, to get you into the next octave.

UNIT 6

SECTION 2

COMPOSING AND IMPROVISING

Whether you want to write a full-scale piano concerto or just to improvise the odd tune in private or with friends, you'll need more theory than if you are just reading and playing music composed by other people. You'll need to understand the rules that determine how chords are used: the theory of **harmony**. Classical harmony came before non-classical harmony, so let's start with that. (We'll get started on non-classical in Unit 9.)

HARMONY

Chords

Chords are combinations of notes played simultaneously so that we perceive them as a single unit. In traditional classical music, they're combinations that sound especially **consonant** – they don't clash. (Notes that do clash are **dissonant**.) The basic form is a **triad**, meaning three notes separated by intervals of a third. Take a five note scale: play the first, third and fifth notes, omitting the second and fourth.

We already know that there are two types of thirds: major thirds and minor thirds. There are four ways of combining major and minor thirds to produce a triad, which means four **chord types**:

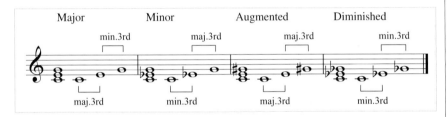

We get a whole family of triads by building one on each note of a scale, using only the notes of that scale. (The technical term for a set of chords using only notes from one scale is **diatonic** harmony. The opposite is **chromatic** harmony, since in traditional classical music the only common scale apart from the major or minor scales is the chromatic scale.)

Here are the chord types created when you build on the notes of a major key or scale. Make a careful note of which type of chord appears on each degree of the scale:

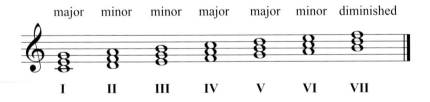

And now the chord types for a minor key or scale. The scale we are using is called the **harmonic minor scale**: there are other types. Notice how the chords appearing on each degree of the scale differ from those associated with the major scale.

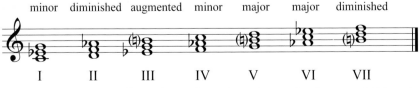

Triads can appear in different **inversions**. Inverting a chord means shifting the bottom note to the top, so a different note sounds at the bottom of the chord, even though the notes of the chord have stayed the same. (Broken chords are really a way of practising moving between inversions of the same chord.)

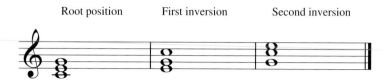

Root position   First inversion   Second inversion

Keys

Chord structures in traditional classical music are based on the **major-minor system** of **tonal harmony**, meaning the chords are derived from their position in the major and minor scales, as we've just seen. It also means that they work in terms of a **key**.

We learned about keys in the first section of the book (see **key signatures**). At any moment, traditional tonal music is in one key or another, meaning it is built around the major or minor scale that starts on a specific note. Tonal music gravitates towards that note as a **tonal centre**, trying to reach 'home base' by whatever means possible.

So there are **chord functions** within a key. But there are also **key relationships** – that is, relations between keys. Let's look at those first. Key relationships reflect the number of notes that any two keys have in common. For example, G major has a key signature with one sharp, F-sharp: so all its notes are the same as those in C major except that one. The more notes in common, the more closely the keys are related. This is reflected in the key signatures. A key with four sharps is closer to one with three sharps than to one with one sharp: the same with flats. We can show this by arranging the keys around a circle, in order of increasing numbers of sharps in one direction, and flats in the other. (It's a circle because F sharp major, with six sharps, is the same key – with the same notes – as G-flat major, with six flats. That's an example of what we call an **enharmonic key relationship**.)

Note that for every major key there's a **minor** key with the same key signature: this **relative minor** is always a minor third (three semitones) down from its **relative major**. These minor keys can then be arranged around the inside of the circle. For both major and minor keys the result is a series of keys, each a perfect 5th away from the previous one: the **circle of fifths**.

Learning keys

The quicker you learn the order of keys and key signatures shown in this diagram, the sooner you'll become confident in understanding how all aspects of harmony work. The distance between any two keys around the circle determines the effect of changing from one of those keys to the other in the course of a piece of music – what we call a **modulation**.

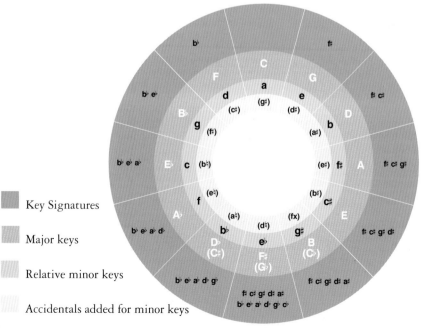

■ Key Signatures

■ Major keys

■ Relative minor keys

■ Accidentals added for minor keys

Chord functions

In classical music, the functions of chords are much the same for major and minor keys, since they principally reflect where the **root** of the chord is located in the scale (rather than the chord type). Hence the technical names for chord functions (see the chart below) also tell you the scale degrees the chords are built on. They are shown with roman numerals:

Degree	Technical Term	Function
I	TONIC	**Tonal centre** (most important chord)
		Point of maximum harmonic resolution
II	SUPERTONIC	5th above dominant
		Substitutes for subdominant chord
III	MEDIANT	5th above submediant
		Substitutes for dominant chord
IV	SUBDOMINANT	**5th below tonic**
		Main source of harmonic tension with dominant
V	DOMINANT	**5th above tonic** (second most important chord)
		Main source of harmonic tension with tonic
VI	SUBMEDIANT	5th above supertonic
		Substitutes for tonic chord
VII	LEADING TONE	5th above mediant
		Rarely used chord

As with keys, the interval of a 5th is crucial in determining the relations between chords. The most important chords are the **primary triads**: I, IV and V. Each chord works like a magnet, trying to become the centre of gravity. I is the strongest, the home chord, but V asserts itself as a rival centre of attraction a 5th higher, eventually resolving back to I. But IV establishes a counter-weight to V by creating another attraction: it is a 5th lower than I as well as a 4th above. (The same logic applies to the relation between tonic, dominant and subdominant as keys.)

Just as V relates to I, so each of the secondary triads, II, III and VI, can be heard as functionally related to the chord a 5th lower. However, in a major key they can also function as substitute minor chords for the major chords two steps higher (the primary triads). (Compare the way the relative minor is derived from a major key.)

Because classical music tends to treat minor key harmony as derived from major, the same principle of substituting for the chord two steps higher is sometimes applied in minor keys, even though the chord types are quite different.

These functions then determine which **chord progressions** sound effective.

The perfect 5th

The importance of the perfect 5th interval reflects its role in the acoustic origins of the major scale itself. The ancient Greek mathematician Pythagoras discovered that all notes in the scale can be derived mathematically from successive intervals of a perfect 5th, which can be reproduced on a stringed instrument by stopping or fretting the string at two-thirds of its length. Only the octave, produced by stopping the string in the middle, is based on a simpler ratio. **Frequency** is the term used by scientists to refer to the speed of vibration of a string, but it also determines intervals between pitches. If a string remains at the same tension, the ratio between frequencies corresponds to the ratio between string lengths. If you halve the length of a string, you double its frequency, creating the octave. To make a perfect 5th, you reduce the string's length by a third.

CHORD LAYOUT AND FINGERING

The basic layout for chords consists of three notes in the right hand and one in the left ('the bass'). Since most chords are triads, one note of the triad appears in two different octaves: it gets **doubled**. Usually this means the left hand note, because the easiest thing for the right hand is to play a triad in **close position**, in one of its inversions. (You'll see why if you try playing Ex.6.5. Compare it to Ex.6.4.) More important is which note lies at the top of the chord, since this may be heard as forming part of a melody.

Close position right hand   Open position right hand

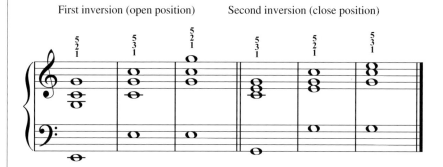

Viewed hands together, these chords are all **root position** chords: they have the root at the bottom. Sometimes, though, especially in classical music, we use chords in **first inversion** or **second inversion**, for variety. These sound less resolved. There are rules for which note to double:

- Root position chords: double any note.
- First inversion chords: don't double the bass (ie, not the 3rd).
- Second inversion chords: *only* double the bass (ie, the 5th).

This means close position triads will also work well as second inversion chords, but not as first inversion chords.

First inversion (open position)   Second inversion (close position)

Note the right hand fingerings. However, these are for isolated chords. It is important to realize that chord fingering can be much more complicated than this (especially for close position chords), since it also depends on how they connect up with preceding or succeeding chords. This can happen in all sorts of ways, so often you may need to rethink fingering to link chords together smoothly with the minimum of changes of hand position.

VOICE-LEADING

The way a chord links up with preceding or succeeding chords depends on **voice-leading** (or 'part writing'). This refers to the way each note in one chord can be heard as moving melodically to a corresponding note in the next, like when each singer in a group takes responsibility for sounding a particular note in the chord. It is what makes for the sense of smooth transition between one chord and the next, which is highly prized by classical composers. It allows us to hear **chord progressions** as combinations of unfolding lines or 'parts'. The rules for voice-leading can be complex, but you should know the basic principles:

Golden rule: each note moves to the *nearest* note in the next chord.

There are three different ways in which two parts may relate to one another:

In parallel motion, the parts move in the same direction; in oblique motion, one part moves while the other stays fixed; in contrary motion, they move in opposite directions.

Other rules:
- avoid parts moving in parallel a perfect 5th or octave apart ('parallel 5ths/octaves');
- aim for contrary or oblique motion between the upper voices and the bass.

Note how these two rules are related. If the *hands* move in contrary motion, you avoid 'parallel 5ths' or 'parallel octaves'. This general principle is worth remembering if you're improvising your own chord arrangements in practically any style.

Chord progressions and cadences

A **chord progression** is a sequence of two or more chords which works by respecting the functions of chords and using these to create patterns of tension and resolution that sound 'logical'. Think of them as combinations of certain basic sorts of **root progression**: these in turn work because they're strong enough to displace the first chord with the second while keeping a sense of continuity.

Great root progressions:
- up or down a 5th or 4th
- down a 3rd

Other root progressions:
- up or down a 2nd
- up a 3rd

The second group can work, depending on context and the particular chords. For example, IV-V works well in classical music, but V-IV is sometimes avoided, though you'll hear it a lot in blues-based and rock music. (That's because blues emphasizes

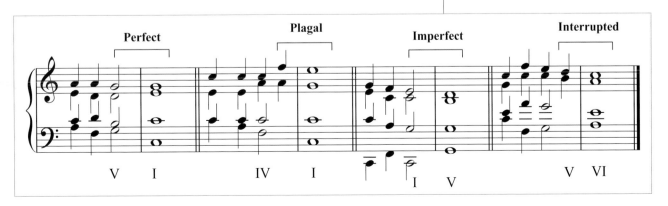

the subdominant region of tonal harmony, whereas classical music typically emphasizes the dominant.) You can learn a lot about chord progressions just by noting down the numerals for any sequence that strikes you when you're playing pieces or just messing about at the keys.

There are special rules about using chords in second inversion. Either the bass should be approached and left by step (a 'passing six-four'), or the chord is followed by a root position chord with the same bass note (a 'cadential six-four'). The term 'six-four' refers to the old way of showing chord inversions by specifying the intervals of the notes above the bass as numbers. In the Baroque period, composers would just write the bass line with these numbers, leaving the keyboard player to decide how to realize the **figured bass** according to his or her style or mood. As we'll see later on, something similar happens in jazz when we use a **lead sheet** that just gives the melody with chord symbols. The modern system of classical chord notation uses the following abbreviations:

Root position:	I, II, III, etc. (or I^a, II^a, III^a, etc.)
First inversion:	I^b, II^b, III^b, etc.
Second inversion:	I^c, II^c, III^c, etc.

MELODY AND HARMONY

There are two ways to think about the relationship between melody and harmony.

- Harmony comes from melody: chords can spell out a harmonic structure already implied by a melody; they provide a **harmonization** – a series of chords that can be played alongside the tune.

- Melody comes from harmony: chord sequences provide source material from which melodies can be developed, through **decoration** of the uppermost part of the progression in various ways.

In the first case, you may want to create the melody yourself before harmonizing it, in which case you'll need to think about **contour** (the shape of the melody), rhythm, and **phrase structure**, as well as harmony.

A good melody develops by rising and falling in interesting but consistent ways, while introducing subtle variations to a regular underlying rhythm. In early music the melody line often reflects the character of dance forms – a bit like some popular styles today. **Classical** melodies often divide up into phrases of equal length, creating 'question and answer' effects. **Romantic** melodies usually build up gradually to a high-point or climax, which can often be delayed for emotional effect.

Have another look at the melodies in the pieces you've played so far in this book. Which of the above categories would you place them in? Why not try analying the chord structure of the melodies. Could the chords have been realized in other ways? Can you make up a tune of your own that works with those chords?

Once you've an idea for a tune of your own, the hardest thing is knowing what to do next. So here's what to do:
- Try to work out what key and time signature it's in;
- Try writing it down (you'll need some blank manuscript paper);
- Write out the chords for each degree of the scale of the key of the tune;
- Look to see if the notes in each bar, half-bar, or beat, form a pattern that corresponds to some or all of the notes of one of the chords from the scale;
- Once you've found the implied chords, try extending the chord progression;

Melody or harmony first?

Right from the beginning of classical music, composers, music theorists, and even philosophers have disagreed about whether melody or harmony comes first in music. They probably never will agree. Even great theorists like Schoenberg and Schenker have struggled to make sense of the way they seem to unfold together.

◗ Look for **motives** (small but distinctive musical shapes within each phrase) that could be repeated or developed.

One way to extend a melody is through **development**: this usually consists of taking a motive and subjecting one or more of its aspects to a series of changes, but in such a way that it remains recognisable. For example, a common technique is to repeat the tune a step higher or lower, forming a rising or falling **sequence**.

Another way is **variation**: here we repeat the same basic idea, but each time altering some of the details, for example by adding faster notes to fill in the gaps between long notes – what we call **embellishment**. This was especially important in early classical keyboard music. When keyboard instruments such as harpsichords and early pianos had limited sustaining potential it was necessary to decorate long notes to avoid awkward gaps in the musical line or texture.

Embellishment

Embellishment is another way of deriving a melodic line from the top part of a harmonic progression. It can even make the **inner parts** or the bassline more melodically interesting, so it's worth looking at more closely. Many of the standard techniques of embellishment are also used by composers to create tunes, as well as by jazz improvisers who want to create their own versions of existing material. Thinking of the tune itself as an embellishment helps us to see how it relates to a harmonic structure, and what that harmony should be.

Classical embellishment techniques are ways of connecting up **non-harmony notes** (which don't belong to the chord over which they sound) with **harmony notes** (which do).

A **passing note** is a non-harmony note moving by step between two harmony notes, sounding off the beat:

An **accented passing note** also moves by step between harmony notes, but is itself on the beat, creating a dissonance

Escape notes precede a step or leap with one or more steps in the opposite direction:

An **auxiliary note** moves to the note a step above or below, and back again:

An **anticipation** sounds before the harmony it belongs to, and then again with the chord:

An **appoggiatura** sounds on the beat as a dissonance, then moves by step to a harmony note:

A **suspension** is like an appoggiatura, but prepares the dissonance by first sounding the note as a consonance against the previous chord, then holding it over onto the next beat (as a tied or repeated note) before achieving **resolution** by step to a weaker beat (or off the beat).

Dominant 7ths

The use of embellishment became more and more sophisticated as classical music developed, especially with the increasing importance of instrumental music and operatic singing in the period of the **Renaissance**. As people started to get used to hearing melodic dissonances, it became acceptable to include a dissonance as part of the dominant chord: a 7th above the bass that only resolves with the resolution of the chord itself.

Note how the 7th (here, the F) resolves downwards by just a semitone to the 3rd of the next chord. It's natural to hear the 3rd (the B) of the dominant chord rising a semitone to the tonic. This is called a **leading note** effect. These movements of just a semitone are especially powerful. In the 19th century the revolutionary composer Wagner used them to introduce more and more chromatic notes into harmony. You'll find similar things when we look at jazz. (However, in the example above, the 3rd in fact moves down to the 5th of the next chord, as marked. This is only permitted at cadences.)

This relaxation of the rules of consonance and dissonance set a precedent for later composers to add other notes to chords to increase the dramatic and expressive tension in their music. This led to the dissolution of tonality in modern classical music, and produced the looser relationship between melody and harmony that makes jazz improvisation possible (as we'll see in Unit 9).

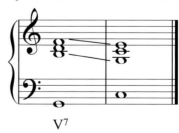

V^7

Note how the 7th (here, the F) resolves downwards by just a semitone to the 3rd of the next chord. It's natural to hear the 3rd (the B) of the dominant chord rising a semitone to the tonic. This is called a **leading tone** effect. These movements of just a semitone are especially powerful. In the 19th century the revolutionary composer

---

The Renaissance

This was a turning point in the history not just of European culture, but of Western music. The 'rebirth' of ancient Greek and Roman values in music took the form of an emphasis on sung melody lines with chordal accompaniments, so decoration and drama became more important than the smooth textures required by the Church in medieval times. Melody was freed up, reflecting the influence of Arabic and Islamic musical cultures, and the emergence of the major-minor system allowed chords to be treated as an independent aspect of musical structure.

Wagner used them to introduce more and more chromatic notes into the harmony. You'll find similar things when we look at jazz. (However, in the example above, the 3rd in fact moves down to the 5th of the next chord, as marked. This is only permitted at cadences.)

This kind of relaxing of the rules of consonance and dissonance set a precedent for later composers to add other notes to chords to increase the dramatic and expressive tension in their music. This led to the dissolution of tonality in modern classical music, and produced the looser relationship between melody and harmony that makes jazz improvisation possible (as we'll see in Unit 9).

Exercises

Using the piano, try to realize the following chord sequences as four-part harmony with appropriate voice-leading. Where possible play three notes in the right and one in the left. Write each realization down as you do it. Then embellish the top part to produce melodies.

1. Key of C major: I IV I IV I VI II V :‖

2. Key of G major: I VI IV V I II^b I^c V :‖

3. Key of F major: I V^b VI III^b IV I^b II V^7 :‖

4. Key of A major: I V I V I V^b VI V^7 :‖

5. Key of A minor: I V I IV I^b II^b V7 VI :‖

Notice how these chords often fall into regular groups of two or four that suggest a kind of harmonic rhythm. This gives the music its sense of forward motion. Now see if you can add more chords to round off each progression with a cadence.

Heinrich Schenker (1868-1935) was, along with the composer Arnold Schoenberg, one of the two most important music theorists of the early 20th century. He was born in Galicia (now western Ukraine) and worked in Vienna, first as a practical musician and composer, and then as a critic. This led him to investigate the formal basis of the great musical masterpieces, to try to understand what made them special. From the publication of his *Theory of Harmony* (1906) to the end of his life, he concentrated on theoretical work, producing a series of analytical studies culminating in *Free Composition*. Schenker sought to analyse the extended unfolding of classical forms in terms of tonal forces, emphasising how harmonic direction is shaped and revealed by underlying polyphonic structures of voice-leading, embellished on different levels.

This approach became increasingly influential in the latter part of the 20th century: it was taken up by American music theorists and applied more flexibly to a wider range of musical idioms. Schenker's approach emphasises the linear unfolding of music in time, as opposed to sectional and thematic contrasts, and points to a sense of structural depth (foreground and background) in music. Also, the importance given to embellishment reveals how even the complex works of great composers may reflect the melodic vocabulary of improvising musicians in unexpected ways.

UNIT 7

SECTION 3

TONE CONTROL

When musicians talk about tone control, they mean all the ways in which you can control the quality and volume of the sounds you produce. Different instruments allow the player more or less control over different aspects of sound. This is especially significant with the piano.

First the bad news. Here's what you can't do on the piano:
- control the colour (brightness, etc.) of individual sounds;
- control the tuning of individual sounds;
- control the way individual sounds unfold once they have been begun.

The last point is important, especially where dynamics are concerned. You can't make a sound get louder, or even keep it at the same level, once it has already begun.

Sounds on the piano die away automatically, but how long this takes (if they're not cut off by releasing the keys) depends on their initial loudness and pitch: louder and lower will last longer than softer or higher. These changes in sound level within notes are outside your control, so they don't get shown in the written music. This makes it easy to forget that they are occurring. But staying aware of the level of the sound after it starts means you can decide how other sounds relate to it (as louder or softer). And this affects how the original sound gets heard.

This trick is central to classical piano playing. In classical piano we often want the instrument to 'sing' rather than sound percussive, which means achieving maximum smoothness, continuity, and evenness of tone. And this means creating the illusion that each sounds sings on until the next one, when in fact it dies away.

Now the good news. Here's what you can do:
- control the overall dynamic level (loudness) of sounds, unlike with the organ or harpsichord);
- control when the sound is cut off;
- let the sound continue until it dies away naturally;
- control the **sympathetic resonance** of other strings (with right-hand pedal);
- alter the tonal quality of the whole instrument to a duller, softer sound (using the left hand pedal, which works like **mutes** do on other instruments).

Because you can't control individual sounds directly, except in terms of how loudly they start and how long they last, you have to make those aspects work much harder than on other instruments. This calls for something all good musicians need to have anyway: imagination. In fact, it allows for much more complexity in the kind of music one person can play. Differences of tone colour can be evoked through connecting up sounds in different ways, so playing at an advanced level often feels more like being in control of a whole orchestra.

Using the wrist in phrasing

Keep the wrist loose and relaxed. Letting it sink down slightly (top) makes for a relaxed but full tone. Lifting the wrist near the end of a phrase (bottom) lightens and shortens the last note, leaving a gap that indicates that the phrase is over.

PHRASING AND STRESS

We've already seen how swinging the hand round sideways with a lateral movement of the wrist is necessary to keep broken chords flowing smoothly. As with passing the thumb under in scales, this requires keeping the wrist as loose as possible. But we can also use the wrist to shape phrases. Lifting the wrist as we approach the end of a phrase simultaneously lightens *and* shortens the last note, making a gap which can also mark the end of the phrase. Conversely, letting the wrist fall as we play a note produces an accent that can emphasise the strong beats of a bar. Again, this requires looseness of the wrist. The illustration (right) shows, slightly exaggerated for clarity, how the hand naturally gets drawn in under the wrist slightly as it lifts.

Exercise 7.1

The simplest form of this exercise is known as couplets. The first note in each pair is stressed and joined smoothly to the second, with the wrist low and relaxed, but as we come to play the second note we are already beginning to lift the wrist, which both makes the second note lighter (softer) and makes us release the key sooner. Start by trying this on the piano lid, then begin playing the notes. The wrist controls tone (volume) and length at the same time, which makes for musical playing. The second half of the exercise uses this technique with extra notes in each phrase. Combining this with lateral wrist movement will further enhance the character of the phrases and help to keep the wrist loose. Play it through hands separately, with the left hand an octave lower than written.

Exercise 7.2

Notice how this exercise reverses the combination of lightening and shortening. Each phrase ends on a strong beat with a short, strong note approached smoothly from a lighter note on a weak beat. The accents come more from the fingers, with a slight kicking into the key from the wrist as you lift it off, so once again stress and shortening come from the same movement.

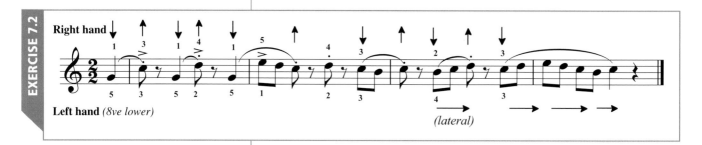

Next we're going to work on a piece called 'Clowns', by the Russian composer Dmitri Kabalevsky. Let's start with some exercises to prepare you for the main technical points.

Exercise 7.3

The left hand needs lateral movement for the octave jumps, even though these are staccato, so here's an exercise to get this going.

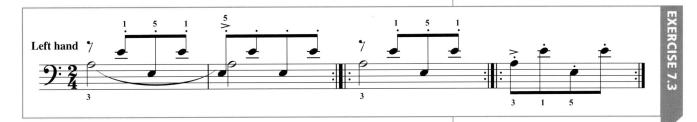

Exercise 7.4

The right hand calls for couplets just like in Exercise 7.2, so practise lifting and dropping. Here's an exercise to practise shifting the right hand finger position between the black and white notes, in blocks.

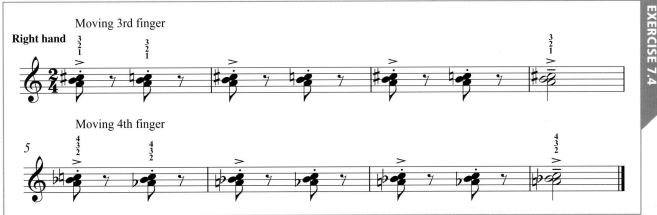

Exercise 7.5

Exercise 7.5 shows how to combine the hands by concentrating on the underlying pattern, so you see how the fingerings of the hands link up. Notice how frequently both hands use the same finger at the same time. Start very slowly and speed up gradually. Keep the thumbs light, especially when they play together.

Exercise 7.6

CD: **TRACK 24**

Now here's the whole piece. Remember, accidentals affect the note in question for the whole of the rest of the bar, unless cancelled by other ones.

EXERCISE 7.6

Exercise 7.7

'Country Gardens' is a traditional folk tune associated with English Morris dancing. The left hand calls for couplets at the start, while the right hand has quite a few changes of hand position within the melody. Getting the hands to lift off on different beats of the bar can be tricky here. Watch out for the change of clef in the left hand in the second line, and for the unusual chromatic thirds fingering there.

CD: **TRACK 25**

EXERCISE 7.7

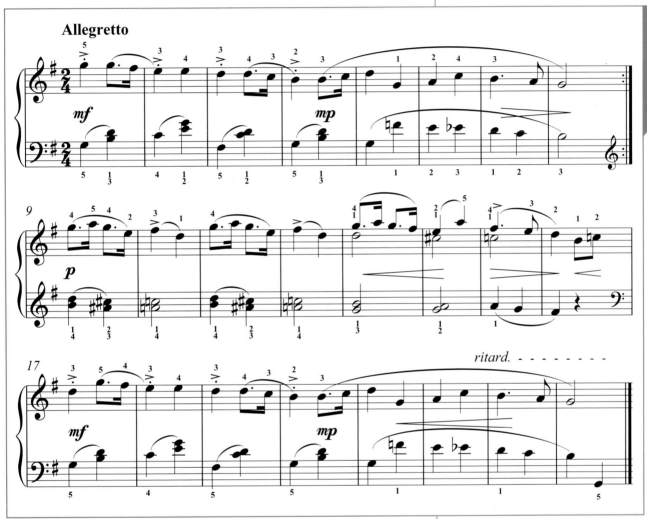

Morris Dancing is a traditional style of English folk dancing, mainly from the Cotswolds and north-west of England, danced in groups using handkerchiefs, sticks or swords, and with bells attached to knees so the dancers make a rhythmic noise. Each dance has a specific folk tune. Many of these tunes were saved from extinction at the end of the 19th century when Cecil Sharpe and others went into the countryside to record them, since rural traditions were dying out in the face of industrialisation and migration into cities. Some claim that Morris Dancing dates back to primitive pagan times, but there are no records of it before the 15th century. Others claim that this is a myth, and that the participants invented this colourful history for themselves. The name 'Morris' seems to derive from 'Moorish', leading some to suggest North African origins for the dance. Originally all male, the dances are now often performed by women.

MAJOR SCALES ON BLACK NOTES

Major scales starting on black notes have a different kind of fingering, based on the need to pass the thumb under to a white note after a black note. In B flat major, this means we don't always get the same combination of fingers (between the hands) on the same black notes. Also, the second finger is put in at the start of the right hand, and at the top of the left hand.

B flat major

E-flat major is easier, since the fourth finger is always used when two black notes are played one after the other, but never when there is only one.

E flat major

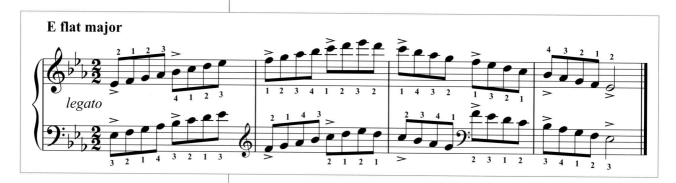

A-flat major works on similar principles, except that there are two pairs of black notes, one followed by a single white note and one followed by two.

A flat major

Remember that for every major scale there is a **relative minor** (see Unit 2) with the same key signature but with accidentals added. However, the relative minors for the above scales follow the fingering patterns for major scales starting on the same pitch, rather than for the relative majors. (So G minor follows G major rather than B flat major, etc.)

G minor

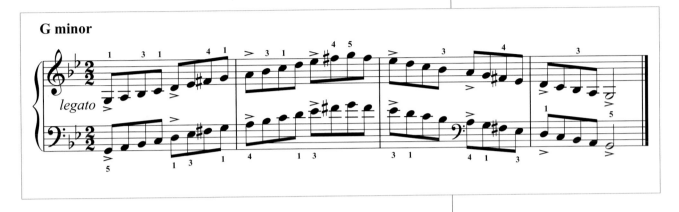

C minor

F minor

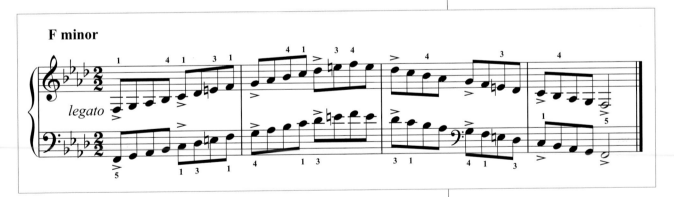

BROKEN CHORDS WITH BLACK NOTES

Four-note broken chords can be played even when they include black notes that require thumb to be used on them at some point. When this situation approaches, move the hand further into the black keys, even when actually playing white notes. This can be tricky, especially if you don't have slender fingers, but try to get used to it. Practise hands separately only.

B flat major

G minor

UNIT 8

SECTION 3

TONE PRODUCTION

It's never enough just to know what level of loudness you want – you need to know how to produce it without sacrificing control over other aspects of playing. You'll find that you want to strike the keys harder for more sound, which may make your arms and wrists tense up: they can become stiff and lose the freedom of movement they have when relaxed. Your muscles may tire more quickly and get strained, leading to injuries.

Before you know it, people will say you're 'banging' – playing everything too loudly in an awkward and tense way. As a result, you may feel you have to make a special physical effort just to play quietly. But than can just increase the underlying physical tension.

So you need to learn how to produce different levels of volume in a relaxed way, by controlling how much of the dead weight of your body is released into the keys as you play them.

Make sure you're sitting up straight, with relaxed, loose shoulders. Close the piano lid and hold your arms so your hands are some way above the lid, ready to fall and land where the keys would be. Let go completely so they drop, noticing how hard the impact feels when they hit the lid. Then do it again, but when your hands reach the lid, keep them resting there for a bit, with the weight still pressing down so that you can feel the lid actually taking your weight and supporting you, like when you lean against something. Feel the weight of the upper part of your body and arms pressing down on the lid through your hands. Remember how that feels.

Now open the lid and try the same thing with each hand in turn, so that you end up holding down a simple chord (like the one in Exercise 8.1). Can you feel the weight pressing through your hands and fingers and into the keys?

The next thing is to control how much of your own weight you release. We do this by thinking of different parts of the body as having their own weight. Letting go of more of the body releases more weight, starting with the hands themselves, and working upwards to include the forearms, whole arms and even the shoulders. For maximum loudness, we tilt forwards to throw the whole weight of our back into the piano.

Exercise 8.1

Try playing and holding the chords in just one hand, adding more weight with each chord, then gradually taking the weight back up into your body until you are left with just the gentle pressure of the hands and fingers. Then do the same with the other hand, and hands together. Notice how the wrist plays the role of a support throughout, keeping the hand from collapsing under the weight of the arms.

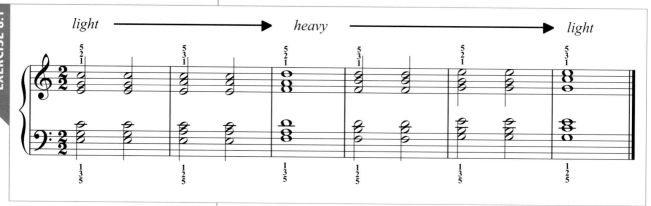

Exercise 8.2

You need to develop your own sense of level for each of the basic dynamic markings (pp, p, mp, mf, f, ff), giving a sort of scale of evenly spaced degrees of loudness. In this exercise, try to remember how much weight you released for each dynamic level, so that when you return to it you know in advance how much to use. This helps you achieve consistent dynamics.

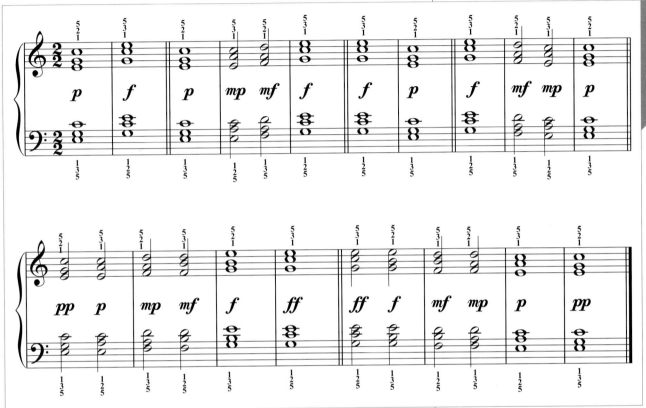

Play the same chord one or two octaves higher or lower, and you'll notice that different registers of the instrument have different volume characteristics: the lower and middle registers require more care in producing softer levels, the octaves just above middle C are naturally softer, while the topmost register is bright but has a more limited dynamic range. This can also alter the balance between the hands.

GRADATION OF TONE

Now you have a sense of the different dynamic levels – of what it feels like to produce them as well as what they sound like – it's time to see if you can make smooth transitions between them.

The golden rule is not to change too suddenly. **Crescendo** and **diminuendo** are always gradual processes of getting louder or softer, starting from the place indicated, which means you shouldn't hear any change in the music until *after* the indication in the music. Equally, you mustn't reach the new dynamic level ahead of the point marked in the music.

Exercise 8.3

Remember that a gradual change of level means a gradual change in the amount of weight as you pass from one chord to the next. Also, 'prepare' each chord by moving your fingers into position and feeling your fingertips in contact with the keys before actually 'letting go' into the piano to play the chord.

LEGATO PEDALLING

In the preceding exercises, I'm sure you noticed the awkward gaps between chords when shifting the hand into position or releasing keys to restrike them. These are typical situations where it is physically impossible to create a smooth join with the fingers alone. The sustaining pedal can be useful here.

Legato pedalling uses the right pedal to create a legato that would otherwise be impossible. Remember, legato is really a slight overlap between the end of one note and the start of the next. We can create this by 'catching' the first note or chord in the pedal, keeping it down so that the sounds carry on even when we let go of the keys to move to the next note(s). Then we release the pedal immediately after sounding the new note or chord.

Try it. Take the first few chords of Exercise 8.3. Try joining just the first and second chords, then do the same with the second and third. That's the easy part...

To join all three chords in one go, you'll need to make sure the pedal goes back down to 'catch' the second chord immediately after you have released it to 'clear' the first chord. The pedal has got to be down before you release the fingers from the second chord in preparation for the third. Once you get to the last chord you can relax a bit, since you won't need to get the pedal back down before releasing the keys to find another chord. But it still makes sense to put the pedal back down again after 'clearing' the previous chord, in order to maintain continuity of sound. Remember what we learned in the last chapter: using the sustaining pedal will alter the colour and texture of the piano's sounds.

112

Exercise 8.4.

Notice the usual way of indicating legato pedalling, as in the second half of this exercise. You'll see for yourself that the hard thing is lifting the pedal fractionally after playing the notes, yet lifting off the fingers while keeping the pedal down. Start incredibly slowly, and only speed up gradually when you feel confident about it.

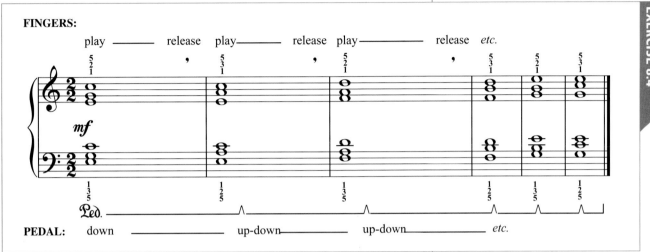

Now go back and do Exercises 8.1, 8.2, and 8.3 again, using legato pedalling. Note how pedalling not only adds to the volume of sound, but also makes it harder to control it, since the foot movements can interfere with your attempts to control the release of weight. Practise with a long pause on each chord at the point where it is held in both the fingers and pedal at the same time. Try to keep all your movements smooth, controlled and economical.

Make sure the rapid release and depression of the pedal occur *after* the playing of the new chord. The 'up-down' of the pedal should be swift, so that the overlap between chords doesn't become noticeable and blur the harmonies together. At the same time, the foot movement must be controlled and easy, so as not to jolt the body or cause unwanted accents in the music.

The 'Prelude in C Major' (from the 'Forty-Eight') is a well-known piece by Johann Sebastian Bach (1685-1750), which shows why he's still considered the greatest harmonist of all time. Who else could write such a piece with just chords and no melody? First we'll do a couple of preparatory exercises, so you can see how to practise chord-based patterns to get them fluent.

Playing the notes of each chord-pattern together as a single 'block' chord helps to get the changes between chords going fluently. This way you avoid hesitating at the end of each bar while looking for the next hand position. Practising 'in blocks' like this is useful wherever you have awkward changes of position.

Exercise 8.5

Here are the first few chords of the Prelude, as blocks. You can get the rest from looking at the piece itself, but make sure you note the fingerings carefully. Play each chord twice the first time round, then go back and try again with each chord played just once. Notice how beautiful the harmony is, and finally try using legato pedalling as well.

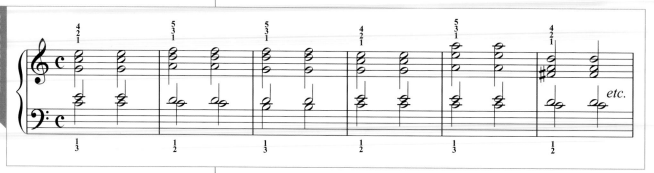

Exercise 8.6

Notice how in the actual piece the left hand holds both first and second notes of each bar right through to the end of the measure, whereas the right repeats a three-note pattern across two beats – part of a broken chord. This means we use lateral movement to achieve a flowing legato and to make the dynamics reflect how the pattern shifts in relation to the beat. The wrist describes a circle as it moves sideways around the hand, swings back, and then begins the second group of three, all as one movement. Moving the wrist round towards the top note itself produces first a crescendo (arriving at the 2nd/4th crotchet beat of the bar), then a diminuendo (after the beat). The lateral movement and change in weight form a single action.

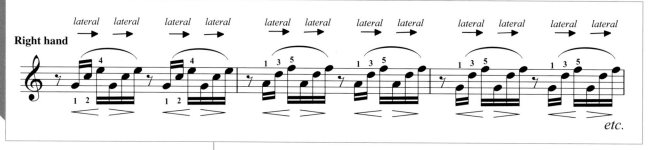

Exercise 8.7.

CD: **TRACK 26**

Time to try the Prelude itself. Because it was originally written for harpsichord, Bach didn't include expression markings, so you must decide the tempo, dynamics, and pedalling for yourself. In practice, not every possibility will sound musical. The gentle character of the piece clearly requires a moderate tempo, while the flowing texture demands legato playing, with or without legato pedalling. We've added basic dynamics. Notice how they echo various features of the music: changes of texture as it shifts between registers and between harmonic tension and release, and the build-up to the close, created by holding the bass fixed while the chords above are changing. (This 'dominant pedal' allows the upper voice in the left hand to hint at a line, but you'll only hear this and be able to bring it out if you are in the habit of listening carefully to the results of your own playing – the number one rule of good musicianship.)

114

Moderato

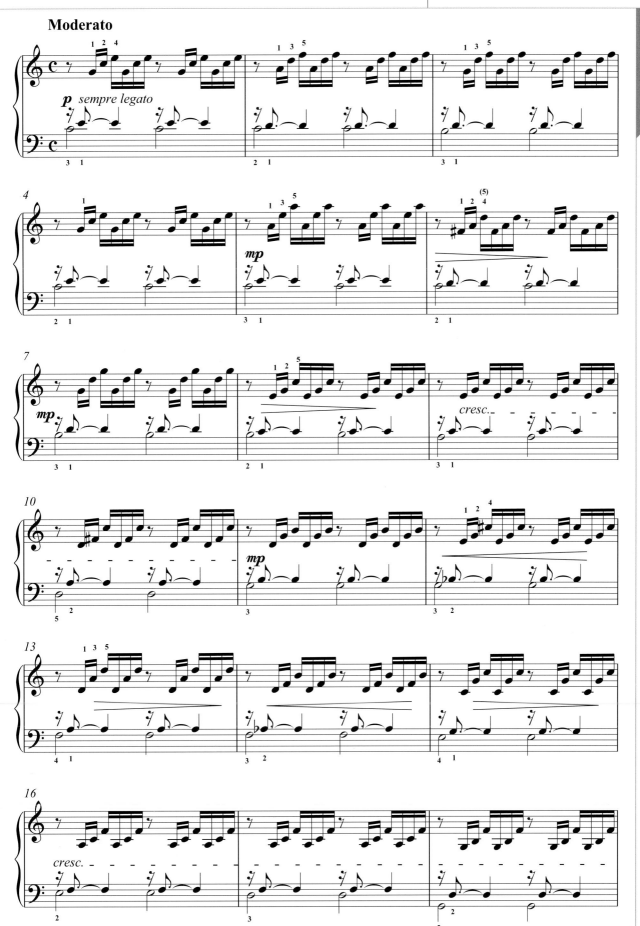

HAND STACCATO

When we talk about staccato, we don't just mean making notes as short as possible. Different ways of producing staccato produce different results that work better in different contexts. We adjust the degree of staccato (ie, of shortness) to suit the style and character of the music. The choice of staccato technique often depends on the speed and loudness of the music, and on what other technical challenges are involved. **Hand staccato** is useful for fast and light passages, and especially for rapid repetitions of notes or chords.

Exercise 8.8

Hold one arm up and flap the hand loosely up and down, like when you wave goodbye to someone. Notice how the hand moves loosely from the wrist. Bring the hand down and hold it just above the closed lid of the piano. Make the same kind of flapping, so all the fingers strike the wood at once, with rapid repetitions. Now do the same thing again, but with only thumb, third and fifth fingers actually hitting it the lid – like in a chord. Then lift the lid and try the two exercises below. Afterwards go through the whole process again with the other hand.

Although Johann Sebastian Bach (1685-1750) held a number of important official posts in his lifetime, it was not until well into the next century that his music began to be appreciated for its greatness. Bach absorbed all the stylistic elements of his day and developed new possibilities on the basis of them. His music is characterised by a supreme spiritual and intellectual honesty, while also reaching the highest level of technical sophistication that any western composer has yet achieved. He found a new balance between the demands of harmony and counterpoint, together with clearly defined themes and a satisfying architectural sense of formal equilibrium. He composed vast quantities of cantatas, as well as masses and oratorios, and a large quantity of instrumental music, including many keyboard masterpieces, both for organ and for harpsichord and related instruments. J.S.Bach's *Art of Fugue*, whose instrumentation remains unspecified, epitomises the tendency to focus on formal aspects of musical unfolding at the expense of instrumental colour and dynamics – elements that are more dependent upon how the music is actually performed. This way of treating music as a self-contained art with an almost abstract character, independent of its social context, is possibly unique to the culture of European art music, and is important to some modern music.

LEFT-HAND MELODIES

Jazz and popular styles usually treat the left hand as just bass line and/or accompaniment, but classical music often treats both hands as equal and independent units. This means that sometimes the left hand plays the melody, while the right hand is in the background.

Burgmüller's 'Ballade' contains hand staccato and left-hand melodies. Try transposing the left hand tune two octaves up and playing it in the right hand; then see if your left can make it sound equally musical. You'll need to practise the opening a great deal hands separately before putting the hands together. When you do combine them, start really slowly and get the speed up gradually.

Exercise 8.9

Here's a preparatory exercise to help combine the hands.

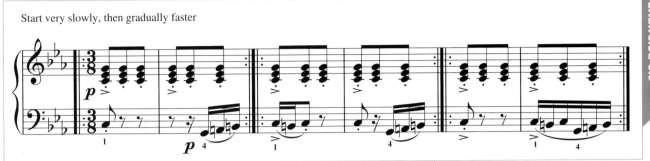

Start very slowly, then gradually faster

Exercise 8.10

CD: **TRACK 27**

Now the whole piece. Keeping the right hand loose and bouncy at the start while the left stays smooth is not easy. Co-ordination should emerge naturally from each hand doing its own thing, rather than being forced. Accenting the first beat of every bar will help, but don't overdo this. Notice the change of key signature for the middle section. Here the left hand chords should stay light, with the second of each pair softer than the first. Focus on using weight to get the dynamics at bars 45-48 and 71-74. The sforzandi (sfz) are sudden, so use arms rather than shoulders or back. Staccato passages each have a different character, which should be brought out: the descending chord at bars 16-18 calls for a very short and sharp style, whereas the left hand chords in bars 18-44 accompany a singing melody, so they should be gentler, with fingers keeping closer to the keys and only a slight movement of the hand. This keeps them in the background. The chords in bars 19-22 also require a kind of staccato action: drop and lift from the forearms to get the slower, heavier movements that naturally result in heavy, sustained yet separated chords. Dynamics and articulation emerge together from the same physical movement.

EXERCISE 8.10

Allegro con brio

STACCATO SCALES

We also use hand staccato for rapid staccato scales. Take a scale that you know well, and try playing it fairly quickly, with wrists raised and fingers flatter than usual. You only need a slight flapping of the hand as you play each note, but it's much harder to keep the wrist loose, isn't it? The fingers themselves hardly do any work at all, which makes this quite an advanced technique – so don't expect to master it straight away.

CHROMATIC SCALE ON A-FLAT AND C

Talking of scales, it's time you played your two-octave chromatic scale beginning on some notes other than D, so try it on A-flat, and then on C (hands separately). We use the same fingering as before, starting with fingers that play those same notes in the original chromatic scale on D. (In other words, the pattern is basically the same whatever note you start from.) On A flat, that means starting with the 3rd finger in each hand. On C, we get the thumb in the left at the start, but we also begin with the thumb in the right, instead of 2nd.

TWO-OCTAVE ARPEGGIOS

A two-octave arpeggio goes up through the notes of a chord, carrying straight on over into a repetition in the next octave before coming down again with the same notes in reverse order. The main challenge is maintaining a legato join and an even tone as you stretch the thumb under the fingers, or the 3rd or 4th finger over the thumb, to get from one octave to the next. Make the wrist do the work here, and check that your elbows stay close in to the sides of your body. Practise slowly to begin with, and listen carefully for breaks in the legato. Notice how the rhythmic grouping in fours stresses different notes in each octave, which helps to achieve an even sound and constant flow. By now you should be familiar with the notes that make up all of the chords mentioned below.

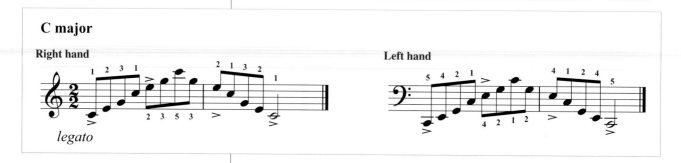

Now try F major and G major with the same fingering.

We use the same fingering for minor arpeggios when all the notes are white:

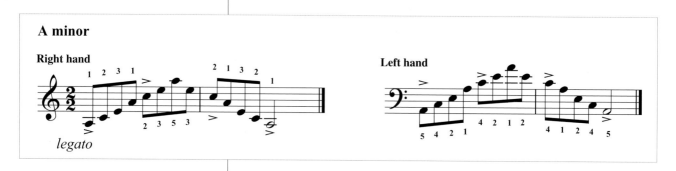

Try D minor and E minor this way too.

When the 3rd of the chord is a sharp, the left hand uses 3rd finger instead of 4th, but the right hand stays the same:

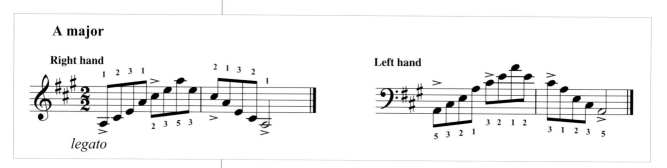

D major and E major will work like this too.

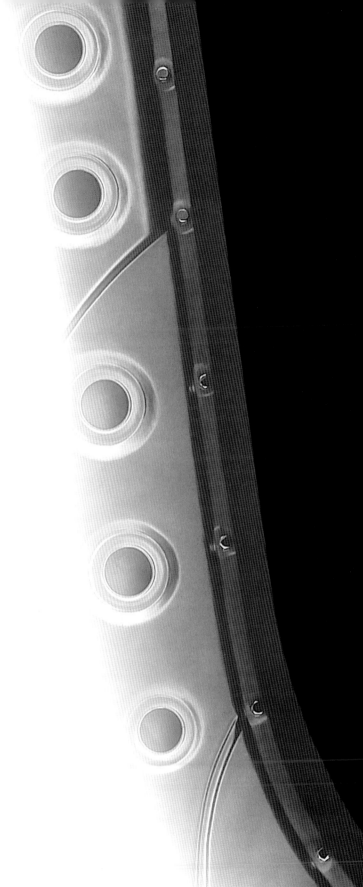

UNIT 9

- Jazz, rock, & blues (1) •
- Scales & scale theory •
- Jazz chord progressions •
- Two-hand voicings •
- Chord embellishment •

SECTION 3

SCALES AND SCALE THEORY FOR JAZZ, ROCK, AND BLUES

In classical piano playing, scales tend to be treated just as technical warm-up exercises. But if you want to be creative and compose or improvise your own music, you'll need to understand scale *theory*. This tells you how different kinds of scale are organised, and how they relate to each other, so you can use them to make music for yourself.

Traditional classical music really only uses three scales: major, minor and chromatic. By contrast, jazz, rock and blues draw on a wider range of scales to provide source material for chords and melodies, though these are still often understood in terms of the major-minor distinction. The best way to learn these is as alterations to the major scale that could be built on the same note, shown using numbers to represent scale-degrees. This will allow you to find the notes of any scale in any key, providing you're familiar with the major scale for that key. For example, the classical harmonic minor scale can be written as:

1   2   *b*3   4   5   *b*6   7

Within the seven-note major scale is a more basic five-note scale, found in almost all musical cultures across the world. This is the **pentatonic** scale. Notice how it misses out the 4th and 7th of the major scale:

1   2   3   5   6

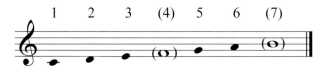

This means that instead of tones and semitones, it consists of tones and minor 3rds. Because it's found within the major scale, it's known as the **major pentatonic**.

The equivalent **minor pentatonic** uses the same notes, but starts a minor 3rd lower. Note that 4th and 7th degrees of the scale are not omitted, as they are in the major pentatonic, but the 2nd and 6th degrees.

Notice how the 7th of the minor pentatonic is already flattened, when compared to the raised 7th of classical major and minor key harmony. Adding an extra note, the 5th, to this scale gives us the **blues scale**. This note is also flattened, and the flattened 3rd, 5th and 7th produce a bluesy, out-of-tune sound when the scale is played over major key harmony:

Now here it is on C, to make it really obvious how it relates to the major. (Take away the G-flat and you'd get a minor pentatonic on C!):

Mainstream rock and popular music often uses a form of the minor scale that incorporates the notes of the pentatonic minor, especially the flattened 7th. It's the **rock minor** scale:

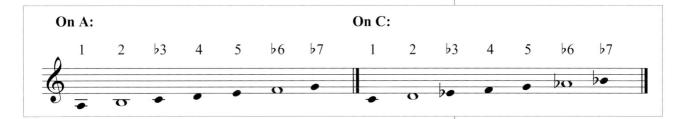

Jazz uses its own minor scale, with raised 6th and 7th degrees; so it's like an ascending melodic minor scale in classical music, except that in **jazz minor** these notes also get used for harmony and descending lines:

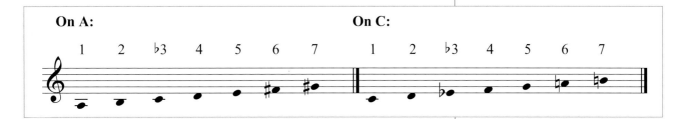

Scale theory gets more complicated in jazz when we start interpreting the scale itself in terms of its relationship to the different chords that it gives rise to (ie, as source material for improvising freely over those chords). This leads to the concept of **modes**, and to a more complex role for minor-scale-based harmony, especially in modern jazz. As with all styles that have evolved since the introduction of keyboard instruments, the chromatic scale is also available to jazz players. Jazz also introduces chromatic notes into existing scales and modes to form **bebop scales**.

NON-CLASSICAL HARMONY

As we saw in Unit 6, classical harmony has strict rules for **voice-leading**. This approach originated in early church music, where melodic lines sound together, each sung by a separate voice or group of voices, making a smooth texture known as **polyphony**. But the priorities are different in jazz, rock and blues. Here the basic model consists of a tune sung by a singer or played by a soloist, accompanied by chord changes that often have a rhythmic as well as a harmonic function. In the case of jazz, this then gets used as a basis for freer **improvisation**. So in these kinds of music we learn how to play chord progressions according to certain formulae that automatically fulfil voice-leading requirements. Other chords and progressions are then treated as variations on these.

In non-classical styles the main difference is that we write the actual letter name of the **root** of the chord rather than its position in the scale. So a chord built on G in the key of C is just written as G rather than as V. You don't have to analyse the harmony of the whole passage just to figure out what chord is meant. The **chord-type** is specified using a special symbol that tells you what its function is. There are several different sets of these symbols in use in jazz, rock and blues, but they share certain features. But first let's clarify the different chord-types themselves.

You can get a good sense of the difference between classical and non-classical harmony from looking at how they deal with **dissonances**. Classical treats all notes that don't belong to the chord (ie, the triad) as potential dissonances to be **resolved**. (See Unit 6.) Non-classical harmony just tells you which note in the scale to avoid (because it's *really* dissonant), meaning that all the others are okay. Try playing a major scale of C over a C major chord, and you'll hear that F doesn't sound too good when you linger on it. That's because the 4th of a major scale is what is sometimes called an **avoid-note**. (These notes are usually a minor 2nd or perfect 4th above the root of the chord.)

CHORD-TYPES, EXTENSIONS AND ADDED NOTES

Remember the four kinds of triad from classical harmony? These provide the basic chord-types for non-classical harmony:

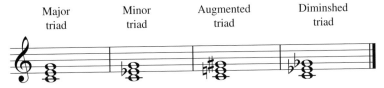

Major triad   Minor triad   Augmented triad   Diminshed triad

We looked at dominant 7th chords in Unit 6. That showed us that a chord need not consist just of a triad, but can be extended to include other notes, in line with the principle used to arrive at the notes of the basic triads. That is, by superimposing more intervals of a 3rd on top of the original triad we get the 7th, 9th, 11th, and 13th, as elements of the chord rather than as melodic elaborations. We call these **chord extensions**.

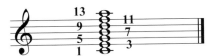

In non-classical music, we can do this on practically *any* chord in a key, not just the dominant. The most important form consists of just adding the 7th. Depending on which scale-degree we do this on, we get different kinds of 7th chord. The result is several more chord-types.

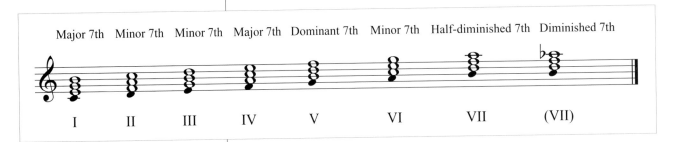

Major 7th   Minor 7th   Minor 7th   Major 7th   Dominant 7th   Minor 7th   Half-diminished 7th   Diminished 7th

I   II   III   IV   V   VI   VII   (VII)

Except for the diminished 7th, we're just dealing with extensions of major scale harmony at this stage. That's because minor scale harmony works differently depending on how jazzy or bluesy or mainstream you want it to be. Jazz uses its own version of the minor scale to generate all kinds of extended chords, but this is quite advanced, so we'll deal with it later.

You can see how these types of 7th chord relate to each other if we lay them all out over a single root. Then they look like a series of **chromatic alterations** of the initial 7th chord. Each one flattens (or lowers) an extra note by a semitone. This highlights an important relationship between them.

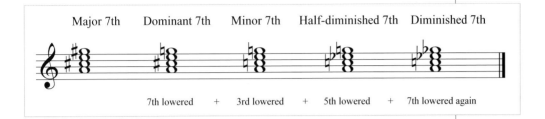

Here are the most common alternatives for indicating chord-types in non-classical music. We'll use 'shorthand' notation here, as a compromise between what works best for advanced jazz and what you'll most likely encounter in more mainstream popular music. But try to get familiar with the others too.

Chord symbol notations

CHORD TYPE	Basic notation	Shorthand	Advanced (jazz)
Major triad	C	C	C or CΔ
Major 7th	Cmaj7	CM7	CΔ7 or CΔ
Dominant 7th	C7	C7	C7
Minor triad	Cmin	Cm	C-
Minor 7th	Cmin7	Cm7	C-7 or C-
Diminished triad	Cdim	Cdim	Co
Minor 7th, flat 5th ('half-diminished')	Cmin7b5	Cm7b5	Cø7
Diminished 7th	Cdim7	Cdim7	Co7
Augmented triad	Caug	Caug or C#5	C+ or C+5

In jazz, the 7th tends to get taken for granted as part of the basic harmony, with other extensions automatically implied by the resulting 7th chord. But maybe it's occurred to you that the 9th, 11th, and 13th are the same notes as the 2nd, 4th and 6th of the scale, plus one octave. So why not call them by their original positions as notes in the scale? Well, sometimes we do, depending on what the underlying chord-type is like. Then we call them **added-notes**.

> ### Chopin and jazz
> Extended and added-note harmonies have precedents in classical music from the late 19th and early 20th centuries. Many of the unresolved, extended harmonies common in jazz can already be heard in the piano music of Chopin, Ravel and Debussy.

NON-JAZZ HARMONY

Whereas jazz harmony uses all types of 7th chord and related extensions, blues-based harmony focuses more on just the dominant 7th and its extensions. Rock, folk and country, on the other hand, have far fewer 7th chords, but use added-note chords. They also use **sus chords**, in which the 2nd or 4th substitutes for the 3rd, like in guitar harmonies. ('Sus' refers to the idea of an unresolved **suspension**.)

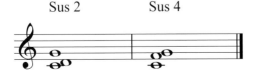

Outside jazz, simple chords are voiced and connected along similar lines to classical music, though with the rules loosened up a fair bit. Just how far this goes depends on the style of the music and the situation – and on personal preferences, of course. If you're playing a solo arrangement of a song on just piano or keyboard, or a solo instrumental backing for a voice, then you'll be sufficiently exposed to justify taking time out to polish up the voice-leading in your chord arrangements, along the lines dealt with in Unit 6. You'll hear the difference: the whole thing will start to sound a lot more professional.

JAZZ PROGRESSIONS & TWO-HAND VOICINGS

Because jazz can be more complex harmonically, as well as being directed more towards improvisation, you really need to familiarise yourself with the basic voicings and progressions. Do this and you'll automatically be taking care of most of the voice-leading problems. Remember, in jazz it's not enough just to see on paper how a progression should go. Jazz lives in and for the moment, so when you're improvising or working with other players you must really have those chords in your *fingers*, so you can use them without even thinking about it. This means learning how chords feel and look when you play them, not just what notes they have. On the piano this depends on what key you're in, so you'll have to practise them in lots of different keys.

In jazz, you also need to know when to treat a note as an extension or an added note, which depends both on the extra note and on the underlying chord-type. The further away from the basic triad, the more likely it is to be an added note. On the other hand, dominant chords naturally support the most extensions. Remember that the 4th is an **avoid-note** in major-key harmony. As a result, 11ths or added 4ths over major or dominant chords either get treated as **passing notes** (like in classical) or raised a semitone (especially from **Bebop** on – see Unit 18).

Chord extensions or added-notes

Major	9th		Added 4th*		Added 6th
Dominant	9th	11th*		13th	
Minor	9th	11th			Added 6th

* usually sharpened

THE II-V-I PROGRESSION

3-Note Voicings

The cornerstone of jazz is the II-V-I progression. This gives us the three most important chord types in a logical succession of increasing tension, then resolution, like a classical **cadence** (see Unit 6). The simplest way is to split the progression between the hands in 3-note voicings. (Because we're doing jazz, we need the 7ths, so we'll leave out the 5th of each chord for now.) Note how the bass moves in intervals that form a root-progression of falling 5ths (or rising 4ths – the same thing). This will be significant later on. The neat thing here is the way the 7th of each chord falls a semitone to the 3rd of the next chord, while the 3rd of each chord becomes the 7th of the next chord, producing perfectly smooth voice-leading. Play through the jazz and classical versions of the same sequence and just listen to the difference in sound. (Compare also how the chords are indicated below the music.) With the jazz voicings, either voice can be on top.

Classical: **Jazz:**

4-Note Voicings

Now let's try adding another note to each chord. 4-note voicings have a slightly richer feel. We get the same kind of exchange between the 5th of one chord and the 9th of the next as we have with the 3rd and 7th, with one voice staying the same while the other falls a step, then the other way round.

The example at the top of the page shows the way jazz tends to keeps to root position chords, whereas classical harmony uses inversions to emphasise the independent melodic contour of the bass line. Inversions are less common outside of classical music, and are written as **slash chords**, meaning that the bass note is specified after the slash. This also lets us write down complex jazz harmonies, treating them as simpler chords combined with unusual bass notes.

A jazz **sus chord** is a dominant 7th with an added 4th. It can also be written as a slash chord.

Sometimes you'll even find it written as Dm7/G, to show its **function**. That's because in jazz, II, V and I are the basic harmonic units (corresponding to minor, dominant and major chord types). Other chords get treated as modifications of those. The sus chord has the 3rd and 7th of Dm7, but the root and 7th of G7, so it can function as II and V merged together.

In jazz from the 1940s onwards you'll hear sus chords with the 3rd kept in alongside the 4th. This makes it more dissonant, but how much you hear of this depends on the internal **layout** of the chord, which is where the real art of jazz chord-voicing begins. Listen out for the contrasts between 'close' and 'open' spacings of the notes, between different registers, and between different inversions and/or positionings of dissonant intervals within the chord. For example, can you hear the difference with the 4th *above* the 3rd, as in last of these sus chord voicings? Note how the **function** of the sus chord stays the same even when the 6th is also added.

Gsus

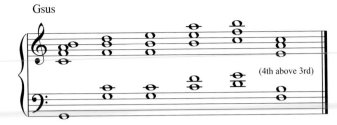

(4th above 3rd)

The real challenge is familiarising yourself with the harmonies enough to use them freely and creatively. This is mainly a question of learning **transpositions.** For each of the examples in this section, try transposing down a perfect 5th, then the same again, and so on until you've gone through all 12 keys and made it back to where you started. If you need help, use the Circle of Fifths diagram on p92. Note that descending in 5ths means progressing anti-clockwise around the circle – adding flats or taking away sharps. And this happens a lot in jazz anyway. When you've done this, try transposing chromatically, descending a half-step at a time.

Just to start you off, here's a II-V-I taken through all keys in the circle of 5ths. When you've gone through it a few times, try with the book closed. Then try adding 5ths and 9ths to make 4-note voicings along the lines of the example on the previous page. Then try substituting a single sus chords for both the II and the V.

EMBELLISHING A SEQUENCE

In music, 'embellishing' means taking a simple musical idea and making something more complex out of it. Jazz improvisation developed out of increasingly free embellishments of **standards**. These are well-known melodies and chord sequences by early jazz composers, whose structures provide a shared basis for improvising, having been made famous in recordings of jazz musicians.

The top voice of a series of chords gives us a basic melodic outline to work with. By filling-in this outline we create our own melody lines, which still work with the chords underneath. This is the first step towards working creatively with harmonic structures. (We'll keep the rhythmic aspect pretty free for now.)

Here's a II-V-I moving down by whole steps. (Why not practise taking this through as many keys as possible, like we did just now? This time it only passes through every other key in the Circle of Fifths.)

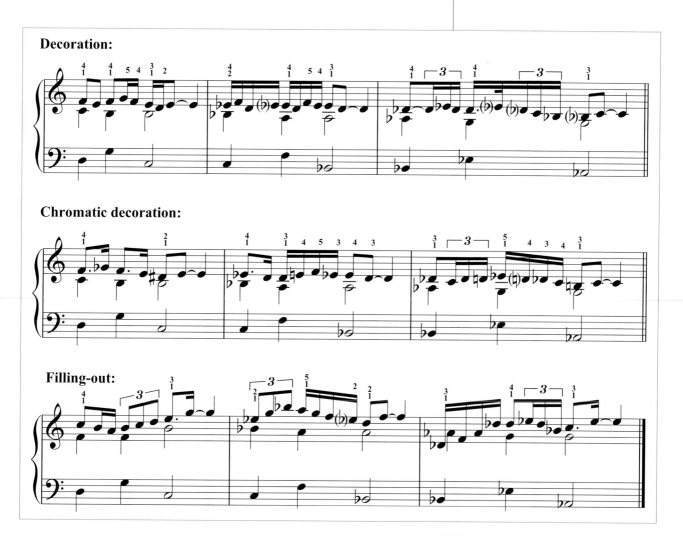

Decoration:

Chromatic decoration:

Filling-out:

Now let's see what we can do with it. (When playing this through, you need to adjust your right hand fingerings to accommodate the extra melody notes, using legato pedalling to get some of the smooth joins between notes. This tends to result in a more relaxed approach to legato fingering than is acceptable in classical playing, relying more on the sustaining pedal.)

Look at how we decorate the notes of the top voice with adjacent notes, either from the scale of the key of the music or from the chromatic scale. And observe how we open up the contour of the line by introducing other notes from the chord, filling in gaps with stepwise movements. Remember those classical decorative devices (passing and auxiliary notes, appoggiaturas, and suspensions) that we learned about in Unit 6? How many of them can you find in the example on the previous page? Try taking the progression through the other keys again, as we did before, but putting in some embellishments of your own.

Later on we'll give a tune this treatment, and learn to vary harmony and rhythm. Embellishing gets you started if you want to make music more creatively. But be careful: if the source is familiar to others, you'll be playing with their expectations in a big way.

Embellishing

Each time you experiment with different ways of playing the same tune, you're embellishing, and this happens all the time in rock, blues, gospel, and other mainstream popular styles – not to mention most non-European musics. It is not limited to jazz or freely improvised music. Even a great deal of classical music, at least until the 20th century, can be shown to contain written-down forms of embellishment. Heinrich Schenker, a celebrated Austrian musical theorist, claimed controversially that all musical structures were embellishments of a single voice-leading progression – a perfect cadence. (Recently his approach has been used to analyse jazz as well.) Hearing how embellishments relate to underlying structure creates a sense of 'structural depth' in music – like perspective in painting. It's even been compared to the way language is organised, with rules that can be endlessly varied by individuals while remaining comprehensible to others.

Jazz pianist Thelonius Monk (1917-1982) was the archetypal improviser. Improvisation in music naturally leads to a focus on performers as individuals. And an emphasis on solo improvising over a steady rhythmic and harmonic background is one of the defining features of jazz. Monk was a total individual in terms of personality, style, and technique (so much so that even many jazz players thought he was crazy). From the early 1940s, Monk introduced many of the features associated with 'bebop' and, more specifically, 'hard bop', including much more complex rhythms and harmonies than those used in jazz at the time. Economical and sporadic, punchy and irregular, with lengthy gaps between solos, his style was at first taken as indicating an inferior technique.

Only later, when bebop jazz had been assimilated, with its freestyle soloing over chords, did people realise that Monk was ahead of them all and, in his own way, far more original. His disjointed, quirky approach got closer to what improvisation in jazz is really all about than the fluid virtuosity of his contemporaries. His playing seems to capture the fracturing of experience into dissolute moments, each holding a clue to a lost meaning, typical of modern urban life.

Monk's *Brilliant Corners* album became a classic, and many of his songs became standards, used by others as a basis for their improvisations. In the 1970's he began to develop problems with mental illness and retired. He remains a model of uncompromising individuality in jazz and improvisation, contrasting with the uniform virtuosity of so many of today's jazz performers.

Monk's example teaches the most basic lesson of all for anyone seeking to improvise seriously: you can't learn how to do it except by doing it!

UNIT 10

SECTION 4

INTERPRETATION

When you learn classical pieces, you're presenting music that was written by someone else, so you have to make judgements about how the music was intended to sound. That's what **interpretation** is all about.

In Unit 5 we looked at ways of making a melody sound more expressive by subtly adjusting the dynamics as we go along, to reflect the structure of the line and its relation to harmony and metre. We can also use slight adjustments of **tempo**, and of the timing of particular notes or chords, to heighten the listener's expectations.

There are all sorts of ways to put across the mood, feeling or character of a piece, but only if we've first become aware of it for ourselves. To achieve proper interpretative awareness, think about these issues as you learn the piece:

STYLISTIC: When was the piece written, and what were the conventions for playing that sort of music at the time? (Don't panic: we'll go into this later.) Who wrote it? Does it belong to a particular **genre**?

EXPRESSIVE: What sort of mood, emotions or character does the piece have? Does it suggest a personality? Is it song-like, dance-like, or like a conversation or a march?

DRAMATIC: What dramatic features or contrasts could you bring out? Where does the climax come? How is it resolved?

NARRATIVE: Does the music tell a story? What do you think happens in the story, and how does it end?

By now you should be getting the message: interpreting music is creative. It takes imagination.

Italian	Abbreviation	Explanation
forte-piano	*fp*	loud, then immediately soft
subito forte	*sf*	suddenly loud
subito piano	*sp*	suddenly soft
sforzando	*sfz*	with a sudden accent

See the Glossary for more Italian musical terms and their abbreviations. At an advanced level you will also be expected to know French and German terms.

TEST YOUR INTERPRETATIVE SKILLS

The Schumann piece 'First Loss' (opposite) offers a perfect chance to exercise your interpretative abilities. With a title like that, it's obvious it's going to be sad. (Like a lot of Romantic music, it's about that forbidden subject: death.) It's clearly an expressive piece, so we can do a lot with shaping dynamics and timing to bring out the intensity of the line, and we can also use speed and timing to heighten the overall sense of an unfolding musical story or drama. Note how Schumann cleverly integrates melody and accompaniment to form a single texture, while retaining a sense of melodic shape and motion at all levels.

Develop your interpretation

Don't just learn the notes first, in the hope of working out an interpretation and then imposing it later on: that never succeeds. Let your interpretation develop gradually as part of the process of mastering the playing, so technique and expression are coordinated from the outset.

A musical romance

Robert Schumann (1810-56) was one of the most important composers of the Romantic period, which lasted from towards the beginning of the 19th century to the beginning of the 20th. He was also a great pianist, writing a lot of fine music for the instrument. He fell in love with and married Clara Wieck (1819-96), the leading piano teacher of her day; her students established some of the great schools of piano playing of the last hundred years. The romance between Robert and Clara – the leading composer and the leading pianist of the time – was one of the great events of the German musical world. Legend has it that when Schumann was trying to drown himself in the river some people passed by in a boat and fished him out of the water. He immediately threw himself back into the water again. Like several Romantic poets, philosophers and composers, he eventually went mad and ended up in a mental asylum.

Exercise 10.1.

'First Loss' starts with just the right hand, inviting you to focus on the expressive value of each note even more than usual. Although the first note is individually marked loud (fp), this is relative to the overall character of the phrase and not aggressive. Hold it for slightly longer, so it has a chance to die down a little. That way it will connect up with the line. (Note the way the left hand then fills out the harmony with overlapping notes: these produce a sustained texture and echo the falling intervals of the melody.) The music only gradually picks up momentum, and really starts to flow from bar 6 down towards the cadence in bars 9. Then the expressive return of the opening can coincide with a slight pulling back of tempo, so it gets drawn out yet again. Chromatic alterations (D-sharps and A-sharps) should also be highlighted. The second half of

CD: **TRACK 28**

Precious silence

Rests are as important as notes. Music isn't just about hearing sounds in more intense ways than you would in everyday life – it's also about learning to hear and appreciate silences.

'First Loss' has some difficult passages, especially where each hand plays more than one voice. Practice each voice with the correct fingering before combining voices slowly within each hand, listening for balance between voices and legato. (Bring out the upper voice where this is part of the principal line. Only then combine the hands, and try to continue listening to the inner parts as well.) Notice the tempo changes indicated, and that pedal is only used where a legato would otherwise be impossible. In bar 31, the right hand chords marked with staccato dots and slurs should be neither legato nor staccato. Feel the dramatic impact of the rest in bar 30 – silence is an important part of this piece, and it's there even when you don't hear it.

MIXING UP THE HANDS

Sometimes the hands interact or relate to each other in unusual ways while playing. For example, they may dovetail together to form a single texture or line, or overlap by playing in the same region of the keyboard at the same time, or cross over to play on opposite sides of the keyboard. It's always important to know exactly how they should move in and out of these positions: for example, which hand goes above and behind, or below and in front of, the other. This may be indicated in the music (eg, 'l.h. under', 'r.h. over'), or left to you to work out.

Non-legato

In the next piece you'll see some more places where notes or chords are marked with both staccato dots and slurs. This is called non-legato, meaning that each note or chord has some feeling of length, *and* a slight gap before the next one: a sort of relaxed staccato that keeps a sense of line and connectedness, like someone speaking rather than singing.

Arpeggiated chords

The wavy vertical lines in front of certain chords in the next piece (bars 15, 59 and 61) mean that they should be 'spread'. **Spread chords** begin with the lowest note, sounding each note in rapid succession up to the top one, yet still holding them as a chord as specified by time values. The effect is like strummed chords on a lute or guitar, or harp textures produced by drawing fingers over several strings in a single movement. (A single wavy line across both staves means you should spread both hands in succession rather than simultaneously, as one big spread.) Use lateral movement from the wrist to make arpeggiations sound natural rather than forced.

Exercise 10.2

CD: **TRACK 29**

'Avalanche' by Heller has lots of dovetailing of hands, and a bit of overlapping too. The opening figure consists of triplets, which must relate accurately to the crotchet pulse stated in the second bar. The division between staves shows how both hands participate in the line, with the division of hands shown by direction of note stems. First practise the flowing line by itself, until you can't hear the switching of hands. (Fingers close to keys will help here.) Then introduce the staccato chords in the background. Note how each long minim note in the melody continues to be held after the chord, and how pedal is added just to 'colour' the held note, without losing the staccato release of the chord. The non-legato in bars 13-14 can be done with light 'dabbing' movements from the arm rather than wrist.

Bring out top notes in the right hand chords in the middle section, focusing on contrasts of dynamic level. (Think about your 'scale' of volume levels – are they consistent throughout the piece?) Dovetailing of hands means there's no point in practising them separately: instead, analyse the music into levels (melody and accompaniment, foreground and background) and practise each level before combining them. Apply this approach to the final section (bar 57 onwards) as well. But bars 67-9 revert to a normal combination of the hands, so they do need to be practised hands separately! Think about

the contrast of a light 'snowflake' touch with dramatic textures and sonorities that require release of weight into the keys, and use the wrist to get good leverage on louder staccato chords. The runs in bars 25-28 and 41-44 should sweep down the piano rhythmically (so accent on the first beat of the bar), with a crescendo as they approach the bottom. After all, these really are meant to be 'avalanches'.

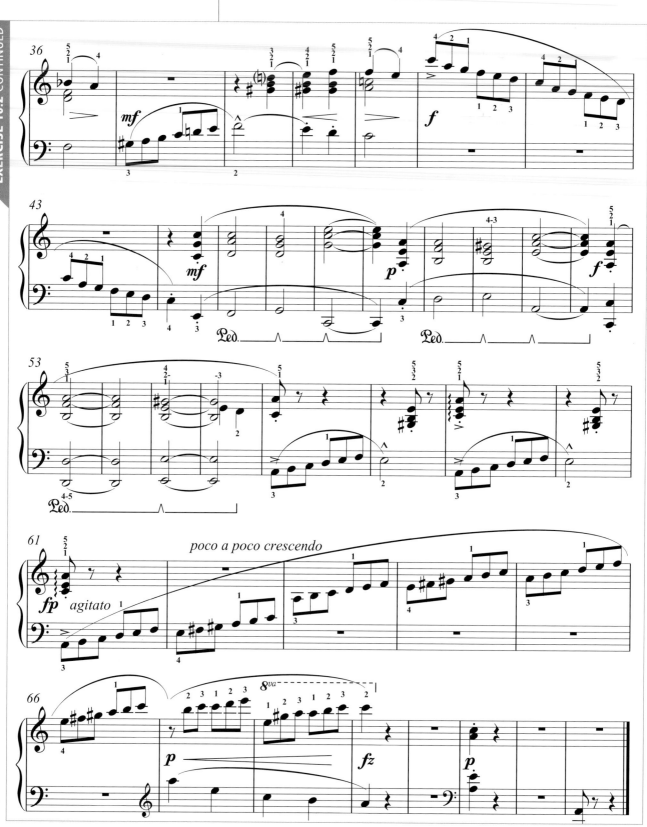

Exercise 10.3

In this study the hands overlap throughout, so the right hand must stay above and behind the left, playing right up on (and between) the black keys. Marking each rhythmic group with an accent helps maintain rhythmic evenness. For accuracy and control, keep fingers close to the keys, with a minimum of hand movement for the staccato playing. At the same time, note how repetitions of notes between the hands require you to control speed while maintaining a sharp and precise staccato touch.

CD: **TRACK 30**

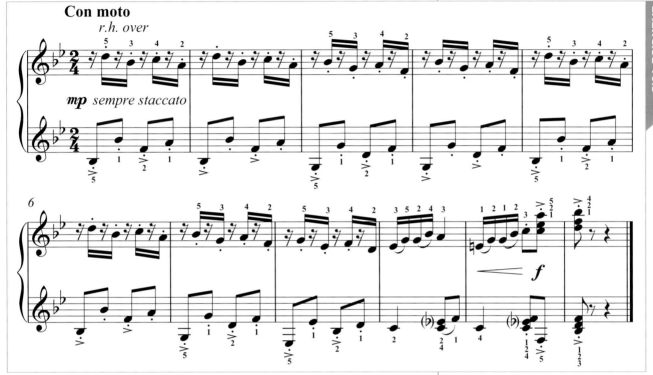

BASIC ROTATION

Take a look at the next piece (Ex.10.5). Notice the alternating pattern of semiquavers, first in the left hand, then the right, then the left again.

If you try to play these passages by themselves (ie, hands separately) you'll notice how quickly your hand stiffens up and your forearm gets tired and tense, disrupting the evenness of rhythm and tone. We use a special technique to overcome this problem, called **rotation**.

Forget the piano for a moment. Imagine you're opening a door by turning one of those door handles that have to be grasped and twisted round. (If you've got a real door handle like this in your home, that's even better. Go and try opening it, and observe carefully what your arm and hand do.)

Notice how your whole forearm, wrist, and hand move as one, in a kind of circular, twisting movement. That's rotation. Now try repeating it, first in one direction, then the other, so that the arm continually turns to and fro. Now try with the other hand. That should give you an idea of the kind of arm movement you will need when you play the following exercise.

EXERCISE 10.4

Exercise 10.4

Start slowly and gradually speed up, stopping for a rest as soon as your hand starts to feel tired. Accent the first note of each group slightly to maintain rhythmic evenness. The left hand plays the same notes, an octave lower.

Right hand

Left hand *(8ve lower)*

Franz Joseph Haydn (1732-1809) lived a long life, most of which was spent as court composer to the aristocratic Austro-Hungarian Eszterhaza family. This enabled him to develop gradually as a composer, absorbing local Viennese musical influences over a long period and responding to changing tastes, while emerging as an increasingly mature and inventive composer. His music is characterised by a gentle and good-humoured wit, and by the dramatic use of form to surprise the listener in countless ways. Haydn wrote a huge number of symphonies, string quartets and piano sonatas, many of which are masterpieces. He was influenced by his encounter with Mozart, and his own risk-taking made an impression on Beethoven, who briefly studied with him. Later in life, Haydn made visits to London, and wrote some of his finest symphonies to be performed there, as well as a number of superb piano trios. Haydn's long career means that his music spans the evolution of the music of the classical period, from baroque and galante origins through to the drama of early Beethoven. His keyboard compositions begin as works for harpsichord and end as full-length sonatas, exploiting the expressive range and dynamic possibilities of the piano.

Exercise 10.5

This piece by Haydn requires good rotation from both hands. The left plays rather high up at the start, so avoid unnecessary leaning back. Better to lean in the direction of where the right hand is to give space to the left, with feet firmly on the ground, apart and in front, to support the body's need for balance. You'll also need to work to bring the right hand melody out, as the left hand plays in a stronger register at the beginning, so it should be kept from dominating. Rotation also helps you to master independence of hands from the point of view of articulation: right hand must be phrased with couplets and staccatos, lifting off, while left hand stays legato; then the roles are reversed for the middle section. Watch out for left hand octaves in bars 13-16: keep the wrist loose and relaxed, sinking in on crotchets, and practise with eyes closed to memorise hand shifts. Haydn had a great sense of humour, so aim for a lively and light-hearted feel.

CD: **TRACK 31**

MELODIC MINOR SCALES

Classical music uses two versions of the minor scale: **harmonic minor** and **melodic minor**. So far we've only learned to play the former, which is the one that chords are based on in minor keys: hence the name. However, this scale contains an unusually large step – a chromatic interval of an augmented 2nd (see Unit 2) – from flattened 6th to sharpened 7th (ie, the **leading note**), which makes it unsuitable for melodies, since this is hard to sing. So there is a special version of the scale for melodic lines, which evens out the intervals by raising both the 6th and 7th on the way up and flattening both on the way down. Hence this melodic minor scale has different notes in ascending and descending forms, though the fingering is normally the same.

A melodic minor

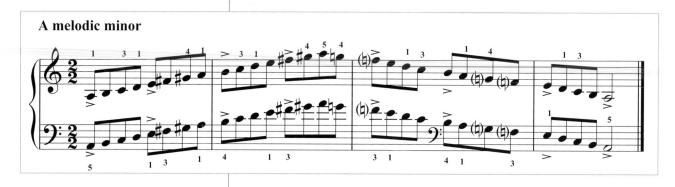

D melodic minor

E melodic minor

B melodic minor

G melodic minor

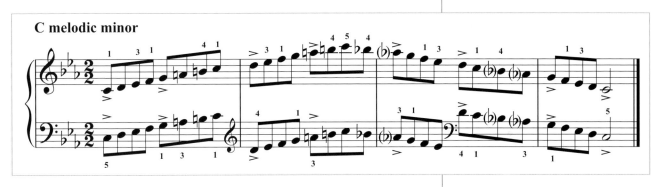

C melodic minor

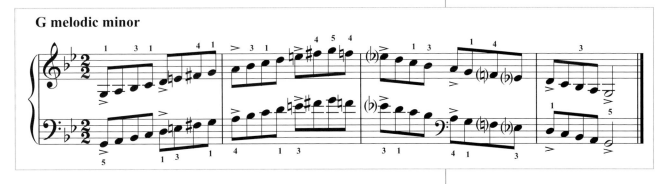

F melodic minor

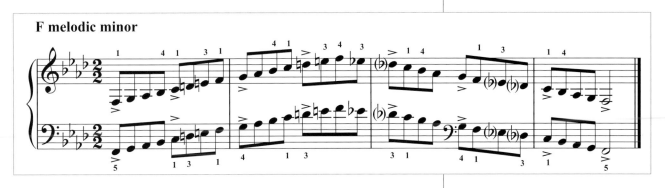

ARPEGGIOS AND CHROMATIC SCALE – HANDS TOGETHER

Combining the hands for arpeggios (in the same direction only) will not be a problem if you've mastered them hands separately; but be careful, it's easy to forget to join notes smoothly when stretching under or over into the next octave when both hands are playing. Slow them down to start with.

It's time to try playing the chromatic scale hands together: first in opposite directions (**contrary motion**) then in the same direction (**similar motion**). Start with one octave, then extend it to a second octave with the same fingering.

Note how in contrary motion we get matching fingering at the same time between hands when we start on D or A-flat, since these are the only two notes around which black and white notes form a symmetrical pattern.

In similar motion 3rd fingers come together on black notes, but thumb and 2nd work in reverse order between the hands. You should be able to figure this out for yourself on D and A-flat, so here it is on C, where we have the added feature of beginning with thumbs together. (You may need to glance back at Unit 3 just to check out the fingering again.)

UNIT 11

SECTION 4

FINGER INDEPENDENCE

As the music you're learning gets more demanding, you need to develop your physical abilities to allow you to play it without muscular strain: otherwise you won't be able to meet your own artistic standards, which should also be developing by now.

The more closely you listen, the more you'll notice any faults in your own playing, such as inequalities of tone or rhythm, or breaks in legato. This is good: it probably means you're becoming more self-critical. But the chief cause of all these problems is tension, which may be a result of poor practising habits. It can take time to develop real control and independence of the fingers without forcing them.

So here are two exercises to develop relaxed independence of the fingers. Use them as warm-up exercises before practising scales, arpeggios or pieces.

Exercise 11.1

This exercise uses extremely slow practise to make you aware of how each stage of playing a note needs to be executed in a natural and relaxed way.

Place one of the hands in a simple five-finger position on the keys. Check that hand, wrist, arm and shoulders are all relaxed (with fingers rounded, knuckles level, etc.). Lift one finger, holding it raised well above the key for a few seconds, keeping all the others resting on the keys, and the hand, wrist and forearm relaxed.

Now let go of the finger so it falls on to the key, and release enough weight to depress the key. Keep on feeling the hand weight pressing down through the finger into the resistance of the key-bed, with the hand relaxed and supported from the wrist. Hold the note for a few more seconds, and remember how this feels, with the hand relaxed and other fingers just sitting on the keys.

Now release the key by releasing the weight of the finger, and feel the hand revert to being entirely supported from the wrist. Concentrate on relaxing for a few more seconds (in the playing position), then begin with the next finger.

As you play each note, think: 'lift – play – relax!'

Perfect practice

Do you start off practising by trying to play right through the piece at full speed? Or do you begin by practising just the difficult passages, starting slowly and gradually increasing speed?

When you get to a problem passage, do you just keep on struggling in vain to play it again and again, so that you're actually practising your mistakes, or do you stop and try to find out why you can't play it, and what you're doing wrong?

What do you think are the correct answers to these questions? A handy trick when learning difficult music is to begin with the end of the passage, gradually adding on the earlier bits until you reach the beginning. This reverses the order in which different parts of the piece come to your attention, helping you to achieve technical consistency.

Exercise 11.2

This is an advanced trill study. (Trills are rapid alternations between adjacent notes: see the section on ornaments, later in this unit.) It will help you to achieve equality between fingers and develop evenness of tone and a relaxed legato. Note that there are three elements to be controlled simultaneously: the finger holding the long note (with release of hand-weight into the key-bed); the fingers playing the alternating notes (which must be even in tone and time, and perfectly legato); and the fingers not playing, but sitting on the keys. In the last case, try closing your eyes and feeling the fingertips just touching the surface of the keys. If you can't control all three elements while staying relaxed, you're playing too quickly, so slow right down.

ORNAMENTATION

Ornaments are stylised musical decorations, used to embellish a melodic line. In early classical music they were especially important, particularly for keyboard instruments such as harpsichords, clavichords and early pianos, all of which had more limited sustaining abilities than the modern piano. Like the stylised movements of ballet, they were important expressions of the spirit of elegance and formality of the aristocratic culture prevalent in Europe in the 17th and 18th centuries. This was the **Enlightenment** period, dominated by the rise of science and **humanism**, when instrumental music and opera began to achieve greater independence from sacred music. Opera singers would show their virtuosity by decorating arias in dramatic and extravagant ways. This greatly influenced the feeling for melody in classical music.

Classical ornaments need good finger control and independence, since they often require very rapid notes to be fitted into the existing rhythm of the line without sounding forced or awkward. Keep the hand relaxed and the fingers close to the keys. Many ornaments correspond to the classical embellishments used in melodic composition (Unit 6), which reappear as standard jazz techniques for embellishing chord sequences (Unit 9).

Ornaments were frequently indicated using shorthand symbols, whose exact realisation might be left to the performer. The conventions for how this was done changed gradually over the 17th and 18th centuries, and are only imperfectly recorded. Only the principal forms are given here, and you should be aware of them, but the rules are by no means fixed or certain.

Grace notes look smaller than usual, and do not affect the way the rhythm of other notes relates to the beats of the bar. A single grace note is usually written as a quaver with a diagonal slash, which makes it an **acciaccatura** ('crushed note'). Two or more grace notes are written in the same way, often without the slash, and with shorter time-values. Grace notes are normally played very quickly so as not to alter the underlying rhythm, though their speed may be varied to suit the character of the music. They usually sound just *before* the beat on which the main note sounds, though in the 18th and early 19th centuries single and multiple grace notes were also commonly played on the beat.

An **appoggiatura** ('leaning note') looks like a single grace note without the slash, but also corresponds to the appoggiatura as a melodic embellishment. The appoggiatura sounds *on* the beat, delaying the main note to afterwards, so the value of the main note gets split into two equal subdivisions or, for dotted notes, usually into two-thirds (for the appoggiatura) and one third (for the resolution).

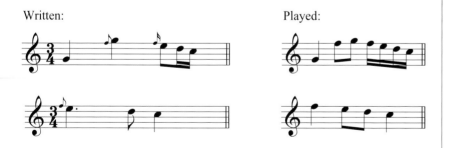

A **turn** is a decorative figuration passing quickly through the note above the written note, the written note itself, the note below, then the written note itself again. In classical period music, or where the turn is placed after the note rather than on the note, the figure will be preceded by the written note itself. Inverted turns are upside-down versions of the same. Note also how the rhythm of the turn is adapted to suit different speeds or dotted notes.

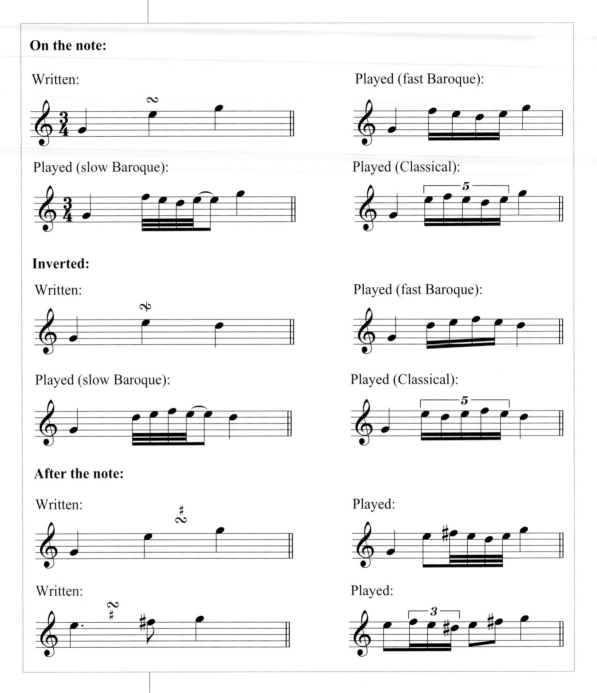

On the note:

Written:

Played (fast Baroque):

Played (slow Baroque):

Played (Classical):

Inverted:

Written:

Played (fast Baroque):

Played (slow Baroque):

Played (Classical):

After the note:

Written:

Played:

Written:

Played:

A **trill** is a rapid alternation between the main note and the note a step higher. Trills begin on the upper note in Baroque music (eg, J.S. Bach or Handel) unless preceded immediately by this same note, but as the Classical period developed (Mozart, Haydn, Beethoven) this practice gradually shifted to starting on the written note (unless preceded by the upper note as a grace note). Because the trill normally ends with a turn (in preparation for the melodic resolution that follows, if the latter is not already anticipated melodically), the later style requires inclusion of a triplet to fit all notes into time. (The last two notes of the turn often appear as grace notes before the resolution note.) Trills were employed to round off cadenzas in concertos or vocal arias, coinciding with a final resolution of dominant harmony to the tonic, and may not continue through the entire duration of the note. Trills on short notes in fast music become single alternations, turns, or a combination of the two.

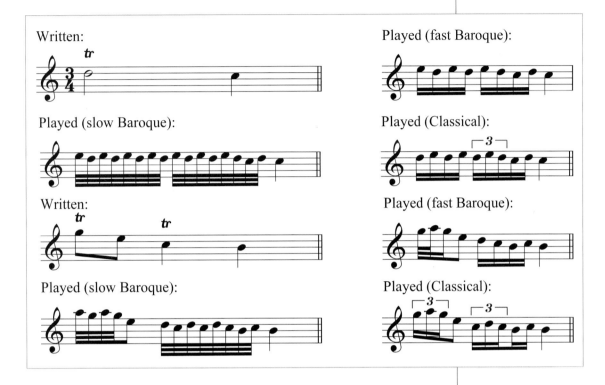

Mordents evolved out of trills on short, fast notes ('Schneller' in German). They later came to consist of a single alternation with the note above or below (like upper or lower auxiliary notes).

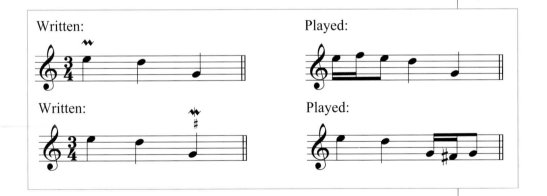

Note how the small accidentals placed above or below ornament signs signify chromatic alteration of the note above or below the written note.

Exercise 11.3

CD: **TRACK32**

The Classical period ornaments in this theme from Haydn's A major Sonata should reflect the relaxed character of the music. Watch out for the difference between acciaccaturas (bars 2, 4, 8, 10 and 12) and appoggiaturas (bars 5-6 and 13-14.) Grace notes before the final bar tell you to finish the trill with a turn, while the appoggiatura in the last bar takes two counts, resolving only on the final beat. Practise the melody without ornaments first, then hear how decorations embellish the line without distorting its underlying character and shape. The repeat marks means that in performance you could play each section first without, then with ornaments.

LEFT HAND LEAPS

A lot of piano music requires the left hand to alternate between low notes (a bass line) and chords in the middle register to create a rich harmonic texture as an accompaniment to a right hand melody. This requires good control of left-hand leaps, which must not result in unwanted accents and which are often combined with legato pedalling, making the latter much more difficult to coordinate. The left hand should move over the keys within a more or less horizontal plane, and should not release the bass note until after the change of pedal. Move into position for each chord slightly before you need to play it ('preparation'), and first practise the chords and bass line individually, fingering chords as if moving directly between them. Control of volume is essential, especially when pedalling is involved.

Exercise 11.4.

Practise this left hand pattern, first between the hands, then entirely in the left hand. Aim for the same control of volume and texture in both cases. Then practise the same material, using the rhythm from the actual piece below.

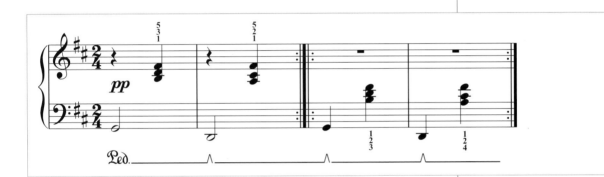

Erik Satie (1866-1925) was a lonely eccentric who lived in Paris in the early part of the 20th century. At that time the city was a great centre for radical artistic movements such as Surrealism, Futurism and Dada, and home to colourful individuals like Picasso, Breton, Stravinsky, Diaghilev and many others. Satie, however, was a quiet man, always polite and elegantly dressed. Only when he died did it emerge that he had been living all the while in one of the poorest parts of the city, with almost no possessions except his collection of identical, perfectly pressed, grey suits. His music has a strange and subtle combination of irony, sadness and detachment, and expresses nostalgia for ancient Greek culture.

Exercise 11.5

Gymnopédie No. 1 by Satie is a slow piece that requires perfect control of tone and texture. Try to obtain the pianissimo levels required for both hands without resorting to the soft pedal, grading crescendos carefully. Keep strictly to time, to maintain the sense of poise, and avoid adding expressive nuances beyond those marked in the score. Your touch should be soft and velvety. Notes in chords should be perfectly synchronised, so listen carefully, monitoring balance between the hands and the effect of the sustaining pedal. A Gymnopédie was an ancient Greek ceremonial dance performed by several dancers, probably moving in unison.

CD: **TRACK 33**

Lent et douloureux
(slowly and mournfully)

Carl Phillip Emmanuel Bach (1714-1788) is one of the most important figures in the history of classical keyboard music. One of the many sons of the great German Baroque composer J.S. Bach, he was a great composer in his own right. He really developed the arts of keyboard composition, improvisation and embellishment to an unprecedented level of originality, shocking audiences with his experimental, freestyle approach. He paved the way for the great giants of the Classical period (Mozart and Haydn) and especially for the greatest rebel of them all: Beethoven. C.P.E. Bach's *Essay on the True Art of Playing Keyboard Instruments*, published in 1753, is still widely studied today. Bach preferred the clavichord to the harpsichord, but his late keyboard works were probably written with the piano in mind.

He developed an intensely personal style of playing and improvising, reflecting his involvement with the trend towards free-ranging emotionalism (Empfindsamkeit) in the arts in Germany in the 1760s and 1770s (also known as Sturm und Drang, meaning 'storm and stress'). Later composers brought this tendency under tighter control. He was probably the first to recognise the individualistic potential of the keyboard, and to set about realising it to the full. The English historian Dr Charles Burney describes encountering Bach's involvement in his own performances, which was quite new and shocking for its time: 'He played till near eleven o'clock at night. During this time he grew so animated and possessed, that he not only played, but looked like one inspired. His eyes were fixed, his underlip fell, and drops of effervescence distilled from his countenance.' He used ornamentation and phrase structure in such a way that the music seems to dramatise the unfolding of the personal moods and thoughts of the composer-performer himself.

In this way, C.P.E.Bach also moved music in the direction of a closer resemblance to expressive speech, and to the rhetorical structures of oratory. He thus made the performance itself into a confrontation between artist and audience, in contrast to the more impersonal collective music making of public events that previously dominated. In contrast to earlier composers, it can be hard to tell whether some elements in his style have their origin in improvisation or in composition.

In his autobiography, he complains of the conflict between his own artistic aspirations and the life of professional musicians at the time. As Mozart himself said, C.P.E.Bach was '...the father of us all – without him, nothing would have been possible!' He kicked off the European tradition of keyboard improvisation and piano playing as creative forms of performance – a tradition that in the 20th century shifted from classical music into jazz (except for organ music). It's the spirit of that great tradition that this book is dedicated to keeping alive.

DOVETAILING AND OVERLAPPING THE HANDS

Exercise 11.6

CD: **TRACK 33**

This piece by C.P. Bach requires continuous dovetailing of the hands, as well as overlapping. There should be an even flow of rhythmically accented semiquavers throughout. Notice how few dynamics there are, and use your imagination to develop a dramatically interesting interpretation, matching the sudden shifts of register. The line should be shaped with dynamics that match rising and falling melodic contours, and right hand octave alternations should employ rotation. Feel your hands transporting you between different regions of the keyboard, letting the rest of your body follow, but keeping firmly balanced. This piece will strengthen your weak 4th fingers.

BLACK-KEY ARPEGGIOS

It's time to add some more two-octave arpeggios to your repertoire.

B major and B minor follow standard white-note arpeggio fingerings, with left hand 3rd on the D sharp in the former, left hand 4th on D natural in the latter. However, we haven't mentioned them until now because they call for fingers well into the black keys, just like the arpeggios starting on black keys below.

When arpeggios start on black notes, the fingering must change to keep the thumbs on white notes. B-flat major is unusually tricky, since thumbs play on different notes.

B flat major

By contrast, in E-flat major thumbs play together, making life simpler and producing a standard fingering used whenever the third of the chord is the only white note. (Try A-flat major like this too.)

E flat major

Arpeggios in the equivalent relative minor keys have a flattened third. They take the same fingering as ordinary arpeggios with just white notes. For instance, major key arpeggios start on the same notes. You can try G, C and F minors this way: just take G, C and F majors, flatten the third in each hand, but keep the same fingering.

UNIT 12

SECTION 4

RHYTHM IN JAZZ, ROCK AND BLUES

The fundamental contrast between classical and non-classical musical cultures comes from their different ways of dealing with the most elemental aspect of music: rhythm. Both kinds of music are rhythmical, but they treat the relation between rhythm and other aspects of music differently, reflecting different feelings about rhythm itself.

- **Classical music** (until the 20th century) integrates rhythm, melody and harmony systematically at the level of motifs, themes, and melodies.
- **Non-classical** music explores rhythm, melody and harmony more independently, or in separate combinations, combining them more freely later on as separate layers. This gives more flexibility to performers, who don't have to calculate the precise effect of combining all elements at once in the way that classical composers do.

Because non-classical music such as jazz, rock and blues evolved from the music of black slaves shipped from Africa to North America in the 19th century, it reflects African traditions of drumming and singing, as well as the European harmonies used in American revivalist hymns. African drumming makes rhythm central, in a way that reflects dance, and when Africans dance, they really dance, letting go with the whole body until they fall into a trance. That's a world away from the controlled elegance of European courtly dances, in which the body is held fixed and upright. It's this spirit of surrender to the dance that emerges also in rock music and modern dance music idioms.

Because rhythm in non-classical music relates to drumming, it reveals a whole new side to the piano: that it is, in fact, a *percussive* instrument. Something similar happens in 20th century classical piano music, with composers like Bartok and Stravinsky (See the Bartok piece in Unit 17.)

- Rock pianists play the instrument percussively using their whole body, releasing much more physical energy than classical pianists.
- Jazz pianists also feel rhythm more strongly in their body, but work against this in more exploratory ways, channelling their physicality such a way that the movements of their hands over the keys can take on a life of their own in improvised melodic lines and **figurations**.

The other side of this coin is that melody tends to be rhythmically freer in music with an Afro-American base, such as jazz, which evolved from **blues,** religious **gospel** music, and the **spirituals** (the work and recreational songs of slaves).

In blues, the conflict between African scale-tunings and European harmony produces expressive "out-of-tune" effects ("blue notes") that evoke the sense of suffering and displacement of Africans and poor people generally in America, especially as they moved into big cities in search of work.

The blues musician usually tells a story, with a style of **declamation** that lies between emotionally heightened speech and song. This lets the rhythm and shape of the melody line reflect the irregular rhythms and continuous **inflections** of speech much more closely, since it is not bound strictly by constraints of metre and scale tuning. Instrumental phrases comment on the unfolding story, echoing this "raw" feel of melody as heightened speech, resulting in a distinctive feel for shape and rhythm in improvised lines, which underlies not just R&B and blues-based rock styles, but also much jazz improvisation. The downside is that our system of musical notation isn't really designed to show these things, so it misrepresents them. You need to listen to old recordings to get the feel of how blues works. The point about

From jazz to house

The 20th century saw an explosion of new styles of music, largely made possible by the influence of Afro-American music on urban cultures in which the commercial entertainment industry and the demands of youth culture have played an ever-increasing role. From jazz, ragtime and boogie-woogie through to rock'n'roll, rhythm and blues (R&B), rock, pop, punk, funk, reggae, disco, heavy metal, death metal, acid, house, and whatever makes the charts and clubs this time next week, popular musical styles have become part of the cultural landscape against which most young people today define themselves. This means that musical styles closely reflect the preferences of particular generations and subcultures, as well as their approach to social activities, especially dance.

Afro-American idioms is not just that melody can relate more flexibly to the underlying rhythm and metre of the music, but that this freedom brings melody closer to its own origins in the expressive characteristics (the rhythms and inflections) of speech. See the Listening Guide at the back of this book for examples of the many Afro-American styles.

In **gospel**, Christian (pentecostal) and African (shamanistic) traditions merge together, with individual members of a congregation bursting spontaneously into freely extemporised song above a chorus, 'taken over' by the Spirit. The same thing used to happen in European religious singing, and can still be encountered on remote Scottish islands. All this fed into the way popular singers and jazz musicians work using melody to extemporise.

Jazz over the last half-century has drifted away from the traditional improvisatory styles of New Orleans and Chicago ('trad jazz') and the entertainment-orientated big band arrangements of the 'swing' era. From bebop in the Forties, through Fifties 'cool jazz' to Sixties 'new wave', **modern jazz** has become a progressively more sophisticated and experimental art form with its own connoisseurs. It's also become increasingly reliant on compositional techniques from classical music. These days, you're more likely to find the tradition of free-style keyboard extemporisation – stretching from C.P.E Bach through Mozart, Beethoven, Liszt and Chopin to the greats of jazz and rock – being kept alive by 'free improvisation' specialists working the 'alternative' music circuit.

The only real way to learn popular styles is get out there and experience the dance cultures of the day (if you don't already do so), and, as with jazz, to learn by listening to what other musicians are doing. In this book, we can only hope to sketch the most basic features of rhythmic styles and the differences between them. It's up to you to get into the 'feel' of the 'groove' (ie, the particular rhythmic style), and that's more about how you relate to your own body than it is about any techniques you could ever learn.

SYNCOPATION, GROOVES & SWING

The principal distinguishing features of rhythmic styles derived from Afro-American music are:

- **offbeat** emphasis: the weak beats of the bar (normally the 2nd and 4th beats). In rock and heavy rock this can be extreme, creating what drummers call a strong **backbeat**.
- **syncopation**: displacing the rhythmic accent away from its normal position in the metre, usually on to a subdivision of the beat.

(It's worth pointing out that syncopation is a concept that properly belongs to classical music. In African music, syncopation is the norm rather than the exception, whereas in classical music it is treated as a 'rhythmic dissonance' – between actual rhythm and implied metre – that has to be resolved.)

Rhythmic styles also divide into those that subdivide the metre into twos or threes. The latter will often be heard as also dividing the beat into two parts, but of unequal length, approximating to a triplet rhythm of two-thirds, then one-third of a beat. In blues and slow styles, you'll often see this written out as a **shuffle** rhythm in 12/8 compound time, but in jazz it becomes so normal that it's assumed even when the music is shown as even quaver divisions or as dotted rhythms. This effect of a permanent triplet **feel** in simple time is known as **swing**.

Written:

Played:

Swung rhythms in jazz also reflect the strong awareness (in black and white American folk music traditions) of how melody can work rhythmically against metre, to create a distinctive 'upbeat' or 'downbeat' feel. Country music (which has strong links to Celtic folk music traditions in Scotland and Ireland) will often **push the beat** by making melody notes consistently anticipate it slightly, whereas blues tends to create a dragging atmosphere of frustration by **leaning on the beat**, delaying the main notes so they sound slightly after. (Not all blues does this, since not all blues is downbeat.)

The particular combination of speed, subdivision, degree of swing or syncopation, and strength of offbeat, will define the **groove** of the music, on which the whole feel of the style may rest. Harmonic devices, melodic elaborations and bass line figurations often derive their sense from this, especially as different rhythmic idioms open up gaps in the texture for melodic elaboration in different ways. Let's try and get a glimpse of some of the most widely used rhythmic idioms of Afro-American popular music, at least in their simplest forms.

The great rock session pianist Nicky Hopkins, seen here playing electric piano.

RHYTHMIC IDIOMS

The examples that follow just illustrate the most basic forms of groove – on which there are endless variations. Play each one through over and over until it's in your bones, and your own body will begin to tell you how to vary the rhythms.

Ragtime & jazz

Ragtime was one of the first syncopated styles, developed mainly by black musicians who found employment in cities by playing pianos in bars. Left-hand **stride** patterns provide the basic rhythmic pattern, with syncopated semiquaver right-hand figures on top. Composers like Scott Joplin developed this into something closer to classical music. Turn to Unit 16 and you'll see the most famous ragtime of them all: 'The Entertainer'.

Early jazz also uses left hand stride patterns and **walking bass** effects in piano solos as a substitute for the rhythm section of the jazz ensemble. These can support swung rhythms like those in Example 12.1. Unless you have large hands, you'll have to spread the walking tenths, starting on the lower note.

Later jazz moves away from this in order to create rhythmically freer styles of melodic improvisation over the subtle background textures of the jazz rhythm section (ie, drums and bass). The pianist often contributes syncopated chords as accompaniment for instrumental solos (known in the lingo as 'comping'), or the more economical left-hand voicings that we'll be looking at in Unit 15. The patterns here are designed to work over a rhythm section, so they stay off the beat, and you can feel the difference between 'comping behind and ahead of the beat by practising them with a metronome. When 'comping, try to keep out of the register of the soloist. Don't worry about the voicings for the moment – we'll investigate those in due course.

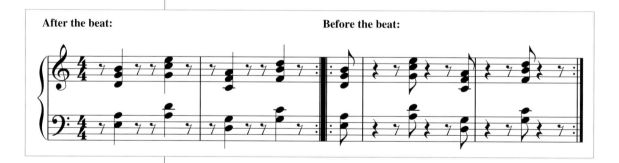

12/8 styles

Boogie-woogie offers an insistent rhythmic background – the **shuffle** rhythm – as a basis for bluesy improvisation over a strong beat:

Rock 'n' roll in a **ballad** style has a relaxed feel, with right hand providing a kind of even quaver (eighth note) **ride** pattern while the left makes the bass line move around the middle and end of the bar (the 'rock' and the 'roll'). **Rock shuffle** or 'rock-a-boogie' combines this with the more powerful left-hand patterns of a boogie-woogie, with right-hand breaks for soloing.

CD: **TRACKS 35 AND 36**

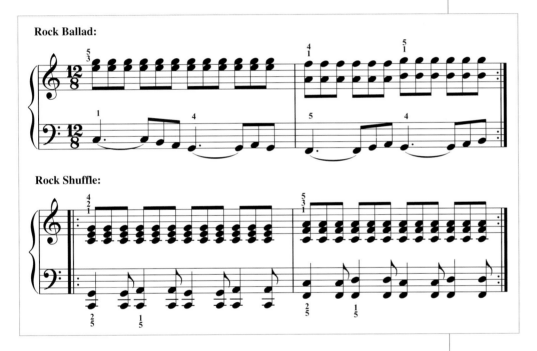

Country shuffle then adds **country** harmonies and feel by avoiding bluesy flattened 7ths on the tonic and using **fretted style** right hand elaborations. The latter copies guitar fingerpicking, with alternations of fingers and thumb, and guitar hammering-on and pulling-off techniques, using added 4ths or chromatic notes on or before the beat that resolve by shifting quickly up or down by step to chord notes. Actually sliding fingers between black and white notes in 3rds adds to the effect.

CD: **TRACK 37**

4/4 Straight ahead styles

Straight-eight New Orleans style and **Cajun** use two-handed grooves to push the beat, while **straight-eight boogie** drives the rhythm harder with eight left-hand **pounding** quavers (eighth notes) to the bar, bass-line movement on offbeats, and right-hand stabbed chords (called **chops**) helping to **turn the rhythm around** (ie, leading the cycle of syncopation or offbeats back to where it starts again). **Straight ahead** or 'get down' rock then develops this with left-hand octave alternations and funkier right-hand figures, especially around chord changes, making for the standard rock dance groove. **Country (L.A. style) rock** has more relaxed right-hand arpeggiations in quaver eighth notes (like guitar strumming), with the bass moving to the 5th of the chord at the half-measure in a dotted rhythm. Straight-eight **rhythm and blues** mixes blues (lots of flat 7ths) and gospel harmonies (see below) with melodic **turnaround** figures that mark the move from one section to the next with an upbeat pushing of the beat that varies in intensity as the music picks up or subsides.

CD: **TRACKS 39 TO 43**

Straight-Eight New Orleans

Cajun

Straight-Eight Boogie

"Get Down" Rock

LA Style Country Rock

Straight-Eight R&B

Gospel styles:

Gospel harmonies feature block chords, V^9 or V^{13}, and a harmonic figure that moves from I to IV^c and back again (I - IV^c - I) – a bit like the I^c - V progression in classical cadences. The stately 6/4 gospel style combines two 3-beat rock-waltz figures in a single bar, with shuffle (triplet) subdivisions and a strong backbeat lift (accent) on the half-measure of each bar: full of ecstatic solemnity! Straight-eight gospel offers an upbeat alternative with semiquaver (sixteenth note) syncopations over flowing left-hand quaver (eighth note) rhythms.

CD: **TRACKS 44 AND 45**

Funk

The 1970s saw the emergence of **funk** grooves operating in **halftime,** ie, with a single backbeat punctuating the middle of every group of sixteen (semiquaver) notes rather than eight (quaver) notes, but in 4/4 time. On the piano, two-hand funk grooves create repeated patterns that bend the metre by holding back or pushing forward the rhythm, often using repeated blues-scale melodic figures (**riffs**). Changes of feel between sections (**releases**) keep the music fresh, while 'laying in the groove' makes it possible for others to solo freely, especially in chorus sections. **Halftime pop-rock** is a sweeter and smoother piano style: the halftime spacing between backbeats gives more freedom to vary levels of rhythmic tension, eg, by shifting syncopations between hands to make them more or less prominent. Funk grooves figure in **pop** music and **disco** as mechanical repetitions of rhythmic patterns.

CD: **TRACK 46**

167

All these styles have strong Afro-American roots. **Latin-American** music, however, forms a separate but related category, with a distinctive mixture of Afro-American, European and 'Latin' influences. The 'Latin' element here itself reflects a Hispanic (Spanish) culture that combines European and Arabic/Moorish influences – we'll explore this in the last unit of the book (Unit 18). Between these lie Afro-Cuban and Afro-Caribbean styles (like reggae), whose hypnotic rhythms you should certainly get to know.

RIFFS & LICKS

Riffs are repetitive melodic figures that help to set the groove, thanks to their rhythmic character (pushing or pulling back the beat). Left hand bass-line riffs on the piano pitted against offbeat right hand chords are a good way to catch the feel of a rhythm section in rock. Doubling a riff line at the octave or double octave with hands in sync (known as **locked hands** to rock and jazz musicians, or **rhythmic unison** in classical music) can be a great way to increase the power of the sound. (Adding 4ths or 5ths gets something quite like a classic 'hot' electric rock guitar sound.)

    Licks are brief embellishments that take advantage of gaps in the rhythmic texture to add some interest beneath the solo (**lead**) line, often in a kind of informal rhythmic dialogue with the underlying groove. Rock is eclectic, so you're free to mix up fretted styles, bluesy off-note figures, pentatonic scales or R&B style figures to get to your own personal style, and **glissandi** (sliding the hand down across the black or white keys) may be used for dramatic effect at the **turnarounds** (the move from one section into the next).

Other special rhythmic effects include:

- **Breaks:** brief episodes where the metrical rhythm suddenly breaks off, leaving free melodic figures exposed for the equivalent of a couple of measures

- **Out-of-time passages:** rhythmically free **intro** sections before the beat clicks in, or winding down from the beat at the end

- **Change of 'feel':** altering the character of the groove, or even the speed, between sections

- **Double tempo:** superimposing passages with a halftime feel by subdividing the beat into four instead of two (drummers do this a lot)

- **Pitch-based rhythm:** using higher-pitched or denser chords to accentuate offbeats creates the same kind of intensity of sound and rhythm as high-energy (African-style) drumming, where volume distorts drum sonorities and this further heightens elements of the beat.

SONG FORM

Everyone knows the way Americans soldiers chant when on training: one guy (the leader) calls out a line of a song, then all respond in chorus, and so on. The songs of the black slaves working in the cotton fields or building the railroads across America had the same practical logic. (According to ethnomusicologists, aspects of musical cultures across the world often reflect the everyday activities of the people.) That's why Afro-American melodies and rhythms have a strong element of **call and** response, alternating a musical idea from one player with a collective response. Similar effects on piano can be achieved between one hand and both hands, or by exploiting the wide expressive range of the instrument for contrasts of volume and **register** (high and low textures).

One of the most basic formal structures in all music (including classical as well) is **song form** (also known as **strophic form**): here the alternation of verse and chorus also reflects a call and response pattern, with the same music used for different words in the verse sections, and words and music returning together in the choruses, often to release the tension built up in the verses. **Song-writing** requires an imaginative grasp of the different possibilities of this, such as story-telling alternating with ironic commentary, contrasts of mood, or just plain tension and release. Try to listen to as wide a variety of songs as you can, noticing differences in how the form is used to expressive effect.

Jazz tunes often follow a special kind of song form. Instead of simply alternating verse ('A section') and chorus ('B section'), they tend to play through the A section twice, then pass once through a short B section (known as the **bridge**), then play the A section once more: the resulting AABA pattern can be played over and over again as a basis for improvising.

12-BAR BLUES

This is probably the most basic and important chord sequence in popular music, and is often used by rock musicians for **jamming** together, for example as way of 'getting to know one another' musically. You should know it thoroughly, as it can give a feel for how harmony works in general in rock and blues, where subdominant and dominant function differently to the way they work in classical harmony. (Subdominant tends to be more important, especially in blues-based harmony. So is the switch from V to IV, which classical composers tend to avoid because it weakens the dominant.) Notice how the chords are basically major key harmonies, whereas the blues scale has a minor 3rd and flattened 5th, producing the classic blues grating between major key harmony and 'out-of-tune' blue-notes.

The basic pattern is:

‖ I | I | I | I | IV | IV | I | I | V | IV | I | I :‖

This was slightly altered in the 1930s to:

‖ I | IV | I | I | IV | IV | I | I | V | IV | I | V :‖

> **Blues ability**
> If you can't realise a simple 12-bar blues in most keys without even thinking about it, then it's probably best to keep out of sight of other jazz and rock musicians. They might consider you musically illiterate.

In blues, all of these chords would be dominant 7ths. Don't worry about getting authentic blues voicings for the moment. Just get the feel of the changes, with standard two-hand chord layouts (three notes in the right hand and one in the left – see Unit 9), then try adding notes, changing the rhythmic feel, transposing, and generally exploring. The sequence may also be elaborated with a range of **chord substitutions**. (See **reharmonisation** in Unit 18.)

Why not try putting some of those rock grooves we've just learned about through the 12-bar blues cycle, in a variety of keys?

LEAD SHEETS & STANDARDS

Both well known hit songs and jazz **standards** (tunes famous for the improvisations based on them, as recorded by the great jazzmen) can be learned and played from a lead sheet. This is a reduced version of the song, used by rock musicians to work out an arrangement of their own, or in jazz as a basis for improvisation. Jazz standards are published in collections known as **fake books**, while hit songs can usually be obtained either in lead sheet or **sheet music** form (ie, simple voice and piano arrangement): look for these in popular anthologies covering particular bands or periods of rock music history like the 1960s or 1970s.

Don't take the chord symbols in **lead sheets** too literally. Sometimes they include only the most basic structures, leaving it to you to decide how to make the harmony more stylish and interesting. Other times they'll include jazz reharmonisations already, which may sometimes be optional or even plain wrong (though they won't tell you that). Always look at the key signature first, which may only be given for the first line (in contrast to classical scores and sheet music). It affects all of the music, but not the chord symbols (unlike symbols used for analysing chords in classical music). Diagonal strokes may be used to indicate beats of the bar when specifying exact points in time, especially in **chord charts** for band musicians. The tune will normally be put in the middle register for ease of reading, so feel free to transpose parts of it into other octaves for effect. If you plan to work with a singer, it's worth learning to transpose chord progressions at sight into other keys, so that you can find the best key for the song for their particular voice.

Here's a typical lead sheet for a well-known Bud Powell **number**, based on George Shearing's 'Lullaby of Birdland':

CD: **TRACK 47**

Buy the book

Head down to your local music shop and pick up some song collections and a **fake book**, so you've got a range of sheet music and lead sheets, then work through the chords experimenting with different rhythmic styles like those we've learned about here.

Try combining the changes in this lead sheet with different grooves. Which ones give you space for a right hand treatment of the melody line as well?

EMBELLISHING A TUNE

We've already looked briefly at how you can embellish the top voice of a chord sequence to get a melody or improvised line (Unit 9). This is not just central to jazz, but also to traditional classical composing (see Unit 6), where melodies and harmony are often conceived alongside each other. But with a standard or a hit, the tune is already given, so you're embellishing a line that already has a familiar and distinctive shape. This brings in a few extra considerations.

Producing a rock piano rendition of a hit song is more about **arranging** the tune and chords in a pianistically interesting style (in terms of texture, feel and groove - see Unit 18) than it is about producing complex melodic variations At the other end of the spectrum, jazz elaborations often veer towards loose successions of melodic or rhythmic **sequences**: patterns repeated with the same melodic shape moved up or down a step or two, or just keeping the rhythm the same. These may bear little resemblance to the original tune. They're really more concerned with translating the subtle colours of chord **reharmonisations** into melodic form, often as arpeggio-like figures (see Unit 15).

Between these extremes lies a rich field of possibilities for working creatively with melodies. It's here that you can really tap into the great tradition of spontaneous melodic embellishment coming from blues, gospel and folk music generally.

In addition to **diatonic** and **chromatic** forms of decoration and **filling out** of intervals, which we looked at in Unit 9, you can do a lot through responding to the structure of the melody itself. Consider delaying and complicating the arrival at key moments (high-points or climaxes and harmonic resolutions), extending and expanding figures or motifs embedded within the line, or isolating a simpler shape of which the line itself is already an embellishment, then substituting your own embellishment or taking the existing one further.

Here's an extract transcribed from my own improvised embellishment of the Bud Powell number we just looked at. I've left out the sophisticated reharmonisations or chord-based improvising of jazz, since we're not quite ready to tackle these yet, and the rhythms are written as played (ie, classical-style) to show exactly what's going on. Note how in the opening phrase the F resolution-note gets pushed back to the second bar, and the way the **cross-rhythms** in bars 5-6 emerge naturally from the rhythmic independence of the hands. The narrow melodic range in the chorus invites one to open up with larger intervals, while the chromatic movement of the original line provides the material for decorative runs. And by the way, you'll find similar techniques in classical music in any **Theme and Variations** by Mozart or Beethoven.

CD: **TRACK 48**

Now you try producing your own version. Start by just playing through the melody several times, then feel where it wants to go.

There's really nothing to stop you experimenting right now with your own arrangements of tunes like this one, combining the changes and the line with different grooves and piano styles. It's all about that magical sense of playfulness and

172

exploration, about surprising yourself and others with the unexpected, and losing yourself in the moment. Your first attempts are sure to sound a bit hesitant and primitive, but stick at it and you'll be amazed how quickly you turn into a skilled improviser. But it does need practice.

PENTATONIC & BLUES SCALES

Rock and blues soloing require familiarity with fingerings for pentatonic and blues scales, which may vary greatly depending on key and context, especially as notes are more irregularly spaced than in classical scales. Here are just a few typical possibilities. Try to apply the fingering principles to other keys as well. We'll only look at the right hand for now, as left-hand soloing is rare.

Note that it can often be more effective to develop your own fingerings as you

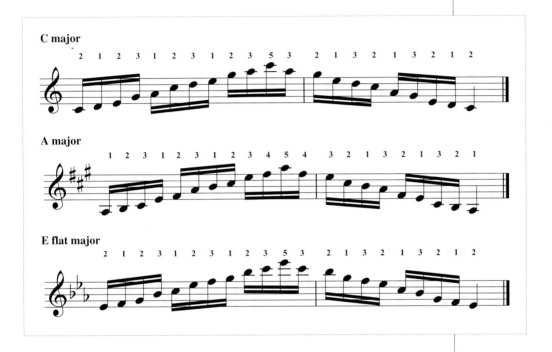

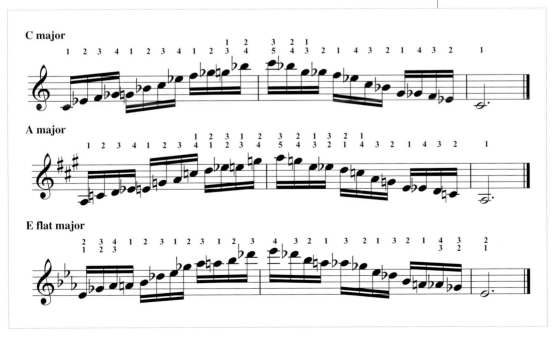

build up your own personal repertoire of licks, riffs and other right-hand elaborations. Many of these will interweave fragments of different scales and arpeggio chords with added notes or extensions, including the 7th chords whose fingerings are shown below. These play a more important role in chord-based jazz improvisations, and practising them will help you familiarise yourself with the principal structures of jazz across the full range of keys. Try out fingerings for other keys as well, and note that fingering may vary depending on the size of your hands.

7TH CHORD FINGERINGS

Root position 7th chords on white notes follow a simple logic for fingering: use 1234, passing thumb under for the next octave and 5th at the top. (This works for all chord types.) However if the chord begins on a black note, begin in the middle of the pattern so that thumb appears on the first white note, as below, adjusting the fingering to minimise the first stretch under. (Don't worry about inversions just yet.)

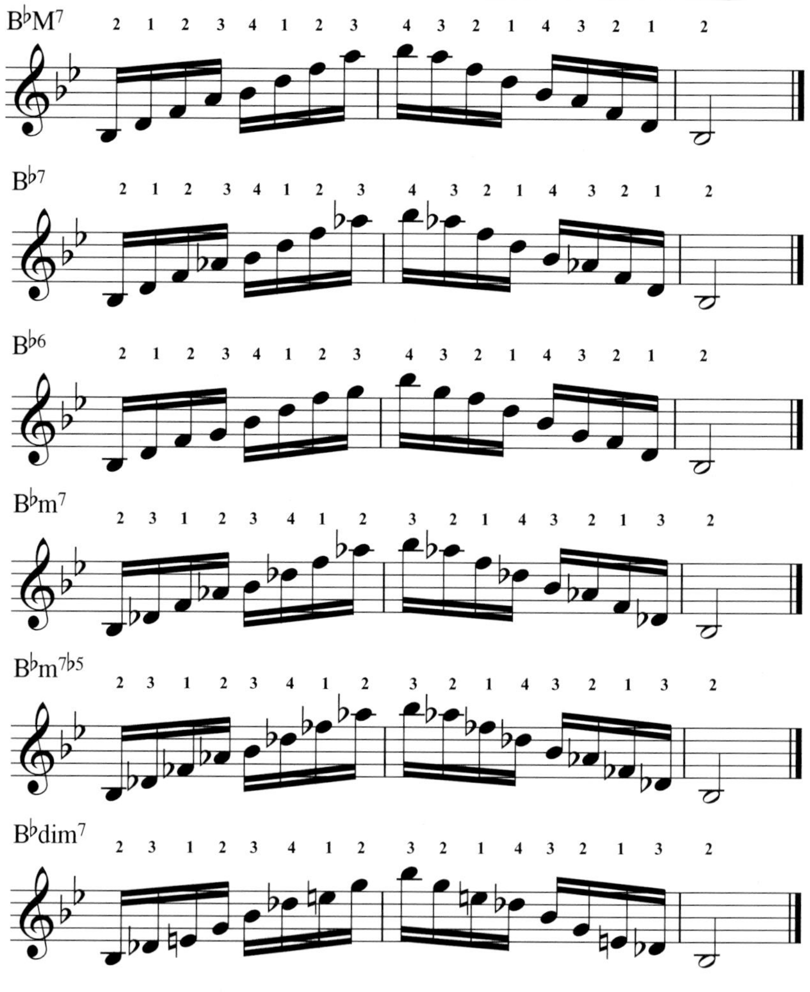

Practise all of these 7th chords as arpeggios and broken chords, through all keys, with the appropriate fingering; diminished 7ths and dominant 7ths should also be practised hands together as classical arpeggios.

Watch out for **enharmonic equivalents:** F-flat is the same as E, (and E-sharp would be an F), but it's written this way to show it's the flattened 5th of the chord. Likewise a diminished 7th on B-flat should strictly include an A **double flat** (written as two flat signs next to each other), which is a G on the piano. (Note that a **double sharp** is written as an *x*, not as two sharp signs. God knows why!)

Enharmonic equivalents

Because the piano is tuned to **equal temperament**, with the tuning fixed to be the same in all keys, enharmonic equivalents really only serve to ind+icate harmonic function, and we can compromise this in practice to avoid unnecessary accidentals. (It's common to see diminished 7ths written more freely, as they often function ambiguously in terms of key, since any note can be the root when they're all equally spaced.) But be careful writing or arranging for stringed instruments or voice, where enharmonically equivalent notes produce real differences of tuning.

UNIT 13

SECTION 5

CLASSICAL STYLE

The late 18th century saw the emergence of what is known as the classical style of composition. ('Classical music' is a much broader term, referring to European art-music as a whole, not just music written during this 'classical period'.) The classical style emphasises clarity of form and naturalness of unfolding. The music is divided into phrases that follow a question-and-answer pattern, while also forming carefully balanced structural divisions. By this time opera had emerged as a major art form, leading composers to emphasise melody as the focus for drama and expression, even in instrumental music.

It was now that the piano replaced the harpsichord as the principal keyboard instrument. Technical improvements allowed composers such as Clementi, Mozart and Haydn to start exploring its musical possibilities. The classical style of playing is generally restrained and delicate, with dynamic contrasts less pronounced than in later styles. It also requires a clear distinction between foreground (melody) and background (accompaniment). To get a sense of how this works, get hold of some of the pieces mentioned in the Repertoire guide at the back of this book.

The key concept in playing classical period music is that of **phrasing.** This refers to how we present various elements of the music so that they combine together to create the sense of an unfolding series of ideas. Phrasing includes:

- shaping of line with dynamics;
- maintaining line with legato and singing tone;
- stressing rhythmically important notes, in line with metre;
- creating breaks/gaps between phrases (often by shortening last note of phrases).

A good pianist will be aware of how particular movements of arm, wrist, hand or fingers affect several of these elements at once. The wrist must be especially flexible, as it is often responsible for both the accentuation and the lightening and shortening that mark phrase divisions. Arm weight is only used in rare moments for a full and dramatic sound. Staccato articulation must be carefully judged to fit the character of the music in respect to lightness and shortness, and real evenness of tone is necessary, especially in scale passages and arpeggio patterns. All of this requires a state of relaxed control which can only be achieved by careful practice, and never through forcing the hands. Sustaining pedal is rarely used, if at all. (Note: phrase markings may not be given in the music – or may have been added by editors.)

Muzio Clementi (1752-1832) was an important figure in the evolution of the European piano tradition. Clementi arrived on the scene as the more powerful English piano was being developed. He developed a style of writing for the instrument that features richer and more dramatic textures than anything Mozart or Haydn had dared to write. Clementi made more use of the powerful lower registers, with thicker chords, unusual modulations, octave doublings and sudden changes of mood. He had an almost symphonic approach to sonata movements, in which the unfolding of a work is anticipated in an introduction that recurs later as a dramatic recall. In this respect, and in his development of specifically pianistic techniques and textures, he provided an important model that was taken much further by Beethoven, who also prescribed Clementi's sonatas as daily practice when he was teaching his nephew.

Exercise 13.1.

Muzio Clementi was one of the first composers to develop a style of writing specifically for the piano. In later life he turned to manufacturing and selling the instruments. Musically, he was influenced by Mozart. This movement from his Sonatina in G illustrates the concise, logical form and clarity of phrase structure that Beethoven admired in his works. The opening theme captures both the singing character of the upper register of the piano and its capacity for detailed phrasing and contrasts of legato and staccato. The left hand provides a smooth and flowing accompaniment that can be softened by overlapping notes within each chord and keeping fingers in contact with keys. Rotation helps the right hand in bars 13-14 and 50/52, while louder passages in the middle section call for a lively staccato touch to set off quavers against the semiquavers, which must be played legato. Watch for couplets and phrase endings that need lifting from the wrist to lighten and shorten notes.

CD: **TRACK 49**

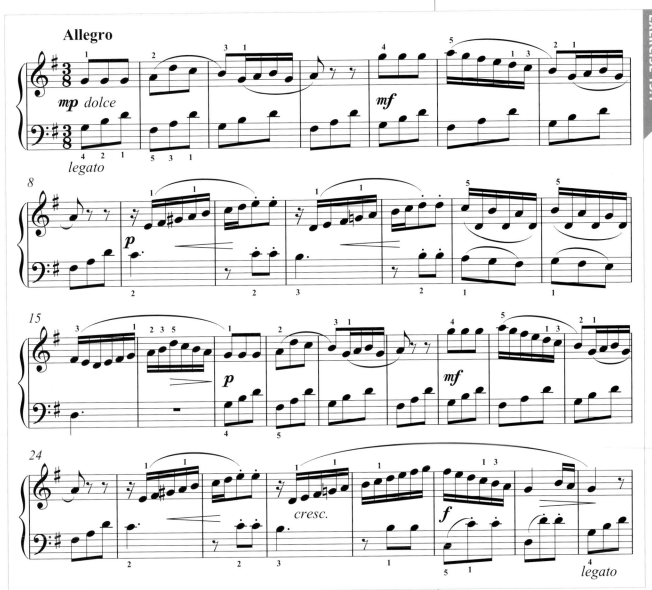

SONATA FORM

The classical period saw the emergence of more sophisticated musical forms in various instrumental **genres**, such as the **symphony, concerto, string quartet** and **wind quintet,** and in other chamber music combinations, including **sonatas** (instrumental works for solo piano or solo instrument with piano accompaniment). All sonatas have several movements and tend to follow the same sort of formal pattern. Classical composers also liked to write wrote **rondos** as self-contained works. Try listening to C.P.E. Bach's *Rondo in A* (Wq.58/1) and *Rondo in C minor* (Wq.59/4) (see the Listening Guide for recommended recordings). Or try Mozart's exquisite *Rondo in A minor* (K511).

Normally, a first movement exploring thematic contrasts at a fairly fast tempo is followed by a **minuet and trio** (a relaxed dance movement with a contrasting middle section). Then comes a slow movement (in a song-like **strophic form** rather similar to that described in Unit 12 for modern popular songs), and finally a fast, flowing movement called a *finale*, often with a more **contrapuntal** character. The last movement is usually a **rondo,** with something like an ABCBA pattern of sections: that means it presents two contrasting forms of material, passes through a third section with different material, and then repeats the first two kinds of material, possibly in reverse order.

This idea of a contrast between two kinds of material with a third middle section before a repeat is taken much further in the first movement form, which is what the term **sonata form** actually refers to. This consists of three main sections:

- **exposition:** a statement of the two contrasting types of material (1st and 2nd **subject** or **subject group**), the second in a different key to the first;
- **development:** elements of the material transformed with rapid changes of key;
- **recapitulation** (or **reprise**): a written out repeat of the first section with altered key relationships and other changes that produce a greater sense of resolution.

The movement may begin with a slow **introduction**, and is frequently rounded off with a short additional closing section, called a **coda**. Similar additional material at the end of the exposition is called a **codetta**. If the movement is in a major key, the 2nd subject will most likely be in the **dominant**; if it's in the minor, the 2nd subject will probably be in the **relative major**. The subject groups are linked by **transitions**. The exposition is usually played twice, and some sonatas also call for a separate repeat of the rest of the movement as well.

Sonata form was something that composers such as Mozart, Haydn and Beethoven arrived at through intuition, and in many different variants. The basic schema was only formally identified later by historians. Beethoven (see Unit 16) expanded the whole conception dramatically, with far greater contrasts of material and extensive development sections. His sonata movements unfold organically, working through the tensions and contrasts latent in musical ideas and their relations with an inexorable logic. This led to the romantic conception of the symphony, and eventually to modern music (see Unit 17).

The main alternative to sonata form in the classical period was variation form, also known as **theme and variations**. Whereas sonata form embodies the increasing emphasis on linear unfolding and development in music at this time, variation form holds on to the more static and sectional character of baroque dance forms. A theme is followed by a sequence of relatively self-contained sections that each have the same underlying harmonic structure as the theme, but vary the melody, harmony and texture in different ways. That makes it much closer to the sort of structures you'll find in jazz, where musicians improvise on the chords of a song over and over again but in different ways.

For a good example of classical variation form, try getting to listen to Beethoven's monumental *Diabelli Variations* (see the Listening Guide at the back of the book).

Alternatively, you might consider learning to play Mozart's fabulous *Sonata No.11 in A* (K331): the first movement (Andante Cantabile) is unusual in that it's a theme and variations. The last movement (Rondo alla Turca) is one of his most famous rondo compositions, so you might try that too.

Haydn's *Sonata in A* (Hob.16/30) also includes a theme and variations of only moderate difficulty: if you've played through the Haydn piece in Unit 11, then you've already learned the theme.

ALBERTI BASS

Classical period music for piano makes much use of left hand repeated chordal patterns to provide flowing textures as background for melodies. These are known as the **Alberti bass**. Practise the pattern as block chords to master changes of hand position, then aim for a rhythmically even pattern. Slight forearm rotation can help here (with the fingers staying in contact with the keys) so long as it doesn't spoil the balance of volume between hands. Notes on the beat (or half-beat) should be stressed slightly more to reflect their relation to the metre. Some overlapping may be appropriate, especially if pedal is not used, but not in the muddy lower registers of the piano.

Here's how to practise the Alberti bass at the opening of the Mozart piece we're going to look at next. The second exercise is important for learning to restrain the thumb, which has to play the weakest notes of the pattern in spite of being the hardest digit to control: direct the rotation onto the weaker fingers more, but keep the thumb in contact with the key when it's not actually playing.

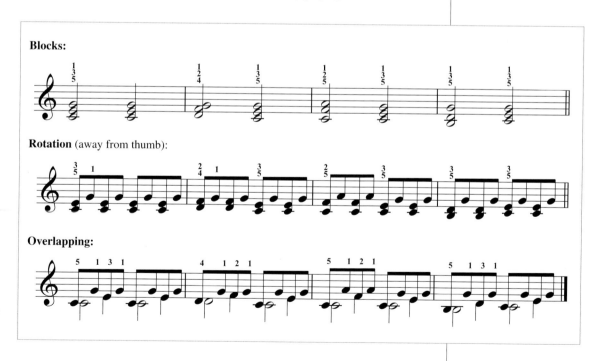

Exercise 13.3.

Now it's time to tackle a complete classical sonata movement: the first movement of Mozart's Sonata in C, K545 (overleaf). We've put in a few suggestions for dynamics, but it's up to you to figure out the detailed phrasing and shaping. Aim for a smooth

CD: **TRACK 50**

181

and singing tone and an even flow throughout. The opening puts the left hand in the more penetrating middle register, so you've got to work for a proper balance between hands. Lift and drop lightly with the wrist to articulate left hand crotchet upbeats and downbeats from bar 5 on, with the right hand semiquavers flowing evenly but heading towards the first beat of the next bar. (Feel the arm drawing the hand and fingers across the keys – also in the left hand scales starting at bar 50.)

Practise bar 11 slowly, with left hand lateral movement to kick back round from the thumb to the 5th, and a crisp right hand staccato. You will certainly need rotation for the left at bar 13, and the speed at which you play the trill over this will set the upper limit for the speed of the piece: there's no point starting quickly if you have to slow down here. Lateral movement and blocks will help for seamless flow between hands from bar 18.

The long trill in bar 25 is best played as quickly as possible, but in free time: use rotation to assert the rhythmic independence of the left hand, but synchronise the arrival on the first beat of the next bar between the hands. (A forte-piano followed by a crescendo is effective on long trills of this kind.) The arpeggio-like figure in bar 26 will also benefit from lateral movement.

A good interpreter needs an analytical understanding of the music being played. Can you analyse the form of this Mozart movement? Where do the exposition, development and recapitulation start and finish? What key is the second subject group in? How does the recapitulation differ from the exposition?

MORE BLACK-KEY SCALES

Scales of D-flat major and G-flat major work like B major: they have all five black notes, plus two white notes, so they are distinguished by the white notes they have, not the black notes. Thumbs play together on white notes, with 3rd going over on to groups of two black notes, 4th on to groups of three, like in B major. Check out the key signatures in the circle of 5ths (Unit 6). Here are the white notes for these scales:

B major:	B, E
D-flat major:	F, C
G-flat major:	B, F

G-flat major can also be written as F-sharp major, since the former has six flats, the latter six sharps. In G-flat, the white notes are C-flat and F. In F-sharp they're B and E-sharp – the same keys on the piano since they're **enharmonic equivalents**.

B-flat minor (harmonic) is the relative minor of D-flat major, and follows the same fingering pattern, even though the A-flat is raised to A natural. In other words, it's fingered as though it had all five black notes. (The melodic minor uses the same fingerng with G and A naturals going up and G- and A-flats coming down.)

B flat minor (harmonic)

The same goes for E-flat minor, which is the relative minor of G-flat and uses the same fingering. Note how the raised 7th produces an awkward stretch from C-flat to D natural, but we still pass the left hand 3rd over onto the D as if it were a black note. (The melodic minor uses the same fingerng with C and D naturals on the way up and C- and D-flats on the way down, so it's easier to play.)

With these scales, keep the hands well into the black keys and the fingers rounded: try to get used to playing white notes up in between the black keys.

MORE BLACK-KEY ARPEGGIOS

The arpeggio of D-flat major is like A-flat and E-flat majors. Only the 3rd of the chord is a white note, so 2nd and 4th fingers come together on the D-flats and A-flats, with thumbs together on the Fs between (see Unit 11).

However, B-flat minor (the relative minor) is different, since here the white note is the 5th of the chord. Note: the left hand follows the fingering for B-flat major.

By contrast, arpeggios of G-flat major and E-flat minor have *only* black notes, so we finger them as if they were white notes. G-flat major has 3rd finger on the second note in the left, whereas E-flat minor has 4th finger as the gap from the first note is smaller. Aim for rounded fingers, playing on black keys as confidently (ie, with the same hand shape) as on white keys.

FIVE-FINGER EXERCISES

This is an excellent warm-up exercise for strengthening fingers and moving in and out of black keys with confidence. Note the formula for passing through all possible keys, by going from major to minor, then to the major scale a semitone higher but starting on the leading note, then moving up and starting again on the first note of the new scale. Try hands separately and together, in contrary and similar motion, and with different rhythms (eg, dotted rhythms). Aim for evenness of tone and time, and pay close attention to hand shape and thumb independence. You can also vary the melodic pattern so that the weaker 4th and 5th fingers work more, or create more irregular patterns that increase finger independence.

More music...

There are many published collections of exercises like this. They will help you build up the finger strength and independence required to play more advanced classical works. See the Repertoire Guide for some suggestions.

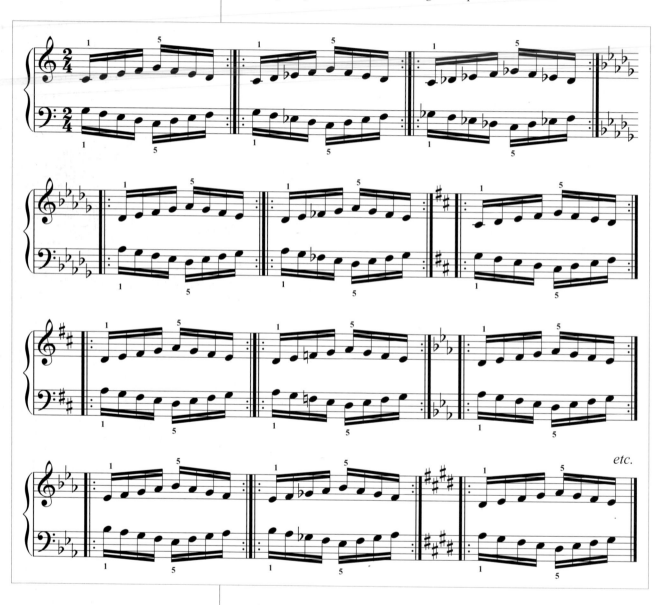

UNIT 14

SECTION 5

Romantic playing

In the wake of the French Revolution, and the careers of rebels such as Napoleon and Beethoven, the culture of 19th century Europe was dominated by Romanticism. The dramatic fates and overpowering emotions of individuals were emphasised. The piano developed into an instrument of great power and subtlety, with a much wider compass, and the introduction of the sustaining pedal made possible a richer palette of textures.

Great pianist-composers such as Liszt and Chopin dominated the artistic salons of European cities, transforming piano playing into an exercise in virtuosity and drama. Romanticism continued through the 19th century and into the early 20th century, with composers such as Fauré and Rachmaninoff stretching to the limit the instrument's capacity for subtleties of mood and virtuoso drama.

Interpreting Romantic works requires not just a good technique, but a good understanding of human psychology. You need to be sensitive to the complex feelings and moods that the music evokes. But playing with intensity should never mean surrendering control or critical awareness. Pedalling is used more freely, but this brings challenges, since the accumulation of sound in sustained textures needs to be controlled to reflect the unfolding of the melody line.

Timing is also more flexible, as we'll see when we come to look at the concept of rubato. The wider range of the instrument means you need to be aware of tonal differences between registers.

Johannes Brahms (1833-97) was a composer of the Romantic period who emphasised the importance of classical forms, especially in his symphonies. He was also a superb pianist. His love for the great pianist Clara Schumann was never fulfilled, since she married his close friend Robert Schumann. As he grew older, Brahms composed wistful and beautiful piano music as he reflected on the joys and disappointments of his life. Considered somewhat conservative, his music influenced such 20th century Austrian-German composers as Mahler and Schoenberg by its emphasis on the logical unfolding of formal structures.

Exercise 14.1

CD: **TRACK 51**

This Waltz by Brahms has a melody that unfolds and expands gradually, so dynamics must be graded to reach a climax at the appropriate place. The disjunct intervals in the right hand can be made more expressive by overlapping the first note with the second note. (Remember: intervals, not notes, make the line expressive, so feel the intervals.) Larger or more chromatic intervals should be brought out for expressive effect, but dynamics should also follow the arch of the melody as a whole. Always think about where the music is going: where is the point of arrival? Notice the embedded line, moving between the hands in the inner voices from bar 19 on, and listen carefully to the effect of pedalling on texture and dynamic level, adjusting left hand dynamics to reflect the nuances of the melody.

LEGATO PEDALLING IN ROMANTIC MUSIC

Romantic music often requires continuous legato pedalling, not just to create sustained textures, but also to join notes of the melody line together smoothly. The fingers often can't do this because the same hand is also involved in playing parts of the background texture or chords at the same time. This can lead to rapid pedal changes to avoid unwanted overlapping between melody notes. You need a good pedalling technique for this: try to calculate exactly how much of a lift is necessary to clear the pedal, and don't have too much foot on the pedal. It can also be acceptable to overlap melody notes (in the pedal) when they belong to the same harmony. Remember that pedal changes alter the volume of the texture as a whole, which should also fit with what is happening in the melody.

Franz Schubert (1797-1828) was a great composer of songs. Even his instrumental melodies have a magical singing quality. He lived in Vienna at the beginning of the 19th century, in poor and uncomfortable circumstances, and depended on the subsidy of his admirers before dying in his early thirties like Mozart. He was an admirer of Beethoven, but only met him when the older composer was on his deathbed. Schubert carried a torch at the funeral. At that time there were frequent epidemics of tuberculosis and cholera, and Schubert – by nature a happy young man – had premonitions of death. His music became more dreamy, but tinged with sadness and foreboding. Even his happiest tunes have an underlying sense of melancholy yearning. He wrote many great piano and chamber music works, and symphonies that were never performed in his lifetime. See the Repertoire Guide for more of his piano music.

Exercise 14.2

CD: **TRACK 52**

This is just the theme from the 'Impromptu in A flat' by Schubert. The melody must be played with great sensitivity to recapture the natural expressive qualities of the singing voice. Aim to bring out the top line and shape it while playing the chord notes at the same time. (This requires greater differentiation when it switches to the higher register.) Lean on accented passing notes in the melody, eg, at the start of the second and third full bars. Direct weight on to fingers responsible for melody notes. (These fingers can also be slightly more rounded than others, to play more 'deeply' into the keys). Check that individual chords remain properly synchronised, and be aware of the bass line as a melody line as well. The right hand should shift smoothly and in a controlled way between chords with octaves stretches (bars 6-8), with a minimum of movement and keeping close to the keys. When you've worked out pedalling, write it in. The greatest challenge is to make the whole thing pianissimo, so it sounds hushed and intimate. If you like this theme, why not learn the whole piece?

RUBATO

Rubato means 'robbed time'. It refers to the ways in which tempo is varied in Romantic music to reflect its expressive and structural features. It is especially associated with the music of Chopin. However, it's a myth that we 'take out' time from one place in the music and 'put it back' in another, so that speeding up and slowing down cancel one another out. What's really important is that rubato reflects the actual structure and expressive character of the music: the sense of arrival at key moments, of building to a climax, delayed resolution, and so on. It's something you have to develop a 'feel' for, and the best way to do this is to listen carefully to great performers. (See the Listening Guide at the end of the book.)

A good rule of thumb is that moments of expressive importance, such as unexpected 'turns' (changes of direction) of the melody or chord changes, need a little more time to be absorbed by the listener. This can be achieved through a slight delay of the note or chord in question, but you should never let it become a mechanically applied formula. The whole point of rubato is to be spontaneous and human (it should actually be a sort of improvised variation of timing and speed – within certain limits, of course). So trust your instincts and 'live in the moment', like in jazz.

Frederick Chopin (1810-1849) was a deeply sensitive individual who wrote almost exclusively for the piano. His music captures something essential about the instrument in a unique way. He was born in Poland, which remained occupied by surrounding countries throughout the 19th century, when other nations were achieving independence from the big empires that dominated Europe. But all the revolutions in Poland ended in tragic failure, forcing artists such as Chopin to live in exile in France. His music often evokes deeply felt moods of nostalgia and sadness. But the piece below expresses a dark fatalism, more typical of 20th century Polish composers like Lutoslawski or Szalonek. See the Repertoire Guide for more on Chopin's music.

Exercise 14.3

'Prelude in E minor' by Chopin requires very sensitive playing to achieve the right mood of reflective sadness. Carefully judge the amount of tone needed for each melody note to sound through to the next: the rising/falling semitone figure should sound like a mournful moaning or sighing.

CD: **TRACK 53**

Clear the pedal when necessary to keep the left hand texture from accumulating too much sound. Individual repetitions of left hand chords should hardly be discernible, and should keep well in the background, except when rubato is used to heighten the shifts of harmony. Bar 13 should be played without pedal. Change pedal for each stepwise movement of the melody in bar 18, but hold the pedal on through the triplet in the next bar. Smorzando means 'dying away'.

Let the silence sink in before attempting the final chords, which should be carefully coordinated and balanced, with top notes and bottom notes clearly audible: prepare each chord in advance, feeling fingers on the keys, then let the hands sink in together as blocks, as if invisibly connected.

Listen to the last chord dying away before releasing keys and pedal together: the piece isn't over until the chord has actually finished sounding.

MORE MINOR BLACK-KEY SCALES

Harmonic minor scales on F-sharp and C-sharp involve changes to the equivalent major scale fingering, in the right hand.

F sharp minor (harmonic)

C sharp minor (harmonic)

G-sharp minor doesn't, but note the F double sharp (equivalent to G natural).

G sharp minor (harmonic)

F-sharp and C-sharp melodic minors follow the fingering of the equivalent harmonic minors on the way down, but require different fingering on the way up for the sharpened 6th.

F sharp minor (melodic)

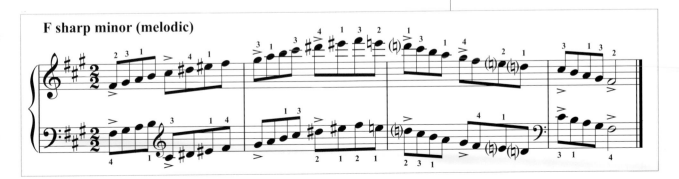

C sharp minor (melodic)

G-sharp minor melodic isn't affected in the right hand, since the raised sixth is an E sharp, which is still a white note (equivalent to an F natural); however the left hand fingering must alter on the way down, since F double sharp is lowered to an ordinary F-sharp, which is a black note. (Notice how we write the accidental cancelling the double sharp to a single sharp.)

G sharp minor (melodic)

THREE MORE BLACK-KEY ARPEGGIOS

Arpeggios of C-sharp minor and G-sharp minor follow the same fingering patterns as D-flat major and A-flat major, since the 3rd is still a white note when flattened. F-sharp minor follows the same principle, so it's different from G-flat major. In each case the notes will be the 1st, 3rd and 5th of the equivalent minor scale.

UNIT 15

SECTION 5

THE INTERPLAY OF LINE AND HARMONY

In this unit we're going to look at the way harmony, melody, form and texture work in the freer kinds of jazz improvisation, and at how this relates to similar techniques used in composition. Jazz improvising works by turning the subtle colours and shadings of harmonic structures directly into melody. So what's important about the improvised line in the first instance is just the way it expresses the harmony as melody. On top of this, the line can also work against the harmony, either by adding notes foreign to it, or by deliberately suggesting a different harmony from the one that is actually sounding. It's the interplay of line and harmony – expressing one another, but also pulling against one another – that gives jazz its musical subtlety.

MODES

Because jazz melody expresses and explores harmony, the underlying chord changes are treated more as particular kinds of melodic resource than as precise combinations of notes sounding together. This is a logical extension of the technique of treating extensions such as the 7th, 9th, 11th or 13th as part of the chord, since that means, in effect, that practically all the notes of the diatonic scale are included as potential harmony notes. So it's simpler just to think of the chord in terms of the scale material it gives rise to. This corresponds to what we get by playing the scale that the music is based on over the root of the chord in question: notes of the scale are then heard in terms of their relation to that *root*, rather than to the normal starting note of the scale, the *tonic*. When we treat a scale as starting on a different note from normal, even though its actual notes are the same, we call it a **mode**.

Here are the modes created when we play the notes of a C major scale, starting not just on C but on each of the scale's notes in turn. Each mode has its own sequence of tone and semitone steps, and thus its own character. Learn which degrees of each mode (indicated by Arabic numerals) are flattened or sharpened relative to a major scale starting on the same note. That way you will be able to use modes independently of the underlying key when you wish to. Observe also that the intervals in each mode correspond to those in a chord built on the same starting note (the Roman numerals show this).

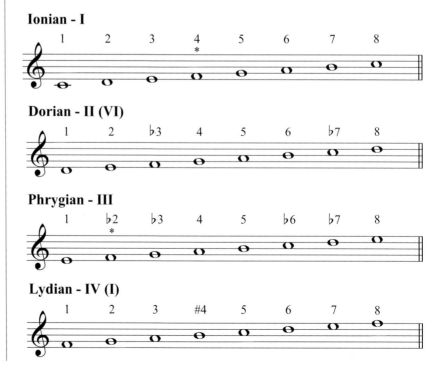

Ionian - I

Dorian - II (VI)

Phrygian - III

Lydian - IV (I)

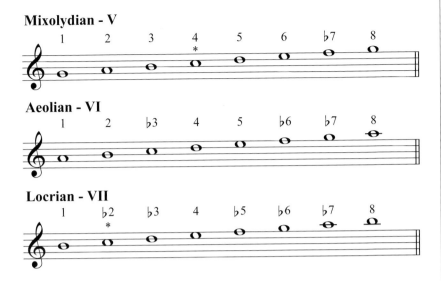

Mixolydian - V

Aeolian - VI

Locrian - VII

The notes marked with an asterisk are considered dissonant – that is, they're heard as clashing with the implied root of the chord (we looked at the treatment of dissonance in non-classical music in Unit 9). We therefore tend to avoid using them at prominent points in the line or at the same moment that the chord itself actually gets struck. In these cases, we would substitute a raised (sharpened) note instead.

For example, a I chord in a major key gives us the Ionian mode (which happens to be the same as the major scale itself), and here it's the 4th degree of the mode that's problematic. So we just sharpen the 4th to make it less dissonant.

However, do this enough times in the solo and you start to hear the sharpened 4th itself as part of the mode. So it can sometimes be simpler just to think of the Lydian mode (which already contains the sharpened 4th) as providing the scale material for soloing over chord I, rather than the Ionian. (Parallel to this, Dorian can function as VI, but sharpening dissonant notes in other modes, such as over II itself, gives rise to more advanced jazz modes that have to be derived from the jazz minor scale rather than from modes of the major scale. See Unit 18.)

Which way you think of this is up to you: seeing it as a change of the actual mode used on the chord is really just a kind of shortcut to getting the right **alterations**: it's handy if you generally prefer to avoid dissonant scale degrees in favour of a cooler or sweeter sound, but not if you like to maintain a continuing tension between melody and harmony. In the latter case it's better to still treat the raised notes as the exception rather than the norm, since this keeps you aware of how the line is working both with and against the underlying harmonic structure.

The best way to grasp how modes relate to one another is to see how alterations accumulate as we move away from Ionian (as chord I), ascending the circle of 5ths. So when jazz progressions have the root descending in 5ths, as they frequently do (think of VI-II-V-I), the resulting modes gradually converge with Ionian, which is the major scale of the underlying key:

CHORD:	MODE:	ALTERATIONS FROM MAJOR					
VII	Locrian	b2	b3	–	b5	b6	b7
III	Phrygian	b2	b3	–	–	b6	b7
VI	Aeolian	–	b3	–	–	b6	b7
II (& VI)	Dorian	–	b3	–	–	–	b7
V	Mixolydian	–	–	–	–	–	b7
I	Ionian	–	–	–	–	–	–
IV (& I)	Lydian	–	–	#4	–	–	–

OFF-NOTES

Take another look at the notes with asterisks in Ex.15.1. Note that different modes have different dissonant notes to be avoided. But there's another aspect to how dissonance works in relation to modes. Because each mode uses seven notes of the twelve-note chromatic scale, this leaves a set of five unused notes for each mode: these are called **off-notes,** used when we want to deliberately go against the harmony and sound "out-of-tune". (That's a concept you should be familiar with by now from blues.) When you're familiar with each mode as a set of alterations from the major scale on the same note, try learning the off-notes for each mode in the same way.

CHORD:	MODE:	OFF-NOTES					
VII	Locrian	2	3	-	5	6	7
III	Phrygian	2	3	-	$b5$	6	7
VI	Aeolian	$b2$	3	-	$b5$	6	7
II	Dorian	$b2$	3	-	$b5$	$b6$	7
V	Mixolydian	$b2$	$b3$	-	$b5$	$b6$	7
I	Ionian	$b2$	$b3$	-	$b5$	$b6$	$b7$
IV	Lydian	$b2$	$b3$	4	-	$b6$	$b7$

LEFT-HAND VOICINGS

Voicing chords between the hands (as shown in Unit 9) limits the freedom of your right hand to solo over them, so it's handy to have a way to voice chords entirely in the left hand. We do this by omitting the root, which is often provided by the bass player in a jazz ensemble, and even if it isn't, is heard as implied by the functional character of the chord. Left hand voicings have the same voice-leading characteristics as the II-V-I progressions we've already looked at (ie, alternate stepwise descents), but also include the 13th for the V chord. There are two voicing patterns, distinguished by whether 5th finger plays the 3rd - 7th - 3rd or 7th - 3rd - 7th at the bottom of the chords. Chord voicings are colouristic, but the choice of voicing pattern also depends on the key you're in, since this affects where the voicing lies in relation to the middle register of the piano. Note the variations on chord I, which produce different degrees of harmonic resolution. Outside of II-V-I progressions, we generally move to the position for the next left hand voicing nearest to the one we've just played. These voicings emerged in the 1950s, associated with players like Bill Evans and Wynton Kelly, and were widely used in the 1960s. (Note that the chord symbols above the music here only specify the type of 7th chord, rather than all added notes, as in classical music or ordinary popular music. In jazz, indicating the 7th chord is enough to give the chord function for standard unaltered progressions, but added notes that are chromatically altered would be specified.)

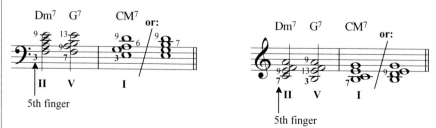

These voicings are too dense to use lower down in the left hand register, so if you want fuller sonorites go for the pared-down voicings of earlier 1950s **bebop** players like Bud Powell: these are two-note or three-note root position voicings.

Exercise 15.1

Take all of these left-hand voicings through all keys in descending 5ths, major 2nds and semitones, just like we did with the two-hand voicings. Then try playing the appropriate mode for each chord of the II-V-I progression in the right hand at the same time. Hear how each mode expresses the harmonic flavour of the corresponding chord, in melodic terms. Then try improvising figures over the left hand voicings with the modes.

CHROMATIC HARMONY

Classical

Chromaticism is a major feature of jazz, but your appreciation of it will be far richer if you're also aware of how it works in classical music. Make sure you take the time to play through each of the following musical examples several times, listening carefully to the voice leading. One of the main features of the development of classical music was the gradual introduction of ever more chromatic forms of harmony for colouristic surprises and expressive contrasts. This started back in the Baroque period with J.S.Bach, whose harmonies often anticipate jazz and can be highly chromatic. Look at this famous harmonisation of the chorale 'Es ist Genug' (quoted later by the 20th century composer Alban Berg in his *Violin Concerto*). The chromaticism emerges naturally out of the melodic voice-leading of individual parts, but still gives rise to strange chords with an 'other worldly' feel:

Es ist genug;

Bach's chromaticism partly results from his unique approach to composing, which emphasises the horizontal or **polyphonic** aspect (the relationship between lines unfolding simultaneously) and the vertical or harmonic aspect with equal force, so neither can be reduced to the other. (You can see this in the Fugues from the 'Forty-Eight'. See the Repertoire Guide.) Before Bach, composers let either polyphony or harmony dominate; after Bach, music became more focussed on the relationship between individual melody lines and harmony, at least until the 20th century. However, this didn't prevent composers from expanding the range of chords in the tonal system and introducing chromatic harmonies. Let's look at some of the ways they did this.

Classical harmony centres on tonic-dominant relations, so a chord can be treated *as* a tonic even when it isn't one by introducing its own dominant, as though it had modulated to that key for a moment. (When this actually happens it's called a **passing modulation**.) These are called **secondary dominants**: they introduce notes into the harmony that don't belong to the underlying key of the passage, and are then heard melodically as chromatic alterations of the scale. (The most important of these is the 'dominant of the dominant', shown as V of V.)

C: IV   V of V   V   I   V of II   II   V   I

Note how V of V introduces the raised 4th of the scale, which is the leading tone in the dominant key, and so can resolve upwards chromatically. (Where the chromatically altered note comes just after a chord with the same scale degree unaltered, these are normally both placed in the same part to avoid a **false relation** or **cross relation**, though there are cases where these are allowed.)

Augmented 6th chords also produce chromatic movement on to the dominant, with the raised 4th over the flattened 6th of the minor key scale. The name refers to the interval between these two notes. Technically, the chord can be analysed either as a chromatically altered II^c (with sharpened 3rd and flattened 5th, omitting or including root or flattened 9th) or as a iv^b chord (with chromatically raised root) originating from stepwise contrapuntal movement. It comes in three forms that all resolve on to V. (Note how the last one avoids parallel 5ths by moving to V^c).

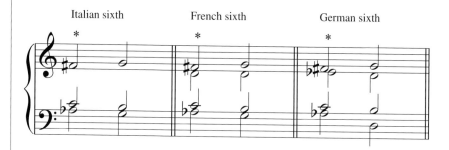

Italian sixth   French sixth   German sixth

The **Neapolitan 6th chord** is a first inversion chord over a flattened supertonic root, producing a strangely colourful progression, normally in a minor key. Note how it substitutes for the ordinary supertonic chord (which would be a diminished triad in a minor key) in the classical equivalent of a II-V-I cadence. It may be heard as a kind of altered V of V.

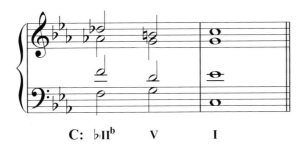

C: ♭II♭   V   I

Using notes from the minor key as chromatic alterations in major key harmony allowed other developments: the chords that result are called **borrowed chords**. The flattened 6th of the minor scale may be introduced as part of a minor subdominant chord, or to heighten the tension of the dominant 7th as a more dissonant flattened 9th (V7b9). Omitting the root of the latter then produces a diminished 7th chord (dim7) with several possibilities to resolve through chromatic voice-leading in otherwise quite remote keys. This allows for dramatic modulations. V7 in a major key also allows for a 9th that isn't flattened, which gives the half-diminished 7th chord, common in jazz and Romantic music.

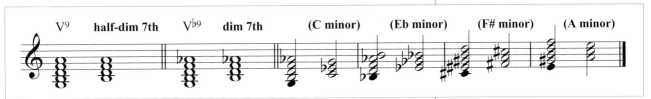

Note how the various resolutions of the diminished 7th are to keys a minor 3rd apart, depending on which note functions as leading note, and that the notes are in fact the same in spite of enharmonic differences. (The best way to see this is by playing them. Implied dominant roots are also shown.) This corresponds to the indirect connections between keys opened up when major and minor keys are increasingly treated as interchangeable. (The exquisite modulations resulting from these sort of key relations are a feature of Austrian composers such as Schubert and Bruckner, who both studied with the great teacher Simon Sechter, whose ideas were later developed by the 20th century composer Schoenberg in his late work, *Structural Functions of Harmony*. In Units 17 and 18 we'll see how this approach relates to the way jazz composers such as John Coltrane treat key and chord relations, and the way modern music and jazz develop harmony in both parallel and contrasting ways.)

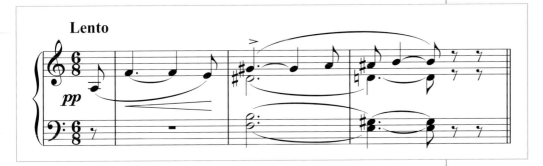

In the second half of the 19th century the idea of harmonic resolution by stepwise chromatic ascent was used by Wagner to open up a whole new approach to harmony: leading-tone progressions could allow unrestrained chromatic movement between chords otherwise hardly related at all. Here's the opening of his most famous opera, *Tristan und Isolde*, in a **piano reduction**. The famous 'Tristan chord' at the beginning of the second bar still hypnotises audiences with its sensuality and mystery, and ambiguous implications for where it will go to next. We can analyse the chord in terms of **functional harmony** as an augmented (French) 6th chord with a G sharp appoggiatura resolving to an A, *or* as a self-contained half-diminished 7th chord. Notice the chromatic accented passing note in the next bar as well.

Jazz

The main form of chromatic harmony in jazz comes from the important technique known as **tritone substitution**. This is just one of a whole range of devices that jazz musicians use to vary existing chord structures. (See Unit 18: **Reharmonisation**.) Substituting the chord of the same type a tritone away ('tritone' means either augmented 4th or diminished 5th, since the interval equals three whole tones) produces a chromatic descent in the bass line. This may be done on the V of a II-V-I, but players like Bud Powell and Thelonius Monk go further and introduce the II of the substitute V chord as well. The important thing to grasp is the pivot role of the tritone between the 3rd and 7th of a V chord: **interval inversion** (see below) means that the same notes also form the 3rd and 7th of the V chord a tritone away, so any two V chords (or keys) a tritone apart can be linked in this way.

Notice how this relates to several of the classical devices mentioned in the previous section: tritone substitution of ♭II for V is a bit like a Neapolitan 6th, while adding ♭VI to give a II-V in the key of ♭II begins to sound like a passing modulation a tritone away from the real key (ie, to ♭V), which it could also turn out to be if I is also substituted for, as in the last example.

You'll also encounter straightforward chromatic descent (or ascent) of block chords, a technique influenced by the ability to slide freely between chords in guitar-based music. In Unit 18 we'll look at some more sophisticated ways of arranging block chords in jazz using diminished 7th harmonies. If you don't omit the 5th of each chord to avoid parallel 5ths the effect will be rather coarse and more suited to blues and rock than jazz. (Note the contrast between the last two chords and the classical resolution of the German 6th shown on p202.)

CONTRAST IN IMPROVISATION

The worst thing that can happen to an improvisation is to lose all sense of contrast and get trapped in endless variations of the same thing. That usually means you've run out of ideas. But if you're clever you can make sure that never happens.

If you're using a standard or a chord chart you've worked out with other musicians, you'll normally have some sort of plan of what comes where in each part of your performance. How much you decide in advance depends on how free your approach to improvisation is. But whatever style it's in, the same point is valid if you want it to be interesting: be creative about what you plan and what you don't. Don't just plan technical or tangible things like harmony or changes of groove. Plan in some contrasts of a more thematic or general kind, of texture or register or even type of material: that way you're sure to sustain the interest of the listener throughout rather than sounding like you've got lost in your own private world.

THEME & MOTIVE

Classical music generates a powerful sense of logical unfolding and forward progression, since it has identifiable materials or musical ideas from which it appears to evolve organically, rather like a living creature or growing plant. These ideas are usually recognisable **motives** or **themes** that integrate different aspects of the music at a deep level, creating an overall feeling of unified underlying shapes (called Gründgestalten by Schoenberg). This approach became increasingly important in late Romantic music with the evolution of large-scale forms in **symphonies** (eg, the works of Franck, Bruckner, Mahler or Sibelius), but you'll also see it in 19th century piano works like Liszt's *Sonata in B minor*.

Jazz and popular music are not normally thematic in this deeper sense: melodies are usually tied to the words of a song, while riffs function as part of the underlying framework provided by the rhythm section, whose processes of cyclical repetition and sectional contrast are more suited to song and dance-based forms. (In terms of form, modern popular music is therefore closer to Baroque classical music, in which dance forms are also central.)

DEVELOPMENT & VARIATION

In classical music, themes can be subjected to **variation** when restated, or progressively transformed as the music unfolds from one moment to the next, often being dissolved into constituent motives which are then recombined in new ways. The latter process is known as musical **development**, which both 'works out' and 'works through' the tensions and contrasts within and between musical ideas. Variation reflects a more static and cyclic approach to form, close to popular music and jazz, whereas development treats form as a linear unfolding, so you won't find it so much outside of classical music, except in advanced jazz. The AABA form of jazz leaves room for variation each time the melody returns, but it also tends to be interspersed with 'breaks' for soloing, in which a good improviser may also develop and transform motives lifted from the main melody. This sort of playing around with a melodic idea often uses the same techniques as classical development, but much more freely and spontaneously, without any underlying feeling of a logically unfolding process.

One of the main techniques for developmental transformation in classical and non-classical music is **interval inversion**. You should be familiar with the inversions of all intervals, which also informs the way they are named. Note that minor intervals always become major (and vice versa), augmented always become diminished (and vice versa), and perfect intervals remain perfect. You can see now why tritones are special: they remain tritones when inverted. This feature is exploited by jazz in tritone substitution, and in a lot of chromatic or **atonal** modern music. (See Unit 17.)

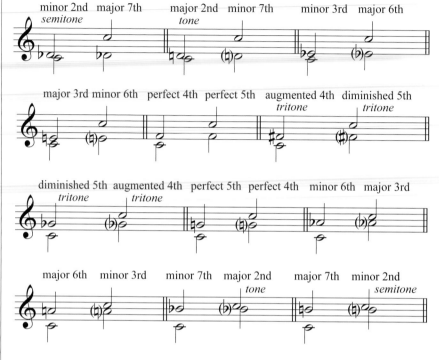

In jazz and popular music, a melody appears in a lead sheet in the register where it's easiest to read, but in practice individual players alter the octave transposition to suit their own taste. If this happens in the middle of the tune, the interval at that point gets inverted, and this can then become part of the new character of the line. Improvisers freely invert parts of the tune to generate new material and new motives when soloing.

Classical music uses **rhythmic augmentation** and **diminution** to vary the rhythm of a theme or motive while keeping the pitches the same: in augmentation, all time values are increased by the same ratio (ie, doubled), while in diminution, they're all shortened by the same ratio (ie, halved). However, the timing of parts of the theme may also be altered more freely than this.

In jazz and popular music a more important device consists of keeping both the pitches and the timing of a figure the same while repeating it so that it shifts in its relation to the underlying beat or metre. (See the opening chordal pattern and the dotted rhythm figures of the melody of the contrasting section in 'Take Five' in Unit 18 for classic examples of this.)

TEXTURE

When composing or improvising, it's easy to get so focused on sorting out technical things like harmony that you become blind to more obvious things that make a piece or a performance interesting. The way register, colour, and density of harmony and texture evolve and create contrasts of character, and reinforce the enjoyment of the sheer sound of the music, can make the difference between a spectacular musical experience and a run-of-the-mill routine that never gets noticed by anyone. Try describing textures with words, or comparing them to colours, to light and shade, to pictures and images, tastes, smells – or whatever gets your imagination going.

JAZZ SCALES AND SOLOING

Jazz improvisation uses diatonic major and minor scales, but the **jazz minor** scale uses notes of the ascending melodic minor (with 6th and 7th sharpened from the minor key signature) in both directions, since in jazz this scale is also an important harmonic resource. (See Unit 18.) When the descending melodic minor form (with 6th and 7th flattened from the major scale on the same note) is used as a scale (in both directions), it's called the natural minor scale, which corresponds to the Aeolian mode. (Remember that jazz refers to all scales as alterations of the major scale.)

Jazz minor:

| 1 | 2 | ♭3 | 4 | 5 | 6 | 7 |

Natural minor scale (Aeolian mode):

| 1 | 2 | ♭3 | 4 | 5 | ♭6 | ♭7 |

Whereas scales in classical music are used to develop physical aspects of playing technique, in jazz they're a basis for **soloing**, so the really important thing here is knowing the (notes of the) scales, so fingers automatically find the right scale notes for the chord structure at each point in the music. Two things are important here:

- connecting up scale material for one chord directly with that for the next chord, as part of a continuous line;
- developing a repertoire of melodic figurations (different melodic shapes, or 'riffs') that can be reused over different scale material (as melodic sequences).

The first point is one that needs careful practice, just to develop the right way of thinking about melody and harmony: as you play over one chord, think ahead to where your right hand will need to be to begin the line over the next chord on a note that belongs to that chord. Then once you know where your melody is heading, you

The shape of music

Projection occurs in all music, and not just when we're playing it ourselves. When we listen to music, we are aware of how what we're hearing right now implies future continuations, just as what we're hearing right now is revealed as a continuation of what came before. Philosophers have always been fascinated by music's distillation of the character of time or temporality itself, especially when trying to explain why we find music interesting and expressive in the first place. Schopenhauer thought that music embodied the essential striving of life itself (the 'will'), in contrast to the world of mere 'appearances'. Edmund Husserl believed that the strange phenomenon of hearing a succession of tones as a line or shape – which suggests that the notes both coexist together and come after one another in our mind – reflected the nature of our consciousness of time itself. Suzanne Langer claimed that the shape of music's unfolding mirrors the way our emotions unfold in time as we feel them. Peter Kivy argues that music resembles expressive physical gestures. Aaron Ridley describes how we come to empathise with feelings in music. Carl Erik Kühl shows how structural projection in music follows the same logic as change and motion in the real world. There is more on this in Recommended Reading.

can try out more indirect ways of getting there in the time available. This **projection** of the future destination of the line to inform what you do right now can seem strange if you're coming to jazz from classical music. But most human actions set a goal in advance before attempting to achieve it, and it's no different from the way we phrase classical music in terms of points of arrival and departure. You'll be surprised at how quickly it becomes natural to play in this way. See *Ways of the Hand*, by David Sudnow for a rich description of how this works when learning to play jazz piano. (Details in Recommended Reading.)

Notice how the embellished line moves towards the goal note, but avoids anticipating it, so that a sense of imminent arrival is created. You'll find the same thing in piano music by Chopin and Liszt, when the right hand breaks into **arabesques** (flowing runs, often written as grace notes): that's how they improvised too. Here are three versions of the theme from Chopin's *Mazurka in A minor*.

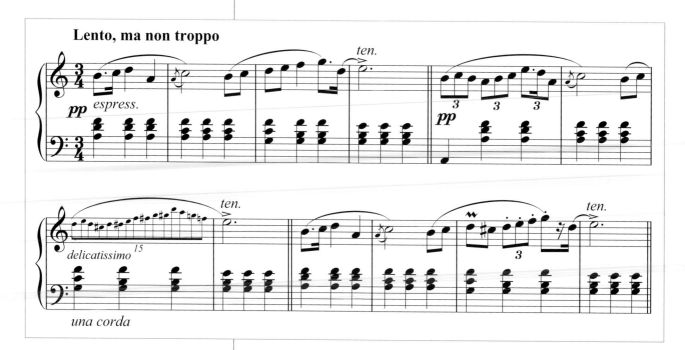

When you've got the hang of this, try taking simple melodic shapes (preferably of your own invention) and repeating them in transpositions – creating what we call melodic **sequences** – so that they arrive in the right place for the next harmony too. (You'll find sequences all over the place in classical music too, when phrases of a tune are repeated a step or so higher or lower.)

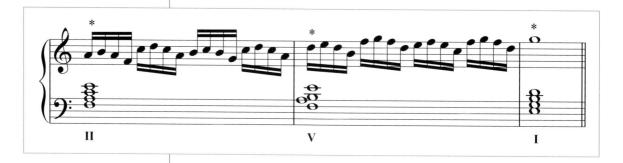

The second point is really down to you. The whole point of jazz and improvisation is to develop your own style of creative playing, so there are no standard tricks or formulas worth learning, unless you want to sound boring. You need to develop your own personal repertoire of licks and riffs and other melodic figurations.

Listen to what others do, but don't waste time practising melodic patterns parrot-fashion. (There are loads of books that encourage you to do this. Don't buy them – they're guaranteed to turn you into a mediocre musician who plays the same tired phrases as everyone else. Do you think the jazz greats of the past used them? You must be joking!) Take your own ideas seriously from the start by keeping a musical notebook, in which you jot down the ideas that you discover through playing, and that excite you, and then be disciplined about practising these, taking them through all keys and building sequences that work over chord changes and different scale material.

RHYTHM CHANGES

After the 12-bar blues, the most important set of chord changes used in jazz are those based on the American composer Gershwin's popular number 'I've Got Rhythm'. The chords from this song were used as a basis for many famous jazz **heads** (ie, melodies composed by jazz musicians on the basis of existing chords): hence they're known as Rhythm Changes. Like 12-bar blues, they're often used as a basis for improvising together, so you should be familiar with them if you want to be taken at all seriously by jazz players!

George Gershwin was a classically trained composer and virtuoso pianist, who improvised and composed in a style strongly influnced by jazz. Notice the recurring VI-II-V-I sequence, and the **borrowed chord** from the minor key in bar 6 (the E flat minor chord). This is a minor subdominant chord, just like in classical music. It reasserts the tonic after the V7 on B-flat in the previous bar, which in classical terms suggests a passing modulation to E-flat (as V of IV, a secondary dominant). But in jazz it could equally mark the start of a move through the circle of 5ths (like that of the 'bridge' section).

George Gershwin (1898-1937) was an American composer who bridged the gap between classical concert music and the more populistic culture of the American 'Broadway' musical. He began as a songwriter, but had hits with theatrical songs based on lyrics by his brother, Ira Gershwin. The combination of classical structure and jazzy or bluesy harmonic and melodic elements have made some of his songs and chord progressions important as jazz standards. Consequently they have often been used as the basis for improvisation by jazz performers. *Porgy and Bess*, Gershwin's opera, also crosses the boundary between classical and popular, and has been produced in both as operatic and Broadway musical style. And *Rhapsody in Blue* mixes jazz with the techniques and textures of Romantic piano music.

Now here's a later version of the same piece. Note how it varies the harmony, introducing the following:

- diminished 7th chords that substitute a stepwise chromatic bass line at the start;
- slash-chord inversions for stepwise bass-line movement (bars 5 & 7);
- secondary dominants in bars 3 & 7 (II-V of II, or V of II);
- augmented 5ths on V chords towards ends of sections.

Welcome to the world of jazz **reharmonisation**. We'll be looking at this in more depth in the last unit of the book.

Exercise 15.2

Try out both versions of the Rhythm Changes: first work out your own two-hand voicings, then put these into left-hand voicings; then try soloing over both, using your own melodic ideas.

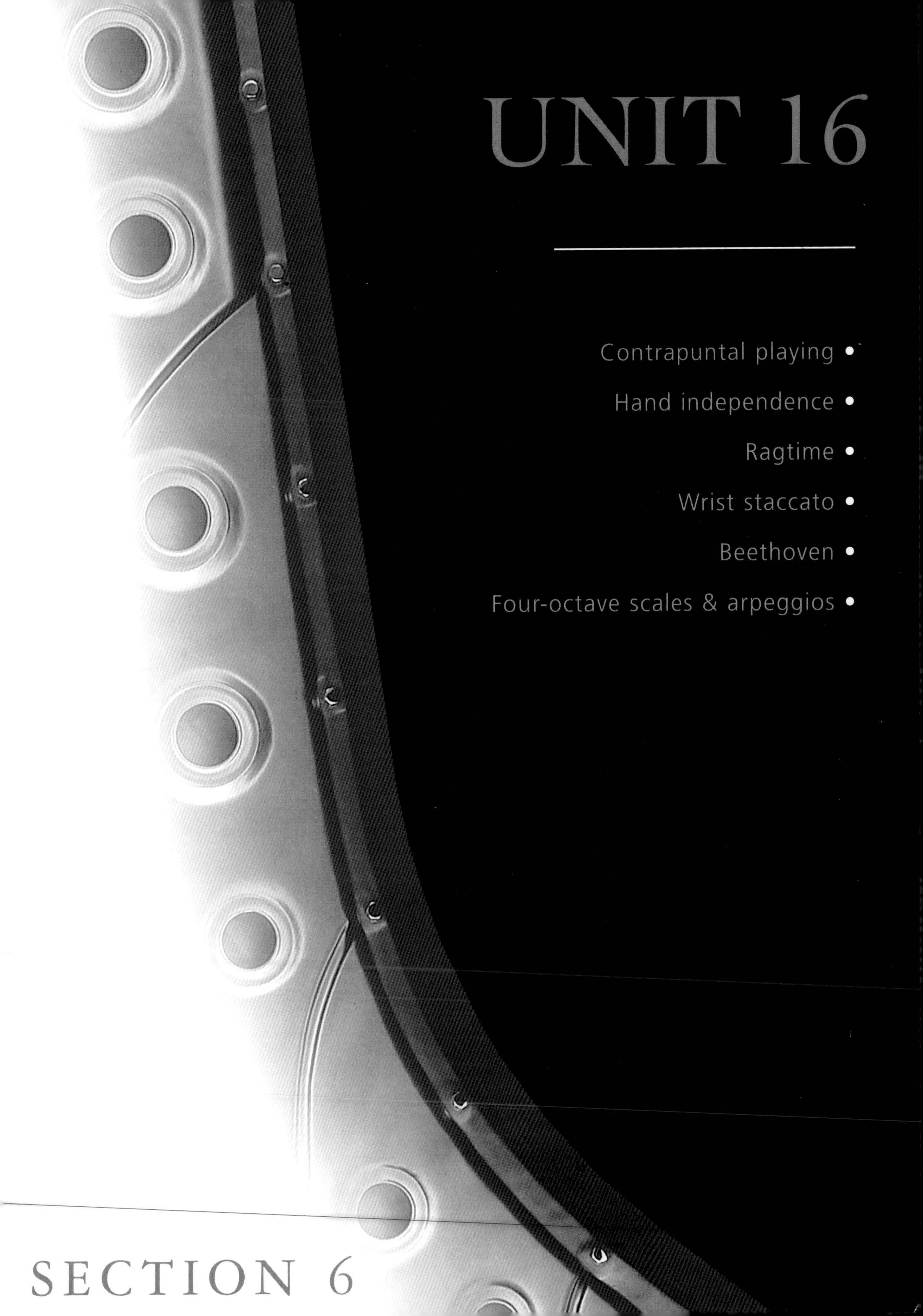

UNIT 16

Contrapuntal playing •
Hand independence •
Ragtime •
Wrist staccato •
Beethoven •
Four-octave scales & arpeggios •

SECTION 6

CONTRAPUNTAL PLAYING

Music of the Baroque period is often characterised by **counterpoint**. This refers to the relationship between two or more independent lines of equal importance unfolding simultaneously, differentiated by rhythmic contrasts, but linked through **imitation** of one another (each 'voice' or 'part' echoing material already given in other voices, often at a different transposition). The most sophisticated contrapuntal form is the **Fugue**, whose greatest master was J.S. Bach (1685-1750). His *Forty Eight Preludes and Fugues* (*Das Wohltemperierte Klavier*) explore the possibility of writing in all keys with equal effectiveness, exploiting the invention of the tuning system known as **equal temperament**. (A **clavier** was a term applied to any keyboard instrument at the time of Bach.)

It's worth bearing in mind that Bach was almost certainly not writing with the piano in mind, but rather the harpsichord or clavichord. Although he wrote with a deep practical understanding of the instruments to be used, his priorities were different from those of Romantic or modern composers, who are usually more concerned with exploiting the distinctive characteristics of individual instruments. It seems that for Bach instruments are interesting because they too can embody the ideal of musicality presented in the first instance by the voice, and even extend that ideal. So when playing Bach on the piano we probably get closer to the spirit of the music by aiming for this universal quality of musicality than by trying to copy the character of a harpsichord or clavichord. Many musicians since Bach speak of the unique spiritual and intellectual fulfilment of playing the 'Forty Eight' – the sense of encountering something truly universal.

HAND INDEPENDENCE

Contrapuntal music requires a fundamental independence of the hands, since each line must be phrased according to its *own* requirements, not treated as background accompaniment to what other parts are doing. This means that one hand may be legato just when the other is staccato, or may get louder when the other gets quieter. In two-part counterpoint this can be achieved by practising hands separately, matching up articulation and shaping of equivalent material between the hands. With more than two independent parts, each individual part should be practised (even if it's split between hands), then the hands combined, practising hands separate where necessary at points of difficulty. The best guide to phrasing is always to sing lines yourself, and learn from the natural feeling for melodic phrasing that we all have when we sing.

Here are some of the clichés of *bad* Bach playing that emerged in the 19th century:

- hammering out every entry of a **subject** (the contrapuntal equivalent of a theme);
- *always* playing legato semiquavers against staccato quavers;
- treating it as a mindless exercise in technical self-discipline, with insistent rhythmical precision but no trace of human feeling.

Equal-temperament

This was a crucial development in western music, since it allowed keyboard composers to move freely between keys and chromatic chords with consistent results, thanks to the subtle compromise that hid discrepancies of tuning by spreading them equally across all keys. The result was that all key and chord relations could be explored within the single framework of the chromatic scale and its division of the octave into twelve identical semitone steps. This made the development of complex chromatic harmony in 19th and 20th century music possible, but also creates a fundamental tension: between harmonic relations defined by the slightly abstract unity of the system, and the natural tunings whose elasticity and vagueness helps to make melodic intervals expressive in the first place. Try accompanying a singer or string player, both of whom can control intonation themselves, and you'll be aware of this. (Singers and string players move between different kinds of intonation to suit different relationships of melody to harmony.) Some modern composers have experimented with smaller divisions of the octave than the semitone, such as quarter-tones, to produce **microtonal music**. Others have tried to reintroduce the natural tunings of **just intonation** as microtonal adjustments.

Exercise 16.1

This is the first of Bach's Two Part Inventions. Pay close attention to the rise and fall of individual melody lines and always listen to the balance between the parts. Try different articulations, such as staccato quavers and legato semiquavers, or both legato, or even slurred couplets (on the mordents). Avoid an unwanted accent on the last note of the opening left hand phrase: generally feel the music heading towards the strong beat at the start of the next bar, keeping speed steady throughout. Practise without ornaments first, then introduce them at a reduced speed: they should not disrupt the easy flow of the music, and should be played with a relaxed hand and fingers close to keys. From bar 15 onwards tied minims in both hands should sing through to the next note, which in turn should reflect the level of sound reached at the end of the previous tied note, to preserve continuity of line. Where is the climax of the piece?

CD: **TRACK 54**

RAGTIME

Ragtime was one of the precursors of jazz in America (emerging at the end of the 19th century), and has many common features with it, but it remains closer to European classical music in other respects.

The rhythm of the right hand melody is syncopated over a regular beat, but not swung. The left hand already features the familiar 'stride' pattern, and makes greater use of dominant 7th harmonies, while chromatic passing notes in the right hand have the same 'out-of-tune' character as blues or country music. Rags were often heard played brutally at tremendous speeds on mechanical piano rolls, but in fact should travel at a fairly relaxed tempo, with an ironical and suave feel.

Like contrapuntal playing, ragtime requires independence between hands, but of a different kind: counterpoint requires the hands to be equal partners in melody, but ragtime treats them like two separate instrumentalists in a syncopated relationship to each other.

Exercise 16.2 (Over the page)

CD: **TRACK 55**

The most famous ragtime composer was Scott Joplin, whose best-known rag, 'The Entertainer', was made famous in the movie The Sting.

Here's the main part, with the right hand slightly simplified. Lean slightly on the quavers leading in to the main theme, and let the offbeat accents created by the syncopated melody speak for themselves. Notice the rapidly shifting right hand octaves and 3rds, beginning at bar 6: keep wrist loose and notes coordinated, without forcing speed, and use dynamics to contrast with more restrained parts of the melody in the middle register.

Get your left hand leaps absolutely fluent before combining hands: a good test is whether you can play the left hand without looking at the keys at all. You can vary the touch in the middle section, possibly with a more 'flaky' mezzo staccato feel (ie, notes very slightly detached, with a loose right hand wrist). Feel the bass-line movement as a melody in its own right, and let the 'backbeat' effect of the left hand chords come through a little, in contrast to classical music.

Use direct pedalling to connect up left hand bass notes and chords, but be careful about pedalling in softer passages or where stepwise movement of the melody is exposed, as in bars 24-5.

Not fast

WRIST STACCATO

Let's remind ourselves of the kinds of staccato we've learned so far:

- **Finger staccato** creates crisp accents on individual notes through individual finger movements.
- **Hand staccato** uses a loose flapping of the hand from the wrist for rapid staccato sequences, with less emphasis on articulation of individual notes than on overall consistency of speed and attack.

Sometimes the musical context requires slower and more relaxed forms of repeated staccato. In these cases we use the wrist as a lever:

- **Wrist staccato** uses a lift of the wrist to kick slightly into the keys and lift off at the same time, shortening the note, just like in **couplets**.

Go back and try playing the Bach Invention (Exercise 16.1) at a leisurely speed, focusing on achieving a loose and relaxed wrist staccato for quavers. Can you hear how much more natural the music sounds? Then try playing at a faster speed: note how this requires you to change over to hand staccato.

An extension of wrist staccato consists of using the arms themselves as levers, kicking in to the keys to individually articulate chords, to produce accents with a more sluggish recoil or shortening. This technique sets up a natural (physical) correlation between volume and length of sound – a feature common to percussion instruments. This is sometimes called **arm staccato**, and can work from the forearm (levering from the elbow) or whole arm (levering from shoulder and back), depending on the volume and length required.

When a very short and sharp staccato on loud chords is needed, we use **clenched hand staccato**: a sudden clenching of the hand that draws all fingers off the keys at once with a sharp, snappy feel.

Exercise 16.3

CD: **TRACK 56**

This octave study practises maintaining the octave stretch over shifting hand positions, but also offers opportunities for wrist, arm staccato and clenched-hand staccato, depending on the speed. Let your body guide you in matching the right staccato technique to the musical situation. Notice fingerings for moving between white and black notes in octaves. To use 4th finger and thumb on black-note octaves you need large hands, so you may prefer to stick to thumb and 5th. Focus on speed of shifting and quality of attack, but without arms stiffening up.

EXERCISE 16.3

BEETHOVEN

The German composer Ludwig van Beethoven (1770-1827) was a titanic genius who changed irreversibly the face of European music. Inspired by the French revolution and Napoleon, he asserted his uncompromising artistic individuality with unprecedented disregard for both social and musical conventions. His fiery yet profoundly sensitive personality transmitted itself directly into music of startling originality, while the deafness that eventually isolated him from others left him increasingly introverted. We've already looked at one of his most famous melodies ('Für Elise') in Unit 5. The evolution of his compositional style divides into three phases, known as the early, middle and late periods.

The **early period** reflects the priorities of the classical style (he studied with Haydn), but with a more intensely dramatic approach, especially where thematic development is concerned.

Beginning with the *Symphony No.3 ('Eroica')*, the **middle period** shows Beethoven opening up classical forms into a much more expansively dramatic and lyrical idiom, the inspiration for composers of the Romantic period that followed.

In his **late period** Beethoven retreated more and more into his inner world, affected by his deafness and other tragic circumstances. The late piano sonatas and string quartets transcend classical and Romantic tendencies into something unique, rediscovering and transfiguring earlier techniques such as fugal writing while exploring new formal possibilities combining improvisatory freedom and decoration with deeper forms of structural unity, anticipating 20th century music. Audiences could not understand these strange works, which they blamed on the composer's deafness. Some thought he'd gone mad. His 32 sonatas are technically demanding works that reflect his dramatic yet intellectual approach to the instrument. There are more details in the Repertoire Guide.

Beethoven's pupil Carl Czerny taught Liszt, who then taught many great players of the late 19th century, some of whom were still around when the first recordings were made. So if you take the time to *hear* and learn from them, you'll be a step closer to knowing how Beethoven himself might have played his works. The Listening Guide at the back of the book has recommendations on recordings.

Beethoven became ill and died because he was so poor that he had to travel home from a performance of his music in the back of an open cart, in the cold and rain. Legend has it that his last gesture was to shake his fist in defiance at his fate. His late works only began to be appreciated much later, when composers like Wagner rediscovered them. He was constantly frustrated by the limitations of the pianos of his day, which he often wrecked. A piano was made especially for him by the English maker, John Broadwood, whose instruments can still be bought today.

Exercise 16.4

This Scherzo, No.2 from the Bagatelles (Op.33) is probably an early composition that Beethoven re-used. Notice the sudden leaps of register and contrasts of loud and soft, both of which anticipate the fragmented, disjointed character of modern music. You'll need to practise the physical movements across the keyboard to get the combination of speed and control needed to land in the right place at the right time. Notice the sudden switches between legato and staccato as well. Kick in with wrist and forearm for the louder staccato crotchets, with a light and springy hand staccato for the softer repeated chords. Make the final chords short to the point of dryness (with clenched-hand staccato) to compensate for the greater resonance of the lower register.

EXERCISE 16.4

Exercise 16.5

Now let's turn to the beautiful theme from the slow movement of Beethoven's famous
C minor Sonata (Op. 13), known as the 'Pathétique' for its atmosphere of pathos,
which looks forward to the composer's middle period works.

CD: **TRACK 58**

    Legato pedalling should reflect changes in harmony as well as movement in the
melody and bass line, which must be carefully balanced against each other. You
really need to listen carefully. Dynamic shading and timing should be sensitive to
the shape and destination of the melody, especially the contrast between larger and
smaller intervals within the line: sink in to the right hand top notes. The
accompanying texture should reflect this, with right hand thumb used delicately.

    Rethink balance when the melody moves up the octave at bar 9 and the texture
thickens, and tail off sensitively on appoggiaturas at ends of phrases. The middle
section could move on just a little, but decorative passages will need space for their
relaxed lyricism. The falling couplets from bar 24 move the focus into the darker and
richer lower register, as does the left hand in bar 25, which should sing. Why not
learn the complete movement?

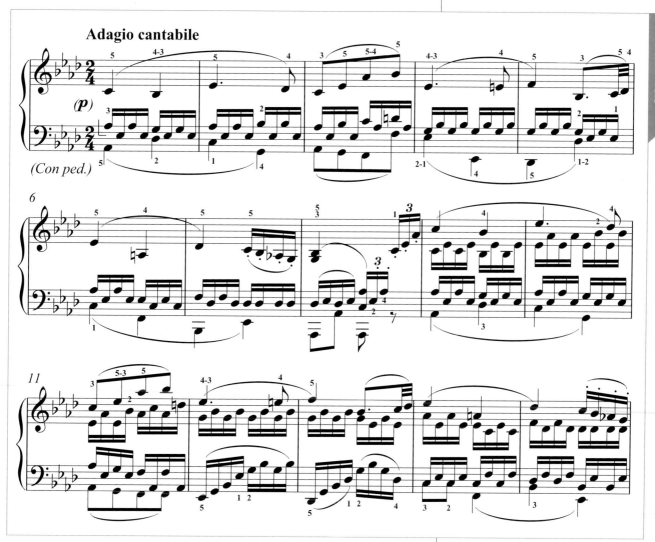

2

Exercise 16.6

This Andante, No.11 from the Bagatelles (Op.119), gives a glimpse of Beethoven's later style. The music passes through a succession of pianistic idioms in a highly condensed way, with practically no thematic repetition: first a singing melody, then an improvisatory cadenza-like passage, then extremes of register evoking tranquillity and spaciousness, and finally a chorale-like texture. Each stage of

unfolding melody feels like a new idea, yet all share the same few notes and intervals – giving the music a rhapsodic feel in spite of its extreme economy of material. (This resembles the fusion of rhapsodic expressionism with austere and condensed structural thinking that dominated early 20th century in the works of atonal composers like Schoenberg and Webern.) The line needs to be projected in the upper register, especially if long notes are to sing. Pedalling should be sparing and extremely subtle. Don't be deceived by the apparent simplicity of the music: let every note speak for itself, even when it's just part of a scale.

FOUR-OCTAVE SCALES & ARPEGGIOS

It's time to start practising scales and arpeggios over four octaves. This requires no changes to the fingering. For scales, think of rhythmic groups of eight instead of four, with arms drawing the hands across the keyboard in a single grand sweep, and consistent release of weight, leaning into the keys for full but even tone. Adjust posture as you move between registers, leaning just a little towards where your hands are, with a straight back and good support from feet, which should be firmly on the ground but sufficiently apart to support leaning over. You should be confident enough to focus on overall shaping and character and let individual fingers look after themselves. The same goes for arpeggios.

UNIT 17

20th century piano music •

Tonal colour •

Modern music •

Irregular metres and rhythms •

Contemporary music •

Scales in 3rds & octaves •

SECTION 6

20TH CENTURY PIANO MUSIC

Performing 20th century piano music requires a highly developed awareness of the physical aspects of playing and how these relate to the wide contrasts of attack and colour required by the music. The complexity of some scores will test your analytical skills, and requires patience. Interpreters of this music often place more emphasis on precision and clarity than on emotional involvement, though extremes of technique and expressive characterisation may be relevant in ways that would be inappropriate for more traditional music. You may have to count rhythms that are hard to feel in terms of their relation to the underlying pulse, which in turn must be actively projected into the music to achieve a sense of carefully measured timing. Wherever possible, analyse the music as you learn it, and think about the effect of texture, register, dynamics and articulation. Gesture can play an important role: the process of playing may be part of the unfolding musical event, and may affect the sound of the music in ways hard to calculate.

The classical music of the 20th century is a complex and confusing affair, with competing artistic tendencies evolving alongside each other or superseding one another. People use the term 'modern music' to refer to developments that marked a radical break with earlier traditions when they first emerged. However, these are pretty familiar to most musicians now, even if many are not comfortable with them. The term 'modern' may perhaps be more significant as an indication of the continuing indifference of the wider listening public. Recently written modern music is also called 'contemporary music'. Much 20th century music is not 'modern' at all, but continues 19th century Romanticism or draws on alternative sources and inspirations unrelated to any attempted musical revolution.

COLOURS AND TEXTURES

The arrival of the 20th century coincided with a reaction against the dominating influence of Wagner's hypnotically sensuous and emotional music. This was linked to developments in other art forms, such as painting and literature. In France, Impressionism led painters to emphasise the richness of the senses rather than the drama of emotions, influencing writers like Proust and composers like Debussy and Ravel, who explore the sensuality of piano textures, colours and sounds in ways also influenced by oriental music. Like many composers of the time, they preferred the detachment of the satirist or the craftsman to the inspirational involvement of Romanticism.

Unlike wind and stringed instruments, or the voice, the **tone colour** or **timbre** of the piano is mechanically fixed. However, this doesn't mean it lacks colour. Different registers have different colouristic qualities, and these also depend on the volume and attack of notes. These are part of what the composer intends to be heard when he writes for the instrument. Harmony and texture (and pedalling) also contribute to pianistic colour, which gains an added dimension through its ability to evoke orchestral instruments and percussive or bell-like sounds. Don't be deceived into thinking that these aspects of music don't matter by the fact that they're not shown in the score, and learn to savour the colours and textures of music for their own sake.

Exercise 17.1

This piece ('The Little Negro') by Claude Debussy (1862-1918) parodies the syncopated rhythms associated with minstrels (black entertainers). The opening rhythm should be crisp, but not overstated. Notice the fingering for left-hand chromatic 3rds, which should be played mezzo staccato with a loose flapping hand. In bar 9, the right hand plays over the left and into the black keys, while the left-hand octaves call for a lively finger staccato accenting the bass notes slightly. Notice the static and oriental bell-like texture in bars 17-22. The doubling of the melody line between hands from bar 23 should also be a colouristic effect, so perfect coordination and legato are needed, without pedal. Everything should sound subtle and precise.

CD: **TRACK 60**

MODERN MUSIC

At the start of the 20th century, Art Nouveau decadence and Futurism influenced the Italian composer and virtuoso Ferrucio Busoni, who proposed a range of new composing techniques (artificial scales, metreless music, texture music).

At almost the same time, Expressionism and Abstraction in painting influenced composers in Germany and Austria, notably Schoenberg and his pupils Webern and Berg. Freud's theory of the irrational and Einstein's relativity theory added to the sense that the old certainties of European culture were disintegrating. Schoenberg's music became so dense and chromatic that it crossed the threshold into **atonality** and **athematicism**, where all sense of key and thematic identity are suspended, because all notes have equal claim to be regarded as tonal centres or fundamental elements. This led Schoenberg to his **emancipation of dissonance**, in which clashing intervals and harmonies are no longer resolved, and towards his **twelve-tone method** of composition. In cosmopolitan Paris, Stravinsky's ballet scores reflected the primitivism of art influenced by African culture, superimposing unrelated keys or rhythms to create **polytonality** and **polyrhythms**.

World War I destroyed the faith of people in the old structures of society, making political movements such as socialism and fascism popular. In Russia the communists swiftly imposed strict constraints on composers, prompting Prokofiev and Shostakovitch to use traditional idioms in bitterly sardonic ways. Stravinsky and the French composers of the inter-war period also adopted an ironical attitude to the past, known as *Neo-Classicism*, subjecting earlier styles to **parody** and **pastiche**. (Stravinsky later took to using the twelve-tone technique.)

Other Eastern European composers, such as Bartók, were influenced by the irregular rhythms, modes and microtonal elements of folk music. World War II caused many musicans to flee to America or Britain to escape the Nazis: Schoenberg went to California, Berg died prematurely, Webern was accidentally shot by an American soldier. Two centuries of domination of classical music by Austro-German culture was brought to an end.

The piece below was written by Arnold Schoenberg (1874-1951) just before the outbreak of World War I. It shows the composer's 'free atonal' style: his music is atonal and freely dissonant, but he is not yet using the twelve-note method (in which all the notes of the chromatic scale are organised into a sequential series that must be stated before any notes are repeated, and from which all thematic and harmonic material is derived). This piece could be analysed on several levels:

- as **blocks** of harmonic material, forming progressions with chromatic voice-leading characteristics (ignoring octave transpositions); eg, the descent from B to B♭ between the notes in the first two lines, or top notes D-C-B in the right hand of the last line;
- as **interval structures**; eg, the superimposed 4ths in the opening left hand chord (G-F-C), extended in bar 6 from below (E-[A]-D) and above (C-F-B♭), and transposed into the left hand of bar 9 (C♯-F♯-B);
- as **motives**; eg, rising and falling semitones presented consecutively in bars 4-5 (D♯-E), then simultaneously in bar 9 (E-E♭ and F♯-G); also the descending whole tone in bars 7-8 (left hand) which becomes the falling major 9th at the end.

Theorists have also developed an advanced system for analysing the deeper theoretical properties of atonal music, called **pitch-class analysis**. See Recommended Reading for more on this.

The idea of basing chord structures on intervals of a 4th instead of a 3rd is known as **quartal harmony**, and was developed by Schoenberg in his famous *Harmonielehre*. Later in the 20th century it also came to be used in jazz. (See Unit 18.) The

Recommended Reading section at the back of this book explains where you can read more about this development.

Exercise 17.2

CD: **TRACK 61**

This is the last of Schoenberg's Six Little Pieces (Opus 19). The absence of a tune or regular rhythm makes it resemble abstract art: just pure colour and shape, but each chord should be measured precisely in terms of time and sonority.

Note how the left hand crosses over for the high D-sharp (bar 4), which colours the right hand note like an overtone. Use pedal to keep the left-hand chord sounding, and to join chords where a note has to be restruck (bar 6): in both cases note how the pedal isn't depressed until well after the attack of the chord, in order to minimise resonance and maintain consistency of sound quality. Pressing the pedal half-way down in the last bar will sustain higher notes but not bass notes, so the melodic motion between the last two notes is clearly audible.

The big leap between the first two notes of bar 8 must be heard to be joined legato (between the hands): delay the second note and overlap a little more, so we have time to really register the join in spite of the large interval. Listen to how silences work as part of the music, and to how they relate to the dying away or release of notes and chords. What state of mind do you think this piece expresses?

Sehr langsam *(very slow)*

mit sehr zartem Ausdruck
[with the most delicate feeling]

genau im Takt
[strictly in time]

wie ein Hauch
[like a breath]

Arnold Schoenberg (1874-1951) was the most controversial and radical composer and theorist of classical music in its modern phase. Coming from a Slovakian family, but based in Vienna, he dominated Austro-German music until the rise of Hitler forced him to flee to California, where he then exerted an influence on American musical life. In his early works, Schoenberg pursued Romantic music's tendency towards increasing extremes of chromaticism, rhapsodic comlexity, and richness of texture. He took it beyond anything that had appeared even in the works of such composers as Wagner, Wolf, Mahler or Richard Strauss. This led to increasing levels of tension and dissonance, and to the suspension of tonality (the sense of key) in music.

At the same time, he reintroduced stricter formal techniques associated with Brahms and the classical masters. In this way he reintegrated the two opposing sides of the Austro-German musical legacy (which at the time were identified with Wagner and Brahms respectively), but under extreme circumstances. Schoenberg's move into atonal music reflected his sympathy for expressionism in art (he was also a painter), and led him to develop the 12-tone technique, which continued to influence the way modern composers worked throughout the 20th century.

His work *Pierrot Lunaire*, for female voice and chamber ensemble, introduced a half-speaking, half-singing style of declamation called Sprechstimme. Later, when the composer returned to his Jewish roots, he composed an opera, *Moses und Aaron*, which explores the conflict between the truth of ideas and the eloquence of earthly communication. This reflected his conception of music as an art that should remain true to its inner formal and expressive principles – its ideas rather than its surface style.

This has made him a figurehead for classical composers and musicians throughout the 20th century who seek to distance themselves from the growing influence of popular culture and commercialism on western society. Schoenberg was an important teacher, who developed important theoretical concepts relating to how classical music should be understood and analysed, emphasising underlying unifying melodic and rhythm shapes, and illuminating the workings of tonal harmony and traditional forms.

While many composers influenced by him have seen their music accepted into the repertoire after initial protests, Schoenberg's own works remain difficult and challenging to this day. What do you think that tells you about them?

IRREGULAR METRES AND RHYTHMS

The music of the 20th century often makes use of irregular and shifting time signatures: these can make it hard to judge the timing of the music in the normal intuitive way.

Irregular metres have an odd number of beats to a bar, so these don't fall into obviously regular groupings. (Jazz players know these as 'odd time' – see Unit 18). This means feeling every equal subdivision in its own right instead of as divisions of larger groupings: it is called **additive rhythm**, which is also a feature of complex rhythmic systems such as those of classical Indian music (see Unit 18). Notice how five, seven or eleven beats in a bar are irrational, but nine is just compound triple time. In some cases there is a regular division into unequal groupings.

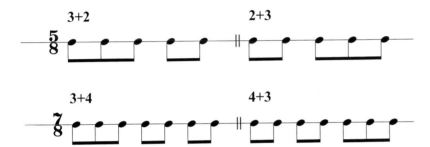

Irrational rhythms are also a feature of modern music. These divide the beat into a different number of equal subdivisions from that implied by the metre (ie, the time signature). We've already encountered **triplets**. The general term for these alternative divisions is **tuplets**, which are often indicated as ratios in modern music. We normally learn to feel them by intuitively judging the speed required to fit the correct number of subdivisions into the available time-span, but occasionally it's necessary to calculate the exact relationship to normal subdivisions, to achieve the cross-rhythms that result when normal and irrational divisions are superimposed.

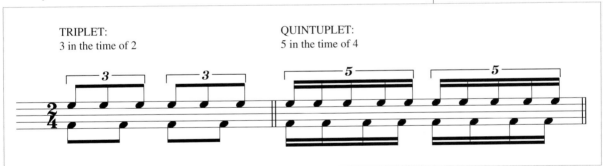

TRIPLET:
3 in the time of 2

QUINTUPLET:
5 in the time of 4

The Hungarian Béla Bartók (1881-1945) was possibly the most important Eastern European composer of the first half of the 20th century. Bartók spent time studying the folk music of countries such as Hungary and Bulgaria, and of the gypsies, and his music draws on the unusual features he discovered, especially the use of irregular metres and modal scales quite different from those of western classical music. He was also a virtuoso concert pianist, and developed many original formal compositional techniques that influenced later generations of composers across Europe, such as the use of special 'Golden Section' mathematical ratios and tiny chromatic **cells** from which larger structures of melody and harmony evolve.

CD: **TRACK 62**

EXERCISE 17.3

Allegro pesante

Exercise 17.3

'Change of Time' is from Book Five of Bartók's Mikrokosmos, a series of modern pieces composed especially for piano students. It's a study in shifts between regular and irregular metres. This means switching between counting crotchets (for 2/4 and 3/4) and quavers (for 3/8 and 5/8). If you keep both levels of counting in mind for bars with crotchet counts, it's easier to switch over to just quavers for irregular bars. Stress the first beat of every bar, but avoid turning 3/8 patterns into triplets by rushing them. Quavers must also remain at the same speed for the final 6/8 bars. Repeated lower notes in each hand must be released in time to be restruck, so a degree of staccato is required throughout, with strong rhythmic movement from the wrist backed up by arm weight. Bartók's unusual right-hand fingerings emphasise percussiveness and rhythm over line, since thumb and 5th finger are maintained through rapid shifts of hand position.

CONTEMPORARY MUSIC

After World War II a new generation of composers emerged in Europe, many studying with Messiaen, the French composer whose music reflects exotic cultures and birdsong, who opened their minds to other possibilities outside European music. The highly cerebral music of Webern and the futuristic music of Edgar Varèse also became models for the **Darmstadt School**, who in the 1950s subjected all aspects of music (pitch, rhythm, dynamics, articulation and tone colour) to abstract principles of organisation inspired by Schoenberg's twelve-tone method. This **total serialism** aimed at a completely new start, eliminating all conventions in favour of permanent innovation, in line with the ideas of **modernism** and the **avant-garde**. But the most radical composers were not necessarily the best: Jean Barraqué, for example, is now recognised as a more important figure in post-war French music, especially for his monumental *Piano Sonata*.

The idea of an avant-garde, always shocking audiences, went further in the 1960s with the chance-based **aleatoric music** of Cage, and Stockhausen's conceptual music. (Cage had already experimented with placing objects inside the piano to alter its sound for particular notes, creating the **prepared piano**.) **Minimalism**, which reintroduced simple tonal harmonies in repeated patterns that shift gradually in and out of phase, spread from America to Europe, and remains fashionable, since it marked the start of a convergence between modern and popular music now associated with **postmodernism**. The Mexican-American composer Conlon Nancarrow created works of unplayable complexity, full of fantastic polyrhythms, written for **player piano**, and the Polish composer Witold Szalonek developed ways of writing for instruments that capture the characteristics of vocal **inflection** that had almost disappeared from western classical music. Others such as the British composer Brian Ferneyhough pushed atonal and serial techniques to new expressionistic extremes. Computers led to developments in **live electronics** (the electronic modification of sounds in live performances) and to the compositional techniques of **spectral music**, influenced by research into the acoustical properties of sounds.

The 1980s saw the commercialisation of contemporary music, with the introduction of modern marketing techniques by music publishers, the growth of international festivals and competitions, and the various **crossover** fusions between different traditions that reflect the increasing multiculturalism of western urban societies. The 1990s saw affordable computer **sequencing** software for composing, and the Internet, whose long-term implications for music have yet to be seen. More significant was the striking absence in the last three decades of the 20th century of real developments in the underlying compositional language of contemporary music.

SCALES IN 3RDS & OCTAVES

You'll often come across passages where a single hand plays two lines, moving in parallel a 3rd apart. These may have to sound legato even where only one part is actually joined in the fingers, so it requires a special approach to fingering to create the illusion that both parts are joined, through careful coordination and joining of the notes that *can* be joined. Notice how fingering for major and minor scales still works in terms of a group of three and a group of four: at the end of the group the 2nd or 3rd finger must stretch past the 5th, which takes careful practice. With some scales the patterns have to be reversed, or begun in the middle, to avoid thumbs on black notes. Practise staccato first to two octaves, aiming for crisp coordination and even rhythm, then slow right down to master legato playing. You'll need a really flexible wrist to join past the 5th finger and to make the movement in reverse, and elbows should remain close in where possible. When you're ready, try combining the hands.

The basic C major pattern also works for major and minor scales on C, G, D, and A, and for E minor. (Try these.) Notice the change of fingering for E major to avoid left hand thumb on a black note, and how F major has a change to the right hand to

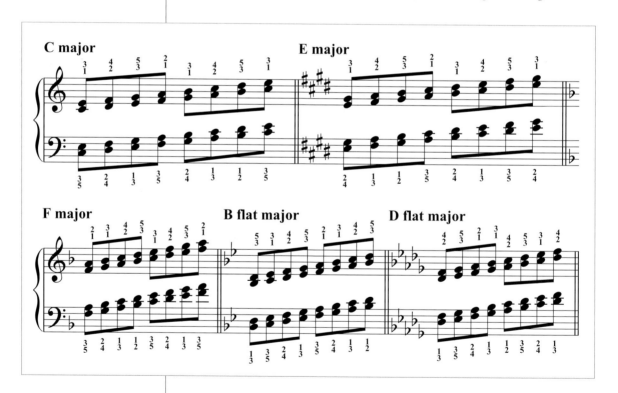

avoid using thumb on B-flat. B-flat major is given as an example of how black note scales involve a permutation of the fingering for the white-note scales close by (in this case on C). Eventually thumbs on black notes become unavoidable, as shown here for D-flat major.

Here's the best fingering for a chromatic scale in 3rds. Practise staccato before legato, and hands separately before hands together.

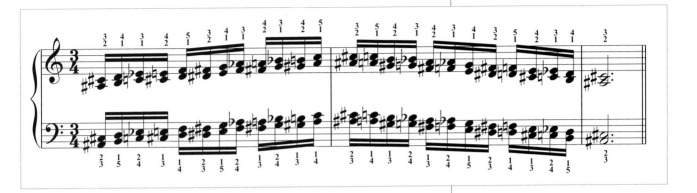

Staccato scales in octaves can be practised with thumb and 5th throughout, or changing to thumb and 4th for black keys if your hands are large enough. The same goes for chromatic scales. (Notice this way of writing a chromatic scale to avoid suggesting any particular key: accidentals are shown as sharps ascending and flats descending.) Avoid straining the muscles to play these, but accent the first of each rhythmic group clearly.

UNIT 18

SECTION 6

LATIN STYLES

The term *Latin* refers to music from Latin America – a large area that contains many related regional musical idioms. These are very diverse and reflect a wide range of musical influences, of which the most important are Spanish, Portuguese, African, American Indian, and American (ie, jazz). Here are just some of those idioms:

Country	Idiom
Argentina	tango
Cuba, Puerto Rico, & USA	salsa
Brazil	samba, bossa nova
Mexico	mariachi
Trinidad	calypso
Jamaica	reggae
Dominican Republic	merengue

Argentinean, Afro-Cuban, and Brazilian idioms are probably the most relevant for pianists, so we'll concentrate on these.

Tango

Tango reflects strong Spanish influences, and is the most European of the Latin idioms. Tango harmonies may echo the modal (Phrygian) flavour of Spanish music. Here's the basic rhythm, which underpins the fiercely sensual and passionate feel of the music.

Salsa

Salsa is a term invented to refer to music with an Afro-Cuban basis, connected with the interaction and interchange of musicians in Havana, Puerto Rico, Miami and New York: consequently it also reflects the continuous influence of jazz. The main feature is the reliance on a strict underlying rhythmic pattern known as the **clave** (pronounced 'clah-veh'), which comes in two principal forms: forward and reverse. A third form, the **rumba clave**, is also used.

Forward clave (3+2)

Reverse clave (2+3)

Rumba or African clave (3+2)

Salsa melodies will fit consistently over one or other of these patterns, but since Latin jazz often involves arranging a jazz standard in a Latin style, the melody line may not fit so naturally and may require adaptation or a looser approach. Salsa uses a rich rhythm section, with a wide array of hand percussion instruments and hand drums such as conga and bongos that produce a wide and subtle range of colouristic effects. Consequently salsa pianists frequently resort to octave doublings and two-handed chordal figures to cut through the texture. Salsa tends to have extremely simple harmonic patterns (sometimes just a two-chord progression such as II-V), and it often features a repeated highly syncopated 2-bar melodic figure called a **montuno**. Here's an example.

CD: **TRACK 63**

You should learn to feel the interplay between continuous syncopation and the underlying crotchet pulse, playing the figure in both hands while maintaining the normal pulse as a foot-tap. Then you might try to get a feel for how the same pattern works over typical percussion and bass patterns such as the **cáscara** (played on cymbal or sides of drums) or **tumbao** (played on bass). You can do this by programming a drum machine or putting the tumbao into your left hand. Even better, team up with a bassist and percussionist or drummer – they'll be delighted to have a pianist versatile enough to play Latin.

Notice how syncopations in Latin are shown as single notes even when they run across the 3rd beat of the bar (which in classical music would require the use of tied notes).

Samba and bossa nova

Samba is the dynamically energetic, explosively physical style of music and dancing associated with Brazilian carnival celebrations. It features a distinctive up-tempo kick drum pattern (the samba 'feet') and two-bar rhythmic figures that move in and out of syncopation (the rhythmic equivalent of preparing and resolving a dissonance).

Bossa nova is more relaxed and subtle, with a pattern similar to the clave of salsa, but used more loosely.

The most famous example is 'The Girl from Ipanema', a sensuous and sultry number written for Dolores Duran by Antonio Carlos Jobim (the inventor of the bossa nova). Can you see how the melody begins by suggesting the pattern of the clave, but then mixes up elements of it more freely?

Bossa nova clave

General features

Many Latin idioms have similar rhythmic and harmonic features. For example tango, clave, samba and bossa nova patterns all highlight the 'and' of the 2nd beat of the bar, but in different ways.

Tango

Samba feet

Salsa clave (3+2)

Bossa nova clave

241

Syncopating over the bar line and the halfway point of the bar are general features of Latin music. They often combine with the distinctive use of chromatically descending bass lines (and the resulting chord progressions) to create a sinister, trance-like feeling of irresistible forward propulsion. This feature is responsible for Latin music's atmosphere of demonic sensuality, of raw passion and energy spinning out of control. You'll also find it in fusion idioms such as Latin rock.

CD: **TRACK 64**

Fast and rhythmic

ARRANGING

Arranging is the art of adapting material (such as a popular tune or standard) to suit a particular instrument or group of instruments (what non-classical musicians call a **line-up,** and classical musicians call an **ensemble.**).

A common way to harmonise tunes 'as you go along' in jazz piano (ie, freely and flexibly) is known as **block chords**: the hands move in parallel, providing a chord for each note of the melody. This often uses a technique derived from the way jazz arrangers write for four **horns** ('horns' in jazz means saxophones, not the brass instruments of classical music) or four trumpets: this is called **four-way close.** Alternate notes of the scale are harmonised as inversions of the basic chord or as diminished 7th chords that imply the corresponding V7♭9. A chromatic passing note is added to the scale to maintain the alternation (see **Bebop Scales**). On the piano the hands can then move in parallel (known as **locked hands**) either by letting the left hand double the top line (in the style of George Shearing) or by dropping the second note from the top by an octave into the left, known as **drop two.** This kind of voice leading works in either direction (ascending or descending).

Four-way close

Doubled-melody style (Shearing)

Drop two

Just like when you're 'comping for a singer or soloist, arranging for piano involves learning to fit an interesting and appropriate texture behind your own presentation of the melody. Look for spaces in the tune (ie, long notes or rests) that leave room for freely realising the rhythmic textures of the style. In the lead sheet for 'The Girl from Ipanema' the B section has long notes that leave room for bossa nova patterns: these can suggest a rhythm section, contrasting with the triplet crotchets of the melody (marked). On the other hand, the A section calls for chords that underline the flexible rhythm of the tune itself, by coinciding with the equivalent melodic notes in each phrase (technically speaking, the 'points of departure and arrival', marked with an **x** in Example 18.1 overleaf). That way we are made aware of their shifting rhythmic position.

Eddie Palmeiri (left), one of the great Latin-jazz pianists of the 20th century.

243

Exercise 18.1

Try to create your own piano realisation of Jobim's The Girl from Ipanema, based on the lead sheet given above, with a bossa nova feel. When you've worked through the next section, come back and try introducing some reharmonisations. (Write them down.) Then take your new changes and solo over them. Try to hold on to the Latin rhythmic feel.

Now let's have a glimpse of what a master like Bill Evans can do with a jazz standard. Here's the original version of the opening of Duke Ellington's 'In a Sentimental Mood', followed by a transcription of Evans' version.

CD: **TRACK 65+66**

Evans often had an almost Zen-like focus on disjoined and sparse left hand voicings.
Even so, in contrast to some other bebop players, his right hand does indirectly track
the original line, but as a haunted wandering from moment to moment through
strange chromatic twists.

Notice the elastic treatment of the rhythmic shape of the line in terms of its
relation to the musical metre, as well as the changes to the chords in bar 5: the twist
on to the D minor chord (a sort of interrupted cadence in the original) becomes a II-
V-I in D minor, with the II (E7#5) itself altered to V of V, a **secondary dominant**,
and the V also chromatically altered, with raised 5th and flattened 9th. This is a
typical example of modern jazz **reharmonisation**.

Play through both versions for yourself.

REHARMONISATION

A major feature of jazz is the reharmonising of standards or well-known tunes,
substituting more unusual chord structures that fit the original tune but provide
more striking and individual opportunities for voicing and soloing. We've already
looked at basic forms of chord substitution such as **tritone substitution**, and
replacing V with II-V. Now it's time too look at a few more tricks that jazz pianists
carry around in their fingers and heads.

Altered-note harmonisations

For basic functions such as II, V and I there are a range of alternative harmonisations
that change the character of a chord by chromatically altering one or more notes
within it. This then affects the scale used to solo over that chord (since this will
incorporate the same alteration).

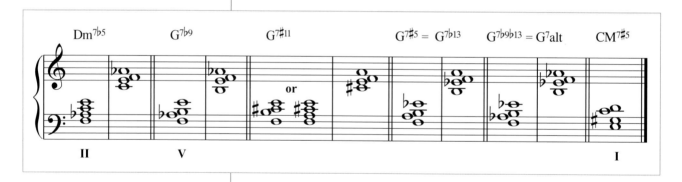

Also there are chords that don't correspond to any of the basic II-V-I major key
functions, such as when a minor key or modal tonality is implied for chord I.

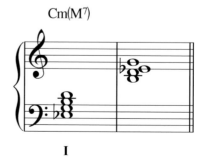

As well as seeing these as alterations of more familiar voicings, jazz scale theory
derives many of them from modes of the **jazz minor scale**. (Left-hand voicings still
produce the corresponding harmonies.)

Major-minor - m(M7) - I

sus b9 - II

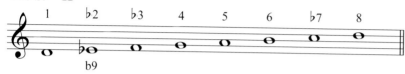

Lydian augmented - M7(#5) - I

Lydian dominant - 7#11 - V

Locrian #2 (half-diminished) - m7b5 - II

Altered - b9#9#11b13 - V

Note especially the alternative harmonisations on V produced by the **altered mode** scale. This is very important to jazz, and contains four alterations; even when all the altered notes aren't present in the chord, they are still implied for the corresponding scale. Note how a V7alt has the same notes as an unaltered V7 voicing a tritone away – so here's **tritone substitution** again.

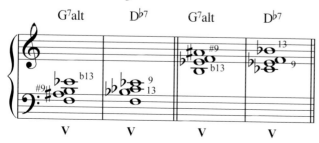

Now turn back to the Jobim number earlier in this unit ('The Girl from Ipanema') for a moment. Remember the two V7♭9 chords near the end of the B section, with a sharp 5th in the melody? Technically, this note is an accented chromatic passing note, but if we're soloing over the chord we can reflect it by treating the chord as altered-scale harmony, which has 7♭9 *and* #5.

The Lydian augmented scale offers an alternative treatment of I, which resembles the **whole-tone scale**. (That's a scale made from dividing the octave into six equal whole-tone steps – you'll find it especially in the music of 20th century French composers such as Debussy). The **half-diminished scale** resembles the Locrian mode with a raised 2nd, and is used for half-diminished chords, including II chords in a minor key. (If you want an interesting experience, go back to Unit 15, and try treating the famous 'Tristan chord' as a half-diminished chord, improvising over it with this scale.)

Like the whole-tone scale, the **diminished scale** offers an alternative to normal diatonic scales, this time by alternating tones and semitones, beginning with either a semitone or a tone. Notice how both whole-tone and diminished scales can only be transposed once to produce a different set of notes: this led the French composer Messiaen to call them **modes of limited transposition**. (A diminished scale beginning with a half step has the same notes as one beginning with a whole step on the note below or above.)

Lydian augmented - M7(#5) - I

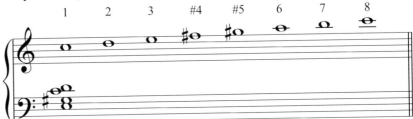

Locrian #2 (half-diminished) - m7b5 - II

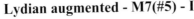

Diminished scale: half/whole tone - V7b9

Diminished scale: whole/half tone - dim7

Jazz minor scale harmonies are quite chromatic already, so they aren't notes to be avoided: this means that the same voicing can take on different functions depending on context, making for rich ambiguities. You can get a feel for this by substituting alternative roots in the bass.

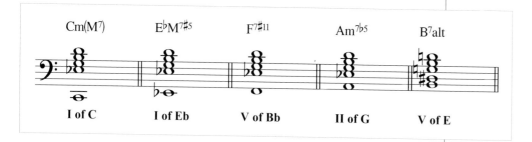

Here's a version of the Rhythm Changes, reharmonised post-Bebop style. Note the increased number of V chords, which replace the diminished 7ths in the simpler reharmonisation in Unit 15. Chords realised as V7♭9 could equally be treated as Valt, and vice versa.

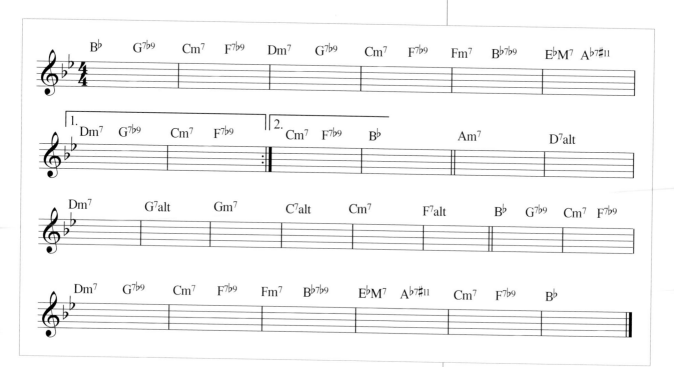

Multi-purpose chords

The reusability of jazz chord voicings is an essential feature of jazz, since it gives the player much greater freedom and flexibility, and isn't confined to chromatically altered harmonies. 'So What' chords consisting of three perfect 4ths and a major

3rd, and **4th chords** (also known as **quartal harmony**) built entirely out of superimposed 4ths, both embody this multifunctional character. The same chord-voicing can be heard in terms of several different functions, corresponding to different roots that may be implied or stated. This is the basis for the sort of modal jazz improvisation associated with **bebop** and the likes of Charlie Parker (see below). If you know that the chord has several functions, then you just can treat all of those chord functions as freely interchangeable voicings within a single mode.

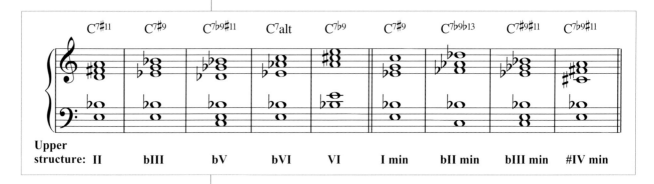

"So What" chords

4th chords

Upper structures superimpose a triad over a left hand tritone to create complex altered harmonies by simpler means. They're identified by the interval difference between the root of the triad and that of the tritone, taken as part of a V7 chord. Just like 'So What' and 4th chords, they provide an easier way of visualising otherwise complex harmonies, making them more readily available to be used spontaneously while 'on the fly'. (Except where the root is present, swapping 3rd with 7th in the left-hand tritone produces another upper structure a tritone away, making advanced tritone substitution much easier.)

Play through all of these and listen carefully to how they sound. Try inverting them to get new voicing sonorities. Then transpose them all around the circle of 5ths.

Coltrane changes

In his tune 'Giant Steps' John Coltrane introduced direct modulation between keys a major 3rd apart. This was a big new development for jazz improvisers, and became known as **Coltrane changes**. Subsequently (in the early 1960s) other jazz musicians also tried out modulation between keys a minor 3rd apart. In both cases the effect is to create striking tonal shifts between basic progressions as simple as V-I and II-V-I.

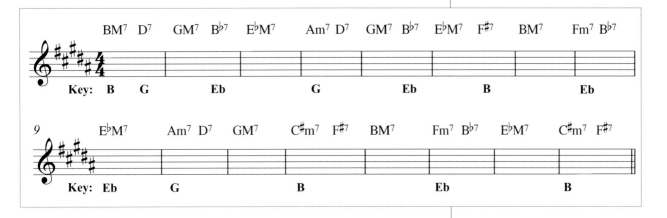

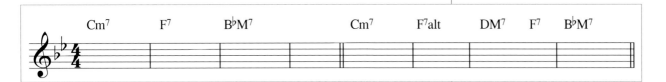

Coltrane then developed a handy way of interpolating these changes into the middle of II-V-I progressions to reharmonise them. Here's a typical example.

Classical composers on the other hand had long been familiar with this trick: you'll find modulation by 3rds in Schubert and late Beethoven (eg, the 'Hammerklavier' Sonata), not to mention Bruckner. In his later theorising Schoenberg mapped out these extended key relationships in classical terms through combining relations between major and minor keys on the same tonic, and those between relative major and minor keys, into a single system. This also illuminates jazz modulations. See the chart of key relationships below. Major keys are in capitals, minor keys in lower case. Each key has its relative major or minor on one side and its *tonic* major or minor (the major or minor key built on the same keynote) on the other. Each row corresponds to a move up or down the circle of 5ths.

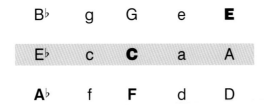

From this we can grasp how keys a minor 3rd apart are linked (sideways) through major-key equivalents of relative minors, while keys a major 3rd apart relate in the same way, with the addition of a step up or down the circle of 5ths (ie, diagonally). Jazz has also produced original theorists of its own, notably the composer George Russell, whose theory emphasises the linear character of modal-chromatic jazz harmony. There is more on this in Recommended Reading at the back of the book.

Exercise 18.2

Try taking these new harmonic resources through different keys, then solo over them with your own musical ideas. Take some standards from a fake book and reharmonise the changes, then use the resulting chords as a basis for your own improvising, referring more or less freely to the original tune.

BEBOP & MODERN JAZZ

Bebop (or **bop** for short) developed in the early 1940s, marking the beginning of the era of modern jazz. The move from embellishing familiar melodies to improvising freely over chords altered from those of the original standard often resulted in quite new melodic material. It produced a new kind of jazz, with a culture of greater technical sophistication and musical brilliance. Bebop had a distinct rhythmic feel, produced by irregular phrase lengths and mid-bar accents, and featured rapid-fire soloing. It's this approach, associated with the likes of Charlie ('Bird') Parker, Miles Davis, Thelonious Monk and others, that led to the development of reharmonisation and chord-based soloing techniques, as well as the adoption of short routes between keys.

Bebop scales involve the addition of a chromatic note to the basic scales of jazz: these are usually the Ionian, Dorian or Mixolydian modes, or the jazz minor scale. By turning scales from 7-note to 8-note scales, they produce a more regular alignment of harmony notes with the beat. (We've already seen the advantages of this for block chord arranging.) Note how scales for chords in the same II-V progression keep the same added note.

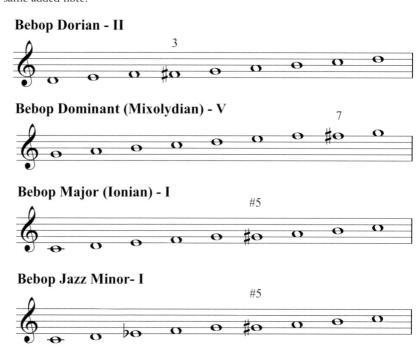

Bebop Dorian - II

Bebop Dominant (Mixolydian) - V

Bebop Major (Ionian) - I

Bebop Jazz Minor- I

Modern jazz is a term used to apply to all jazz that reflects the innovations of bebop, but also refers to the more wildly experimental approaches that it spawned from the 1960s on. These often feature the device known as 'playing *outside* the changes' (known as playing **outside** or **out**, for short), in which the soloist's line switches between passages using scale-notes belonging to the underlying chord and passages with notes completely foreign to the chord (and even to the key). (The concept of **off-notes** is relevant here. See Unit 15.) At the same time what counts as 'out' is often relative to the time: Bird and Coltrane were heard as 'out' when they were performing, but might not be now, especially in the light of atonal and **free jazz**, which have no chord structure at all. In this respect, players such as Anthony Braxton and Cecil Taylor might be said to be permanently 'out'.

ETHNIC, URBAN, FUSION, CROSSOVER

Both modern classical music and non-classical music have become increasingly open to outside influences. Indian and Arabic classical music offer alternative approaches to improvisation, based on their own long and highly sophisticated traditions. The Indian **ragas** are a system of scales that each give rise to different collections of melodic formulae and principles of unfoldin. The gradual opening out of a melodic compass – the range of pitches covered by the melody – is a particularly subtle feature of this music, and something from which western musicians could still learn a great deal. The Indian rhythmic system of **talas** is far more sophisticated than western approaches to metre, with complex 'rhythmic modes', which can combine fixed-length and variable-length beats according to certain rules, producing highly extended and elaborated rhythmic cycles. Arabic music has similar features: the (Iran-Persian) **dastgah** system interweaves freer elaborations with more formulaic melodic cadences.

The **fusion** of idioms to produce hybrids such as jazz-rock can be dynamic, but is often greeted with suspicion and disdain by purists on either side. Some of the most interesting fusions have come from the interaction between the dance music scene of increasingly multicultural western urban societies and their own ethnic minority subcultures. The synthesis of strikingly different ethnic dance feels such as Bhangra with urban dance beats, whose irregular, fragmented **break-beat** feel exploits drum machines and sampling and sequencing technologies, can be exciting even for those who think they've heard and tried everything.

The ability of the piano to set up two-handed grooves makes for rich possibilities for layered rhythmic textures similar to those of sequenced dance-music beats. Many drumming patterns are based on **linear grooves** that work by dividing up a single, even stream of notes between the two hands to create a rhythmic counterpoint of syncopated patterns: the piano can do just the same. Here's the basic stick pattern known as the **paradiddle**, in which the same 4-note pattern is swapped around between the hands (l = left; r = right):

l r l l r l r r

Here's how it looks in rhythmic notation, first as a linear groove, then as two separate parts, showing the resulting syncopations. The whole 8-note pattern has to be repeated several times to get the feel.

CD: **TRACK 68**

CD: **TRACK 69** Try it away from the piano, then transfer it onto the keys as a two-handed texture, for example: right-hand rock-style chords over a left-hand bass-line pattern.

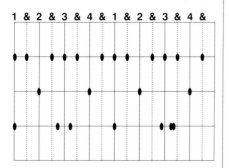

If you like this sort of thing, get your hands on a few drum-kit playing manuals and start working through the patterns. Then take a look at drum and percussion patterns in Latin music – they're *really* interesting.

On the other hand, the grid-based charts used by drum-machine and keyboard programmers offer a highly visual way of representing beat-structures, allowing you to work with these in more creative and sophisticated ways. You can then transcribe the results into traditional musical notation. Notice how the half-bar accent gets displaced around the beat, producing a funky, jittery dance feel that adds tension to the backbeat.

Crossover is often used to refer specifically to the fusion of classical or contemporary classical approaches with non-classical, ethnic, jazz or popular elements. Often the impetus has come from classical performers such as the Kronos Quartet, the violinist Nigel Kennedy (his arrangements of Hendrix, for example) or the pianist Joanna MacGregor; however, in many cases the motivation seems to be nakedly commercial.

Exercise 18.3

Take a dance track number that has an interesting feel and transcribe the rhythm section. Then use this as a basis for two-handed piano grooves. How would you fit a tune over this in your right hand? Try composing a tune whose melodic movement fits into places where the groove leaves the right hand free. Then try the reverse: fit bassline movement into the gaps in the left-hand part of the groove.

ODD-TIME

An early example of crossover was **Thirdstream** music: the interaction of jazz and classical approaches in the 1960s, associated with the likes of Dave Brubeck, the Modern Jazz Quartet, or the composer Gunter Schuller. Brubeck studied with the classical composer Darius Milhaud (a master of polytonality), but is looked down on by jazz aficionados as not being a real jazzman. The complex syncopations and swung rhythms of jazz rely on an underlying regular metre: a reliable two or four in a bar. But Brubeck introduced **odd-time** metres (irrational metres) into jazz, such as five, seven or eleven beats in a bar. Do you think that composed jazz combines the best or the worst aspects of classical and jazz music?

John Lewis of the Modern Jazz Quartet (left) was a concise and gifted player, as well as a notable composer and arranger.

Mixing it

Terms like fusion and crossover have become rather debased since the 1980s by the incessant attempt to hype new trends. It's tempting to think that all possible fusions of style have now been tried. The bad side of crossover is a tendency to dilute difference and contrasts by blending all styles into different shades of grey. The good side comes when the confrontation between traditions forces musicians on both sides to rethink old habits, to find deeper and fresher perspectives from which they can appreciate both differences and similarities between idioms. That's what this book has tried to do. If you've worked through the book from the beginning, you'll know that the intermixing of musical cultures and styles and techniques is nothing new, and that western classical music itself originated in just this way.

Exercise 18.4

Here (overleaf) is the tune from 'Take Five', a well-known Brubeck number, written by another member of the group, Paul Desmond. It's normally played fairly quickly: straight (eighth-note) quavers aren't swung, but dotted rhythms are. The syncopated character of the opening two-handed figure can be brought out by emphasising the bass note both on and off the beat, but keep the left hand light and controlled once the right hand takes up the melody. The middle section requires careful practice and attention to accidentals, with phrased couplets working across the beat. Left-hand leaps should be loose but controlled to prevent an unwanted accent on the thumb, again stressing the bass notes with the 5th finger. (You should be able to play on the black keys with as much confidence as if they were white keys.) When you've mastered the opening tune, try keeping the left hand figure going by itself and improvising freely over it with the same scale: the melody interweaves pentatonic and blues-scale elements in E flat minor. Even better, get hold of a bassist and/or drummer and work out an arrangement, and even find a sax player or clarinettist to solo the line: then take it in turns to improvise in the breaks.

CD: **TRACK 67**

Moderately fast

FREE IMPROVISATION

Some of the most advanced aspects of jazz and contemporary classical music meet and overlap in the area known as **free improvisation.** This has evolved into a separate and alternative culture of its own, operating 'underground' – quite independently of mainstream circuits.

Musicians attracted to exploring radical forms of spontaneity are often attracted to this approach: in their performances they may emphasise immediacy of physical involvement, the relationship between gesture, timing and musical expression, or the theatricality, mysticism and ritual of musical 'happenings'. They'll usually try for a closer and more intimate relationship with an audience over the course of an evening, responding imaginatively to the shared atmosphere as it develops, and treating every performance as a fresh situation to be reflected in the playing itself. Free improvisation is often highly eclectic and individualised from a technical point of view, resisting categorisation in terms of traditional or mainstream stylistic forms. Indeed, it aims precisely at breaking down the stereotypical categories that sometimes seem to dominate the wider music scene.

Free improvisation may lead you to want to find more radical ways of exploring the role of your own body in live performance, for example through bringing to the fore aspects of the musical material whose character is directly tied to that of the physical movements that you make while playing. This can heighten the experience of sensory feedback during performance, and gets channelled back into the sounds you make, generating a spiralling sense of involvement. This can also be an opportunity to explore the uncharted territory that lies between the very different physical styles of playing involved in classical and non-classical approaches to the piano: for example, between treating parts of the body such as the hands, or hands and arms, as more or less self-contained ('encapsulated') physical systems (like in certain classical piano exercises, or ballet, or even modern robotics), and letting the whole body flow in a single current of energy and movement (as in hard rock and modern dance, for example).

From here you may find yourself getting curious about the nature of performance itself. In what sense is the source of your playing 'inside' you? When is your playing expressive because of the musical sounds it gives rise to, and when are these sounds expressive because they come from your playing – from your actions as a player, which are perhaps already expressive? When is a musician like an actor performing a role, and when are you just being (and expressing) yourself? Thinking about these sorts of issues may help you to understand how you yourself personally relate to playing the piano, giving you the confidence needed to fully develop and realise your own individuality as a player. Explore this aspect of musicianship by referring to the Recommended Reading section at the end of the book.

CREATING A PERFORMANCE

Whatever your own preferred style of playing, when the time comes to give a performance you'll need to remember that it's not enough just to play the right notes in the right way: a performance should also work as a performance. What that means of course depends on what you're performing. You'll need some basic **stage-presentation** skills, and you'll need to consider how to put together an interesting **programme** (the order of pieces).

Stage-presentation is a rather personal matter, but it's common sense that you should be sensitive to the cultural connotations of the sort of music you're playing. Classical music is normally played in an atmosphere of respectful concentration: stage presentation tends to be formal, and body language while playing tends to be focused on meeting the technical demands of the piece. Excessive swaying and lungeing will be viewed with suspicion and distaste by the concert-going public, especially if the music itself emphasises grace, elegance and refinement. With the exception of some Romantic show-pieces, the performer is there to serve the music, not the other way round. Jazz and popular music, of course, require a much more physically demonstrative style of playing, and often aim at producing a visual spectacle, without any of the classical constraints on correct posture, etc. One of the hardest things is to insulate these two approaches from each other, since the body has a memory of its own that tends not to differentiate between styles or cultures.

Programme planning is an art of its own. A good programme (for any style) should first win the audience over by getting them involved, then work that involvement into a climax, then provide closure. Classical recitals often have an interval, and it is normal to place a longer, more serious work in the second half. Just like a good composition, a good programme achieves a balance between unity and contrast. Contrasts of period or character or key may be considered, as well as thematic links, similarities of idiom, or works linked by a common origin (eg, the same composer, or composers of the same nationality) or by common extra-musical associations. Jazz and other non-classical performances are of course much more informal: you may well converse with the audience between numbers, contextualising pieces and helping to break the ice, but try this in a classical recital and you'll get a very different reaction, except in the context of an **encore**.

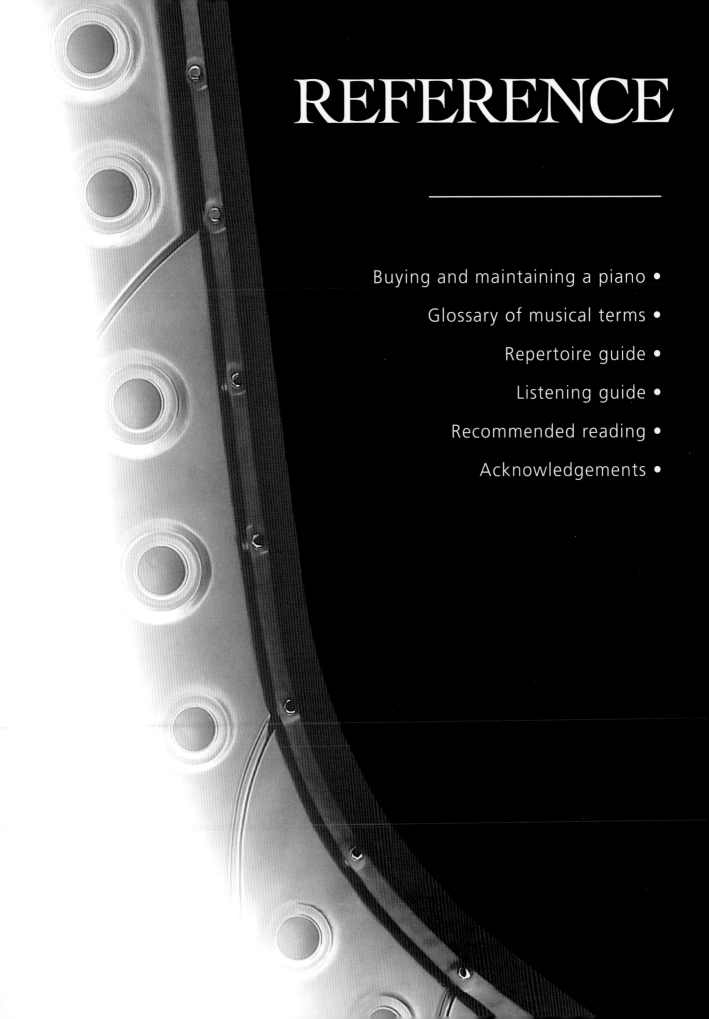

REFERENCE

CHOOSING AND BUYING A PIANO

CHOOSING A PIANO

There are various factors to bear in mind when choosing a piano, but never forget that the really crucial thing is how *you* feel about the instrument you're going to buy, since *you* are the one who's going to be playing it.

When viewing second-hand (used) pianos, it is difficult to generalise: each instrument will have different strengths and weaknesses. If you know of a local piano technician, it can be worth arranging for him or her to accompany you, especially when viewing older instruments, so that you don't end up with a piano with serious structural flaws.

Here are the ten key points to look out for.

MAKER'S NAME

Top-name pianos will always command a higher price, especially if brand new. A top-of-the-range **Steinway**, **Bösendorfer**, **Blüthner** or **Bechstein** will set you back the equivalent of a new car, or if you're buying a grand, even the equivalent of a house! If you've just won the lottery, you might even consider a luxury hand-produced grand piano from the Italian firm of **Fazioli**.

If you're not a millionaire but want to make a serious investment, you can either go for a second-hand instrument from one of these top names, or opt for a new piano from the next rank down of piano makers, which are also fine.

German pianos are generally thought to possess more character than others: many of the smaller firms active there in the first part of the 20th century produced fine instruments, reflecting longstanding family traditions of piano making. **Förster** (the German rather than the Czech firm), **Schimmel** and **Ibach** are all excellent, and have many of the qualities of the top rank German and Austrian piano houses. In the UK, **Broadwood** and **Chappell** should both be taken seriously, as should the French firm of **Pleyel** and, in America, **Baldwin** and **Boston** (a cheaper Steinway product made in Asia).

The new Japanese and Korean producers such **Yamaha**, **Kawai** and **Young Chang** can be superb value for money. Often the tone is not a match for European instruments, but the actions can be very good, and their competitive pricing may be the only way to bring a decent-sized grand or a brand new instrument within reach of your budget.

Other German makes to watch out for include **Feurich**, **Grotrian-Steinweg**, **Pfeiffer**, **Sauter**, **Seiler**, **Steinberg**, **Steingraeber** and **Steinmann**, to name but a few. Respectable British names include **Welmar**, **Collard & Collard**, **Marshall & Rose**, **Kemble**, and **Rogers**, though these are generally tonally inferior to German makes. **Chickering** is a well known American brand, and you'll still see French pianos sold under the name of **Érard**, though older ones may have a primitive action with poor repetition. Central European firms such as **Petrof** (Czech) have successfully returned to the market, and **Betting** (Poland) had a good reputation in their day.

Be warned: in recent times many familiar brand names of the piano world have regularly changed hands and are now produced by different companies or in different places, with consequences for the resulting instruments. Their reputations are primarily based on instruments produced in the early and mid-20th century.

AGE

When buying second hand, try to assess the age of the instrument. Sometimes this will be marked on the piano itself, and sometimes the owner may know. Three basic signs of whether it dates from the modern age are the following:

Is it overstrung? (Do the strings run across each other diagonally?)

Is it underdamped? (On an upright, do the dampers operate from *behind* the strings?)

Does it have an iron frame?

An instrument that does not have these three features should be treated with caution: it almost certainly dates from before the final stages of the evolution of the instrument, as so will be a very old instrument, and will be much more likely to develop problems.

CONDITION

The condition of a used piano can vary enormously, regardless of its age. To assess the condition, establish the following points.

Has it been regularly maintained and tuned? (Check the tuning for yourself. Take a tuning fork and try the A above Middle C. If the instrument is generally significantly below concert pitch, it probably hasn't been regularly tuned throughout its life.)

How much felt is left on the hammer-heads? (Try inspecting these from sideways-on.)

Is the sound-board intact. (Search for cracks.)

Have several individual strings been replaced recently? (New strings won't be discoloured in the way that the others are.)

Has the instrument been reconditioned in the recent past? What work was done?

SIZE

Of course, a *larger* piano will generally produce more tone, but so will a *better* piano. Also, grand pianos will almost always tend to have a more responsive action than uprights of equivalent quality or condition, since they have longer keys and the action works in alignment with gravity. But they're also more expensive. Check the amount of space in your home before viewing or purchasing an instrument.

TONE

Whether you're looking at a new or used instrument, you'll need to check for evenness of tone, and dynamic range.

First, try playing across the full range of the keyboard to see whether the tone is consistent. Is the bass noisy or richly and sonorous? Is the very high register thin? Do notes in the upper middle register sing on, without being too bright?

Then try playing at different volumes to assess the dynamic range.

The most important feature is the *tonal character* of the instrument, which is partly a matter of personal taste. Remember that this can be hard to judge if the piano you're trying out is out of tune.

In a shop, try a range of instruments from all price ranges so you get a feel for how good and bad pianos sound and feel. Your teacher may be able to advise you on this, so try dragging them along to the shop as well.

Don't be deceived by sheer brightness, especially if you want to play classical music, though some jazz pianists tend to opt for brighter instruments.

TOUCH

Touch – how it feels to actually play the keys – can also depend on your personal taste and technique. A light touch will suit younger children or women who have weaker, more delicate fingers, or those who are attracted to music by composers where subtlety is more important than power, for instance Mozart or Debussy. Conversely, a heavy touch might be more appropriate if you have robust hands, or if you plan to concentrate on heavy-duty rock, romantic or modern music.

ACTION

Test all notes for repetition. Try some rapid trills or tremolos, and repeated notes or chords. Check to see if all notes damp cleanly by listening carefully: do notes cease sounding immediately when the keys are released?

PEDALS

Check that the pedals work smoothly and quietly. Do all notes sustain when the right pedal is depressed, and do all notes damp together when it is released? Is there a middle pedal for quiet practising?

KEYS

Most modern new pianos use synthetic key-covering instead of ivory or ebony, out of respect for environmental concerns. Decide if this is acceptable to you. Some pianists feel that synthetic key-surfaces are more slippery, others don't. If you don't like synthetic keys, consider a used or reconditioned piano.

CASEWORK AND DESIGN

Bear in mind that pianos also come in a variety of designs. Many earlier instruments have attractive decorative casework, while current models are usually available from producers in a number of different stylings to blend with your other furniture.

However, just because a piano looks nice, it doesn't mean it's a good instrument, or the right instrument for you as a player.

BUYING A PIANO

When you decide to buy from a showroom, don't be afraid to haggle. If you don't look as though you would buy the instrument anyway, you might be able to persuade them to throw in a stool for free. Remember, a piano stool is *only* worth having if you can adjust the height. Check that delivery and the first tuning (after the piano arrives) are included in the price. There should also be a service guarantee, entitling you to free maintenance from a technician if problems develop within an initial period.

You may also consider renting instead of buying, though this is not usually good value for money in the longer term. Remember, a piano is one of the few investments that can last for a lifetime, so take your time to make sure you are getting exactly what you want.

MAINTAINING YOUR PIANO

You should arrange for your piano to be tuned regularly by a professional tuner, between two and four times a year, depending on how heavily the instrument gets used. Your instrument will also need to be retuned after any move to a new home or building. A good tuner will also alert you to any other emerging problems that he might not be able to fix on site.

Beware of damp and central heating. Humidity (the moisture level in the atmosphere) is always an issue with pianos. There are many small wooden parts and felts involved in piano actions that can swell with damp to the point where they cease to work smoothly. Equally, central heating can dry the instrument out to the point where the wood will crack. If the piano is placed close to a heater, or is exposed to bright sunlight, the resulting changes in temperature can also seriously affect tuning stability.

After a while you may find that a certain amount of dirt builds up on the surface of the keys. When you notice this, don't be afraid to wipe them with a cloth, which should be *slightly* dampened with water or milk so that no liquid runs down into the action. Do not use corrosive fluids of any kind. If you look after your piano it will serve you faithfully throughout your life.

GLOSSARY OF MUSICAL TERMS

Abbreviations: esp. = especially; It = Italian; Fr = French; Ger = German; L = Latin.

aber [Ger] but

a cappella [It] unaccompanied (referring to church music)

accent the attacking of a note or chord more strongly for melodic or rhythmic emphasis

accented passing note a note that moves by step between harmony notes, but is itself on the beat, creating a dissonance

accelerando (accel.) [It] gradually getting faster

acciaccatura grace note played very quickly on or just before the beat; written with a diagonal slash (when a single note)

accidental sharp, flat or natural sign placed before a particular note in the music to alter it from the key signature, with that note remaining altered for the remainder of the measure

adagio [It] slow

added-note where the 2nd, 4th, or 6th forms part of a chord without being heard as an extension of the series of 3rds forming the basic triads of tonal music

additive rhythm rhythms whose note lengths are counted in terms of the shortest common subdivision of the notes themselves, rather than through treating the notes themselves as subdivisions of a regular beat (esp. Indian classical music)

ad libitum (ad lib) [L] play freely or not at all

agraffe [Fr] a metal stud or staple through which the piano strings are passed, which improves stability of tuning and tone

Alberti bass rhythmically regular repeated pattern based on notes of a chord, passing from bottom to top, then to middle, then back to top note of the chord again, used as left-hand accompaniment to a melody (esp. classical period music)

aleatoric music music in which the decisions of the composer or performer are replaced by random, chance-based ingredients, such as dice, accidental circumstances, etc. (esp. John Cage)

aliquot [Fr] this refers to the overtone series: aliquot scaling (invented by Blüthner) adds an extra string for each note in the high register that is not struck by hammers and resonates sympathetically to enhance tone

alla breve [It] 2/2 time

allargando [It] broadening out

allegro [It] fast

allegretto [It] quite fast

als [Ger] than

alteration a note incrementally raised or lowered from its original pitch, but still heard as occupying the same functional position in a scale or chord

altered mode jazz scale used to embellish and reharmonise V chords, corresponding to the 7th mode of the jazz minor scale (esp. bebop and modern jazz)

andante [It] leisurely, at a walking pace

andantino [It] slightly faster (or slower) than *Andante*

animando [It] becoming more lively

anticipation a note that sounds just before the harmony it belongs to, and then again with the harmony

appoggiatura [It] a note that sounds on the beat or strong beat as a dissonance, before resolving by step to a consonance on a weaker beat (or subdivision); also, a grace note corresponding to this (written without a slash)

arabesque a rhythmically free melodic figuration, often ornamental or improvisatory in character

arm staccato heavier or more accented staccato, achieved by producing the movement of attack and release by levering with the arm rather than from the wrist or hand or fingers

arpeggiation playing the notes of a chord in rapid succession rather than together, as on the harp

arpeggio [It] similar to an arpeggiation, but with notes played rhythmically to produce a melodic pattern, often as a basis for practising chord fingerings and lateral freedom

arranging adapting a melody or piece of music so that it can be played effectively on other instruments or groups of instruments

articulation how individual notes are played in relation to one another, where this is understood from the point of view of the performer's playing techniques, eg legato, staccato, accents, slurs

assai [It] very, extremely

assez [Fr] enough

attacca [It] go straight on to the next section or movement

a tempo [It] back to the original speed

athematicism music that does not unfold or develop distinguishable musical ideas, but is organised in terms of motives or pitch relations heard in terms of the harmonic textures they give rise to

atonal music music not composed or heard with reference to the tonal (diatonic) system of key relations

augmentation the lengthening of rhythmic values by a consistent ratio, to preserve a rhythmic contour through changed durations

augmented chromatic alteration of an interval that enlarges it by one semitone

augmented sixth chord chord combining the flattened (minor) sixth and sharpened fourth of the same scale

Ausdruck [Ger] expression

ausdrucksvoll [Ger] expressively

authentic performance a controversial approach to the performance of early European classical music, increasingly popular in the last part of the 20th century, attempting to make use of playing styles, techniques and instruments thought to have been in use when the music was originally composed

auxiliary note a note that moves to the note above or below and back again as a melodic embellishment

avant-garde [Fr] those who regard themselves as ahead of the majority in dissolving artistic conventions, discovering new and radical forms, etc.

avant-garde jazz experimental jazz that dispenses with many of the principal features of both traditional jazz and bebop, in favour of unfamiliar harmonic structures rhythms and textures

avec [Fr] with

avoid-note a note in a jazz scale that is considered too dissonant to be played against the underlying chord, and so is either avoided or chromatically altered

baby grand a small grand piano designed for the modern living room

backbeat a strong accent placed consistently on the weak (2nd and 4th) beats of the bar to heighten the sense of rhythm and metre, originating in African music and typical of rock music

ballad a slowish song or song-like composition that tells a story

bar a segment of music enclosed between adjacent bar lines for purposes of measurement and identification, also called a measure, and usually corresponding to a metrical cycle

bar line a line drawn vertically across the stave or staves to indicate the end of one bar and the beginning of the next

baroque classical music from the late 17th and early 18th century 'Enlightenment' period in Europe, often characterised by elaborate decoration or contrapuntal unfolding

bass clef the symbol placed at the start of a line of music to indicate that the note on the fourth line is the F below middle C: the normal clef for the left hand part in piano music (also called 'F clef')

bass line a melody line formed by the succession of notes lying at the bottom of a harmonic texture or chord sequence, possibly with melodic embellishment (usually of a stepwise character) or some rhythmic elaboration

beat a measure of musical time corresponding to a single count of the basic pulse or metre, or a point in a bar where such a measure begins (as defined by the pulse or metre)

bebop an approach to jazz that emerged in the 1940s, led by Charlie Parker and (later) Miles Davis, featuring free improvisation with scales and melodic figures derived from the chords (themselves often altered) of a well-known song

bebop scale a scale that adds one chromatic passing note to the usual 7-note scales of jazz to produce a scale that allows complex melodic sequences to retain a regular rhythmic relationship to chords

ben, bene [It] well, very

bewegt [Ger] with movement, agitated

bhangra dance music derived from a fusion of traditional Indian folk elements and modern urban dance grooves

bis [It] twice

bitonality music that implies two distinct keys at the same time, usually in distinct parts of a texture: used in modern classical music and post-bebop jazz

block chords harmonising a melody line with all parts moving in similar motion to preserve the same chord shape (classical) or to move between inversions of the same chord in alternation with diminished 7ths (see *four-way close*) (jazz)

blue-note a melodic scale-note corresponding to the flattened 3rd, 5th or 7th of a chord, clashing with major-key harmony to produce the out-of-tune (major-minor) character typical of Afro-American blues

blues a genre of Afro-American folk and popular song in 4/4 time originating in the narrative songs of black slaves in the southern states of America; popularised in the early 20th century, then influenced by jazz and the use of electrified instruments and leading to R&B, soul, and urban blues

blues scale a minor pentatonic scale with the addition of the flattened 5th

boogie-woogie blues based solo piano style with repetitive left-hand rhythmic figures, influenced by the pounding style of piano playing typical of 19th century American bars and barrelhouses

bop short for 'bebop'

borrowed chord a chord introduced into major-key classical harmony that is taken from minor-key harmony with the same key note, or vice versa

bossa nova a Latin-American dance-based song idiom with a relaxed feel, using syncopated rhythms drawn freely from a repeating rhythmic pattern related to the *clave* patterns of salsa; first associated with the music of the Brazilian composer Jobim

boudoir grand a medium-sized grand piano, larger than a baby grand but smaller than a concert grand

break a point in jazz where one player is given free reign by other musicians to improvise as a soloist

break-beat rhythm highly syncopated, irregular, and repetitive rhythmic grooves typical of drum tracks used in contemporary dance music

breit [Ger] broad

bridge the contrasting chords of the middle 'B' section in jazz song form, usually linking the earlier A sections with a final repeat before recapitulating the song as a whole

brillante [It] brilliant

brio [It] vigour

broken chord a classical pattern in which the notes of a chord are stated melodically in ascending or descending order in groups of three or four, each beginning on the next note of the same chord; also used as an exercise for chord fingerings and technique

cadence a chord progression used at the end of a phrase, section, or movement to generate a stronger or weaker sense of completion and finality through degrees of tonal harmonic resolution

cadential six-four a chord progression in which a second inversion tonic chord resolves downwards by step to a dominant chord in root position over a dominant bass, forming an imperfect cadence

cadenza a soloistic passage, usually in a classical concerto or operatic aria and originally improvised, in which the soloist performs music of a more improvisatory character, often with little or no accompaniment

Cajun accordion-based style folk-dance music from southwest Louisiana, with Creole, French and Anglo-Saxon elements

calando [It] getting slower and softer, dying away

call and response alternating juxtaposition of musical ideas, often corresponding to soloist and group respectively, typically found in African drumming, Afro-American work songs, and popular musical idioms influenced by these

canon a piece of music whose principal formal feature is the imitative relationship between different melodic voices or parts

cantabile [It] in a singing style

cáscara repeated rhythmic pattern played on a cymbal or the side of a drum in Brasilian salsa

casework the decorative designs featured on the exteriors of earlier keyboard instruments

cédez [Fr] relax the speed

chamber music classical music composed for small ensembles, suited to performance in the more intimate environment of private residences

Chicago jazz a style of jazz that developed in the twenties, associated with stride and Dixieland jazz bands, often with collective and then solo improvisations, together with horn riffs

chops punchy individual chords used to punctuate the texture of heavier rock piano styles

chord a grouping of three or more notes of different pitch based on the effect of sounding them together, and treated as a functional unit

chord chart a chart indicating only the chord changes and metre of a song, used by jazz and popular musicians as a basis for their own arrangements or for improvisation

chord extension the inclusion of further notes as part of a chord in addition to the root, 3rd and 5th, usually by continuing the principle of accumulating ascending 3rds.

chord function the identity that a chord has as part of a larger functional system of relations between chords (and, traditionally, keys); typically the system is that of western major-minor tonality, itself often equated with the term 'functional harmony'

chord inversion the particular layout of the notes of a chord, defined in terms of which note is placed at the bottom

chord layout the choice of vertical ordering and spacing of the notes of a chord on some particular occasion

chord progression a distinctive succession of two or more chords whose musical effect reflects their functional relationship

chord substitution a chord that is typically substituted for another with a closely related function to add variety to the harmony

chord type the particular spacing of notes in a

chord that characterises chords based on certain notes of a scale but not others: e.g. major, minor, augmented or diminished triads, and major, dominant, half-diminished or diminished 7ths, etc.

chord voicing the particular layout of the notes in a jazz chord, in respect of spacing, register, vertical ordering, notes doubled or omitted, viewed in terms of the harmonic character, colour or texture that results

chromatic based on the chromatic scale of 12 semitone steps, or on adjustments of another a scale by a semitone

chromatic alterations the practice of raising or lowering the pitch of a note by a semitone in such a way that it is heard as an altered form of the existing scale-degree

chromatic harmony chords, chord progressions and key relationships based on chromatic alterations of ordinary tonal harmony, or derived directly from the chromatic scale itself

circle of fifths the arrangement of key centres in western tonal music to show how the successive additions of sharps or flats needed to reproduce major and minor scales and harmony on different notes produces a sequence in which adjacent keys are separated by an interval of a perfect 5th

classical music western art music traditionally composed in Europe or America to be listened to in the concert hall, opera house, or church, or at courtly occasions

clave a repeated and syncopated rhythmic 2-bar pattern from which the principal rhythms of Afro-Cuban salsa music are derived, alternating a 3-note pattern in one bar with a 2-note pattern in the other (as 3+2 or 2+3)

clavichord early European keyboard instrument that, like the piano, uses hammers to strike the strings, in contrast to plucked keyboard instruments such as the harpsichord, virginals and spinet

clavier a general term used in early classical music to refer to keyboard instruments generally, principally in German-speaking countries

clef symbol placed at the start of a stave to show which position on that stave corresponds to the letter name of note from which the symbol is derived

clenched-hand staccato a sudden clenching of the hand that draws all fingers off the keys at once for a sharp, accented staccato

close position the layout of notes in a chord that puts them in the closest possible vicinity to one another

coda a short additional section added to the end of a movement or work, serving to bring it to a close

codetta a small coda

col [It] with

Coltrane changes a technique of chord reharmonisation used in bebop and post-bebop jazz, that has the effect of introducing direct movements between chords in keys a major or minor 3rd apart

'comping short for 'accompanying' – the art of improvising a rhythmic, chordal accompaniment as background to a solo line in jazz

compound time time-signatures that indicate a metre in which the normal subdivision of the beat is into three rather than two, notated using dotted beats instead of triplet subdivisions

con [It] with

concert grand a large grand piano designed to be played in a concert hall

concerto [It] a work for one or more soloists accompanied by an orchestra

conjunct interval an interval whose size falls within the limits of what can easily be heard or sung as part of a continuous melody line

consonance an interval between two notes sounding together with an internally resolved character

continuo [It] a baroque term for a part performed on a keyboard instrument, usually the harpsichord, whose main purpose is to fill out the harmony implied by the *figured bass*

contour the shape produced by the rise and fall of a melodic line over time, normally reflecting its rhythmical character

contrapuntal music whose character and unfolding is chiefly defined by the use of counterpoint

contrary motion where two parts or voices move melodically in opposite directions, or where the two hands of the pianist move in opposite directions

cool jazz a west coast jazz style popular in the 1950s, featuring elements of bebop and swing in arrangements with dissonances often softened and rhythmic accents smoothed out

corda, corde [It] string, strings

counterpoint music that unfolds as two or more simultaneous and independently heard melody lines, rhythmically complementing one another and often unfolding related material at different times

country a range of popular American musical styles that reflect common origins in the simple songs and twangy sound of traditional rural folk performers and string-based settler bands from various parts of the United States, especially mountainous and southern regions, and ultimately originating in folk ballads from the British Isles

country rock rock music with a country feel, often using guitar fingerpicking styles typical of country music; also known sometimes as 'L.A. rock'

country shuffle country-based music with a relaxed shuffle beat

couplet two notes performed as a single phrase, with a single movement of the wrist controlling accentuation, legato and release, often lightening and shortening the second note

crescendo, cresc. [It] getting gradually louder

crossover any mixture of two distinct musical traditions, but usually understood to refer to attempts to bridge the gap between western classical and non-classical styles

cross-relation see *false relation*

cross-rhythms two or more rhythms that relate to an underlying pulse in radically different ways, so that they each have to be independently felt

crushed note a grace note performed very quickly or as quickly as possible on or just before the beat on which the main note sounds, also known as an *acciaccatura*, and marked with a diagonal slash through the stem

da [It] from

da capo, D.C. [It] from the beginning

dal segno, D.S. [It] from the sign

dampers blocks of felt that automatically fall back onto the piano strings as soon as keys or the sustaining pedal are released, in order to cut off the tone of the sounding strings

Dämpfer [Ger] mute

Darmstadt School a school of avant-garde modernist composers prominent in the 1950s and 1960s, centred on summer courses held annually in the German town of Darmstadt, associated in its earlier years with total serialism and later with electronic and aleatoric techniques of composing

Dastgah a melodic mode in Persian music that uses a scale constructed from smaller segments, composed of a variety of intervals derived from complex tuning ratios, many of which are not to be found in western music

declamation a style of vocal delivery that lies somewhere between actual singing and emotionally heightened speech, as in blues, often associated with storytelling through music or with religious oratory

decoration the introduction of additional notes into a line for decorative effect, in such a way that the underlying structure of the line continues to be heard, often for a more extravagantly formal or playful character, or to fill gaps created by long notes on early keyboard instruments with limited sustaining power

decrescendo, decresc. [It] getting gradually softer

détaché [Fr] detached

development a continuous process of musical unfolding in which the formal implications of one or more ideas are worked out through subjecting them to a series of transformations

development section typically the middle section of a sonata-form first movement, in which the focus switches from simply presenting musical ideas to more intense forms of musical development, often involving rapid changes of key, leading eventually to a restatement of the original thematic material in the home key

diatonic any harmonic or melodic structure based strictly on notes of the major or minor scales, to the exclusion of structures derived through chromatic alteration or based on the chromatic scale

diatonic harmony harmony using chords whose notes are drawn exclusively from the major or minor scale corresponding to the key of the music

diminished chromatic alteration of an interval

that reduces its size it by a semitone

diminished scale an eight-note ('octatonic') scale based on alternating whole-tone and semitone steps, beginning with either interval

diminuendo, dim. getting gradually softer

diminution the reduction of rhythmic values by a consistent ratio, to preserve a rhythmic contour through changed durations

direct pedalling a technique in which the sustaining (right) pedal is depressed at the start of a note, chord or texture and released at its end, adding resonance and/or volume

disco an upbeat teenage dance music style

disjunct interval an interval whose size falls outside the limits of what can easily be heard or sung as part of a continuous melody line

dissonance an interval between two notes sounding together with an internally unresolved character, produced by the phenomenon of audible acoustic interference known as 'beating'

doch [Ger] however, yet

dolce [It] sweet, soft

dominant the 5th step of a diatonic scale, and the harmonic function corresponding to chords based on this step

dominant pedal a note corresponding to the 5th of the scale, usually in the bass, that is held (or repeated) unchanged as the harmony shifts above it, generating a sense of tension and expectancy

double bar line or **double bar** the use of two adjacent vertical bar lines together at the end of a bar to indicate the end of a section, movement, or piece

double escapement a refinement of the piano action mechanism introduced by Erard, allowing each note to be restruck without the key being fully released, making rapid note repetition possible for the first time

double flat the lowering of a flattened note by an additional semitone, indicated with two flat signs

double sharp the raising of a sharpened note by an additional semitone, indicated with an x

doubling the practice of including more than one note of the same letter name in a chord, in different octaves; also, the sounding of a melody simultaneously in more than one instrument or more than one transposition (usually one or more octaves apart)

douce, doux [Fr] sweet, soft

drop two a variation of the jazz block-chord arranging technique known as *four-way close*, in which the second note from the top in each chord is moved down an octave to form the bass

duet, duo a composition for two solo players

duration the length of a note

dynamics the use of varying levels of loudness by players to enhance the musical effect

e, ed [It] and

early music early European music, dating from periods in which playing techniques are thought to have been significantly different from those normally employed now by classical musicians

égal [Fr] equal

eguale [It] equal

ein [Ger] a

emancipation of dissonance the term coined by Schoenberg to describe the move whereby some modern classical composers cease to regard dissonances as automatically standing in need of harmonic resolution, en route to an abandonment of traditional tonality in favour of atonal composition

embellishment a decorative effect, corresponding in classical music to either stylised musical ornaments (often introduced by the performer) or the compositional filling out of basic voice-leading structures with more complex or flowing melodic movements; in non-western and non-classical music embellishment often takes the form of stylised inflexions of tone colour and tuning, as heard in traditional Indian and Arabic music or in the 'note-bending' of western jazz, rock and folk performers

Empfindung [Ger] emotion, feeling

empfindungsvoll [Ger] with feeling

en animant [Fr] becoming more lively

en cédant [Fr] holding back

encore [Fr] the custom of playing one or more additional short pieces (often unannounced) at the end of a classical concert, in response to an audience's enthusiastic applause

en dehors [Fr] standing out

energico [Fr] energetic

enharmonic equivalence, enharmonic relationship the relationship between two notes having different note-names (e.g. F-sharp, G-flat) but corresponding to the same pitch within the system of equal temperament

enharmonic key relationship a relationship between keys based on an enharmonic equivalence, often used as a basis for modulation between otherwise unrelated keys, typically allowing the music to pass right around the circle of 5ths and arrive back in the key in which it started

enlightenment a historical development dating from late 17th century Europe in which respect for human reason and science first came to dominate at the expense of religion and other cultural traditions

en pressant [Fr] hurrying on

en retenant [Fr] holding back

ensemble [Fr] a group of classical musicians who play together; (literally 'together')

equal temperament the system of tuning used on the modern piano, in which the octave is divided into 12 equal semitone steps so that all keys sound equally in tune, making unlimited modulation possible between keys

escapement the device invented by Cristofori, that enables a piano hammer to be thrown against a string by the playing action in such a way that it then disengages itself ('escapes') from that playing action and is free to rebound from the string when the key remains depressed, leaving the string free to continue sounding

escape note, echappé a note inserted between two notes forming a step or leap, to make a stepwise movement in the opposite direction to

the original interval

espressione [It] expression

espressivo, espress [It] an instruction to play with heightened expressive feeling

et [Fr] and

etwas [Ger] somewhat, rather

exposition the first of the principal sections of a sonata-form first movement, in which the main (usually contrasting) thematic ideas are stated in succession, linked by transitions but usually without intensive development

expressif [Fr] expressive

extended hand position any position in which the hand stretches out to cover more than just five adjacent scale notes on the keyboard

extension see 'chord extension'

fake book a collection of lead sheets for standards, used by jazz musicians

false relation the relation formed between an altered and unaltered form of the same note, when these occur in close temporal proximity to one another in different melodic parts: also called a *cross-relation*, and generally avoided in most classical music

feel a term used to refer to the particular underlying quality of rhythmic movement evoked by different sorts of dance-based or African-influenced music

felts the soft material covering the hammer-heads of a piano action, whose condition can affect the brightness or dullness of the resulting tone

figuration any musical figure that can be more or less freely used for purposes of improvisation or composition

figured bass a shorthand system for notating harmony in baroque continuo (keyboard) parts, allowing the performer some flexibility in how chord progressions are realised

filling out the technique of interspersing additional notes between those that form larger intervals, so the intervals are traversed in a more melodically or harmonically continuous fashion; often used when improvising embellished versions of a melody

finale the last movement of a symphony, sonata or sonata-form work, usually characterised by a fast, flowing tempo, possibly with contrapuntal elaboration and in rondo form

fine [It] end

finger staccato a staccato achieved through use of the finger alone, often to emphatically characterise individual notes

first inversion the arrangement of a chord so that the 3rd of the chord is at the bottom

first-movement form the form most strongly associated with the concept of sonata-form, consisting of an exposition, development section, and recapitulation/reprise, in which contrasting themes are first stated, then transformed (developed), then restated once again.

first subject, first subject group the first theme or group of themes to appear in the exposition of a sonata-form first-movement

flat symbol used to indicate that a white note

should be lowered by one semitone

flutter pedalling a technique in which the pedal is intermittently cleared and immediately re-depressed in a rhythmically free manner in order to regulate the accumulation of tonal resonance and texture over passages of music that would otherwise be sustained with the pedal throughout

forte (f) [It] loud

forte-piano (fp) [It] loud, then immediately soft

fortepiano [It] early form of piano

fortissimo (ff) [It] very loud

forza [It] force

forzato (fz) [It] play with sudden force

fourth chord a chord built on successive intervals of a 4th instead of the more normal 3rd

four-way close a technique for readily arranging block-chords in bebop jazz, that enables all melodic scale notes to be harmonised either as inversions of the same basic chord or (for alternate notes in the scale) as inversions of a single diminished 7th chord; see also *drop two*

free improvisation an approach to creating and performing music typically associated with both avant-garde jazz and classical music, in which the possibilities for unprepared or unrestricted improvisation are explored

free jazz an approach to modern jazz in which players are not constrained by the harmonic or rhythmic norms of traditional jazz or bebop

frei [Ger] free

frequency the speed of oscillation of a sound wave, string, column of air, or membrane

fretted style a style of keyboard playing that imitates the country-style guitar techniques such as finger picking, hammerons, pulloffs, and slides between notes

frisch [Ger] vigorous

fröhlich [Ger] cheerful

fugue a strict form of contrapuntal composition widely used in baroque music, in which parts enter imitatively according to a strict sequence of transpositions, usually unfolding according to formal rules that require a final stretto in which all parts enter separated by a shorter time-delay, leading to a final harmonic resolution

functional harmony usually equated loosely with tonal harmony, but applicable to any system of harmony that produces audible harmonic relationships that reflect their place in the system

funk a syncopated dance feel and related musical style derived from soul and associated with disco, characterised by *halftime* syncopations using divisions of the beat into quarters instead of halves

furioso [It] furious

fusion hybrid musical styles formed through the combination of elements of two or more distinct popular styles, such as jazz-rock or jazz-funk, or even country-rock

genre a particular type of music or music-making within a broader tradition, having its

own more specific formal and expressive conventions, e.g. ballads, suites, caprices

gesangvoll [Ger] in a singing style

geschwind [Ger] quick

get down rock aggressive and driving 4/4 rock style, often using syncopated pounding chords over alternating left hand octaves

giocoso [It] joyful, merry

giusto [It] strict, exact

glissando, gliss. sweeping the back or side of the hand over the keys to produce a rapid scale-like run (literally 'sliding')

goal note the note which we feel a melody or improvised figure as heading towards, in advance of it arriving there

gospel Afro-American style of church-based singing popularised in the mid-20th century, rooted in traditional American hymns and spirituals with a distinctive approach to harmony and rhythm and an emphasis on ecstatic improvised solo singing, influencing *soul* music

grace note any note written smaller than usual to indicate that it should be played freely as a *crushed note* or part of a decorative run, or in strict time as an *appoggiatura*

grand short for *grand piano*

grave [It] very slow, solemn

grazioso [It] graceful

great stave the stave formed by combining bass clef and treble clef staves by drawing the line that passes through middle C, producing a single 11-line stave to illustrate the relation between bass and treble clefs

groove the distinctive rhythmic feel created in rock and popular music through repeating one or more rhythmic patterns at a particular speed, especially on drums and bass

half-diminished scale a jazz scale created from the sixth mode of the jazz minor scale, equivalent to the Locrian mode with raised 2nd and used to harmonise half-diminished chords such as chord II in a minor key

half-pedal the technique of depressing the pedal only halfway, in order to achieve a more limited resonance, or so that higher notes can remain sounding thanks to pedalling while low notes still get damped (due to their larger string size)

halftime a rhythmic idiom or *feel* in popular music (especially *funk*), where syncopations are based on subdivisions of the beat into quarters instead of halves

halftime pop-rock a style of rock piano playing that exploits the effect of intermittently superimposing halftime riffs and figures over normal 4/4 rhythms to generate added tension and movement, as with Elton John

hammer the wooden beater caused to strike the strings of the piano when a key is depressed, in order to produce sounds

hand shape the particular shape that the hands are required to assume to achieve musical playing, normally involving rounded fingers, level knuckles and the thumb curved in slightly towards the hand to sit over the keys

hand staccato staccato achieved through an up-and-down flapping movement of the hand from the wrist, suited to rapidly staccato repetitions and runs

harmonic minor scale the form of the minor scale commonly used in classical music as the basis for minor-key harmony, characterised by a large step between the flattened 6th and the leading tone

harmonic rhythm the rhythmic pattern created by a regular succession of chord changes, creating an impression of a certain speed of harmonic unfolding

harmonization the process of fitting chords to an existing melody

harmony the structures and colours created by the vertical sonorities of chords, and the sense of movement, tension and release generated through arranging them in different successions

harmony note a note in a melody line or melodic part that also belongs to the harmony (the chord) heard as sounding at the same point in time

harpsichord the largest of the early keyboard instruments in which strings are mechanically plucked rather than being struck by hammers, sometimes with two manuals and stops for altering tone quality and dynamics

head a tune created by a jazz musician but subsequently used by other players as a basis for their own improvisations and arrangements

hemiola an effect, common in early music, tied notes or accents are used to make two bars of triple time sound like three bars of double time, usually in preparation for the ending of a section

heterophony a musical texture in which different variants of the same material (often a melody line) are played simultaneously; adopted by some modern classical composers after encountering Far-Eastern and South-East Asian traditional musics

homophony a musical texture in which all parts (or block chords) move together in the same rhythm as the principal melody line

horns a jazz term for saxophones

humanism the tendency in western culture, science and philosophy – prompted by the Renaissance rediscovery of Ancient Greek and Roman civilisation, and reaching its peak with the Enlightenment of the 18th century – to treat the human perspective on the world as an authoritative one, and to value individual human beings for their capacity to form rational insights free of external influences

imitation where one melody line enters in succession after another with the same material, sometimes transposed, as in contrapuntal music

immer [Ger] always

impetuoso [It] impetuous

innig [Ger] heartfelt, sincere

imperfect cadence a cadence ending on the dominant chord, producing a sense of only partial completion lacking in finality

improvisation music-making in which the music is more or less created by the players as they go along

inflection the expressive modulation (continuous alteration) of pitch and/or colour while a note lasts, echoing the intonation and colour of expressive and spoken utterances (sighing, crying, etc.); used in extreme ways in jazz and rock ('note-bending'), and in much ethnic music; an important aspect of classical Indian and Arabic music and Japanese Shakuhachi flute music; generally restricted in western classical music to subtle interpretative effects introduced by the performer along with *vibrato* and *portamento*, on instruments whose sound can be continuously controlled (unlike that of the piano, where the effect can only be simulated as a relationship between successive sounds)

inner parts those parts in a harmonic or polyphonic texture that are neither at the top or bottom of the texture

interpretation the art of presenting a piece of music in performance so that its form and character are heard and appreciated to best effect, or as demanded by the composer

interrupted cadence a cadence that proceeds from the dominant to the submediant chord (instead of the expected tonic), creating a sense of unexpected and only partial resolution

interval the size of the gap between two notes of different pitch, measured in terms of steps of a scale

interval inversion transposing one or other of the two notes of an interval by an octave so that the lower note becomes the higher note and vice versa, resulting in a new interval (known as the 'inversion' of the original one), and which added together with original interval makes an octave

intro introduction

introduction a short additional section placed at the beginning of a composition or improvised performance, setting the scene for what follows

inversion any technique in which the vertical arrangement of pitches is reversed: e.g. the arrangement or position of a chord (viewed in terms of the choice of note to sound at the bottom) arrived at through successively shifting the bottom note to the top, or the technique of replacing each interval in a melody or chord with one of equal size but in the opposite direction; also an interval which combines with some other interval to add up to an octave, and which results when the notes of that interval are switched around so the lower becomes the higher;

irrational rhythm any rhythm that involves dividing the beat into a different number of equal subdivisions from that usually permitted by the time-signature (e.g. triplets, duplets, etc)

irregular metre a musical metre where the time-signature specifies an odd number of beats in a bar (above four), so that regular two beat subgroups are not possible (e.g. 5/4, 7/8, 11/8), or where the length of the beats is not constant throughout the bar

jam, jamming informal improvising sessions used by jazz and popular musicians to develop and exchange musical ideas and 'get to know one another'

jazz a musical style that emerged in the United States in the 1920s, originally centred around New Orleans, in which a virtuosic solo instrumentalist improvises more or less freely over the chord progressions of a song presented by the rest of an ensemble; they keep time in the background, interact with the soloist, and may take turns to improvise solos themselves

jazz minor scale a form of minor scale used in jazz, in which only the 3rd of the major scale is flattened; resembling the ascending form of the classical melodic minor scale, and used as a source of many of the modal chord-types used in advanced jazz reharmonisation and bebop-style improvising

joyeux [Fr] joyful, joyous

just intonation the systematic attempt to use the natural tunings of the harmonic (overtone) series in performance or as a basis for composition

key the set of structural relationships between scale-tones and the chords derived from them, heard primarily in terms of their relations to the note and chord that correspond to the starting note of the scale

key-bed the solid horizontal surface beneath the keys of a piano that prevents them from being depressed further than necessary and allows them to be held down

keyboard the arrangement of black and white keys on a piano or similar instrument

key note the starting note of a scale, whose structural relationships to other notes determines their functional significance; normally heard as a central point of melodic and harmonic resolution

key relationship the relationship between two different keys, principally determined by the distance separating them on the circle of 5ths and the number of notes shared by their respective scales

key signature the custom of specifying the sharps or flats corresponding to the key of the music at the beginning of each stave according to a fixed sequential formula

kräftig [Ger] strong

largo [It] fairly slow

L.A. rock see 'country rock'

langsam [Ger] slow

largamente [I] broadly

larghetto [It] fairly slow

largo [It] slow, stately

lateral movement the technique of swinging the hand around from the arm in a sideways direction while keeping it on the keys, in order to change its angle and cover a different range of notes; often used to execute arpeggios and enhance the expressive shaping of legato phrases

lead the role of principal player or melodic soloist in jazz and popular music

lead sheet a form of written-out music that limits itself to showing the melody line, chord structure, metre and form of a well-known song, for use by jazz and popular musicians

leading tone the 7th step of a diatonic scale, which normally manifests a strong tendency towards resolving upwards melodically by step, to the key note a semitone above

leaning on the beat the deliberate placing of notes just after the beat to create a looser or more downbeat rhythmic feel, common in jazz and blues

lebhaft [Ger] lively

legato [It] joining notes together smoothly – achieved on the piano through a slight overlap between the start of one note and the end of the previous one

legato pedalling the use of the sustaining (right) pedal to achieve a legato join between notes or chords where this would not otherwise be possible, by delaying the release of the pedal until just after the next note or chord sounds, then immediately clearing the pedal so that the previous note or chord is damped

legatissimo [It] very smooth, as *legato* as possible

leggiero [It] lightly

left pedal the soft pedal, often indicated with the phrase *una corda* (literally 'one string') in the music, softens and veils the tone on a grand piano by shifting the hammers slightly to the side, so they no longer strike all the strings, or strike the single strings for low notes centrally; a similar muting effect is achieved on upright pianos, where the left pedal causes the hammers to be temporarily positioned closer to the strings so they gather less momentum before striking them

leger line a small horizontal line, used to create lines and spaces similar to those of the musical stave, that indicates the pitch of individual high or low notes that are positioned off the stave

lent [Fr] slow

lento [It] very slow

lick a brief improvised melodic figure that can be interpolated into the gaps between rhythmic textures or longer phrases of an improvised line, to add tension and interest

lieblich [Ger] lovely

linear groove a rhythmic pattern that distributes a single continuous stream of notes of equal length between the two hands to form two or more independent rhythmic layers; modelled on drumming techniques but adapted to two-handed piano playing, notably by rock pianists

line-up the selection of instruments available within a band in jazz and popular music

live electronics the use of electronic devices, including computers, to modify or react to musical sounds as these unfold in 'real time' in a live performance

locked hands a pianistic technique used in jazz, whereby the hands are allowed to move in parallel through a sequence of block chords, permitting a melody to be harmonised on the spot without having to attend to the details of voice-leading

loco [It] at normal pitch (cancelling an octave

higher or lower sign)
lustig [Ger] cheerful

ma [It] but
maestoso [It] majestic
main [Fr] hand
mais [Fr] but
mano [It] hand
major the principal scale of western European music, composed of two identical 4-note scale-segments (tetrachords), each with two tones followed by a semitone; also the sense of key resulting from this scale, and the chord (triad) consisting of the first, third and fifth notes of the scale
major-minor system the tonal system of major and minor scales and related chords and keys, of traditional western European music
major pentatonic a 5-note scale commonly encountered in folk music around the world (with significant variations of tuning), equivalent to a major scale with the 4th and 7th degrees omitted, or to playing just black keys on a piano, beginning on F-sharp (G flat)
maqam a melodic mode in Arabic music that uses a scale constructed from smaller segments, composed of a variety of intervals derived from complex tuning ratios, many of which are not to be found in western music
marcato, marc. [It] an instruction to mark each note clearly with a slight accent
mässig [Ger] at a moderate speed
measure a segment of music enclosed between adjacent bar lines for purposes of measurement and identification, also called a *bar*, and usually corresponding to a metrical cycle
mediant the 3rd step of a diatonic scale, and the harmonic function corresponding to chords based on this step
melisma the effect created when a singer embellishes a single syllable of a word with a sequence of several pitches or inflectional adjustments
melodic minor scale the form of the minor scale used in classical music to produce smooth stepwise melodic movement between 6th and 7th degrees of the scale, neither of which are flattened from the major when ascending (i.e. they are both sharpened from the minor key-signature), both of which are flattened when descending (i.e. neither are sharpened from the minor key-signature)
meno [It] less
mesto [It] sad
metre the organisation of musical pulse into cyclically recurring regular patterns of stronger and weaker accents, as in spoken verse
mezzo, mezza [It] half
mezzo piano (mp) [It] fairly soft
mezzo forte (mf) [It] fairly loud
mezza voce [It] in an undertone
mezzo staccato [It] a moderate *staccato* in which individual notes retain some length
microtonal music music based on divisions of the octave into more than twelve equal semitone steps (e.g. quarter-tones), or on other intervals involving smaller adjustments of pitch than are used systematically in western music

(e.g. Arabic, Indian and Japanese traditional musics)
minimalism a trendy style of contemporary composition that emerged in America in the 1960s (e.g. Glass, Riley, Reich, Young), based on the gradual shifting in and out of phase of elements in continuously repeated rhythmic and tonal-harmonic patterns, influenced by African music and seen as a precursor of musical postmodernism because of its rejection of structural development, abstraction, and expressionism, in favour of monumentalism and detached irony; also the use of repeated musical fragments to create a sense of frozen bleakness and austere depersonalisation by certain German and Polish composers (Zimmermann, Sikorski) from the 1960s onwards
minor the chief alternative to the major scale in western European music, arrived at by flattening the 3rd and 6th and sometimes the 7th of the scale (see *harmonic minor* and *melodic minor*) to produce a sadder effect that may be evocative of Middle-Eastern music; also the sense of key resulting from this scale, and the chord (triad) consisting of the first, third and fifth notes of the minor scale
minor pentatonic a 5-note scale commonly encountered in folk music around the world (with significant variations of tuning), equivalent to a minor scale with the 2nd and 6th degrees omitted, or to playing just black keys on a piano, beginning on D-sharp (E flat)
minuet and trio a classical form consisting of a relaxed dance (minuet) in simple triple time, followed by a contrasting middle section with a more flowing character (trio), and then to a repeat of the first section
misterioso [It] mysterious
misura [It] measure
mit [Ger] with
modal harmony harmony derived from the notes of a modal scale form rather than from the ordinary major or minor scale, as when classical composers base harmony on modal folk tunes (Vaughan Williams, Bartók, Kodály); also, the technique used in 'bebop' and 'modern jazz' whereby the same voicing functions as a realisation of several different chords, allowing continuous improvisation with the same scale material over a stretch of time that originally corresponded to several chord changes, so that a single chord begins to function like a modal equivalent of a key
modal jazz any type of jazz that employs modal approaches to harmony and related scale-based improvising of the kind typified by *bebop* artists such as Charlie Parker and Miles Davies
mode originally the term used to refer to the various scales used in early European and Byzantine church music, and related scales thought to have been used as the basis for ancient Greek music, from which these probably evolved; also used to refer to these same scales when treated as derivations from a major scale through permutation (i.e. just changing the choice of note on which the scale begins, but keeping the actual notes the same),

or to refer to any scale derived from a more basic form in this fashion
mode of limited transposition a term coined by the French composer Messiaen to refer to scales (e.g. whole-tone and diminished scales) whose structure prevents them from being transposed freely by any interval without in some instances duplicating the collection of pitches contained in the original transposition
moderato [It] at a moderate speed
modéré [Fr] at a moderate speed
modernism a broad artistic movement lasting throughout much of the 20th century, emphasizing the capacity of art to transcend social conventions through formal abstraction and experiment, or through exploring extreme emotional or mystical states
modern jazz experimental jazz from the post-bebop era, in which traditional jazz structures and techniques are often taken to extremes
modulation a change of key achieved through careful introduction of notes and chords belonging to the new key but foreign to the original one, while exploiting notes and chords that can be heard ambiguously as belonging to either key to provide a 'pivot'
moins [Fr] less
molto [It] very, much
monody a musical texture consisting of a single melodic line only, with no simultaneously sounding parts, chords or textures
montuno a syncopated rhythmic and melodic figure repeated over one, two, or four bars in the upper registers of the piano in Afro-Cuban salsa music
mordent an ornament consisting of moving swiftly from the principal note to the note above and back again
morendo [It] dying away
mosso [It] with motion
moto [It] movement
motive a short musical figure or idea, often used as a constituent of more extended themes
mouvement [Fr] movement
mute a device that softens or veils the tonal quality of an instrument and reduces its volume

nach und nach [Ger] gradually
natural a sign (usually an accidental) placed before a note to cancel a sharp or flat occurring earlier in the same bar or in the key-signature
natural minor a version of the minor scale in which the 3rd, 6th and 7th are all flattened from the major scale (as in the minor key signature or descending melodic minor scale), regarded as the basic form in rock-based popular music
Neapolitan sixth chord a major chord constructed on the flattened 2nd degree of the minor scale in classical music, and normally used in first inversion
neo-classicism a musical style typical of 1930s Europe, in which modern classical composers such as Stravinsky incorporated elements of earlier classical styles into their works, often distorted for ironic effect, or to achieve a sense of classical clarity, restraint and detachment

New Orleans jazz early jazz dating from the period of its emergence in 1920s New Orleans

new romanticism a movement of contemporary classical composers in the 1970s and 1980s, seeking to revive the emotionally intense atmosphere of late-romantic Austro-German music

nicht [Ger] not

niente [It] nothing

noch [Ger] still, yet

non [It] not

non-harmony notes a note in a melody line or melodic part that does not belong to the harmony (the chord) heard as sounding at the same point in time

non-legato [It] a pianistic touch between *legato* and *staccato*, in which notes are not joined but each retain enough length not to be heard as staccato

note a particular sound, or a particular pitch or letter-name of note

number a colloquial term for a song in jazz and popular music

nuovo [It] new

oblique motion one part or voice moving melodically while another remains stationary (or repeats the same note)

octave the interval from one note to the next with the same letter-name, which then corresponds to the 8th note of a diatonic scale

odd time the use of irregular time signatures (5/4, 7/8, 11/8, etc.) in jazz or popular music, notably by Dave Brubeck

offbeat a beat of the bar not normally accented as part of the metre, such as the 2nd and 4th beats in 4 time, or 2nd and 3rd in 3 time

off-note any note that does not belong to the scale corresponding to the chord sounding, and which is therefore heard as a departure from the harmony, generating tension within the melody

ohne [Ger] without

open position the layout of notes in a chord so that they are no longer in the closest possible vicinity to one another (usually omitting one possible chord note between each adjacent pair of notes)

ornament, ornamentation a stylised melodic embellishment, often indicated in classical music by a shorthand symbol placed above the note to be decorated

ossia [It] or, alternatively (indicating an easier optional alternative)

ostinato [I] persistent (employed to refer to an insistently repeated figure)

out-of-time when one or more jazz or popular musicians (or even an entire group) temporarily play without making specific reference to a metre or pulse

outside, out when a jazz soloist temporarily moves out of the key of the harmony, resulting in chromatic and polytonal effects

overstrung when the strings of an upright or grand piano are arranged in two groups running diagonally across one another in order to maximise string length relative to the size of the instrument

paradiddle a linear two handed drumming pattern used for performing rapid alternations of notes as in rolls, but giving rise to syncopated rhythmic textures when the hands play the pattern on different instruments, or on different notes or chords on the piano

parallel fifths the effect created when two parts move simultaneously in parallel a perfect 5th apart; avoided in almost all classical music before the 20th century

parallel motion two melodic parts moving melodically in the same direction simultaneously and by the same step or leap

parallel octaves the effect created when two parts move simultaneously in parallel an octave apart; avoided in almost all classical music before the 20th century

parlando [It] speaking

parody an imitation of another musical style, usually with ironical or comic intent

part a single melodic line running through a harmonic or polyphonic texture, often corresponding to a single voice or instrument in an ensemble

part- writing the art of composing harmonic and polyphonic textures so that individual parts unfold smoothly in a melodically satisfying way while also producing satisfying harmonies

passing modulation a brief modulation that fails to establish the new key and so either returns almost immediately to the original one or passes on to another

passing note a non-harmony note moving by step between two harmony notes and sounding off the beat

passing six-four the use of a second inversion chord in between the root position and a first inversion form of another chord, so that a stepwise movement is produced in the bass (e.g. I V^c I^b or I^b V^c I)

passing thumb the technique of passing the thumb under the 3rd or 4th finger of the hand, to create a *legato* join between notes in a scale or melody while also moving the hand into a new position

pastiche [Fr] an imitation of another musical style, usually aimed at making it appear ridiculous

pausa [It] pause

pentatonic scale any 5-note scale, including those created by just using the black notes of the piano

per [It] by, for, through, to

perfect cadence a cadence in which the dominant chord is followed by the tonic, creating a strong sense of finality and harmonic resolution

pesante [It] heavily

peu [Fr] little

phrase a series of notes, usually forming part of a melodic line, joined together or played expressively in some other way, so that they are heard to form a single unbroken musical utterance

phrase structure the sense of an unfolding musical structure corresponding to the divisions articulated between musical phrases, often creating a sense of a developing discourse of musical thoughts

phrasing the art of reflecting the stricture and character of musical phrases through expressive shaping of tone, time and articulation

pianissimo (pp) [It] very soft

piano (p) [It] soft

piano reduction a simplified arrangement for piano of a work for originally composed for several instruments or orchestra

piano roll the paper cylinder with punched holes used to store the information about the music produced by a player piano

pitch the change to the experienced character of a sound that results when its frequency is altered; often understood or felt as a change between locations separated by greater or lesser distances, in terms of height and depth

pitch-class analysis a method for analysing atonal music, especially when not based on 12-tone (serial) technique, based on a systematic study of the relations between all possible sets of up to six notes that are derivable from the chromatic scale

più [It] more

plagal cadence a cadence in which the subdominant chord is followed by the tonic, creating a sense of finality and harmonic resolution that is relaxed in character, like an 'amen'

plainchant early form of liturgical chanting from the Middle Ages, usually consisting of a single modal line sung slowly in unison with no fixed metre; occasionally sung in parallel 5ths or octaves

player piano an automated piano that plays itself using a punched roll to trigger the notes, and driven using bellows operated with foot pedals, or by an electric motor

plus [Fr] more

pochissimo, pochiss. [It] very little

poco [It] slightly, a little

poco a poco [It] gradually

poi [It] then

polyphony a texture composed of several independently unfolding melodic lines

polyrhythm the effect created by superimposing two different rhythms that do not stand in any simple relationship to one another

polytonality the effect created by superimposing musical material in more than one key

pop lowbrow and lightweight popular music intended for easy consumption by young people

postmodernism a term used to describe cultural trends thought to have superseded modernism, especially where these trends themselves reflect a loss of belief in overarching historical tendencies, often leading to an impersonal and ironic celebration of the diversity, confusion and directionlessness of 'postmodern' culture

posture the proper way of sitting at the piano

pounding aggressively repetitive and rhythmic striking of piano chords, typically in rock

practice pedal a third (middle) pedal included

on some upright pianos, which mutes the whole instrument dramatically to reduce the disturbance caused to others by practising

prelude a short piece, often intended to precede a more substantial movement

preparation the technique of moving into position to play a note or chord ahead of the moment when it actually sounds, so that the act of positioning the hand does not interfere with the act of playing the notes

prepared piano the insertion of foreign objects and materials into the sounding mechanism of a piano (normally the strings) in order to generate a variety of unorthodox sounds when it is played; first used by John Cage

presto [It] quick

prestissimo [It] very fast

primary triads those triads in a major key that are major chords (i.e. I, IV and V), and the chords based on similar scale degrees in a minor scale

primo, prima [It] first

programme the particular selection and sequence of pieces to be performed in a concert

projection the phenomenon whereby an action or event reaches beyond the present moment to relate to some future goal, in a manner that determines its character or significance in the present

pulse the sense of temporal pattern and rhythmic involvement resulting from hearing and/or feeling a sound or movement repeated at regular intervals

pushing the beat the deliberate placing of notes just in front of the beat to create a looser or more upbeat rhythmic feel, common in jazz and country

quartal harmony the use of chords built from superimposed intervals of a 4th rather than a 3rd

quartet a piece of music for four musicians, or an ensemble consisting of four musicians

quasi [It] as if

quintet a piece of music for five musicians, or an ensemble consisting of five musicians

raga a scale pattern in classical Indian music that also functions as the basis for a particular character of melodic improvisation, in which certain connections between notes are preferred over others

ragtime, rag a syncopated stride-based piano idiom that evolved in the first decades of the 20th century, combining Afro-American and European musical influences; one of the principal precursors of jazz

ralentir [Fr] slow down

rallentando (rall.) [It] gradually getting slower

rasch [Ger] quick

rascher [Ger] quicker

recapitulation or **reprise** the section in a sonata-form first movement following directly after the development, in which principal ideas are restated along similar lines to their first appearance, usually in the home key

register the general sense of whether a note lies towards the top, bottom or middle of an instrument's compass, as opposed to that note's particular functional significance or letter-name

reharmonisation the technique, principally used in jazz of the bebop and post-bebop eras, of altering the chord structure of a familiar tune or progression so that it furnishes new possibilities for improvised embellishment

relative major the major key related to a minor key through having the same key-signature

relative minor the minor key related to a major key through having the same key-signature

release the sense of forward propulsion created when a syncopated rhythmic or melodic figure lands back on the beat at the start of a new bar or section, chiefly in funk and R&B

Renaissance [Fr] the period in European history characterised by a renewal of interest in classical Greek and Roman culture, prompted by the fall of Constantinople to the Turks in 1492, which caused scholars to flee westward with the knowledge of Ancient classical civilisations preserved in Byzantine culture

resolution the release of tension (and/or sense of completion) created by certain melodic or harmonic progressions

rest a musical sign used to indicate a length of time during which a player does not play

retenu [Fr] held back

retrograde the transformation of a sequence of notes produced by reversing their order of succession, so that the original sequence is in effect heard 'backwards'

retrograde inversion the transformation of a sequence of notes produced by simultaneously reversing their order of succession *and* reversing the ascending or descending direction of each melodic step or leap, so that the original sequence is heard 'backwards' and 'upside down'

rhythm the dynamic sense of shape, energy and movement in time created by the organisation of different time-intervals separating successive notes

rhythm and blues (R&B) an urban blues idiom derived from a combination of blues-based melodic material and pounding rhythms or riffs that anticipate rock'n'roll

rhythmic augmentation the lengthening of rhythmic values by a consistent ratio, to preserve a rhythmic contour through changed durations

rhythmic diminution the reduction of rhythmic values by a consistent ratio, to preserve a rhythmic contour through changed durations

rhythmic unison the effect of two or more separate parts moving together in a single rhythm

ride the continuously flowing stream of regular repeated notes, normally played on a suspended cymbal by the drummer; an element of the rhythmic texture normally created with the drum kit in popular music

riff a repeated and rhythmically distinctive melodic figure in rock, jazz, blues or Latin

right pedal the sustaining pedal

rinforzando, rinforzato, rinf., (rfz) [It] reinforced

ritardando, ritard., rit. [It] gradually getting slower

ritenuto, riten., rit. [It] hold back

ritmico [It] rhythmic

rock a broad term for rock'n'roll and the range of popular styles that emerged from it after 1955

rock-a-boogie rock'n'roll with left-hand boogie-woogie-style shuffle rhythms

rock minor scale another term for the natural minor scale

rock'n'roll a rhythmically thrusting musical style that evolved in America in the mid-1950s, influenced by both Afro-American rhythm & blues and white American country music

rock shuffle rock'n'roll with a shuffle-based rhythm

Romanticism an artistic and cultural movement that dominated Europe from the early 19th century through to the beginning of the 20th century and the start of World War I, emphasising the importance and power of an individual's emotions, and associated with emerging nationalism; in classical music, it led to a preference for richer textures, larger orchestras, more expansive musical gestures and lines, and a more demonstrative style of performance, using more striking expressive nuances and rubato

rondo [It] a form in which two contrasting thematic groups lead to a third contrasting section before being repeated, sometimes in reverse order; commonly used for the finale of a sonata or symphony, but also as a self-contained single-movement composition, chiefly in classical period music

root the note in a chord which is also the scale-note on which the chord itself is built

root position any arrangement of notes in a chord which has the root in the bass

root progression the progression between two or more chords, where this functions primarily as an expression of the relations between the roots of the chords

rotation a technique of rotating the forearm from the elbow, causing the hand to alternate rapidly from side to side, and enabling rapid alternations between notes without straining the hand or wrist

rubato [It] the technique of deliberately holding back or speeding up at points in the music for expressive effect, notably in Romantic music and especially Chopin, heightening the sense of a spontaneous expression of feeling; (literally 'robbed time')

ruhig [Ger] peaceful

rumba clave an alternative form of clave pattern used in salsa

salsa a term coined to describe Afro-Cuban music, in which continuously syncopated Latin-American, Puerto Rican and Cuban folk rhythms and melodies interact with Afro-

American and Creole elements in jazz; usually based on a fixed rhythmic pattern known as a clave

samba a rhythmically exuberant Brazilian dance rhythm with a hypnotically powerful sense of forward propulsion and a two-bar rhythmic pattern moving in and out of syncopation

sans [Fr] without

scale the arrangement of a selection of notes in ascending and/or descending stepwise order as raw material from which melodies and chords can be derived

scherzo [It] a lively, often humorous, instrumental dance-like movement in classical period music; often used by Beethoven in place of a minuet, to produce a more rhythmically animated and dramatic contrast to the trio section

scherzoso [It] playful, joking

schnell [Ger] fast

schneller [Ger] faster

Schneller [Ger] an early term for a short trill played as a mordant

score printed or written-out music for several performers showing all parts together

sec [Fr] crisp, dry

secco [It] crisp, dry

second subject, second subject group the second theme or group of themes to appear in the exposition of a sonata-form first-movement

secondary dominant a chord which functions as a dominant in relation to another chord apart from the tonic

secondary triads those triads in a major key that are not themselves major chords (i.e. II, III, VI and VII), and the chords based on similar scale degrees in a minor scale

second inversion the arrangement of a chord so that the 5th of the chord is at the bottom

segue [It] go straight on

sehr [Ger] very

sempre [It] always

senza [It] without

sequence the repetition of a melodic figure at one or more different transpositions

sequencing the use of computer software and/or MIDI technology to create musical effects without the need for performers

sforzando, sforzato, (sfz) [It] with a sudden accent

shake trill

shaping the expressive control of timing, articulation, tone colour and dynamics to reflect the character and form of a musical phrase

sharp symbol used to indicate that a white note should be raised by one semitone

sheet music all printed or written-out music designed to be used in performance by players, in contrast to scores

short score a condensed form of score in which two or more parts share each stave, enabling it to be read like piano music

short route a reharmonisation device in jazz that makes possible direct movement between distantly related keys, often involving Coltrane changes

shuffle an insistent 12/8 rhythm alternating crotchets (quarter-notes) and quavers (eighth-notes), or equivalent triplet rhythms in 4/4, typical of blues, boogie and rhythm & blues, creating a heavy, dragging feel at a slow tempo

similar motion two (or more) parts (or hands) moving in the same direction, but not necessarily by the same distance (i.e. not necessarily in parallel)

simile, sim. [It] continue in the same manner

slash chord a chord symbol in non-classical music that specifies both the chord and the bass note, to indicate either an inversion or a more complex harmony

slur a curved line drawn above or below a series of notes to indicate that they should be joined smoothly

smorzando [It] dying away

sopra [It] above (used to indicate which hand passes above in crossed-hands playing)

sordino, sord. [It] mute

sostenuto [It] sustained

sotto [It] below (used to indicate which hand passes below in crossed-hands playing)

sounding board the large wooden surface inside a piano, parallel to the strings and responsible for resonance

sourdine [Fr] mute

sous [Fr] under

spectral music a movement in contemporary French music of the 1970s focussing on modelling musical structures and textures on the internal characteristics of sounds as revealed through acoustics, often utilising microtonal tunings based directly on the overtone series

spirituals religious songs associated with Afro-American slaves and an Afro-American singing style, dating back to the hymns of the white American revivalist movement of the 18th century

spread chord when the notes of a chord are played in rapid succession ('arpeggiated') but held and/or released together

soft pedal the left-hand pedal on the piano, which veils and softens the tone ('una corda')

soloing the term for solo melodic improvising in jazz or rock, while other musicians in the group play in the background

son a traditional Cuban dance rhythm from which salsa partly derives

sonata any composition for one instrument with or without piano, usually in several movements, often featuring a sonata-form first movement

sonata form a term developed by musicologists to describe the recurrent formal characteristics of 18th and 19th century instrumental compositions, where these tend towards a certain kind of multi-movement work with a first-movement featuring an exposition, development and recapitulation, usually followed by a slow movement and possibly a dance-like movement, and finishing with a faster finale

sonatina a small sonata, originally with little or nothing in the way of a development section

song form the form commonly used for slow movements in 18th and 19th century

instrumental works, based on strophic alternations of material, as found in many song settings

sostenuto pedal a third (middle) pedal developed and patented by Steinway & Sons, which sustains only those notes held down at the moment when the pedal is depressed, so that others continue to be damped in the normal way when the keys are released; favoured by some contemporary composers and pianists, but not in widespread use

'So What' chord a chord voicing used in jazz, built out of three perfect 4ths and a major 3rd, suited to multi-purpose use in the modal harmony typical of bebop

spinet a small, harpsichord-like keyboard instrument, with mechanically plucked strings running diagonally in relation to the keyboard

staccatissimo [It] as short (*staccato*) as possible

staccato, stacc. [It] a technique for shortening the length of individual notes so that they are no longer joined to one another

stage-presentation the art of behaving on stage in a manner appropriate to the spirit of the musical performance

standard a well-known tune familiar to jazz musicians, whose chords (and melody) are used as a basis for improvising

stave or **staff** the five parallel lines drawn horizontally across the page on which notes are positioned to indicate their pitch in western musical notation

Steinway pedal third (*sostenuto*) pedal

straight ahead rock pounding rock piano groove using even (eighth-note) divisions of the beat

straight-eight boogie pounding rock piano groove using left-hand boogie figures corresponding to even (eighth-note) divisions of the beat

straight-eight New Orleans pounding rock piano groove using even (eighth-note) divisions of the beat and New Orleans style harmonic and melodic elements

stress accent

stretto [It] quickening the speed; also, the overlapping entries of a fugue subject, often in preparation for a final resolution

stride a style of left-hand accompaniment that alternates bass notes and chords in a regular rhythm of 2 or 4 beats in a bar

stringendo [It] gradually getting faster

strophic form any musical form that works by alternating verse and refrain-like sections

subdominant the 4th step of a diatonic scale, and the harmonic function corresponding to chords based on this step

subito, sub. [It] suddenly

subito forte (sf) [It] suddenly loud

subito piano (sp) [It] suddenly soft

subject a musical idea or theme in a sonata-form movement, or a contrapuntal idea in a fugal composition

submediant the 6th step of a diatonic scale, and the harmonic function corresponding to chords based on this step

supertonic the 2nd step of a diatonic scale, and the harmonic function corresponding to chords based on this step

sus chord in rock and popular music, a chord in which the 2nd or 4th is used in place of the 3rd as an unresolved dissonance; in jazz, a chord voicing that merges chord functions II and V, usually by playing the 3rd and 5th and 7th of the II chord (equivalent to the notes of chord IV) over a dominant bass

suspension a note like an appoggiatura, but with the dissonance prepared as a consonance over the previous chord (on a weaker beat) that is held over to the strong beat before resolving by step to a consonance on a weaker beat (or subdivision)

süss [Ger] sweet

sustaining pedal the right-hand pedal, used to lift all the dampers off the strings together so that notes sound freely even after keys are released, giving rise to sympathetic resonance resulting in increased volume and richer, smoother textures

swing a term used to describe the rhythmic feel of jazz that results from repeatedly shifting back the halfway subdivision of the beat so that the rhythm becomes uneven like a triplet, even though it is still written as ordinary equal or dotted-note subdivisions; also 1930s big-band New York style jazz

sympathetic resonance an acoustic phenomenon in which strings, for example, pick up and reinforce vibrations in the air around them without actually being struck

syncopation the classical musical term for a shift of rhythmic emphasis away from the beat and on to a subdivision; now widely used to describe the effect of continuously accenting subdivisions and offbeats in Afro-American influenced music (which is really a distinct phenomenon)

tala complex metrical cycles or 'rhythmic modes' used in improvised classical Indian music

tango an passionately sensual Argentine dance-form in two beats to a bar, whose music has a distinctive dotted rhythm figure with a something of a Spanish character

technique physical dexterity and control, achieved through systematic training, as required to perform successfully on a musical instrument

tempo [It] speed (literally: 'time')

tempo primo [It] return to the speed of the opening

tenuto [It] held

theme an important 'musical idea', usually a melodic motif or phrase

theme and variations a classical form in which a theme is stated, followed by a series of short sections in which the thematic ideas and/or chord structure of the original section are systematically varied, while retaining some sort of recognisable underlying form

third pedal the *sostenuto* pedal

thirdstream a movement in the 1960s in which elements of jazz and modern classical music were combined

tie a curved line drawn between two successive (ie, adjacent) notes of identical pitch, indicating that the first note should be held for the combined duration of both of them

tierce de picardie [Fr] the effect of substituting a major form of the tonic chord as the final cadential resolution of a section or movement in a minor key

timbre the tonal colour or character of a musical sound or instrument

time-signature the two numerals normally placed at the beginning of the first line of a piece of music to show how many beats there are in each bar, and what length of note they correspond to

tonal centre a central point of melodic and harmonic resolution, corresponding to the starting note of a scale, and the chord built upon that note, whose structural relationships to other notes and chords determines their respective functional characteristics

tonal harmony harmony based on a tonal centre of the kind that results when major and minor forms of diatonic scale are used as the source of chords and melodies

tone musical sound

tone colour the tonal character of a musical sound

tone control the art of controlling and subtly adjusting the tonal character of musical sounds to suit the expressive requirements of the music; on the piano the colour of each note is fixed and its volume cannot be altered once it is played, so this is only possible at the level of texture and phrasing, through making the relationship *between* notes evoke characteristics normally associated with individual sounds, and through careful attention to dynamic levels, articulation and pedalling

tonic the 1st step of a diatonic scale, and the harmonic function corresponding to chords based on this step; normally the tonal centre and point of maximum resolution

total serialism a movement in contemporary music dating from the 1950s, in which 12-tone techniques of (row-based) serial organisation were applied to all musical parameters, including pitch, duration, dynamics and articulation, resulting in a highly abstract and fragmented type of atonal music with pointillistic textures

trad jazz traditional jazz in the early styles of the pre-bebop era

tranquillo [It] calm

transcription the art of arranging a piece originally written for one instrument or group of instruments so that it can be played successfully on a different one

transition a musical passage that leads from one thematic idea to another instead of presenting important material in its own right

transposing, transposition altering the pitch of all notes in a phrase or chord by the same interval, so that exactly the same structure reappears higher up or lower down

traurig [Ger] sad

treble clef the symbol placed at the start of a line of music to indicate that the note on the 2nd line is the G above middle C: the normal clef for the right hand part in piano music (also called 'G clef')

tre corde [It] release the left (soft) pedal (literally 'three strings')

tremolando, tremolo, trem. [It] (literally 'trembling'); a rapid regular alternation between two notes separated by more than a step, often played as fast as possible; used for left hand octave accompaniments in classical and rock piano, and as a right hand melodic embellishment in blues, where it simulates the strident, warbling vocalisations of blues singers

très [Fr] very

triad a chord constructed from three different notes

trill a rapid and usually sustained alternation between two notes a step apart, often played as quickly as possible for decorative effect

trio [It] an ensemble of three players, or a flowing middle section following on from a minuet or scherzo in classical music

triplet 'three-in-the-time-of-two': three notes of equal length played in the time normally taken to play two of similar time-value

Tristan chord a distinctive chord featured at the beginning of Wagner's opera *Tristan und Isolde*, displaying many of the characteristics that inspired the development of advanced chromatic harmony in 19th century tonal music

triste [Fr] sad

tritone an alternative name for an interval of an augmented 4th or diminished 5th, reflecting the fact that it corresponds to three successive whole tones

tritone substitution a common jazz reharmonisation technique where one or more of the chords in a II-V-I progression is replaced with the equivalent chord a tritone away

troppo [It] too much

tumbao a rhythmically distinctive bass line figure used in salsa

tuning plank the piece of wood into which tuning pins are driven on a piano

tuning pins the metal pins around which the strings of a piano are coiled at one end in order to hold them in place, and which can be adjusted in order to tune the instrument

tuplets where the normal length of each a group of equal notes is altered by a precise ratio so that they can be fitted into the time normally required to play a different number of similar notes, e.g. triplets, duplets

turn a decorative ornament in classical music which proceeds first to the note above, then to the written note, then to the note below, then back to the written note

turnaround a striking melodic figure used to lead the music back to the start of a repeat, in blues and rock-based styles, especially funk and soul music

tutti [It] all, everyone

twelve-bar blues the basic 12-bar chord sequence of the blues

twelve-tone method the method of atonal composition developed by Schoenberg, in which all notes of the chromatic scale must appear in the sequence prescribed by the row (or its transformations) before any may reappear

two-handed groove a rhythmic pattern or groove that exploits the possibilities afforded by distributing notes between the two hands of a drummer, percussionist or pianist

una corda [It] the muted and veiled effect created by pressing the left pedal on a piano, moving the hammers so they engage less fully or less forcefully with the strings (literally 'one string')

underdamped the term used to describe an upright piano where the dampers operate from behind the strings rather than from the same side as the hammers; a sign of a modern upright

unison the name for 'interval' between two notes in different parts that are of identical pitch

unisono [It] all in unison

upper structure an advanced form of jazz reharmonisation in which a triad is superimposed over one or both of the notes of a tritone interval corresponding to the 3rd and 7th of a V7 chord; the complex resulting harmony can then be conveniently referred to by specifying the distance between the root of the 7th chord and the root of the triad

upright a piano devised for use in the home, in which strings are arranged vertically or diagonally so that they run down to the floor

variation a technique whereby some but not all of the features of some musical material are altered, so that we hear that material as undergoing a change rather than being simply replaced by something else

vibrato [It] a rapid 'vibrating' fluctuation of tonal character, consisting of subtle, oscillating alterations of tuning or dynamics

vif [Fr] lively

virginals a small, harpsichord-like keyboard instrument, with mechanically plucked strings running from one side across to the other (perpendicular to the individual keys)

vite [Fr] quick

vivace, vivo [It] lively

vocal score a score of an opera or oratorio in which vocal parts are written out in full, but instrumental or orchestral material is condensed into a piano reduction for rehearsal purposes

voice a term used in music to refer to one of the melodic parts in a musical texture

voice-leading the art of joining chords in such a way that individual notes in one chord are heard to proceed in a smooth and satisfying melodic fashion to those in the next

voicing the art of arranging notes in a chord in jazz to produce an interesting harmonic sonority

voll [Ger] full

walking bass a melodic bass-line pattern based around a steady rhythm of one note per beat, often outlining notes of the chord or connecting harmony notes by stepwise (diatonic or chromatic) movement; based on the

figures used by string bass players in jazz, and imitated by early jazz pianists in their left-hand parts

waltz a 19th century European dance with three beats to a bar

wenig [Ger] little

whole-tone scale a scale consisting of six identical whole-tone steps

wieder [Ger] again

wrist staccato a leisurely staccato produced by lifting the wrist in such a way that the finger playing a note gets drawn in slightly under the hand to lift it off the key

zart [Ger] tender, delicate

ziemlich [Ger] moderately

zu [Ger] to, too

REPERTOIRE GUIDE

This is divided into three main sections: classical; jazz, Latin, rock and popular; and traditional, world and folk. The classical section is further sub-divided, as detailed in the contents list below. At the end of this repertoire section is a list of the abbreviations used throughout for music publishers.

CONTENTS

CLASSICAL MUSIC

In the case of classical music, the range of published anthologies aimed at students is constantly changing. For this reason, where collections are listed below, these mostly correspond to original groupings of works by the composer. (Original collections of this kind may include pieces with varying levels of difficulty, but will be broadly at the level specified.)

Since most of the classical repertoire is available in various editions, individual publishers are not specified here, except in the case of more modern works (whose copyright is likely to continue to be held by one publisher for the foreseeable future) and anthologies.

With advanced classical playing, choosing the best possible edition can be an important issue. 'Urtext' editions of works by the major Austro-German composers are generally authoritatively researched to remain true to the original autograph manuscript (ie, the handwritten score): the main publishers here are G. Henle Verlag and Wiener Urtext Edition, who also publish many works by major composers of other nationalities.

With other composers, try the larger classical music publishers first (eg, Peters Edition, Universal Edition, Schott, Schirmer, Boosey & Hawkes), since these will have hired distinguished editors to research their editions. Some modern works may have separate European (or British) and American publishers.

RATINGS KEY Recommended works or collections are marked here with one black dot (•), works highly rated by some (but not all) get two dots (••), and undisputed masterpieces of the repertoire get three (•••).

SUPPLEMENTARY EXERCISES AND STUDIES

These are grouped by degree of difficulty.

Easy

Burnam *A Dozen a Day* (Willis)
Joan Last •*At the Keyboard* (Books 1-3) (OUP)

Intermediate

Burgmüller *25 Studies* (Op.100)
Czerny *Studies* (Op.139, Op.353, Op.453, Op.684)
Gurlitt *Studies* (Op.50-3, Op.130-2)
Joan Last •*Freedom Technique* (Books 1-3) (OUP)

Harder

Beringer *Technical Exercises*
Heller *Studies* (Op.45-7) (GS)
Tankard & Harrison •*Pianoforte Technique on an Hour a Day* (Elkin)

Advanced

Brahms *51 Technical Exercises* (GS)
Chopin •*Studies Op.10 & Op.25*
Clementi *Gradus*
Cramer-Bülow •*Studies*
Czerny *100 Progressive Studies* (Op.139) (GS)
School of Velocity (Op.299) (PE)
Études de Mécanisme (Op.849) (PE)
Hanon •*The Piano Virtuoso* (PE)
Lyapunov *Études d'Execution Transcendente*
Liszt *Études d'Execution Transcendente*
Phillipp •*Ecole des Arpèges*
Pischna *Technical Studies*
Safonov *Technical Exercises*

ANTHOLOGIES OF STUDENT PIECES

These are grouped by geographical area, preceded by a general list.

General

The Joy of First Classics, Vols 1-2 (Yorktown) (ed. Denes Agay)
The Joy of Modern Recital Repertory for Young Pianists (Yorktown) (ed. Denes Agay)
At the Piano with Women Composers (ALF) (ed. Hinson)
The Century of Invention: Piano Music of the 20th Century (EAMC) (ed. Hinson)
Piano Album: Composers of the 20th Century Collection (Sal/GS)

American

19th Century American Piano Music (Dover) (ed. Gillespie)
20th Century Americans (Associated)
20th Century Americans (GS)
7 Americans – Compositions by Contemporary American Composers (NK) (ed. Banowetz)
12 American Preludes, Vols 1-2 (CF)
12 x 11: Piano Music in 20th Century America (ALF) (ed. Hinson)
American Composers of the 20th Century (SCH) (ed. Schaum)
American Composers of Today (EBM)
American Sonatinas (SCH)

Anthology of Art Songs by Black American Composers (GS) (ed. Patterson)
Black Women Composers: A Century of Piano music (Hildegard)
Changing Faces (EAMC) (ed. Hinson) [works by American composers]
Masters of American Piano Music (ALF) (ed. Hinson) [works by 19th & 20th century composers]
Northwest Passages (Permanent Press) (ed. Beale)
Piano Music in 19th Century America, Vols 1-2 (ALF) (ed. Hinson)
Polka Book (SCH)
Masters of Our Day (CF) [Works by Copland, Cowell, etc.]
Sousa's Famous Marches for Piano Solo (TP) [arr. Levine]
Women Composers of the United States (SCH)

Argentine

Música Viva (Rio de Janeiro)

British

Spectrum (ABRSM)

Canadian

Meet Canadian Composers at the Piano (WC)

Chinese

Chinese Contemporary Piano Pieces

Danish

10 Piano Pieces for Educational Purposes (SUDM) [Various modern composers]
Crisscross, for Piano (WH) (ed. Charlotte Schiøtz) [Various modern composers]

Eastern Europe

Souvenirs for Piano: New Works from Russia and Eastern Europe (FHM)

Finnish

Finnish Piano Pieces (TP) (Fazer)

Hungarian

Easy Piano Pieces by Hungarian Composers (B&H) (ed. Vaczi)
Hungarian Piano Music (B&H) (ed. Szavai)
Piano Works by Hungarian Composersi (B&H)
Small Easy Piano Pieces by Hungarian Composers (B&H)

Jamaican

The Reggae Songbook (MS)

Latin America

Best Known Latin Songs (HL)
Big Book of Latin Songs (HL)
Contemporary Latin Songs (HL)
Latin American Anthology of Music (Rio de Janeiro)
Latin American Art Music (GS)
Popular Latin Teaching Pieces (HH) (ed. Brimhall)
Salsa and Afro-Cuban Styles for Piano (ADG) (ed. Campos)

Russian (& former USSR)

Berlin *From Russia for Youth* (FHM)
Feofanov *Russian Piano Music* (CF)

Children's Piano Pieces by Soviet Composers (B&H)
Contemporary Russian Composers (GS)
Masters of Russian Piano Music (ALF) (ed. Hinson)
Modern Russian Piano Music (Wil)
Play Romantic Russia (Faber/GS)
The Russian Romantics (GS)
19th and 20th Century Russian Pianists' Repertoire (GS)

Scandinavian

Open Sea: Scandinavian Contemporary Music for Beginner Piano Students (NMF) [Various contemporary composers]

Spanish

Masters of Spanish Piano Music (ALF) (ed. Hinson)
Spanish Music for Piano (MB) (ed. Castle)
Spanish Music from the Old and New Worlds (Associated/GS)
Spanish Piano Music (B&H) (ed. Balla)
Spanish Piano Music for the Young Musician (B&H)

CLASSICAL FOR STUDENTS: EASY TO INTERMEDIATE

These are grouped by period, and within that by geographical area.

Early English

Selections from *The Fitzwilliam Virginal Book, Musick's Hand-maid I (1663)* and *Musick's Hand-maid II (1689)*

Early European

Anthologies of early Dutch, French, German, Italian and Spanish keyboard music

Baroque English

Purcell •*Marches, Minuets, Hornpipes,* •*Rigadoons:* in C, in D minor, •*Sarabande in D*

Baroque French

Daquin *La Réjouissance* (plain version)
Rameau *Menuet en Rondeau* (and other menuets)

Baroque German

C.P.E. Bach •*23 Pièces Characteristiques,* •*Fantasia in D minor* (Wq.117/12)
J.C. Bach *Musical Leisure Hours*
J.S. Bach •••*Notebook for Anna Magdalena Bach,* •*18 Little Preludes & Fugues,* •*6 Short Preludes,* •*Clavierbüchlein for W.F.Bach,* •*Minuets:* in G, in D minor, •*2 Polonaises in G minor*
W.F. Bach *Air in A minor*

Baroque Italian

Frescobaldi *Corrente*
Paradies *Presto in B-flat*
D. Scarlatti •*Sonatas:* in D minor ('Aria') (Kp.32), C minor (Kp.40), E minor (Kp.81), in A (Kp.453)

Classical Czech
Dussek 6 *Sonatinas* (Op.19)

Classical English
Attwood *Sonatinas*
Wesley *12 Sonatinas* (Op.4)

Classical German (and Austrian)
Beethoven •6 *Sonatinas*, •13 *Ländlers*,
  •*Ecossaises*, •*Minuets*, •*Sonata in G minor*,
  Op.49 No.1, ••*Sonata in G*, Op.49 No.2
Haydn •*German Dances* (Hob. IX), *Sonata in D*
  (Hob.XVI/37): *Finale*
Kirnberger *Dances*
L. Mozart *Notebook for Nannerl*
W.A. Mozart ••*6 Minuets, Allegro in B-flat*
  (K.3)
Schubert ••*German Dances* (D.972), *Ländlers,*
  Ecossaises

Classical Italian
Clementi •*Sonatinas*, *Pieces from An*
  Introduction to the Art of Playing the Piano
  (Op.42)
Diabelli *First Piano Lessons* (Op.125)

Romantic American
MacDowell *Forgotten Fairy Tales* (Op.4)
  Marionettes (Op.38)

Romantic Argentine
Aguirre *Aires Criollos* (Ric), *Gato* (Ric)

Romantic Czech
Dvořák *Grandfather Dances with Grandmother*
Novak *All Hudebni Matice* ('Youth' for children)
  (Op.55)
Petyrek *Suite (11 Little Children's Pieces)*
Smetana *Trésor des Mélodies*

Romantic Danish
Gade *Canzonette, Romanza & Barcarolle* (from
  Aquareller, Op.19)
Kuhlau *Sonatinas*
Lange-Müller *7 Forest Pieces*
Nielsen *5 Pieces* (Op.3), *Humorous Bagatelles*
  (Op.11), •*Piano Music for Big and Small*
  (Op.53)

Romantic Dutch
Röntgen *Old Dutch Songs Transcribed* (Op.51)

Romantic French
Godard *Studies for Children* (Op.149)
Gounod ••*Les Pifferari (The Italian Pipers)*
Grovlez *Fancies (7 Children's Pieces), A Child's*
  Garden
Le Couppey *The Alphabet* (Op.17), *ABC of the*
  Piano

Romantic German (and Austrian)
Burgmüller *25 Studies* (Op.100)
Gurlitt *Album for the Young* (Op.140), *Pieces*
  (Op.179), *Melodious Little Studies* (Op.187),
  The Friend of the Family (Op.197), *Little*
  Flowers (Op.205)
Hässler *50 Pieces for Beginners* (Op.38)
Heller *Studies* (Op.44-7)

Hofmann *Sketches* (Op.77)
Jensen *Wanderbilder* (Op.17)
Kirchner *New Scenes of Childhood* (Op.55),
  Miniatures (Op.62)
Loeschhorn *48 Progressive Studies for Beginners*
  (Op.65)
Mendelssohn •*Children's Pieces* (Op.72)
Reinecke *Sonatinas, A New Notebook, Fairy*
  Tales, Unsere Lieblinge
Schumann •••*Album for the Young* (Op.68),
  Sketches for Album for the Young
Volkmann *Grandmother's Songs* (Op.27)
Wohlfahrt *Piano Method for Children*

Romantic Italian
Bossi *Children's Pieces*

Romantic Norwegian
Backer-Grøndahl *Fantasy Pieces* (Op.39)
  (Forberg)
Grieg *Poetic Tone Pictures* (Op.3), •••*Lyric Pieces*
  (Op.12)

Romantic Polish
Janotha *Mazurkas* (Willcocks/Bosworth)
Scharwenka *Polish Dance* (GS/Br & H/CF)

Romantic Russian
Bortikievich *Marionettes*
Gedike *Pieces* (Book 1) (Op.36)
Glière *12 Pieces for Children* (Op.31), *24*
  Characteristic Pieces for Young People (Op.34),
  8 Easy Pieces (Op.43)
Glinka *Mazurka in C, Polka*
Gretchaninov *5 Little Pieces* (Op.3), *Historiettes*
  (Op.18), *4 Mazurkas* (Op.53), *8 Pastels*
  (Op.61), *Children's Book* (Op.98), *Glass Beads*
  (Op.123), *5 Miniatures* (Op.196)
Karganov *Album for the Young* (Op.25)
Rebikov *Among Themselves*
Tchaikovsky •••*Album for the Young* (Op.39)

Romantic Spanish
De Falla *Ritual Fire Dance* (JWC)
Granados *Escenas Poéticas Libro de Horas* (UME),
  6 Expressive Studies (UME)
Turina *Danzas Gitanas*, Set I (Sal/GS),
  Miniatures (Schott), *Préludes* (Heu)

Modern American
A.Beach *From Six to Twelve* (Ditson)
Copland *2 Children's Pieces* (CF)
Cowell *The Snows of Fuji-Yama* (AMP)
Griffes *Pieces for Children* (HL) [trad. song
  arrangements]
F.B.Price *3 Little Negro Dances* (TP),
  3 Little Sketches for Little Pianists (TP),
  Variations on a Folk Song (CPE), *At the Cotton*
  Gin (GS), *Cabin Song* (TP)
Schickele *Hollers, Hymns and Dirges* (TP), *Three*
  Folk Settings (EV)

Modern Argentine
Castro *Pequeña Marcha* (PIC)
García-Morillo *Cuentos para Niños Traviesos*
  (Ric)
Gianneo *Cinco Pequeñas Piezas* (ESC), *Música*
  para Niños (PIC), *7 Children's Pieces* (PIC), *3*

Argentine Dances (PIC), *Villancico* (EAM)
Ginastera *Piezas Infantiles* (GS), *Rondo* (Op.19)
  (B&H)
Villoud *Provincianas* (Southern)

Modern Australian
Grainger *The Young Pianist's Grainger*
  (Schott/GS)
Hanson *On Holidays* (Op.1) (CPE)
Penberthy *Aboriginal Song Cycle* (CPE)
Sculthorpe *Landscape* (CPE), *Left Back Waltz*
  (Allans)

Modern Belgian
Absil *6 Bulgarian Dances* (Lemoine)
Peeters *Tango (10 Bagatelles)* (Op.88) CFP •

Modern Brazilian
Fernandez *Children's Visions* (PIC), *Yaya, the*
  Doll (PIC)
Guarneri *Acalanto* (Ric), *As Tres Gracas* (Ric),
  Little Horse with the Broken Leg (AMP), *Maria*
  Lucia (Music Press), *5 Children's Pieces* (Ric),
  Ficarós Sosinha (Music Press)
Mahle *As Melodias da Cecilia* (Vitale), *As*
  Músicas da Cecilia (Ric)
Mignone *Crianças Brincando* (EBM), *Miudinho*
  (EBM), *Quasi Modinha* (EBM)
Pinto *Children's Festival* (GS)
Schmidt *Toada II* (Vitale)
Villa-Lobos *The Toy Wheel* (PIC), *Cirandinhas*
  (Eschig), *Francette et Piá* (ESC), *Petizada*
  (PIC), *10 Pieces on Popular Folk Tunes of*
  Brazil (Mer)
Widmer *Ludus Brasiliensis* (Op.37) Vols.1-2 (Ric)

Modern Chilean
Orrego-Salas *10 Simple Pieces* (Op.31) (Barry)

Modern Chinese
Yip *Memories of Childhood*

Modern Cuban
Ardévol *6 Pieces* (Southern)
Caturla *Un Canto de Cuna Campestre* (CF)
Hernández-Gonzalo *4 Cubanas* (CPE), *Pequeña*
  Suite (CPE)
Lecuona *Danzas Afro-Cubanas* (EBM/GS), *Suite*
  Espagnole (EBM/HL)

Modern Cypriot
Fuleihan *Harvest Chant* (PIC)

Modern Czech
Kabeláč *16 Easy Preludes* (GS)
Kodály *For Children*, Vols.1 & 2, *Children's*
  Dances
Kováts *Slavic Romanticism* (B&H)
Takács *Indian Summer*

Modern Danish
Bentzon *Woodcuts* (WH)
Henriques *Picture Book* (WH)
Ring *The Clever Pianist* (WH)
Tarp *Suite*

Modern Dutch
Badings *Arcadia*

Modern English/British

Alwyn *Suites*
Bennett *Diversions*
Dunhill *First Year Pieces, In Varying Moods, Studies* (Op.74)
Howells *A Little Book of Dances*
Ireland *Leaves from a Child's Sketchbook*
Swinstead *Work and Play* (ABRSM)
Williamson *Piano impressions of New York* (EBM)

Modern French

Koechlin *10 Petites Pièces Faciles* (Op.61)
Martin *Après la Classe* (Dur)
Milhaud *Accueil Amical*
Plé *Les Chants et les Jeux*
Satie *Children's Pieces, Le Piccadilly* (Sal)

Modern German (and Austrian)

Sarauer *To Children*
Toch *Echoes of a Small Town* (Op.49) (AMP), *Pictures of a Small Town* (Op.49) (EAMC)

Modern Hungarian

Agay *Sonatina Hungarica* (MCA/B&H), *2 Improvisations on Hungarian Folk Songs* (TP)
Bartók ••*For Children*, Vols.1 & 2 (B&H), ••*Mikrokosmos*, Vols.1-4 (B&H), •*10 Easy Piano Pieces* (B&H), •*Rumanian Christmas Carols* (B&H), •*First Term at the Piano/Young People at the Piano* (B&H)
Durko *Dwarfs and Giants* (EMB)
Farkas *5 Easy Piano Pieces Based on Hungarian Folk Songs* (B&H)
Kadosa *3 Small Pieces* (B&H), *12 Small Pieces for Children* (B&H)
Károlyi *24 Pieces for Children* (EMB)
Kodály •*12 Little Pieces* (B&H), •*Gyermektáncok* (B&H), •*24 Little Canons on the Black Keys* (B&H)
Kurtag *Games* (164 Miniatures) (EMB)
Ránki *7 Easy Pieces on Melodies from Vietnam* (B&H)
Sugár *Hungarian Children's Songs* (B&H)
Szelényi *Faraway Regions* (FHM)
Takács *From Far and Wide* (Op.37) (UE), *From Far Away Places* (EAMC), *From Far Off Lands and People* (EAMC), *Little Sonate* (Dob)
Weiner *Hungarian Folk Music* (30 Miniatures) (B&H), *3 Hungarian Rural Dances* (EMB/B&H)

Modern Italian

Casella *11 Pieces for Children*

Modern Japanese

Kurokami *Lyric Pieces for Children* (Zen-On), *Wild Flowers* (Zen-On)
Matsudaira *Koromoi-uta* (SZ), *Piano Pieces for Children* (Ongaku-No-Tomo-Sha)
Nakada *Piano Pieces for Little Hands* (Ongaku-No-Tomo-Sha)
Sukegawa *2 Pieces from 'Little Poems of Four Seasons'* (Zen-On)
Yuyama *Children's Land* (Ongaku-No-Tomo-Sha)

Modern Mexican

Jiménez *Pastels* (PS)

Ponce *20 Easy Pieces for Piano* (PIC)

Modern Nigerian

Bakole *Nigerian Suite* (Chap)

Modern Polish

Baird *Little Suite for Children* (PWM)
Ekier *Melodies in Colour* (PWM)
Garscia *Favorite Tunes* (PWM), *Sonatinas* (PWM)
Garztecka *Polish Dances* (PWM)
Lachowska *Polish Polonaises* (PWM)
Lutoslawski *Popular Folk Melodies for Piano* (PWM)
Rybicki *Folk Songs* (Op.46) (PWM)
Szymanowski *Some Polish Songs* (PWM)
Tansman *10 Diversions for the Young Pianist* (AMP), *Pour Les Enfants, Children at Play* (Leeds)

Modern Rumanian

Dragoi *Little Suite of Rumanian Folk Dances* (Simrock)

Modern Russian (and former USSR)

Kabalevsky ••*30 Pieces for Children* (Op.27) (MCA/GS/B&H), *4 Little Pieces* (Op.14) (MCA), *5 Easy Sets of Variations* (Op.51) (MCA), *24 Little Pieces for Children* (Op.39) (ALF/GS/B&H)
Karganov *Album for the Young* (Op.25) (ABRSM)
Khatchaturian *Adventures of Ivan* (MCA/GS), *Album for the Young* (Palmer-Alfred)
Maikapar *Various pieces*
Prokofiev •*Music for Children* (Op.65) (B&H/GS/ALF)
Shostakovitch •*6 Children's Pieces, Sonatinas*
Stravinsky *Les Cinq Doigts*

Modern Spanish

Albéniz *Yvonne en Visite, Malagueña*
Mompou *Fêtes Lointaines* (Sal), *4 Préludes* (Heu)

Modern Swedish

Karkoff *In Front of the Castle* (Geh)

CLASSICAL FOR STUDENTS: INTERMEDIATE TO DIFFICULT

These are grouped by period, and within that by geographical area.

Early English

Selections from *The Fitzwilliam Virginal Book, Musick's Hand-maid I* (1663) and *Musick's Hand-maid II* (1689)

Early European

Anthologies of early Dutch, French, German, Italian and Spanish keyboard music

Baroque English

Arne *Sonatas*
Purcell *Suites*

Baroque French

Couperin •*Pièces de Clavecin*

Daquin ••*Le Coucou, Suites*
Loeillet *Keyboard Pieces*
Rameau •*Le Tambourin, Livres de Pièces de Clavecin*

Baroque German

J.S. Bach •••*6 Partitas*, •••*2 and 3 Part Inventions*, ••*6 English Suites* (selected movts.), ••*6 French Suites* (selected movts.)
C.P.E.Bach •*Presto in C minor* (Wq.114/3), •*Sonata in C* (Wq.55/1): 3rd movt, •*Sonata in F minor* (Wq.57/6): 2nd movt.
J.C.Bach *Sonata in B-flat* (Op.17 No.6), *Musical Studies*
Handel ••*The Harmonious Blacksmith*, •*8 Great Suites*
Telemann *Fantasias*

Baroque Italian

Cimarosa *Sonatas*
Paradies •*Toccata, Sonatas*
D. Scarlatti ••*Sonatas*: in C minor (Kp.11), in F-sharp minor (Kp.25), in F-sharp minor (Kp.67), in G minor (Kp.102), in E-flat (Kp.123), in G (Kp.169), in C (Kp.200), in D (Kp.278), in A (Kp.342), in D (Kp.389), in G (Kp.427), in D (Kp.511), in A (Kp.537)

Baroque Spanish

Soler •*Fandango*

Classical German (and Austrian)

Beethoven •*Sonata in F minor* (Op.2 No.1): 1st/2nd movts., •••*Sonata in C minor* (Op.13 "Pathétique"): 2nd/3rd movts., ••*Sonata in E* (Op.14 No.1), ••*Sonata in C-sharp minor* (Op.27 No.2 "Moonlight"): 1st/2nd movts., •*Sonata in E-flat* (Op.31 No.3): 3rd movt, •••*Sonata in A* (Op.101): 1st movt, ••*Bagatelles*: Op.33, Op.119, Op.126
Haydn •*Sonata in D* (Hob.XVI/14): 3rd movt., •*Sonata in E* (Hob.XVI/31), •*Sonata in E minor* (Hob.XVI/34): 1st movt., •*Sonata in D* (Hob.XVI/37): 1st movt., •*Sonata in E-flat* (Hob.XVI/48), •*Sonata in C* (Hob.XVI/50), Hummel: *Rondo in E-flat*
Mozart •••*Fantasy in D minor* (K.397), •••*Rondo in A minor* (K 511), •••*Sonata No.11 in A* (K331), •••*Sonata No.13 in B-flat* (K 333), •••*Sonata No.16 in C* (K 545), •••*Sonata No.17 in B-flat* (K 570)
Schubert •*Waltzes*, *Sonata in D-flat* (D.567), •••*Sonata No.13 in A* (D.664), •••*Moments Musicaux* (D.780), •••*4 Impromptus* (D.899), •••*4 Impromptus* (D.935)

Classical Italian

Clementi •*Sonatinas*
Diabelli *Sonatinas*

Romantic American

Gottschalk *Bamboula* (Op.2), *Le Banjo, le Bananier, La Savane, La Scintilla, etc.*
MacDowell *Modern Suites, Fancies, Poems, 10 Woodland Sketches* (Op.51), *8 Sea Pieces* (Op.55), *6 Fireside Tales* (Op.61), *10 New England Idylls* (Op.62)

Romantic Argentine
Aguirre *Huella* (Ric), *Argentine National Airs:*
   Vol.1 (*Tristes*), Vol.2 (*Canciónes*) (Ric)

Romantic Czech
Dvořák *13 Poetic Tone Pictures* (Op.85), 8
   Humoresques (Op.101)
Nowak *Sonatinas*
Petyrek *24 Ukrainian Folk Songs, 6 Grotesque
   Piano Pieces, 6 Greek Rhapsodies*
Smetana •*Souvenir* (Op.4 No.3), •*Polkas, 3
   Wedding Scenes, 6 Bohemian Dances, Czech
   Dances* (Vols.1-2)
Vomácka *Intermezzi, Sonata*
Vycpálek *En passant*

Romantic Danish
Kuhlau *Cinq Valses*

Romantic English
Elgar *2 Piano Pieces*

Romantic French
Chabrier *10 Pièces Pittoresques*
Chausson *Paysage, Quelques Danses*
D'Indy *Tableaux de Voyage* (Op.33)
Dukas *Sonata*
Fauré •*Barcarolle No.4 in A-flat* (Op.44)
Franck Pieces from *L'Organiste*
Grovlez *L'Almanach aux Images, 3 Pieces, 3
   Romantic Waltzes, Fancies*
Saint-Saëns •*6 Studies for Left Hand*

Romantic Finnish
Palmgren *Finnish Lullaby, 5 Sketches from
   Finland, The Sea, Pieces*

Romantic German (and Austrian)
Brahms •••*Waltzes* (Op.39)
Bruch *6 Piano Pieces* (Op.12)
Henselt *Spring Song* (Op.15), *Toccatina* (Op.25),
   Lost Illusions (Op.34)
Mendelssohn •••*Songs Without Words:* Op.30,
   Op.38, Op.53, Op.62, Op.67, Op.85,
   Op.102
Schumann •••*Kinderscenen* (Op.15),
   •••*Waldscenen* (Op.82), •••*Warum* (from *3
   Fantasy Pieces*) (Op.12 No.3)

Romantic Hungarian
Liszt •*Consolations,* •*Valse Oubliée No.1, 4 Small
   Piano Pieces*

Romantic Irish
Field •*Nocturne No.4 in A,* •*Nocturne No.16 in F*

Romantic Norwegian
Grieg ••*Lyric Pieces* (Op.71)
Sinding *Rustles of Spring* (Op.32 No.3)

Romantic Polish
Chopin •••*Mazurkas:* in B-flat (Op.7 No.1), in
   A minor (Op.17 No.4), in G minor (Op.24
   No.1), in B minor (Op.33/4), in F (Op.68
   No.3), •••*Waltzes:* in E-flat (Op.18), in A
   minor (Op.34 No.2), in C-sharp minor
   (Op.64 No.2), in A-flat (Op.69 No.1),
   •••*Préludes* (Op.28): No.7 in A, No.6 in B

minor, No.20 in C minor, No.15 in D-flat,
   Nocturne in G minor (Op.15 No.3),
   •••*Funeral March* from *Sonata in B-flat minor*
   (Op.35 No.2)
Moszkowski *20 Melodic Studies* (Op.91)
Tansman *Modern Studies on Polish Folk Songs* (*20
   Easy Pieces*)

Romantic Russian
Gedike *Pieces* (Book 2) (Op.36)
Glière *Sketches* (Op.17), *Preludes* (Op.30)
Medtner ••*Romantic Sketches for the Young*
   (Op.54)
Mussorgsky *In the Country*
Tchaikowsky •*12 Pieces* (Op.40), *Dumka*
   (Op.59)
Tcherepnin *Polka, Rondo à la Russe, Sonatinas,
   Slavonic Transcriptions* (Heu)

Romantic Spanish
Albéniz •*Navarra, Alhambra Suite, Songs of
   Spain, España, Travel Impressions, Spanish
   Dances, Spanish Suite*
Esplá *La Pájara Pinta* (UME), *Lyrica Española*
   (UME)
De Falla •*The Three Cornered Hat* (transcription
   for solo piano) (JWC), *Homenaje* (JWC), *Life
   is Short* (UME), *Pièces Espagnoles* (Dur/TP), *2
   Spanish Dances:* No.1 (TP)
Granados *Stories for the Young* (Op.1), *Spanish
   Dances* (Vols.1-4)
Infante *Gitanerías* (Sal), *Pochades Andalouses*
   (Gregh), *El Vito* (Sal)
Jonás *Spanish Concert Waltz* (CF)
Turina *Suite Pittoresque-Sevilla* (Op.2) (Schott),
   Sonata Romantica (Op.3) (ESC), *Coins de
   Séville* (Op.5) (Schott), *Travel Impressions*
   (Op.15) (IMC/K/UME), *Femmes d'Espagne
   (Mujeres Españolas)* (Op.17) (Sal), *Cuentos de
   España* (Op.20) (Sal), *Danzas Fantásticas*
   (Imaginary Dances) (Op.22) (UME), *Sanlúcar
   de Barrameda* (Sonata) (Op.24), *El Barrio de
   Santa Cruz* (Op.33) (Sal), *Silhouettes* (Op.70)
   (Sal), *Préludes* (Op.80) (Heu), *Danzas
   Gitanas,* Set II (Op.84) (Sal/GS), *Femmes de
   Seville* (Op.89) (Sal/GS)

Romantic Venezuelan
Carreño *Selected Works* (De Capo)

Modern American
Barber *Excursions* (GS), *Souvenirs* (GS)
Copland *Piano Album* (B&H), *Down a Country
   Lane* (B&H), *Fanfare for the Common Man*
   (B&H), *El Salón México* (B&H), *Fantasía
   Mexicana* (B&H)
Cowell *Amerind Suite* (Shawness Press), *Piano
   Works (Vol.1)* (AMP), *6 Ings* (AMP)
Harris *American Ballads* (CF), *Little Suite for
   Piano* (GS), *Streets of Laredo* (CF), *Suite for
   Piano* (Mills)
Harrison *Reel – Hommage to Henry Cowell* (ALF)
Hovhaness *2 Ghazals* (Op.36) (PE), *Mazert
   Nman Rehani* (Op.38) (PE), *Haikus* (Op.113)
   (PE), *Sonatina* (Op.120), *Madras Sonata*
   (Op.176) (PE), *Shalimar* (Op.177) (PE),
   Bardo Sonata (Op.192) (PE), *Komachi*
   (Op.240) (PE), *Ananda Sonata* (Op.303)

(Fujihara Music), *To Hiroshige's Cat* (Op.336)
   (Fujihara Music), *Sonata* (Op.346) (Fujihara
   Music)
Nancarrow *Study No.3* (Soundings Press)
Persichetti *Parable for Piano* (Op.124)
Schikele *3 Piano Sonatinas* (EV)
V.Thompson *Suites* (GS), *10 Etudes for Piano*
   (CF)
Yardumian *Chromatic Sonata* (EV)

Modern Argentine
J.J.Castro *5 Tangos* (PIC)
W.Castro *4 Pieces on Children's Themes* (PIC)
Ficher *5 Songs Without Words* (Op.1) (Ric), *3
   Dances* (PIC), *Sonatas* (EAM)
García-Morillo *Tres Piezas* (Op.2) (Ric),
   •*Conjuros* (Op.3) (ECIC), *Sonata del Sur*
   (Op.4) (EAM)
Gianneo *Sonatas* (CF/Ric), *Sonatina* (PIC)
Ginastera *Estancia* (B&H), *Tribute to Aaron
   Copland* (CF), *Argentine Dances* (Op.2)
   (Dur/TP), *Tres Piezas* (Op.6), *Malambo*
   (Op.7) (Ric), •*12 American Preludes* (Op.12)
   (CF), *Suite de Danzas Criollas* (Op.15) (B&H)
Guastavino *10 Preludes* (Ric), *3 Sonatinas* (Ric)
Paz *10 Pieces on a 12-Tone Row* (Op.30)
   (Ediciones Musicales Politonia), *At the Coast
   of Paraná* (CF), *Canciones y Baladas* (Rio de
   Janeiro)
Villoud *Tres Piezas* (Ric)

Modern Australia
Sculthorpe *Mountains* (Faber), *Night Pieces*
   (Faber), *Sonatina* (Leeds)

Modern Bolivian
Mendozo-Nava *Gitana* (BB), *3 Bolivian Dances*
   (Rongwen)

Modern Brazilian
Bosmans *Lusitanas* (Irmaos Vitale)
Carvalho *Brazilian Dancing Tune* (Ric)
Corrêa *Contrasting Variations on a Popular Theme*
   (Ric), *Variations on Theme of Cana-Fita* (Ric)
Fernandez *3 Brazilian Suites* (IC)
Guarneri *Ponteios* (Vols 1-5) (Ric), *Dances*
   (AMP/Ric), *Improviso I* (Ric), *Lundú* (Ric),
   Sonatinas (AMP/Ric), *Toada* (K)
Lacerda *Brasilianas* (Vitale), *Ponteios* (Ric), *Suite
   Miniatura* (Ric)
Mahle *Sonatina* (Ric)
Mignone *Congada* (EBM/Ric), *Lenda Brasiliera*
   (EBM), *6 Preludes* (Ric), *4 Sonatinas* (Ric),
   Brasilian Tango (EBM)
Nazareth *25 Brazilian Tangos* (EAMC), *Ciclos
   Nordestinos* (Vitale)
Nogueira *9 Brasilian Dances* (Ric)
Peixe *Tropical Preludes* (Vitale), *Sonatinas* (SDM)
Pinto *Negro Dance* (GS)
Santoro *2 Brasilian Dances* (PIC), *Frevo* (Ric), *7
   Sao Paolo Dances* (Vitale), *Sonatas* (Ric)
Vianna *7 Miniatures on Brasilian Themes* (Vitale)
Villa-Lobos *Choros No.5* (ESC/EMB/TP),
   Amazonas (ESC), *As Três Marias* (CF),
   Bachianas Brasileiras No.4 (Consolidated
   Music), *The Broken Little Music Box*
   (Consolidated Music), *Carnaval das Crianças
   Brasileiras* (Napoleão), *Ciclo Brasiliero*

(Consolidated Music), *Cirandas* (Napoleão), *Guia Prático* (Consolidated/ESC/Mer/Southern), *A Lenda do Cabocla* (Napoleão), *Poema Singelo* (Consolidated Music), *Prole do Bébé*, Series I (The Baby's Dolls) (EBM/ESC/K), *Prole do Bébé*, Series II (The Little Animals) (ESC), *Brazilian Forest Memories* (ESC/TP), *Suite Floral* (Op.97) (Consolidated Music)

Widmer *Ludus Brasiliensis* (Op.37) Vols.3-5 (Ric)

Modern Chilean
Allende *12 Tonadas* (Sal)
Lavín *Suite Andine* (ESC)
Orrego-Salas *Variations and Fugue on a Street Cry* (Hargail)
Riesco *Semblenzas Chileñas* (PIC)
Santa Cruz *Imagenes Infantiles* (PIC), *5 Tragic Poems* (Casa Amarilla), *4 Viñetas* (Casa Amarilla)

Modern Chinese
Lam *Uncle Suite* (Op.5) (VPAD Corp.)
Sheng *My Song* (GS)

Modern Columbian
Escobar *Sonatine* (PAU)

Modern Cuban
Caturla *Dos Danzas Cubanas* (Sal), *La Número 3* (Arrow Pr., Havana)
Cervantes •*Danzas Cubanas* (Hansen), *6 Cuban Dances* (GS), *3 Dances* (JWC), *2 Dances* (JWC)
Farinas *Sones Sencillos* (*Tonos*)
Lecuona •*Malagueña* (Marks/GS), *19th Century Cuban Dances* (EBM), *Danzas Afro-Cubanas* (EBM/GS), *Andalucia Suite* (Marks/GS), *Granada* (Marks)
Nin-Culmell *3 Impressions* (Sal), *12 Cuban Dances* (TP)

Modern Cypriot
Fuleihan *Cypriana* (PIC), *From The Aegean* (PIC), *Sonatinas* (MCA)

Modern Czech
Janáček •••*On an Overgrown Path* (Books 1 & 2) (Artia), •*12 Moravian Dances* (Ric)
Kodály *Pieces* (Op.11)
Martinu *Spring in the Garden, Études & Polkas* (B&H), *Butterflies and Birds of Paradise* (Ars Polona), *Borová: 7 Czech Dances* (Leduc), *2 Dances* (Artia)

Modern Danish
Bentzon *7 Small Piano Pieces* (Op.3)
Olsen *6 Small Piano Pieces* (Op.5)
Rasmussen *My Spring Diary* (Vol.1, Duets; Vol.2, Solo Pieces)
Riisager *A Cheerful Trumpet and Other Piano Pieces*

Modern Dutch
De Leeuw *Men Go Their Ways* (Don)
Pijper *Sonatine No.3* (OUP)

Modern English/British
Benjamin *Jamaican Rumba* (B&H)
Bridge *3 Improvisations for Left Hand*
Howells *Sonatina*
Ireland *Greenways, Sonatina, Decorations, London Pieces*
Rawsthorne *4 Romantic Pieces*
Richardson *Sonatina in F*
Ridout *Dance Bagatelles* (Thames)
Roxburgh *Les Miroirs de Miró* (UMP)
Warlock *Folk-song Preludes*
Williamson *Travel Diaries*

Modern Finnish
Rautavaara *Icons* (*Ikonit*) (Frazer), *Fiddles/Folk Musicians* (*Pelimannit*) (Frazer)

Modern French
Absil *Humoresques* (Op.126)
Debussy *The Little Negro* (Dur), *Pour Le Piano* (Dur), *Claire de Lune* (*Suite Bergamasque*) (Dur), •••*Children's Corner* (Dur), ••*Deux Arabesques* (Dur), •••*La Fille aux Cheveux de Lin, Des Pas sur la Niége, La Cathédrale Engloutie, Minstrels,* (*Préludes*, Book 1) (Dur), •••*Bruyères* (*Préludes*, Book 2) (Dur),
Ibert *Petite Suite*
Milhaud *The Globetrotter Suite, La Libertadora* (Ahn & Simrock), *4 Sketches* (Merc)
Poulenc *Mouvements Perpétuels, Suite pour Piano*
Ravel ••*Le Tombeau de Couperin,* •••*Sonatine*
Satie •••*3 Gymnopédies* (Sal), •*6 Gnossiennes* (Sal), *Sports et Divertissements* (Sal), *Pieces in the Form of a Pear* (Sal)

Modern German (and Austrian)
Bloch *Enfantines*
Hindemith *Ludus Tonalis* (Schott)
Krenek *12 Short Piano Pieces* (Op.83), *George Washington Variations* (PIC)
Reger *Traume am Kamin* (Op.143)
Schoenberg •••*6 Little Pieces* (Op.19) (UE)

Modern Greek
Constantinidis *Greek Miniatures* (Vols 1-2) (Rongwen)
Skalkottas *Music for Piano Solo* (UE)

Modern Guatemalan
Herrarte *3 Dances* (PAU), *6 Sketches* (EV)
Ley *Danza Exótica* (PIC), *Danza Fántastica* (EBM)
Marroquin *Chapiniana* (PIC)

Modern Hungarian
Bartók •••*Mikrokosmos,* Vols.5-6 (B&H), ••*6 Rumanian Folk Dances* (B&H), *14 Bagatelles* (Op.6) (K/Dover), *2 Elegies* (Op.8) (Schott/K/B&H), *4 Dirges* (Op.9), *3 Hungarian Folk Tunes* (B&H), *15 Hungarian Peasant Songs and Dances* (UE/B&H), *Improvisations on Hungarian Folk Tunes* (Op.20) (B&H), *3 Popular Hungarian Songs* (K), *3 Rondos on Folk Tunes* (UE/B&H)
Kadosa *55 Small Piano Pieces* (EMB/B&H)
Kodály *9 Pieces* (MCA/K)
Sugár *Baroque Sonatina* (EMB)
Takács *Sonatina* (Dob)

Modern Icelandic
Helgason *Rondo Islanda* (Edition Gigjan), *Sonatas* (Edition Gigjan)

Modern Iranian
Tjeknavorian *Armenian Miniatures* (Ramsey), *Armenian Sketches* (Nov)

Modern Israeli
Ben-Haim *Sonatina* (Op.38) (MCA)
Feigin *Toccata* (IMI)
Haim *6 Israeli Dances* (Leeds Music)

Modern Italian
Casella *Ommagio a Clementi* (Op.35) (Ric)

Modern Jamaican
Russell *3 Jamaican Dances* (Henn)

Modern Japanese
Asakua *Piano-Sonaro* (Eterna/JFC)
Hirai *Sakura-Sakura* (Fantasy for Piano) (EAMC)
Koyama *Kagome Variations* (Zen-On)
Kusagawa *9 Pieces* (JFC)
Matsudaira *Etudes Pour Piano d'Après Modes Japonais* (Zen-On)
Nakada *Time* (Ongaku-No-Tomo-Sha)
Okumura *Dance Impromptu* (Zen-On), *Odori/Sonatine* (Ongaku-No-Tomo-Sha), *Prelude to Three Flowers* (Zen-On)
Tsukitani *Sakura Sakura, Edo Komoriuta, etc.* (6 Pieces) (CPE)
Yuasa *Chant pour 'Do'* (Zen-On)
Yuyama *Sunday Sonatina* (Ongaku-No-Tomo-Sha)

Modern Mexican
Chávez *Early Piano Pieces* (Carlanita/GS), *7 Pieces for Piano* (NME), *10 Preludes* (GS), *Waltzes and Other Dances for Piano* (Carlanita/GS)
Galindo-Dimas *Siete Piezas* (Ediciones Mexicanas)
Hernández-Moncada *Cinco Piezas Bailables* (PIC), *Costeña* (PIC)
Ponce *Elegia de la Ausencia* (PIC), *4 Mexican Dances* (PIC), *Tema Mexicano Variado* (PIC)

Modern New Zealand
Whitehead *Voices of Tane* (Price Milburn)

Modern Norwegian
Egge *Draumkvede Sonate* (EMH), *Gukkoslatten* (Lyche)
Kvandal *Tre Slätterfantasier* (Op.31) (NMF)
Saeverud *Tide Rhythm* (NMF)

Modern Panamanian
Cordero *Sonatina Rítmica* (PIC)

Modern Peruvian
Holzmann *Cuarta Pequeña Suite* (ECIC), *Sonatina sobre Motivos del Folklore Peruviano* (PS)
Sas *Aires y Danzas indios del Peru* (Lemoine), *Arrulo y Tondero* (Op.39) (EV), *Himno y Danza* (GS), *Melodía y Aire Variado* (PIC), *Preludio y Toccata* (PIC), *Suite Peruana* (A La Flute de Pan)

Modern Polish

Baird *Sonatinas* (PWM)
Lutoslawski *Bucolics* (PWM), *Folk Melodies for Piano* (PWM)
Maciejewski *4 Mazurkas* (PWM)
Szymanowski •*Krakowiak* (PWM), *20 Mazurkas* (Op.50) (UE/PWM/EAMC)

Modern Puerto-Rican

Campos-Parsi *Sonata G* (PAU)

Modern Rumanian

Mihalovici *Chanson, Pastorale et Danse* (Sal), *4 Caprices* (ESC)

Modern Russian

Kabalevsky •*24 Preludes*
Khatchaturian *Two Pieces* (MCA/PE/K), *Pictures of Childhood*
Liadov •*Prelude in the Dorian Mode* (Op.11 No.2), *Preludes*, •*Birioulki*
Prokofiev *Sarcasms* (Op.17), •••*Visions Fugitives* (Op.22) (B&H), *Tales of an Old Grandmother* (Op.31) (B&H)
Rachmaninoff •*Preludes*: in C-sharp minor (Op.3 No.2), in F (Op.32 No.7), in G-sharp minor (Op.32 No.12)
Scriabin *Poème in F-sharp* (Op.32 no.1) (INT)
Shostakovitch *Dances of the Dolls, 24 Preludes* (Op.34)

Modern Serbian (and former Yugoslavian)

Tajcevic *7 Balkan Dances* (Schott/EAMC)

Modern Spanish

Gerhard *Dances from Don Quixote* (B&H)
Mompou •*Impresiones Intimas* (UME), *Canciónes y Danzas* (UME/GS), *Charmes* (ESC), *Pessebres* (UME), *Suburbis* (Sal)
Montsalvatge *3 Divertimentos* (PIC)
Nin *Cadeña de Valses* (ESC), *Canto de Cuña para Huérfanos d'España* (ESC), *Iberian Dance* (ESC), *Message à Claude Debussy* (ESC), *3 Spanish Dances* (ESC)
Rodrigo *Bagatela* (Sal), *4 Pieces* (ESC) *Serenata* (Sal), *Serenata Espanola* (EAMC)
Surinach *3 Spanish Songs and Dances* (PIC)

Modern Swedish

Karkoff *Oriental Pictures* (Geh)

Modern Trinidadian

Hazel Scott *Caribbean Fete*

Modern Turkish

Saygun •*Sonatina* (Op.15) , •*Andolu'dan* (Op.25), •*From Anatolia, 12 Preludes on Aksak Rhythms*

Modern Uraguayan

Pedrell *A Orillas del Duero* (ESC)
Tosar Errecart *Danza Criollas* (BB)

Modern Venezuelan

Aretz de Ramón y Rivera *Sonata* (PAU)
Plaza *Sonatina Venezolana* (GS)

OVERVIEW OF CONCERT REPERTOIRE

These are grouped by period, and within that by geographical area.

Early English

Works by Blow, Bull, Byrd, Clarke, Croft, Farnaby, Gibbons, Greene, Locke, Morley
The Fitzwilliam Virginal Book, Musick's Hand-maid I (1663) and *Musick's Hand-maid II* (1689)

Early French

Works by Chambonnières, Clérambault, Daquin, D'Anglebert, Dagincourt, Dumont, Marchand

Early German

Works by Frohberger, Kuhnau, Scheidt

Early Dutch

Works by Sweelinck

Early Italian

Works by Pasquini, Rossi, Zipoli

Baroque English

Purcell *Toccatas*

Baroque French

Couperin *Harpsichord Suites*, Books 1-4 (Ordres 1-27)
Rameau *Les Indes Galantes, Pièces de Clavecin, Nouvelle Suites de Pièces de Clavecin, Harpsichord Suites, 5 Pièces, La Dauphine*

Baroque German

J.S. Bach •••*48Preludes & Fugues (Das Wohltemperierte Clavier)*, •••*Goldberg Variations, Italian Concerto, Chromatic Fantasia & Fugue in D minor, The Art of Fugue, Toccatas*
C.P.E. Bach •••*Sonatas*, •••*Rondos*
Handel ••*Keyboard Suites*

Baroque Italian

Frescobaldi •*Toccatas*
D. Scarlatti ••*Sonatas*

Baroque Spanish

Soler *Sonatas*

Classical Czech

Dussek •*Sonatas*

Classical English

Pinto •*Sonatas*

German (& Austrian) Classical

Haydn •*39 Sonatas*, •*Variations in Fminor*
Mozart •••*18 Sonatas*, •••*Fantasias, Rondos*
Beethoven •••*32 Sonatas, Eroica Variations* (Op.35), *Diabelli Variations* (Op.120)
Schubert •••*21 Sonatas*, •*Wanderer Fantasy* (D.760)

Classical Hungarian

Hummel *Sonatas, Bagatelles*

Classical Italian

Cimarosa *32 Sonatas*
Clementi *Sonatas*

Romantic American

MacDowell *4 Sonatas, Études*

Romantic Czech

von Dohnányi *Rhapsodies* (Op.11), *Humoresques* (Op.17), ••*Variations on a Hungarian Theme (Roszavölgyi)* (Op.29)
Dvorák *Slavonic Dances* (Vols.1-2) (Op.46), *Slavonic Dances* (Vols.1-2) (Op.72)
Nowacek *Concert Pieces*
Nowak *Sonatinas*
Smetana *Concert Study on the Seashore*
Tomásek •*Pieces*

Romantic Danish

Gade *Foraarstoner* (Op.2), *4 Fantasy Pieces* (Op.41), •*Nye Akwareller* (Op.57)
Nielsen •*Chaconne, 3 Pieces*

Romantic English

Delius *3 Preludes, 5 Pieces*

Romantic French

Alkan *Symphony*, *Études*: Op. 35 & Op.39
Chaminade *Toccata*
D'Indy *Fantaisie*
Dukas *Sonata*
Fauré *3 Romances sans Paroles* (Op.17), *Ballade* (Op.19), *Mazurka* (Op.32), *Theme & Variations* (Op.73), *Improvisations* (Op.84), *9 Préludes* (Op.103), •*Nocturnes*, •*Barcarolles*,
Franck •*Prélude, Aria & Final*, ••*Prélude, Choral & Fugue*
Godard *Études*: Op.42, Op.107, Op.149
Koechlin *L'Ancienne Maison de Campagne*
Roussel *Sonatine, Rustiques, 3 Pieces*
Saint-Saëns *Études* (Op.52)
Séverac *The Song of the Earth, On Holiday*

Romantic Finnish

Sibelius *Kylliki* (Op.41), *10 Pieces* (Op.58), *3 Sonatinas* (Op.63), *5 Sketches* (Op.114)

Romantic German (and Austrian)

Brahms *Piano Sonatas: No.1 in C (Op.1), No.2 in F-sharp minor (Op.2),* •••*No.3 in F minor (Op.5), Variations on a Theme of Schumann* (Op.9), *4 Ballades* (Op.10), •*Variations & Fugue on a Theme of Handel* (Op.24), •*Variations on a Theme of Paganini* (Op.35), •*Waltzes* (Op.39), •*Pieces* (Op.76), •*2 Rhapsodies* (Op.79), •*Hungarian Dances*, •*Fantasias* (Op.116), •••*Intermezzi* (Op.117), •••*6 Pieces* (Op.118), •••*4 Pieces* (Op.119)
Jensen *Sonata* (Op.25), *Études* (Op.32), *Erotikon* (Op.44)
Korngold *Fairy Pictures* (Op.3), *Sonatas*
Kreisler *Transcriptions* (of violin works)
Mendelssohn •*Fantasia in F-sharp minor* (Op.28), *Andante & Rondo Capriccioso*, ••*Variations Serieuses* (Op.54)
Raff *Suites*
Schumann ••*Papillons* (Op.2), ••*Davidsbundlertänze* (Op.6), ••*Carnaval*

(Op.9), ••*Phantasiestücke* (Op.12), •••*Études Symphoniques* (Op.13), •••*Kreisleriana* (Op.16), •••*Fantasy in C* (Op.17), ••*Arabesque* (Op.18), ••*3 Sonatas*

R.Strauss *Sonata*

Tausig *Hungarian Gypsy Melodies, Transcriptions*

Weber *4 Sonatas, Rondo Brillant in Eb, Invitation to the Dance*

Romantic Hungarian

Liszt •••*Sonata in B minor*, •••*Dante Sonata*, •••*2 Concert Studies*, •••*Hungarian Rhapsodies*, •••*Années de Pèlerinage, Harmonies Poétiques et Religieuses, 6 Paganini Études, 3 Lieberstraüme, Valses Oubliées, Totentanz, Études d'Exécution Transcendentale*, •*Mephisto Waltz*, •*Transcriptions*, •*Bagatelle without Tonality*

Moscheles *Studies*: Op.70, Op.95, Op.111, *Preludes* (Op.73)

Romantic Irish

Field •*Nocturnes, Sonatas*

Romantic Norwegian

Grieg •*Lyric Pieces*: Op.12, Op.38, Op.43, Op.47, Op.54, Op.57, Op.62, Op.65, Op.68, Op.71, *Sonata* (Op.7), *Album Leaves* (Op.28), •*Norwegian Dances* (Op.35), •*Holberg Suite* (Op.40), •*Norwegian Folkdances* (Op.66), •••*Norwegian Peasant Dances* (Op.72), *Moods* (Op.73)

Sinding *Pieces, Tone Pictures*

Romantic Polish

Chopin *Sonatas*: No.1 in C minor (Op.4), •••*No.2 in B-flat minor* (Op.35), No.3 in B minor (Op. 58), •••*Nocturnes*: Op.9, Op.15, Op.32, Op.37, Op.48, Op.55, Op.62, •••*Mazurkas*: Op. 6-7, Op.17, Op.24, Op.30, Op.33, Op.41, Op.50, Op.56, Op.59, Op.63, •••*Études*: Op.10 & Op.25, •••*Waltzes*, •••*Polonaises*, •••*4 Ballades*, •••*4 Scherzi*, •••*4 Impromptus*, •••*24 Preludes* (Op.28), •••*Fantasia in F minor* (Op.49), •••*Barcarolle* (Op.60), •••*Fantasie-Impromptu*

Godowsky *Renaissance* (Early music transcriptions), *Miniatures*

Paderewsky *Chants du Voyageur*

Romantic Russian

Arensky ••*Sketches on Forgotten Rhythms*

Balakirev ••*Islamey, Sonata, Au Jardin, Nocturne*

Borodin *Au Couvent*

Bortikievich *Six Pensées Lyriques* (Op.11)

Glazunov *Petite Valse* (Op.36), *Sonatas*

Gretchaninov *Pastels* (Op.61), *In the Meadows* (Op.99), *2 Sonatinas* (Op.110), *3 Pieces* (Op.116)

Liadov *Variations on a Theme of Glinka* (Op.35), *Barcarolle* (Op.44)

Liapounov *Études* (Op.11)

Medtner •*14 Sonatas, Pieces*: Op.20, Op.51, Op.58, *Forgotten Melodies, Set of Variations, Fairy Tales*

Moszkowski *Caprice Espagnole, Pieces*: Op.52, Op.56-8, Op.81, Op.83, Op.86

Mussorgsky •••*Pictures at an Exhibition*

Rubinstein *Études* (Op.23), *Theme & Variations* (Op.88)

Tchaikowsky *Sonata, Pieces*: Op.19, Op.21, Op.37, Op.72, •*Dumka*

Tcherepnin *Bagatelles*

Romantic Spanish

Albéniz ••*Iberia (12 Pieces), Malagueña, Sonatas, Tangos, Seguidillas, etc.*

Arriaga *Estudios*

de Falla •*Andalusian Serenade* (JWC), *Andalusian Fantasy* (JWC)

Granados ••*Goyescas* (Vols.1 & 2), *6 Pieces on Spanish Folk Songs* (UME)

Infante *Sevillana* (Sal)

Iturbi *Pequeña Danza Española* (GS)

Turina *3 Andalusian Dances* (Op.8), *Shoes of a Toreador* (Schott)

Romantic Swedish

Stenhammer *Nights of Late Summer* (Op.33)

Modern American

Barber •••Piano Sonata (GS)

Copland •*Piano Variations* (B&H), *Sonata* (B&H)

Cowell *The Banshee, Rhythmicana* (AMP)

R.Crawford *Preludes* (NME)

Gershwin •••*3 Preludes*

Johnson *Sonata* (Merc)

Ives ••*First Sonata* (PIC), •••*Piano Sonata No.2 ('Concord')* (AMP/GS), *Three Page Sonata* (Merc), *The Anti-Abolitionist Riots* (TP), *Varied Air & Variations, Three Protests* (NME), *Study No.20: Even Durations Unevenly Divided* (Merion), *Study No.21: Some Southpaw Pitching* (TP), *Study No.22*

Joplin *Rags*

Ruggles •*Evocations: 4 Chants for Piano* (AME)

Sessions *3 Sonatas, From My Diary, 5 Pieces*

Slonimsky *51 Minitudes for Piano*

Travis *African Sonata* (Univ. of California Press)

Modern Argentine

Ficher *Sonatas* (EAM)

Ginastera •*Danzas Argentinas* (Dur/TP), *Suite de Danzas Criollas* (B&H), *3 Sonatas* (B&H)

Guastavino *Sonata* (Ric)

Modern Belgian

Fontyn *Le Gong* (PIC)

Modern Brazilian

Guarneri *Choro Torturado* (AMP)

Peixe *Suite II Nordestina* (Ric), *Suite II Paulista* (Ric)

Prado *Primitivo* (Ric)

Villa-Lobos *Rudepoema* (ESC)

Modern Cuban

Ardévol *Sonatas* (Southern)

Caturla *Comparsa* (New Music 10/3)

Lecuona *Danzas Cubanas* (EBM/GS)

Modern Czech

Haba *Suites & Fantasia* for quarter-tone piano

Janáček •••*Sonata (I.X.1905)* (Artia), •*In the Mists* (Hudebni Matice)

Kodály *7 Pieces , Dances of Maroszek* (UE)

Martinu *Esquisses de Dances* (Schott), *3 Czech Dances* (ESC)

Modern Danish

Holmboe *Rumanian Suite* (Viking)

Modern Dutch

Schat *Anathema* (Op.19) (Don.)

Modern English/British

Bax *Sonatas*

Bowen *Sonata*

Bridge *Sonata*

Holst *Toccata, Christmas Day in the Morning*

Ireland *Rhapsody, Sonata, The Darkened Valley*

Lambert *Sonata*

McCabe *Variations* (Op.22) (Nov)

Rubbra *Prelude & Fugue on a Theme by Cyril Scott* (Op.69) (Legnick)

Sorabji *Sonatas*

Tippett *4 Piano Sonatas* (Schott)

Williamson *Haifa Watercolours* (EBM)

Modern French

Alain *Mythologies Japonaises, Togo, Little Rhapsody,*

Auric *Petite Suite*

Debussy •••*Préludes*, Books 1 & 2 (Dur), •••*Estampes* , •••*L'Isle Joyeuse*, •••*Images* (Books 1 & 2), •*Études*, •*Suite Bergamasque*

Dutilleux *Sonata*

Emmanuel *Sonatina No.4*

Honegger •*7 Short Pieces* (Eschig), *3 Pieces, Toccata & Variations*

Jolivet *Mana , Ritual Dances, Sonatas* (Heu)

Messiaen *Vingt regards sur L'Enfant Jésus* (Dur), •*Catalogues d'oiseaux, Cantéyodjaya* (UE), *4 Études* (Dur), *Petites Esquisses d'Oiseaux*

Milhaud •*Saudados do Brazil* (ESC/TP)

Poulenc •*3 Pièces, Soirées de Nazelles, Novelettes*

Ravel •••*Jeux d'Eaux*, •••*Gaspard de la Nuit*, •*Miroirs* (Durand), •*Valses Nobles et Sentimentales*

Schmitt *Les Soirs, Les Ombres, Nuits Romaines*

Modern German (and Austrian)

Berg •••*Sonata in B minor* (Op.1) (UE)

Bloch *Poems of the Sea , Sonata*

Hindemith *3 Sonatas* (Schott)

Jarnach *10 Piano Pieces, Sonatina* (Op.18)

Karg-Elert *Partita*

Krenek *Toccata & Chaconne, Suites, Sonatas*

Reger *Variations & Fugue on a Theme of Bach* (Op.81)

Schoenberg •••*3 Pieces* (Op.11) (UE), *5 Pieces* (Op.23) (UE), *Suite* (Op.25) (WH), *2 Pieces*: Op.33a & Op.33b (UE/Belmont)

Toch *Studies*: Op. 55-9, *Sonata* (Op.47)

Webern •*Variations* (Op.27) (UE), *Early unpublished piano works*

Wellesz *Idylls* (Op.21)

Modern Greek

Skalkottas •*Suite No.4*

Modern Hungarian

Bartók •••*Allegro Barbaro* (B&H), •••*Sonata* (B&H), ••*Suite* (B&H), ••*3 Studies* (B&H), ••*Out of Doors (Suite)* (B&H)

von Dohnányi *Ruralia Hungarica* (EMB/B&H), *6 Piano Pieces* (Lengnick), *Variations on a Hungarian Folk Song* (EMB/B&H)

Dorati *Variations for Piano on a Theme by Bartók* (EMB)

Jemnitz *Sonatas* (EMB)

Kadosa *Al Fresco* (B&H), *Bagatelles* (EMB/B&H), *Capriccios* (B&H), *Folk Song Suite* (EMB), *Rhapsodie* (UE), *Snapshots* (EMB/B&H), *Sonatina on Hungarian Folk Tune* (B&H), *3 Suites* (EMB/B&H)

Kodály *Dances of Galanta* (EAMC), *Dances of Marrrosszek* (UE/EAMC), *7 Piano Pieces* (Op.11) (UE)

Laszlo *Sonatina with Coloured Light* (Op.11)

Modern Israeli

Shulamit *Piano Sonatas* (IMI)

Modern Italian

Busoni ••*6 Elegies*, •*Berceause*, •*5 Sonatinas* (Br & H), •*Fantasia Contrapuntistica* (Br & H), •••*Toccata*, •••*Transcriptions*

Casella *Sonatina* (Ric), *Sinfonia, Arioso & Toccata* (Carisch), *New Pieces*

Dallapiccola *Sonatina Canonica* (SZ)

Malipiero *Omaggi, Autumnal Preludes, 6 Pieces*

Modern Japanese

Takahashi *Chained Hands in Prayer* (Zen-On)

Takata *Preludes* (Ongaku-No-Tomo-Sha)

Yamanouchi *Metamorphosis* (JFC)

Modern Mexican

Chávez *Sonatas* (NME/Colección Arion/Belwin-Mills), *Sonatina*

Modern Nigerian

Euba *Scenes from Traditional Life* (Univ. of Ife Press)

Modern Norwegian

Sommerfeldt *Fables* (Op.10 & Op.15) (NMF)

Tveitt *Dance of the Sun God* (NMF), *50 Hardanger* (NMF)

Modern Polish

Bacewicz •• *Sonata No.2* (PWM)

Paderewski *Chants du Voyageur*

Rózycki *Polish Dances* (Op.37), *Nocturnes, Preludes, Intermezzi*

Szymanowski *3 Sonatas* (UE), *Mazurkas* (UE), *9 Preludes* (Op.1), *4 Études* (Op.4), *Variations on a Polish Folk Song* (Op.10), *Metopes* (Op.29), ••*12 Études* (Op.33) (UE), ••*Masques* (Op.34)

Tansman *Sonatas, Preludes, Impromptus, Le Tour du Monde*

Modern Russian (and former USSR)

Gaigerova *Sonatina on Mongolian Themes* (GS)

Gubaidulina *Sonata* (GS)

Kabalevsky *Sonatas*

Khatchaturian *Toccata* (MCA/PE/K/GS)

Mansurian *Sonata* (GS)

Miaskowsky *4 Sonatas, Bizarreries* (Op.25)

Prokofiev •••*9 Sonatas* (B&H), *Toccata*

Rachmaninoff ••*Pieces: Op.3 & Op.10*, ••*24 Preludes: Op.3 No.2* (in C-sharp minor), *Op.23 & Op.32*, ••*Études Tableaux: Op.33 & Op.39, 3 Sonatas*

Roslavetz •*Compositions, Études*

Scriabin •••*10 Sonatas*, •*Vers La Flamme*, •*Preludes: Op.11, Op.15-17, Op.22, Op.27, Op.31, Op.34-5, Op.37, Op.39, Op.48, Op.67*, •*Études: Op.8, Op.42, Op.65*, •*Poems: Op.32, Op.41, Op.44, Op.69, Op.71*, •*Satanic Poem* (Op.36)

Shostakovitch •••*24 Preludes & Fugues* Op.87, *2 Sonatas*

Stravinsky •••*3 Movements from 'Petrushka'* (B&H), *Sonata* (B&H), *4 Studies, Piano Rag Music , Serenade in D, Tango, Pieces*

Modern Rumanian

Enesco *Suite in Ancient Style* (Enoch), *Romanian Rhapsodies* (PS), *Sonata No.3* (Sal)

Mihalovici *Ricercari*

Modern South African

Van Wyk *Night Music* (Galliard), *4 Piano Pieces* (B&H)

Modern Spanish

Mompou •*Cants Màgics*, •*Canción y Danza* ('Song & Dance'), •*Música Callada* ('Silent Music'), *Charmes, Suburbis, Scènes d'Enfants, Fêtes Lointaines, Variations on a Theme of Chopin*

Modern Swiss

Martin *8 Preludes*

Modern Syrian

Succari •*Syrian Suite* (Jobert)

Modern Turkish

Saygun •*10 Etudes on Aksak Rhythms* (PIC)

Contemporary American

Adams *China Gates* (AMP), *Phrygian Gates* (AMP)

Bolcom *12 Études I* (Merion), *12 New Études* (Marks)

Carter *Piano Sonata* (Mercury), ••*Night Fantasies* (Associated)

Cage *7 Haikus* (PE), *Sonatas and Interludes for Prepared Piano* (PE), *Amores* (PE), *Music for Piano* (PE), *Études Australes* (PE)

Crumb *Makrokosmos* (PE)

Feldman *Last Pieces* (PE)

Martino *Fantasies & Impromptus* (Dantalion), *Pianisssimo* (Dantalion)

Nancarrow ••*Studies for Player Piano*

Rzewski *4 North American Ballades* (Zen-On), *Squares and North American Ballades* (EAMC), *4 Pieces for Piano* (Zen-On), *The People United Will Never Be Defeated* (Zen-On)

Sessions *Third Sonata* (Marks)

Wolff *Hay una Mujer Desaparecida (After Holly Near)* (CFP)

Contemporary Belgian

Pousseur •*Exercises* (SZ), *Miroirs de Votre Faust (Caractères)* (UE), *Apostrophe et 6 Réflexions* (UE)

Contemporary Brazilian

Schmidt *Today, I Myself, Tomorrow the World* (Ric)

Contemporary Cuban

León *Momentum* (LP)

Contemporary Danish

Nørgård *Grooving* (WH)

Contemporary Dutch

De Leeuw *Drie Afrikaanse Études* (Don/TP)

Contemporary English/British

Ferneyhough *Epigrams* (PE), *3 Pieces* (PE), ••*Lemma-Icon-Epigram* (PE)

Finnissy *Folklore* (OUP)

Humphries *Going Down*

Contemporary French

Barraqué •••*Piano Sonata* (Bruzzichelli)

Boulez ••*Piano Sonata No.1* (Amph) , •••*Piano Sonata No.2* (Heu), •*Piano Sonata No.3* (UE)

Contemporary German

Rihm *Piano Pieces* (UE)

Stockhausen ••*Piano Pieces I-XIV* (UE)

Contemporary Greek

Antoniou *Sil-ben (Syllables)* (Gerig)

Xenakis *Herma* (B&H), *Evryali* (Sal), *Mists* (Sal)

Contemporary Hungarian

Durko *Psicogramma* (Kultura)

Kocsár *Improvisations* (EMB)

Ligeti *Études* (Schott)

Contemporary Italian

Berio *Sequenza IV* (UE)

Bussotti *5 Pieces for David Tudor* (UE), *Pour Clavier* (Moeck)

Nono ••*Sofferte Onde Serene* (+ tape) (Ric)

Scelsi *Suite X (Ka)* (GS), *Hispania* (Sal/GS)

Contemporary Japanese

Miyoshi •*Chaînes* (Zen-On)

Moroi *8 Parables* (Ongaku-No-Tomo-Sha)

Takemitsu •*For Away* (Sal), *Les Yeux Clos* (Sal)

Contemporary Korean

Yun *5 Pieces for Piano* (Bote & Bock)

Contemporary Polish

Serocki *Piano Sonata* (PWM), *A Piacere* (PWM)

T. Sikorski ••*Hymnos* (PWM), ••*Eufonia* (PWM)

Szalonek *Preludes* (PWM)

Contemporary Spanish

Pablo *Libro Para el Pianista* (UME)

Contemporary Swedish

Nilsson *Quantitäen* (UE)

PIANO FOUR HANDS

These are grouped by period.

Classical

Beethoven *3 Marches* (Op.45)
Mozart *4 Sonatas, 2 Fantasias, Andante &*
  Variations
Schubert *Fantasy in F minor, Marches*

Romantic

Dvořák *Legends* (Op.59)
Fauré *Dolly Suite*
Schumann *12 Pieces for 4 Hands* (Op.85), *9*
  Characteristic Pieces (Op.109), *The Children's*
  Ball (Op.130)

Modern

Debussy *6 Épigraphs Antiques* (Dur)
Messiaen *Visions de L'Amen*
Ravel *Mother Goose*

Contemporary

Boulez *Structures*, Books 1 & 2 (UE)

JAZZ, LATIN, ROCK, AND POPULAR MUSIC

There are now a vast number of anthologies of
jazz and popular arrangements. But the whole
point of these styles is to make your own
realisation after hearing performances and
recordings in the spirit of live playing, since
that's where the essential character of the music
and its creativity are to be found.

That's why the only anthologies listed here
are classical, apart from the books of lead sheets
that real jazz players and popular musicians
actually use. These are known in the trade as
'fake books' or sometimes as 'real books'.

The most comprehensive ones around right
now are listed below (all published by
Sher Music).

The New Real Book, Volume 1
The New Real Book, Volume 1
The New Real Book, Volume 1
The World's Greatest Fake Book
The Latin Real Book

Also useful:

T.A.Brown *Afro-Latin Rhythm*
  Dictionary (ALF)

Another good way to build up a resource of
materials here is simply by trading lead sheets
every time you play with other musicians
involved in jazz or latin – you'll be surprised
how quickly you build up a sizeable collection,
and you'll probably discover some interesting
alternative versions of standards and heads, that
you might want to use yourself.

TRADITIONAL, WORLD, FOLK MUSIC

These anthologies of folk music arranged for
piano are grouped here by geographical area,
preceded by an international section. All the
material listed is at an easy to intermediate
level, unless specified.

International

Agay *Playing Folk Tunes* (MS), *An Introduction to*
  Playing Folk Tunes (MS), *Folk Songs and Folk*
  Dances (MS), *The Joy of Folk Songs* (MS)
Benedict *Folk Song Favourites for Easy Piano*
  (MB)
Brick *The Global Songbook* (WB)
Cass-Beggs *Folk Lullabies of the World*
  (Oak/MS)
De Cesare *90 Songs of the Americas* (WB)
Deutsch *A Treasury of the World's Finest Folk*
  Song (Howell)
Miller *Sing, Children, Sing* (Chappel)
Roth *Piano Chart of International Scales* (MB)
  [Scales around the world]
Sheftel *Sightreading Folk Songs from around the*
  World (ALF)
Smith *29 Very Easy Folk Songs* (BMC)
Vandall *Christmas Improvisations* (MMP) [Carols
  around the world]
Verne *Modes in Miniature* (HL)
Folk Songs of the Sea (Faber/GS)
Folk Songs of the Americas (MS)
The International Book of Folk Songs (Walton)
National Anthems Collection (B&H)
Old Dances for Children (B&H)
Old Dances and Tunes (TP)
Old Songs and Dances (B&H)
Voices of Forgotten Worlds (MIM)

African

Adzinyah *Let Your Voice Be Heard* (MIM) [songs
  from Ghana/Zimbabwe]
S. Coleridge-Taylor *The Bamboula, The Stones are*
  Very Hard, (4 Negro Melodies) (Op.59)
Ourie *Fantasie on l'Africaine* (CPE)
Thompson *African Explorer* (Wil)
Travis *African Sonata* (UCP) [advanced]
Africa Never Stand Still (MIM) [Introduces
  African rhythms & instruments]

Afro-American

Agay *An Introduction to Playing Boogie, Blues and*
  Jazz (Yorktown)
Alain *Negro Spirituals* (EAMC)
Boatner *The Story of the Spirituals* (WB)
S. Coleridge-Taylor *24 Negro Melodies* (Da
  Capo)
Courlander *Negro Folk Music* (Dover)
Fjerstadt *Spritual Songs/Hymns and Folk Songs of*
  Early America (WB)
Nordoff *Spirituals for Children to Sng and Play*
  (TP)
Thomas *Plantation Songs in Easy Arrangements for*
  the Piano (GS)
Hymns of Praise (MS)
Hymns, Spirituals and Sacred Songs (MS)
I Can Play That! Hymns and Spirituals (MS)
Most Beloved Hymns and Spirituals (WB)
Spirituals and Gospels (MS)

Australian

Banks *3 North Country Folk Songs* (CPE)

Balkan

Bresgen *Balkan Impressions* (Lit/Pet)

Baltic

Kasemets *Piano Pieces on Estonian Folktunes*
  (CPE) [Estonian]
Kemp *5 Latvian Folk Pieces* (Waterloo)
Kenius *2 Latvian Folk Dances* (CPE)

Caribbean

Folk Songs from the Caribbean (Faber/HL)

Chinese

Chou *The Willows Are New* (PE)
Shao *Chinese Folk Songs for the Young Pianist*
  (EBM)
Chinese Folk Songs (MIM)
Chinese Piano Music for Children (EAMC)
Dream of Heaven, Music from China (EAMC)

Cuban

Carribean Souvenir Songbook (HL)

Czech/Slovak

Rybicki *This Is Our Garden-Fair* (PWM) [Czech
  & Slovak folk songs]

Eastern Europe

Folk Songs from Eastern Europe (Faber/HL)

Far Eastern

Folk Songs from the Far East (Faber/HL)

Greek

Alevizos *Folk Songs of Greece* (MS)
Greek Songbook (HH)

Gypsy

Sarasate *Gypsy Airs* (Op.20) (CF) [advanced]
Tausig *Ungarische Zigeunerweisen* (Musica
  Obscura) [advanced]

Hungarian

Bartók *3 Hungarian Folk Tunes* (B&H),*15*
  Hungarian Peasant Songs and Dances
  (UE/B&H), *3 Popular Hungarian Songs* (K)
Farkas *5 Hungarian Dances* (ZV), *Old Hungarian*
  Dances from the 17th Century (B&H)
Weiner *Hungarian Peasant Songs* (B&H)
31 Hungarian Peasant Songs (Gen)
Hungarian Children's Songs (B&H) (ed. Sugar)
Hungarian Songbook (Bk.1) (HH)
12 Magyar Songs (Bk.2) (HH)

Indian

Rimsky-Korsakov *Song of India* [various
versions]
Schramm *Bharata Sangita* (MCA), *Javali,*
Kiravani-Ramapriya (AME)
Strickland *Himalayan Sketches* (TP)
Folk Songs from India (Faber/HL)

Japanese

Fukuda *Favourite Songs of Japanese Children*
  (Alfred/MIM)

Hayashi *Suite* (JFC) [based on children's songs]

Kurokami *Suite: 12 Folk Songs in Southern Japan* (JFC)

Okumura *Japanese Children's Songs for Piano* (Ongaku-No-Tomo-Sha), *Japanese Folk Songs* (Vols.1-2) (Ongaku-No-Tomo-Sha)

Japanese Children's Songs (MIM)

Japanese Folk Airs on Piano (Vols.1-2) (EAMC)

Jewish

Beahm *Hannukah Songs* (TP)

Bialosky *10 Jewish Folk Melodies* (Sanjo), *24 Jewish Folk Melodies* (Sanjo)

Bock *Fiddler on the Roof: Selections* (WB)

Engle-Berman *My Hanukkah Song Book* (Wil)

Hajdu *2 Hassidic Tunes* (IMI), *2 Prayer Songs* (IMI)

Jonas *Jewish Songs Religious and Folk Melodies* (WB)

Steiner *Hebrew Songs for the Young Pianist* (WB)

Hebrew Songs for Beginners (MS)

Hebrew Festival Melodies (MS)

Jewish Songs Old and New (HL)

Latin American

De Cesare *Latin American Game Songs* (WB), *Songs of Hispanic Americans* (ALF/MIM)

McLaughlin *Latin American Folk Songs* (ALF)

Songs and Dances of Latin America (MS)

Macedonian

Srebotnjak *Macedonian Dances* (GS)

Mexican

Abril/Hunt *Great Songs of Mexico* (Hansen)

Memories of Mexico (HL)

Mexican Fiesta Album (HL)

Mexican Folk Dances (WB)

North American Folk

Andrews *The Gift to be Simple* (Dover) [Shaker Songs & Dances]

Clauson *Old-Time Cowboy Songbook* (MB)

Crawford *Civil War Songbook* (Dover)

Crawford-Seeger *American Folk Songs for Children* (Doubleday), *19 American Folk Songs* (GS/HL)

Cunningham *American Folk Songs* (Seesaw)

Eckard *Hymns to Play and Sing* (TP)

Ellsworth *Hymn Tunes for Piano* (CF)

Erbsen *Old Time Gospel Songbook* (MB)

Fife *Cowboy and Western Songs* (CC)

Fjerstadt *Spritual Songs/Hymns and Folk Songs of Early America* (WB)

Fowke/Glazer *Songs of Work and Protest* (Dover)

Goldston *Sacred Songs and Solos* (ALF)

Gordon *Gospel Riffs God Would Love to Hear* (ADG Productions)

Guthrie *This Land is Your Land* (GS)

Hayes *Songs of the Old South*

Jackson *Popular Songs of 19th Century America* (Dover) [original sheet music]

Johnston *Folk Songs of Canada* (CPE), *More Folk Songs of Canada* (CPE)

Martin *Country Fiddle Tunes* (BMC), *More Country Fiddle Tunes* (BMC)

Matteson *An Appalachian Christmas* (MB) (Appalachian carols)

Munn *Bluegrass Country* (Wil)

Newell *Games and Songs of American Children* (Dover)

Ralph *American Song Treasury* (Dover)

Seeger *American Favourite Ballads* (MS)

Silverman *Immigrant Songbook* (MB), *Songs of the Western Frontier* (MB)

Taylor *Easiest Country Piano Book* (MB)

All-American Country/Folk/Patriotic/Song Book (4 books) (CC)

American Art Songs of Turn of the Century (Dover)

American Ballads and Folk Songs (Dover)

Best-Loved Hymns (HL)

Bluegrass Complete (CC)

Cherished Hymn Favourites (CC)

Flag Songs (Hansen House)

Folk Songs of Old New England (Dover)

Folk Songs from North America (Faber/HL)

Rockabilly! (HL)

Songs of the Civil War (Dover)

Southern Gospel Music and Proud of It (HL)

North American Indian

Burton *Moving Within the Circle: Contemporary Native American Music and Dance* (MIM)

Carson *The Beige 'American Indian' Songbook* (Hansen House)

Farwell *American Indian Melodies* (Hinson-Henshaw), *Pawness Horses* (GS)

Smith *Native American Songs for Solo Piano* (MB)

Authentic Indian Dances and Folklore (MIM)

Norwegian

Backer-Grøndahl *Norwegische Volkweisen und Volkstanze* (Op.30) (CPE/NMF)

Olsen *Norwegian Folk Songs* (NMF)

Polish

World Charts – The Polish Songbook (HH)

Puerto Rican

Puerto Rico Sings (HL)

Mi Album de Puerto Rico (Hansen)

Rumanian

Bartók *Rumanian Christmas Songs/Carols* (UE/B&H), *2 Rumanian Dances* (K/EMB/B&H), *Rumanian Folk Dances* (UE/B&H)

Russian

Petyrek *Ukrainian Folk Songs, Piano* (EAMC)

Russian Songbook (HH)

Scandinavian

Scandinavian Songbok (HL)

Serbian

Tajcevic *Serbian Dances* (Rongwen)

Turkish

Saygun *Inci's Book (Inci'nin Kitabi)* (PIC)

ABBREVIATIONS FOR MUSIC PUBLISHERS

This index lists principal piano music publishers around the world and the abbreviations used for them in the foregoing repertoire guide. US representatives are shown in parentheses for music publishers based outside of the US.

ABRSM Associated Board of the Royal Schools of Music, London (c/o Theodore Presser, PA)

ALF Alfred Music Publishing, CA

AME American Music Editions, NY

AMP Associated Music Publishers (c/o Hal Leonard, WI)

Amph Amphion, Paris

B&H Boosey & Hawkes, London/NY

BB Broude Brothers, MA

BMC Boston Music Company, MA

Br & Har Breitkopf & Härtel, Germany (c/o Hal Leonard, WI)

CC Creative Concepts Publishing Corp., CA

CF Carl Fischer, NY

Chap Chappel, UK

CPE Composer/Performer Edition, CA

Don Donemus, Holland

Dur Editions Musicales Durand, Paris (c/o Theodore Presser Co., PA)

EAMC European American Music Corp., PA

EBM E.B.Marks, NY

ECIC Editorial Cooperativa Interamericana de Compositores (c/o Peermusic Classical, NY)

EMB Editio Musica, Budapest (c/o Boosey & Hawkes, NY)

ESC Max Eschig, WI (c/o Associated Music Publishers, MI)

EV Elkan-Vogel (c/o Theodore Presser Co., PA)

FHM Frederick Harris Music, NY

GS G.Schirmer, NY

HH Hansen House, FL

Heu Heugel, Paris

HL Hal Leonard Corp., WI

IMI Israel Music Institute (c/o Boosey & Hawkes, NY)

INT International

JFC Japanese Federation of Composers

JWC J.W.Chester, London (c/o MMB Music, MO)

K Kalmus, FL

Led Leduc, Paris

LP Leonarda Prod. Inc., NY

MB Mel Bay Publishing, MO

MCA MCA Music, NY

Merc Mercury Music Corp. (c/o Theodore Presser Co., PA)

MIM Music in Motion, TX

MMP Myklas Music Press, CO

MS Music Sales, NY

NK Neil Kjos Music Co., CA

NME New Music Editions (c/o Theodore Presser Co., PA)

NMF Norsk Musikforlag (c/o MMB Music, MO)

Nov Novello, London (c/o Theodore Presser Co., PA)

Oak Oak Publications

OUP Oxford Univerity Press, Oxford/NY

PAU Pan American Union (c/o Peermusic
   Classical, NY)
PE Peters Edition, London/NY
PIC Peer International Corp., NY
PWM Polskie Wydawnictwo Muzyczne,
   Cracow (c/o Hal Leonard, WI)
Ric Ricordi (c/o G.Schirmer, NY)
Sal Edition Salabert, Paris (c/o G.Schirmer,
   NY)
SCH Schaum Publications WI
SDM Servico de Documentacão Musical da
   Ordem dos Musicos do Brasil, Rio de Janeiro
SUDM Samfundet til Udgivelse af Dansk
   Musik
SZ Suvini Zerboni (Milan, Italy)
TP Theodore Presser Co. PA
UCP University of California Press, CA
UE Universal Edition (c/o European American
   Music Corp., PA)
UME Union Musical Española (c/o Associated
   Music Publishers, MI)
WB Warner Brothers Music Publishers, FL
WC Warner/Chappell, Canada
WH William Hansen (c/o MMB Music, MO)
Wil Willis Music Co. KY

LISTENING GUIDE

This is divided into three main sections: the
top recommendations; a general discography;
and video material.

If you want to develop your sensitivity and
understanding of music through listening, as
well as through playing or composing, then
how you listen is more important than how
much you listen or how many recordings you
own. Especially with classical music,
concentration and attention to structure and
narrative are important. A good listener is
creative: try listening for different things on
different hearings, in surroundings that let you
focus and respond without constraints.

Don't forget that the proper context for
listening to music is not (usually) a sound-
system, but a live concert. A performance by a
lesser-known pianist in intimate surroundings
(such as a private music society concert) may be
a more revealing experience than emptying
your pockets to sit at the back of a huge hall to
hear an international star playing an
instrument designed for maximum projection
rather than subtlety, in contrast to the
composer's likely intentions.

Today's performance culture has been
profoundly influenced by recordings and CD
technology. Many modern players spend their
time working towards studio recordings of
perfect sound quality intended to appear
technically flawless after repeated listenings.
This has pushed classical performing in the
direction of technical precision, often at the
expense of the spontaneity, risk-taking,
atmosphere and audience rapport that make a
great concert. Ironically, you may get a greater
sense of participation in a real event from early
recordings than from many 'live' concerts today
– provided you can hear past the poor sound-
quality present, which to a lesser extent is even
there in digitally remastered versions.

On the other hand, both early and
contemporary classical music tend to benefit
from this shift of emphasis towards clarity and
precision, if not always. The tendency to play
music of the baroque and classical periods in an
essentially Romantic 19th-century style has
now mostly been rejected.

Instead, the aim is to respect the stylistic
conventions believed to have existed when the
music was written: this is known as 'authentic
performance practice'. However, all too often
this becomes a substitute for genuinely
imaginative interpretation.

An additional development has been the
release of collectors' material on video, allowing
one to see as well as hear the playing of
pianistic giants at fairly close range. This
makes for a more vivid encounter with the
sheer involvement and virtuosity that these
musicians were capable of.

Not all recorded material by famous
classical artists is permanently available. The
top recommendations here could all be bought
at the time of writing this book, and the other

recordings mentioned have been publicly
available in recent years. Even when they are
unavailable, you should be able to get them in
public libraries or hear them at friends' houses
or on radio broadcasts. They are also likely to
be reissued within a few years. Many of the
greatest performing artists of the past have
inspired private appreciation societies, whose
members may direct you to alternative sources
for their recordings.

Because many of the most famous
recordings of jazz and of popular music have
been re-released on several occasions – and
often in different collected editions – the
original release details are used here as a
reliable point of reference.

TOP RECOMMENDATIONS

These are one-off historic performances, many
(including most of those indicated as mono)
dating from the early years of recording. Sound
quality may fall a little short of modern
standards, even when the recordings have been
digitally remastered for CD. All were on sale at
the time of writing. For recordings of the same
works with modern sound quality, consult the
discography that follows.

J.S. Bach *Goldberg Variations.* Glenn Gould
(Sony, mono, SMK52594.)
   Here is Gould's legendary early recording of
   the Goldberg Variations, from 1955. A
   religious experience.

J.S. Bach *Dinu Lipatti: The Last Recital.* Dinu
Lipatti (EMI Références, mono, CDH5 65166-2)
   This is Lipatti's recording of the programme
   of his final 1950 recital, given shortly before
   his death from leukaemia at the age of 33. It
   was described by *Gramophone* as "one of the
   great musical and human statements", and
   includes the legendary performance of Bach's
   Partita in B flat, BWV 825.

C.P.E. Bach *Sonatas and Rondos.* Mikhail
Pletnev (DG 459 614-2)
   These performances show the justice of
   Mozart's words: "Without C.P.E.Bach
   nothing would have been possible."

Mozart *Piano Concertos No.20 in D minor, K466
& No.21 in C, K467.* Friedrich Gulda (DG E
4158422)
   Gulda proves with these exquisitely poised
   renditions of two of Mozart's finest concertos
   that it's possible to be a top-rank pianist in
   both jazz and classical music.

Beethoven *Complete Piano Sonatas.* Artur
Schnabel (EMI Références, mono, CHS7
63765-2) (8 CDs)
   Schnabel is unique in capturing the
   explosive intensity and daring of the
   composer, not too mention the deep
   intimacy and poetry of the great slow
   movements. If you can't afford this complete
   edition, try getting one of the four volumes

issued separately on the Pearl label (though the sound quality is poorer).

Schubert (*Richter Vol.5*) *Piano Sonatas Nos.19 in C minor &.21 in B flat.* Sviatoslav Richter (Olympia OCD335)

Richter's 1972 rendition of the first movement of Schubert's great B flat Sonata (D.960) transports the listener into a world of lyrical timelessness.

Chopin *Great Pianists of the 20th Century – Alfred Cortot, Vol.1.* Alfred Cortot. (Philips, mono, 456 751-2.) (2 CDs)

Cortot's remarkable gifts – he was arguably the finest French pianist of the 20th century – are displayed in this selection of seminal works, including both sets of Chopin *Études* and works by Liszt, Ravel, and Schumann.

Brahms *Piano Concerto No.2 in B flat.* Edwin Fischer (Testament, mono, SBT 1170)

Fischer's musical greatness expresses itself as coming from an exceptional human being and charged with humanity and nobility. And there is conducting from the only individual who could match him in these qualities: Wilhelm Furtwängler.

Debussy *Préludes, Books 1 & 2.* Walter Gieseking (EMI Références, mono, CDH7 61004-2)

Gieseking was the master of subtle touch and velvety tone, perfectly suited to the colouristic sound world and atmospheric textures of Debussy's most important cycles of piano music.

Bach-Busoni *Liszt, Bach-Busoni and Chopin.* Ferrucio Busoni (Nimbus NI8810; piano rolls).

Includes the famous transcription of the Bach *Chaconne in D minor for solo violin,* played here by Busoni himself. Taken from early piano rolls.

Schoenberg *Piano Music.* Maurizio Pollini (DG 423 249-2)

Expressionistic modernism, atonality and 12-tone music are all superbly realised by this great Italian pianist, who combines intellectual authority with emotional and technical power.

Jean Barraqué *Piano Sonata.* Herbert Henck (ECM New Series 4539142)

French modernism at its most monumental. Is this what Beethoven would have sounded like had he lived in the 20th century?

Scott Joplin *The Entertainer – The Very Best of Scott Joplin.* Joshua Rifkin (Nonesuch 7559-79449-2)

Rifkin is the authoritative exponent of Joplin, having scrupulously researched and recreated the composer's own style.

Art Tatum *Piano Starts Here* (Sony Jazz 4765462)

Blinding virtuosity from the phenomenal near-blind pianist.

Thelonious Monk *Brilliant Corners* (Original Jazz Classics OJCCD0262)

Monk's quirky originality and individuality are shown here to good effect.

Bill Evans *Waltz for Debby* (Original Jazz Classics OJC202102)

One of the classic recordings with bassist LaFaro, made just days before the latter's tragic death.

Chucho Valdés *Solo Piano* (EMD/Blue Note 7805972)

This shows Valdés at his best, with no distractions.

Jerry Lee Lewis *18 Original Sun Greatest Hits* (WEA/Rhino 0070255RHI)

Classic rock'n'roll piano from the 1950s: this is as hot as it gets.

GENERAL DISCOGRAPHY

CLASSICAL PIANO

This section is divided into periods.

A highlight of recent years has been the series of reissues that forms part of the *Great Pianists of the 20th Century* series on the Philips label. A number of the earlier Philips recordings mentioned below in fact refer to this series, which features the 100 greatest pianists of the 20th century. Beyond this, the suggestions aim to highlight exceptional players and interpretations rather than to give a comprehensive guide to the vast range of recordings currently available. (Inevitably, some of the recordings listed may not available when you try to buy them, but may be reissued in the future on other labels.)

BAROQUE COMPOSERS

Baroque harpsichord music is well illustrated by recordings of French composers such as **Rameau** (Christophe Rousset, on the L'Osieau-Lyre label) and **Couperin** (Lawrence Cummings, on Naxos).

Although the keyboard music of **J.S.BACH** was almost certainly not conceived with the piano in mind, many great pianists have recorded it on the instrument. The most famous example must be Glenn Gould's two legendary recordings of the *Goldberg Variations* (Sony), both of which are classic performances whose pianistic poetry reaches heights of near-religious ecstasy.

Other great interpreters of Bach on the piano are Dinu Lipatti (his recording of the *Partita No.1 in B flat,* originally on EMI), Sviatoslav Richter, Andras Schiff, and recently, Angela Hewitt (on Hyperion). For an idea of how Bach was played back in the 1930s hear the profound Edwin Fischer (his *Forty-Eight Book 1,* on EMI). Rosalyn Tureck (originally on EMI) was a superb Bach player whose style reflects the fact that she played the composer's works on both harpsichord and piano. For great harpischord performances, try older recordings by Ralph Kirkpatrick or Wanda Landowska.

For dazzling pianistic renditions of the **HANDEL** *Keyboard Suites,* try Sviatoslav Richter and Andrei Gavrilov (recorded together on EMI), or Olivier Baumont's versions (on Erato) featuring an interesting range of period harpsichords. The *Keyboard Sonatas* of Domenico Scarlatti received the attention of great players such as Vladimir Horowitz and Emil Gilels; for more recent recordings try Mikhail Pletnev (on Virgin), and for masterful harpsichord interpretations Ralph Kirkpatrick (on DG).

The *Sonatas and Rondos* of **C.P.E. BACH** receive superb interpretations from Mikhail Pletnev (on DG) that capture the style that initiated the European tradition of keyboard extemporisation, influencing Mozart and Beethoven and, through this, 19th century piano music – and maybe even jazz.

CLASSICAL COMPOSERS

Few among even the greatest pianists have achieved the subtlety and pure musicality called for by **MOZART** in his *Piano Sonatas* and *Piano Concertos.* Wiser players have avoided them, and great Mozart interpreters are truly rare. From the early days of recording, Walter Gieseking and Clara Haskil (Philips) stand out. More recently, Friedrich Gulda (DG) shows that one can be a great jazz and classical player. Alfred Brendel (on Philips) applies his remarkable intelligence to the subtlety and elegance of the Viennese style. And Murray Perahia (on Sony) is a model of lyricism, delicacy and sensitivity to the deeper structure of musical lines. Mitsuko Uchida's earlier Mozart recordings (on Philips) are also to be recommended for their subtlety and poise.

For the *Piano Sonatas* of **HAYDN** – which remain undervalued in spite of their huge range of musical lyricism, inventiveness, wit and subtlety – Brendel (on Philips) is the authoritative exponent.

A good sense of why **CLEMENTI**'s early explorations of the piano made a impact on the young Beethoven can be had from hearing his *Sonatas* in the recordings by Horowitz (BMG/RCA) and by Nicolai Demidenko (Hyperion). Demidenko is also famed for his superb recordings of Bach-Busoni transcriptions.

The *32 Piano Sonatas* and *5 Piano Concertos* of **BEETHOVEN** stand at the centre of the classical repertoire. Artur Schnabel's recordings (on EMI and Pearl) from early in the 20th century are still unique in capturing the wild intensity and formal drama of the *Sonatas,* as well as the lyrical inwardness of their slow movements. Two other great exponents from this time were Solomon (EMI) and Edwin Fischer (APR), especially where the extraordinary late Sonatas are concerned. If you have the chance to hear recordings of Myra Hess playing Beethoven, seize it. Other great exponents are the Russians Sviatoslav Richter

(Philips) and Emil Gilels (DG), the early Daniel Barenboim (EMI), Claudio Arrau (Philips), and Wilhelm Kempff (DG).

Maurizio Pollini (DG) captures the intellectual grandeur of Beethoven's extended forms. Stephen Kovacevich (EMI) is a seriously underrated interpreter, and Richard Goode (Elektra) is much admired as a specialist. Beethoven's *Diabelli Variations* and *Bagatelles* lend themselves to the more thoughtful approaches of Brendel (Philips) and Gould (Sony). Fine period-instrument performances, on the fortepiano from Malcolm Bilson (Claves) and on Beethoven's own (restored) Broadwood by Melvyn Tan (EMI), illuminate otherwise hidden aspects of the composer's music.

Where **SCHUBERT** is concerned, the Sonatas were first pioneered by Schnabel (EMI). These and other works have received great interpretations from the likes of Brendel (Philips), Kempff (DG) and Perahia (Sony). An English pianist noted for his Schubert was Clifford Curzon. Imogen Cooper's recordings (on Ottavo) from the 1980s were an important contribution. Performances by Richter, notably of the *'Great' Sonata in B flat* (D.960) (Olympia and Philips) and the *Wanderer Fantasy* (EMI) are majestic, to be sought out amongst the many extraordinary examples of his playing only now emerging to confirm his stature as a giant of the 20th century. Rada Lupu (on Decca) is also rated as a Schubert interpreter.

ROMANTIC COMPOSERS

The *Songs without Words* are the best known of the piano works by **MENDELSSOHN**, with the recommended recording that of Barenboim from 1974 (on DG). You can hear the *Nocturnes* of the Irish composer **JOHN FIELD** (the precursor of the pianistic styles of Chopin and Schumann) played sensitively on period instruments by Joanna Leach (Athene).

For **SCHUMANN** – perhaps the most consistently undervalued of the great 19th century German romantic composers – you might well begin by searching out old recordings by the legendary French pianist Alfred Cortot. Claudio Arrau's aristocratic refinement (on Philips) can also suit Schumann, as does Richter's exemplary pianism, of which there are many instances (on Revelation, Olympia and EMI).

CHOPIN is, of course, the composer most strongly identified with the piano, so the choice of pianists to listen to is extensive and includes early recordings by some of the greatest piano legends. Pre-eminent amongst the latter is the Russian composer-pianist Serge Rachmaninoff (RCA). The wonderful Cortot (Music & Arts) long ago encapsulated the magical refinement and dreamy sensuousness of Chopin's French side with unsurpassed sensitivity. Horowitz was of course a great showman in Chopin, but Artur Rubinstein (BMG/RCA, EMI) reached the quintessentially Polish essence of Chopin's music: its wistful psychological explorations and intense feeling for the moment are expressed in the all-

important *rubato*. Pollini (DG) surmounts the technical challenges in a way that will inspire aspiring pianists, as will Vladimir Ashkenazy's playing (on Decca), and Perahia (Sony). An uncannily modern, Polish reincarnation of Chopin's distinctive musical personality is offered by Krystian Zimerman (DG).

Many of the great pianists have tried their hand at the solo piano music of **BRAHMS**, including Schnabel, Gould, Rubinstein and, most notably, Julius Katchen (on Decca). The great *Sonata No.3 in F minor* (Op.5) receives superb performances from Richter (Decca), Perahia (Sony) and Zimerman (DG). A fine modern interpreter of the late piano music is Rada Lupu (Decca), recorded in the 1970s. For the magnificent *Second Piano Concerto in B flat* (Op.83), one of the composer's greatest works, the recommended recording has to be that by Emil Gilels (DG), also from the '70s. But if you have the chance to hear a recording of Myra Hess playing it, seize the opportunity!

LISZT produced an enormous output for the piano. The technical virtuosity and pianistic character of this music has attracted a large number of exponents. The great *Piano Sonata in B minor* has drawn notable interpretations from the likes of Martha Argerich (DG) and Demidenko (Hyperion) and Pollini (DG). Richter revealed himself as a great Liszt player in an amazing recital recorded live back in 1958 (issued on Revelation).

Other great pianists who have captured the literary and sensuous subtleties of Liszt's music are Louis Kentner (APR), Claudio Arrau (Philips) and Brendel (Vanguard). The composer's reported enthusiasm for dazzling virtuoso showmanship is evoked in the many recordings by Jorge Bolet (Decca), while Leslie Howard has endeavoured to record the complete piano works (Hyperion).

The *Concerto No.1 in B flat minor* of **TCHAIKOWSKY** is one of the most popular piano concertos ever written: if you have to choose one recording, go for Argerich's hugely passionate live 1994 version (DG) with the conductor Claudio Abbado. **FAURÉ** was a late-romantic French composer whose wonderfully subtle piano music remains under-appreciated. There are fine recordings available by Kathryn Stott (Hyperion) and Paul Crossley (CRD).

The Norwegian composer **GRIEG** is best known for his hugely popular *Piano Concerto in A minor* (Op.16), available in numerous modern recordings and, especially, in the classic 1937 interpretation by Gieseking (APR). The *Lyric Pieces* and fascinating *Norwegian Peasant Dances* are available as part of a complete cycle of his piano music recorded by the Grieg specialist Einar Steen-Nøkleberg (on Naxos), while the 1974 Gilels recording of Grieg works (on DG) is an all-time classic.

The four *Piano Concertos* and *Rhapsody on a Theme of Paganini* of **RACHMANINOFF** have been reissued in historic performances by the composer (RCA). However, the *Concerto No.3 in D minor* became uniquely associated with Horowitz (BMG/RCA), while the *Concerto No.4*

in G minor found an unrivalled interpretation in the hands of the fabulous Michelangeli (EMI). For solo piano works, I would suggest that you choose Richter (on Olympia).

MODERN COMPOSERS

The fiery, exotic and mystical piano music of **SCRIABIN** has yet to achieve the recognition it deserves, in spite of promotion in the hands of great players such as Gould and Richter (on Melodiya). An exemplary modern interpreter is Demidenko (on Conifer), while Horowitz fans can now hear his historic interpretations from the 1950s through to the 1970s (BMG/RCA). Going back in time still further, Vladimir Sofronitzky was hailed by the composer's widow as the finest exponent of his music (to be found on BMG and Philips).

For **ALBENIZ**, the pianist of choice has to be Alicia de Larrocha, whose many recordings (on EMI and Decca) imbue the music with a magically Spanish spontaneity and vitality.

In the case of **DEBUSSY**, those who favour sensuous subtlety of tone and colour over ironically dry classicism must hear the classic recordings of Gieseking (HMV and EMI), notably the *Préludes*, while those of the other disposition will be most satisfied by Michelangeli (DG). For the *Études*, Mitsuko Uchida (on Philips) is exceptional.

The *Piano Concerto in G* is one of the most popular works of **RAVEL**, nowhere better played than by Michelangeli (EMI), though if you want to hear the links with jazz made clear, choose the recording by Argerich (DG). For solo works such as the *Sonatine, Le Tombeau de Couperin, Gaspard de la Nuit*, or *Miroirs*, Vlado Perlemuter (Nimbus) offers interpretations informed by having worked directly with the composer, while Jean-Yves Thibaudet has produced authoritative recordings of the collected works (on Decca).

SCOTT JOPLIN's own 1916 ragtime piano-roll recordings are preserved (on Biograph), but the authoritative interpretations of his rags have to be those of Joshua Rifkin (Nonesuch), which emphasise their suave and relaxed classical feel.

IVES's legendary *Piano Sonata No.2* (*'Concord'*) is probably best heard when played by Lubimov (on Erato), though if you can get hold of one of the old John Kirkpatrick recordings, do so.

BUSONI was a phenomenal virtuoso pianist, as well as an important and highly original composer whose works remain unappreciated, in spite of a revival of interest in the late 20th century. The monumental *Piano Concerto* was pioneered by John Ogden (EMI), but reveals less of the composer's originality than other lesser-known piano works. These include the *Fantasia Contrappuntistica*, superbly recorded by Ogden (Continuum), the demonic *Toccata* (of which Brendel was a masterly exponent), and the *Sonatinas* and *Elegies*, which have attracted fine pianistic advocates such as Peter Donohoe. Busoni was better known to many as "Bach-Busoni" – the transcriber of

Bach instrumental (mainly organ) works into virtuoso adaptations for the modern piano that create a unique aesthetic character of their own, blending neo-Gothic darkness with art-nouveau decadence.

For superb modern recordings of these, Demidenko is the only man in town, though the most famous transcription of all, the *Chaconne in D minor* (from the *Partita No.2* for solo violin) has been given an electrifying rendition by Michelangeli and can even be heard as recorded by Busoni himself, originally on a piano roll.

The Second Viennese School composers **SCHOENBERG**, **BERG** and **WEBERN** produced important piano works central to modern classical music. Maurizio Pollini is generally pre-eminent here (DG), though Susan Bradshaw's interpretations should also be studied. Berg's hauntingly post-romantic *Sonata in B minor* (Op.1) is a jewel, also superbly recorded years ago by Barenboim. Gould's renditions of Schoenberg, and also of the Berg *Sonata*, are utterly phenomenal (on CBC).

The highlight of **STRAVINSKY**'s output as far as pianists are concerned has to be the *Three Dances from Petrushka*, with the recording by Pollini (on DG) so electrifying that it outshines all other interpretations. Yet another master with a significantly undervalued oeuvre for piano is **SZYMANOWSKI**, though fine recordings are increasingly available, including those by Mikhail Rudy (EMI) or Pawel Kamasa (Koch Schwann).

BARTOK was legendary as a pianist as well as for his compositions for the instrument, so we are privileged that his own recordings of his piano works have been preserved (on Pearl). A modern pianist who worked with the composer was György Sándor (heard on Sony), and another player who recaptures Bartok's distinctively Hungarian spontaneity in his own terms is Zoltán Kocsis (Philips).

PROKOFIEV's piano works were championed by Richter (DG and Philips), who remains unsurpassed in his renditions, notably of several of the demanding and difficult *Piano Sonatas* and the *Visions fugitives*, not to mention the *Piano Concerto No.5*. There's an old recording out there somewhere that features the composer himself playing the *Piano Concerto No.3*, and Horowitz's Sonata No.7 is legendary (and available on Philips).

SHOSTAKOVICH made a major contribution to the repertoire, especially with his *24 Preludes and Fugues* (Op.87), but also with the great *Piano Quintet* and two *Piano Trios*. The authoritative exponent of the *Preludes and Fugues* is the great Tatiana Nikolayeva (Hyperion), whose playing of Bach inspired the composer to write them, and who was consulted on a daily basis during their creation. The recording of the *Quintet* with the cellist Rostropovitch alongside the composer himself at the piano is a historical document (and it can be found on Revelation).

JANÁCEK's atmospheric piano music is associated with the Czech pianist Rudolf Firkusny (DG), but Mikhail Rudy is also fine (EMI). The titanic *Piano Sonata* by **SAMUEL BARBER** was given a uniquely electrifying performance by Horowitz (on RCA) and this remains one of the pianistic highlights of the 20th century.

For **MESSIAEN**'s piano works, the authority was the pianist Yvonne Loriod (Erato), also the composer's second wife, though Hewitt is also superb (on Hyperion). Peter Hill worked closely with the composer in preparing his interpretation of the birdsong-inspired *Catalogues d'oiseaux* (Unicorn). The exciting two-piano work *Visions de l'Amen* is worth hearing in the recording by Argerich and Rabinovitch (EMI).

There were three highlights of post-war musical modernism as far as the piano is concerned. First, the monumentally Beethovenian *Piano Sonata* of **BARRAQUÉ**, currently available from Herbert Henck (ECM). Then, *Piano Pieces I-XI* of **STOCKHAUSEN**, recorded by the leading 1960s avant-garde pianist David Tudor (on Hathut). And last, the three sonatas of Boulez, whose *Second Piano Sonata* elicited high-intensity playing from the young Pollini (DG).

Pollini should also be heard in his beautiful recording of the highly evocative *Sofferte onde serene...* for piano and tape (on DG) by the Italian composer **NONO**, the most underrated of the Darmstadt brigade.

The *Sonatas and Interludes for prepared piano* by **CAGE** have now been recorded by many pianists, notably Steffen Schleiermacher and Aleck Karis (Bridge), the latter including a lecture-reading from the composer himself. The oriental aesthetic is highlighted in a recording from pianist-composer Yuji Takahashi (Denon). It should however be noted that the adjusted nature of the instrument means that performances of these works can vary considerably in character.

We end now with three of the most striking compositional voices to have emerged in contemporary music in the last decades of the 20th century, each of who has made significant contributions to the piano repertoire.

The English composer **FERNEYHOUGH** exemplifies the high-voltage, expressionistic dissonance and complexity of post-serial music in his *Lemma-Icon-Epigram* for solo piano, recorded by Ian Pace (on NMC).

NANCARROW's dazzling *Studies for Player Piano* inspired much of the fractured eclecticism of musical postmodernism – and these and other works have been given a fresh perspective by Joanna MacGregor (Collins). She makes very effective use of multi-tracking in order to achieve the superhuman excesses that were achieved by the composer's original mechanised performer.

The three books of *Études* of **LIGETI** explore the extremes of textural and polyrhythmic complexity, and have been recorded by one of the leading specialists in contemporary piano music, Pierre-Laurent Aimard (on Sony).

JAZZ PIANO
This section is divided into periods and styles.

EARLY JAZZ
The New Orleans Creole pianist and bandleader '**JELLY ROLL' MORTON** made the transition from ragtime to early jazz. Try his 1923-4 solo recordings (on Indiana Richmond), especially 'King Porter Stomp', or the 1926-1929 recordings with the Red Hot Peppers (on Victor), such as 'Black Bottom Stomp'.

Boogie-woogie was an important influence in early jazz, combining barrelhouse-style left-hand rhythms with blues-based right-hand improvising. (See Blues Piano, below.)

The definitive stride pianist was **JAMES P. JOHNSON**, illustrated in *Harlem Stride Piano 1921-29* (on Hot 'n' Sweet). Johnson's protégé **FATS WALLER** also played stride in the 1920s, before going on to commercial success in the swing era, and demonstrated on *Fats Waller and his Buddies 1927-9* (on Bluebird).

SWING-ERA JAZZ
DUKE ELLINGTON's achievements as the predominant bandleader, composer and arranger of the swing era are well represented on *Early Ellington 1926-31* (GRP/Decca). The solos and big-band recordings of **EARL HINES** are also important, and both can be heard on *1928-1932* (Classics). Hines would break up the rhythm by suspending the left hand during melodic breaks, anticipating modern jazz.

In the 1930s **COUNT BASIE** was synonymous with swing, and the strong rhythm section that his band evolved allowed him to free up his left hand from providing the beat, anticipating bebop. Try his classic 1950s album *April in Paris* (Verve). **NAT 'KING' COLE**'s skill – by 1940 he was one of the top swing pianists – was overshadowed by his later success as a singer, but his trio recordings are well represented on *Hit That Jack Live: The Earliest Recordings* (Decca).

The phenomenal virtuosity of the near-blind pianist **ART TATUM** still amazes, as on *Piano Starts Here* (Columbia/Legacy) or *Classic Piano Solos* (Decca). **ERROL GARNER** emerged in the mid-1940s with his distinctive and uncompromising yet appealing style, in which the right hand lags slightly behind the left-hand beat. His best recording was probably *Concert by the Sea* (Columbia), but there are many others, such as *Too Marvellous for Words Vol.3*, *Dancing on the Ceiling* (Emarcy) and in a Latin mode, *Mambo Moves Garner* (Mercury). **OSCAR PETERSON** was another great virtuoso in the Tatum mould, and like Garner his approach lies between swing and bop. Try *At the Stratford Shakespearean Festival* (on Verve).

BEBOP JAZZ
BUD POWELL paved the way for bebop-style piano playing, completely disposing of the left-hand stride in favour of irregular statements of chords, with fast single-note right-hand lines in the manner of Charlie Parker. Start with *The*

Amazing Bud Powell, Vol.4 (Blue Note). Perhaps the most individual player of the period, **THELONIOUS MONK**, is impressive on *Thelonious with John Coltrane* (Original Jazz Classics) and with other fine players on *Brilliant Corners* (Original Jazz Classics).

WYNTON KELLY is another important figure, best known for his work with Miles Davis and for his distinctive chord voicings: try *Someday My Prince Will Come* (on Vee-Jay).

HORACE SILVER cultivated a funky hard-bop style, evidenced in the classic *Horace Silver and the Jazz Messengers* (Blue Note).

At a time when bop was itself considered revolutionary, the blind **LENNIE TRISTANO** introduced a contrapuntal dimension and other harmonic elements from modern classical music to push in the direction of free jazz, well in advance of others, as is clearly evident on *Intuition* (Capitol).

POST-BEBOP JAZZ
BILL EVANS dominated jazz piano in the 1960s and 1970s with his novel yet sparse left-hand voicings and introverted style. He was reliant on close collaboration with bass players whose contributions play a more important role. A good entry point would be the two complementary recordings from 1961, *Sunday at the Village Vanguard* and *Waltz for Debby* (both on Original Jazz Classics), both of which feature material from a set played with bassist Scott LaFaro, just days before the latter's tragic death. For something more experimentally postmodern, try *Conversations with Myself* (Verve), in which Evans multi-tracks several times to create a haunting yet spontaneous dialogue with himself.

Like Evans, **McCOY TYNER** has been massively influential in post-bebop jazz, especially because of his equally distinctive approach to chord voicing. Try to hear him solo on *Echoes of a Friend* (Original Jazz Classics), his tribute to Coltrane, with whom he worked. Tyner also worked with Afro-Cuban music, on which he exerted an influence.

GEORGE SHEARING, who also played Afro-Cuban jazz and who was born blind, developed the infamous 'locked hands' approach to jazz piano, as well as writing great standards such as 'Lullaby of Birdland' (used for countless bop improvisation – see Tutorial). Try to hear the George Shearing Quintet (with its unique quintet sound, including vibes and electric guitar) on *Lullaby of Birdland* (Verve), including the original number of that name.

The ever-versatile **HERBIE HANCOCK** explored most of the post-bop developments from the 1960s to the 1990s, experimenting with electronic alternatives to the acoustic piano, of which he was also a master. Like Wynton Kelly, he worked with Miles Davis, absorbing the latter's modal experiments: you can hear this in *Maiden Voyage* from the 1960s (Blue Note), but for a taste of his subsequent fusion-oriented experiments, try *Headhunters* from the 1970s (Columbia). **ABDULLAH IBRAHIM** (also known as **Dollar Brand**)

came to America from South Africa, evolving a post-bop style that reflected the influence of Duke Ellington as well as his roots. For solos, get *African Dawn* (Enja); for septet arrangements, you should investigate *Water from an Ancient Well* (Tiptoe).

WEST-COAST JAZZ
West-coast pianist **DAVE BRUBECK** became a household name with his successful quartet, which included the altoist Paul Desmond, composer of 'Take Five' (see Tutorial). Brubeck's synthesis of jazz improvisation included classical modernist elements such as polyrhythms and polytonality (he studied with the French composer Milhaud), and found an ideal audience on American student campuses. But jazz purists tend to regard him with some disdain. *Jazz Goes to College* (Columbia) is a classic, but if you want to hear 'Take Five', look for *Time Out* (also Columbia), one of the most popular of all jazz recordings.

MODERN JAZZ
One of the principal figures here is **CHICK COREA**, whose fusion-based experiments developed between different incarnations of his Return To Forever band: more jazz-oriented in *Light as a Feather*, more rock-oriented in *Hymn of the Second Galaxy* (both on Polydor).

Another pianist who originally worked with Davis was **KEITH JARRETT**. He was renowned for completely free yet extended improvisations, as on *Facing You, Solo Concerts* and *The Köln Concert* (all ECM). He has also worked significantly as a classical player. **KENNY BARRON** was not fully recognised as an important player until the 1990s, but his solo recording *Live at Maybeck Recital Hall (Vol.10)* (Concord) is full of fine originals.

FREE AND AVANT-GARDE JAZZ
Exponents of this style have aroused controversy in jazz, and some from more mainstream bebop have questioned whether they deserve to be considered part of jazz at all. **ANTHONY BRAXTON** has been a leading figure in this area, principally on reeds, but you can hear his 1995 solo piano album, *Solo Piano (Standards)* on the No More label. The most colourful and controversial figure in this area was without doubt **SUN RA**. He was playing 'free' long before the jazz avant-garde became established, while also pioneering the use of early types of electronic keyboard: try *Atlantis* (Saturn) or, for a solo piano session, *Monorails and Satellites* (Evidence). Ra was one of the great originals, but inconsistent, and the personal mythology he built up around himself was ammunition for his detractors.

Perhaps the most advanced exponent of experimental jazz has been **CECIL TAYLOR**, whose uncompromisingly dissonant and percussive piano style, too forbidding for many listeners, was developed well before free jazz took off. *Unit Structures* (Blue Note) from the 1960s and *Silent Tongues* (on Freedom) are both good examples.

BLUES PIANO
The major focus of early blues piano playing was the barrelhouse style that originated in the rough and rowdy atmosphere of barrelhouses and lumber camps in the 19th century in out-of-the-way parts of the United States. This became identified with boogie-woogie, thanks to the early recordings of the style that were made by pianists such as 'Pine Top' Smith and 'Cow Cow' Davenport.

For a good piano boogie, try **PETE JOHNSON**'s *Pete's Blues* (Savoy) or *Boogie-Woogie Mood* (MCA), **MEADE LUX LEWIS**'s 'Honky Tonk Train Blues' or his *Complete Blue Note Recordings* (Paramount), and recordings by **ALBERT AMMONS** (on Blue Note).

Through the 1930s, blues piano developed distinct regional styles, for example in Texas, but became increasingly focused on cities such as Chicago and St Louis, leading to a more restrained, smoother feel. Boogie-woogie was also a major element in swing. However, blues-based piano playing was almost always subordinated to the story-telling and singing aspect of the blues, which had more social relevance during the times of the Depression, so technique remained fairly undeveloped.

The electrification of the blues in the 1940s and 1950s also relegated the piano to a subordinate role (in contrast to the guitar and harmonica), though players like **OTIS SPANN** achieved significant results in this context: try his album *Otis Spann is the Blues* (on Candid). On the West Coast, Jump Blues developed as a synthesis of jazz and blues that left more scope for pianists such as **AMOS MILBURN** (EMI), **FLOYD DIXON** (Specialty) and **CAMILLE HOWARD** (also on Specialty).

Traditional blues piano playing was still on display in the 1960s, however, with the likes of **MEMPHIS SLIM**. Try his *Rockin' the Blues* (on Charly). The style was especially prevalent in Louisiana, where characters like **PROFESSOR LONGHAIR** (Rhino) and **JAMES BOOKER** (on Rounder) were working.

LATIN PIANO
CHUCHO VALDÉS is one of the great Cuban pianists, famous as leader of **IRAKERE**, Cuba's foremost band from the 1970s. Valdes has been likened to McCoy Tyner and described as the Art Tatum of Cuba: try *Solo Piano*, or for quartet playing, *Briyumba Palo Congo* (both on Blue Note).

EDDIE PALMIERI is also famous for bringing the sound of modern jazz pianists to Afro-Cuban music: hear him on *Arete* (RMM). For especially dense chord voicings and polyrhythms, go for **GONZALO RUBALCABA**, as on *The Blessing* (Blue Note).

HILARIO DURAN is particularly known for his *tumbao* bass figures, as on *Killer Tumbao* and *Habana Nocturna* (both to be heard on the Justin Time label).

For rather advanced post-bop Afro-Cuban jazz, try **HILTON RUIZ**, on *Strut* or *A Moment's Notice* (both on Novus). A highly sophisticated pianist whose approach is enriched by a Panamanian background is **DANILO PEREZ**, notably on *The Journey* (Novus). **MICHEL CAMILO** is another great star of Afro-Cuban jazz, with a partly Dominican background, and is well represented by *On Fire* (Epic).

ROCK PIANO

For rock'n'roll in the original New Orleans R&B style, listen to **FATS DOMINO**'s rolling boogie-influenced piano style, especially in 'Every Night About This Time'.

Also, try to get to hear Fats tracks such as 'The Fat Man' (1950, on Imperial), 'Ain't That a Shame' (1955), 'Blueberry Hill' (1956), or 'Blue Monday' (1956). The *Domino '65* collection (available on Mercury) captures the feel of the live act .

For driving, pumping, straightahead (straight-eight) rock, try **LITTLE RICHARD**, especially 'Tutti Frutti' (1955), 'Long Tall Sally' (1956), 'Lucille' (1957), 'Keep A-Knockin'' (1957), and 'Good Golly Miss Molly' (1957), all on the Specialty label.

Also, you really must listen to some classic **JERRY LEE LEWIS** tracks (all of which are on the great rock'n'roll label Sun). Try 'Whole Lotta Shakin' Goin' On' (1957), 'Great Balls of Fire' (1957), or 'Breathless' (1958). Like Elvis Presley (whom I guess you may have heard of), Lewis illustrates the fusion of R&B and country – in other words, of 'black' and 'white' American styles – from which rock music emerged in the 1950s.

For country piano, listen to the 'slip-note' style of **FLOYD CRAMER** (who also backed Presley in his famous 'Heartbreak Hotel'). Cramer's own hits included 'Last Date' (1960) and 'On the Rebound' (1961) and these are available on various compilations; also, later on, he had albums (on the Step One indie label) such as *King of Country Piano* (1992).

For gospel, listen to one of the many US gospel choirs on record – they usually have a piano in the background. (Even better, try walking into a gospel church on a Sunday.) Soul singer **ARETHA FRANKLIN** used piano early on, and in doing so she was reflecting her gospel background.

Starting from the late 1950s, the pianist **RAMSEY LEWIS** took the piano towards soul as well with his jazz trio's instrumental covers of pop hits. (There are various albums originally on Cadet or Argo; try also the Chess compilation *Percussion Discussion*).

Funk is a pretty debased and exhausted genre now, thanks to its use as a basis for endless pop and disco numbers, but you can recognise the halftime feel in the 1970s pop-rock piano style of **ELTON JOHN** ('Candle in the Wind', etc), Britain's answer to **LIBERACE**.

By contrast, **NICKY HOPKINS** was a consistently underrated rock pianist who backed many classic British groups in the '60s and '70s, including The Beatles (Lennon's *Imagine* album), the Stones ('Sympathy for the Devil'), and The Who, and produced albums of his own such as *No More Changes* (1975).

VIDEO MATERIAL

Seeing great pianists as well as hearing them can be an instructive and inspiring experience, even when they're no longer around. For a selection of great classical artists on video, try:

Art of the Piano: Greatest Pianists of the 20th Century (VA: 3984291993)

For jazz, you'll find a number of broad-based historical collections on video, but if you want to focus specifically on pianists, you might want to try some of the following.

Herbie Hancock – Jazz Channel Presents (IX0694BJUKV)
McCoy Tyner – At the Warsaw Jazz Jamboree (MMGV097)
McCoy Tyner – Cool Summer Jazz (QL0617)
Small Jazz Groups; Shearing, Basie, Calloway (SV6006)
Modern Jazz Quartet: 35th Anniversary Concert (MMGV075)

RECOMMENDED READING

If a book happens to be out of print, try your local library, or find a library that specialises in the performing arts, for example in your local arts centre or performing arts college. These are normally open to the public, sometimes subject to certain conditions.

We'd like to draw special attention to some of the books listed, indicated by one of the following symbols:

● Strongly recommended books.
○ Good general-introduction books.
■ Advanced books.

CLASSICAL TECHNIQUE AND INTERPRETATION

Seymour Bernstein *20 Lessons in Keyboard Choreography* (Seymour Bernstein Music) ■
Malwine Bree, Arthur Elson (translators) *The Leschetizky Method.* (Dover) ■
Donald Ferguson *Piano Interpretation* (Williams & Norgate)
Sidney Harrison *The Young Person's Guide to Playing the Piano* (Faber) ●
Joan Last *The Young Pianist* (OUP) ●
Lillie Philipp *Piano Technique: Tone, Touch, Phrasing and Dynamics* (Dover) ■
David Rowland (editor) *The Cambridge Companion to the Piano* (CUP) ○
Gyorgy Sandor *On Piano Playing: Motion, Sound and Expression* (Schirmer) ■
Bela Siki *Piano Repertoire: a Guide to Interpretation and Performance* (Schirmer)
Geoffrey Tankard *Pianoforte Diplomas and Degrees* (Elkin) ●
Harold Taylor *The Pianist's Talent: a New Approach to Piano Playing Based on the Principles of Alexander and Thiberge* (Kahn & Averill) ■
Kendall Taylor *Principles of Piano Technique and Interpretation* (Novello)

WRITINGS BY FAMOUS PERFORMERS

C.P.E. Bach *Essay on the True Art of Playing Keyboard Instruments* (Norton) ■
Leonard Bernstein *The Infinite Variety of Music* (Weidenfeld and Nicholson)
Alfred Brendel *Alfred Brendel on Music* (Robson)
James F. Cooke (editor) *Great Pianists on Piano Playing* (Dover)
Wilhelm Furtwängler *Notebooks, 1924-1954* (Quartet Books) ●
Walter Gieseking, Karl Leimer *Piano Technique* (Dover)
Glenn Gould *The Glenn Gould Reader* (Tim Page, editor) (Faber)
Louis Kentner *Piano* (*Yehudi Menuhin Music Guides*) (Kahn & Averill) ○
Josef Lhevinne *Basic Principles in Pianoforte Playing* (Dover)
Bruno Monsaingeon *Sviatoslav Richter: Notebooks and Conversations* (Faber)

Heinrich Neuhaus *The Art of Piano Playing*
(Kahn & Averill)
Artur Schnabel *My Life and Music* (Colin
Smythe)
Konrad Wolff *Schnabel's Interpretation of Piano
Music* (Faber)

HISTORY OF PIANISTIC PERFORMANCE
Bruno Monsaingeon *Sviatoslav Richter* (Faber)
Geoffrey Payzant *Glenn Gould, Music and
Mind* (Key Porter)
Harold C. Schonberg *The Great Pianists*
(Simon & Schuster) ○

THE INSTRUMENT: HISTORY, BUYING,
CONSTRUCTION, MAINTENANCE
David Crombie *Piano* (Balafon)
Cyril Ehrlich *The Piano, A History* (Clarendon)
Larry Fine *The Piano Book* (Brookside Press)
K.T. Kennedy *Piano Action Repairs and
Maintenance* (Kaye & Ward)

GENERAL MUSICIANSHIP AND
KEYBOARD SKILLS
Sol Berkowitz *Improvisation through Keyboard
Harmony* (Prentice-Hall)
Paul Hindemith *Elementary Training for
Musicians* (Schott)
Reginald Hunt *Harmony at the Keyboard* (OUP)
R.O. Morris *Figured Harmony at the Keyboard*
(OUP)
G.E. Wittlich, D.S. Martin *Tonal Harmony for
the Keyboard* (Schirmer)

JAZZ AND POPULAR MUSIC
Paul Berliner *Thinking in Jazz: The Infinite Art
of Improvisation* (University of Chicago Press)
Avril Dankworth *Jazz: An Introduction to its
Musical Basis* (Oxford University Press) ○
Robert L. Doerschuk *88 The Giants of Jazz
Piano* (Backbeat)
Simon Frith *The Sociology of Rock* Simon Frith
(Constable) ■
Simon Frith, Will Straw, John Street
(editors) *The Cambridge Companion to Pop and
Rock* (CUP) ○
André Hodeir *Jazz, Its Evolution and Essence*
(Da Capo) ●
J. Kember *The Jazz Piano Master: Jazz
Techniques through Pieces and Studies* (Faber)
Mark Levine *The Jazz Piano Book* (Sher Music
Co) ●
Mark Levine *The Jazz Theory Book* (Sher Music
Co) ●
Paul Oliver, Max Harrison, William Bolcom
The New Grove Gospel, Blues and Jazz
(Macmillan)
George Russell: *The Lydian Chromatic Concept
of Tonal Organisation* (Concept Publishing) ■
Keith Shadwick *Bill Evans. Everything Happens
to Me – A Musical Biography* (Backbeat)
David Sudnow *Ways of the Hand, a Rewritten
Account* (MIT) ■
Graham Vulliamy, Edward Lee (editors)
Popular Music, a Teacher's Guide (Routledge)

MUSIC THEORY AND HISTORY
H.K. Andrews, R.O. Morris *The Oxford
Harmony, Vols.1 & 2 (OUP)*
D.J. Grout, C.V. Palisca *A History of Western
Music* (Norton) ○
Dave Stewart *The Musician's Guide to Reading
and Writing Music* (Backbeat)
Eric Taylor *The AB Guide to Music Theory*
(Associated Board of the Royal Schools of
Music) ○

COMPOSITION
Vincent Persichetti *20th Century Harmony:
Creative Aspects and Practice* (Norton) ●
Walter Piston *Counterpoint* (Gollancz)
Walter Piston *Harmony* (Gollancz)
George Pratt *The Dynamics of Harmony,
Principles and Practice.* (OUP) ○
Arnold Schoenberg *Fundamentals of Musical
Composition* (Faber) ■
Arnold Schoenberg *Structural Functions of
Harmony* (Faber) ■

ANALYSIS
Jonathan Dunsby, Arnold Whittall *Music
Analysis in Theory and Practice* (Faber & Faber) ○
Allen Forte, Steven Gilbert *Introduction to
Schenkerian Analysis* (Norton) ■
Allen Forte *The Structure of Atonal Music* (Yale
University Press) ■
Fred Lerdahl, Ray Jackendoff *A Generative
Theory of Tonal Music* (MIT) ■

MODERN MUSIC
Theodor W. Adorno *Quasi una Fantasia*
(Verso) ■
Ferruccio Busoni *The Essence of Music and Other
Papers* (Dover) ●
Carl Dahlhaus *Schoenberg and the New Music*
(CUP) ■
Paul Griffiths *Modern Music & After* (OUP) ○
Olivier Messiaen *The Technique of My Musical
Language* (Leduc)
Harry Partch *Genesis of a Music* (Da Capo)
Arnold Schoenberg *Style and Idea* (Faber) ■
Arnold Schoenberg *Theory of Harmony* (Faber) ■
Anton Webern *The Path to the New Music*
(Universal Edition)
Arnold Whittall *Musical Composition in the
Twentieth Century* (OUP) ○

ETHNIC MUSIC
Elizabeth Axford *Traditional World Music
Influences in Contemporary Solo Piano Literature*
(Scarecrow) ○
John Blacking *Music, Culture and Experience*
(University of Chicago Press) ●
Alain Daniélou *The Ragas of Northern Indian
Music* (Munshiram Mansharlal)
Bebey Francis *African Music* (Lawrence Hill)
Nikhil Ghosh *Fundamentals of Raga and Tala*
(published by the author)
John Miller Chernoff *African Rhythm and
African Sensibility* (University of Chicago Press)
Amnon Shiloah *Music in the World of Islam*
(Scolar)

FREE IMPROVISATION
John Cage *Silence* (Wesleyan University Press)
Cornelius Cardew *Treatise Handbook* (Peters

Edition)
Roger Dean *Creative Improvisation: Jazz,
Contemporary Music and Beyond* (Open
University Press) ○

CONTEMPORARY PERFORMANCE
Mike Huxley, Noel Witts (editors) *The
Twentieth Century Performance Reader*
(Routledge)
Rudolf Laban *The Mastery of Movement*
(Northcote House) ●
Jane Milling, Graham Ley *Modern Theories of
Performance* (Palgrave) ○
T. Richards *At Work With Grotowski on
Physical Actions* (Routledge) ■
Richard Schechner *Performance Studies: An
Introduction* (Routledge)
L. Wolford, R. Schechner *The Grotowski
Sourcebook* (Routledge) ●

GENERAL
Wayne D. Bowman *Philosophical Perspectives on
Music* (OUP) ○
Carl Dahlhaus *Esthetics of Music* (CUP) ●
Eduard Hanslick *On the Musically Beautiful*
(Hackett)
Roman Ingarden *The Work of Music and The
Problem of Its Identity* (Macmillan) ■
Suzanne K. Langer *Philosophy in a New Key*
(Harvard University Press) ■
Aaron Ridley *Music, Value and the Passions*
(Cornell University Press) ●
Christopher Small *Music, Society, Education*
(Wesleyan University Press) ●
Ludwig Wittgenstein *Philosophical
Investigations* (Blackwell) ■

AUTHOR'S THANKS

This book would not have happened had I not been privileged to benefit from the patience and insight of my various teachers in past years, especially Alicia Chislett, Harold East and Witold Szalonek.

I owe a large debt of thanks to friends whose assistance made the task of writing this book an easier one: in particular Carl Erik Kühl, who taught me the importance of clarity and simplicity in thought; and David Braid, whose help and advice made the book happen in more ways than one.

I would especially like to thank my parents, who helped me in countless ways at every step of the process, especially my mother, whose generous advice has led me to hope that a small amount of her own wisdom and experience as a piano teacher may have been captured here. If any single person really deserves credit for this book, it has to be my wife Agnieszka, whose uniquely imaginative way of understanding the world showed me what is worthwhile not just in music but in life. I would also like to thank those involved in the editing and production of the book.

This book is dedicated to my parents, Donald and Christel Humphries.

ABOUT THE AUTHOR

Carl Humphries was born in London in 1966. He studied piano and composition in London, Berlin and Turin, and pursued theoretical studies at the University of Cambridge. He works as a pianist, teacher and composer, specialising in the relationship between theory and performance. His lectures and workshops are in demand at universities and music conservatoires in Europe and in the United States, and he has performed at a number of major classical and jazz venues, as well as for television. He has written extensively on music education, contemporary music, and the philosophy of music.

MUSIC PERMISSIONS

Copyright material reproduced with thanks to the following.
'Change Of Time' (Bartók) from Book Five of *Mikrokosmos*. Boosey & Hawkes Music Publishers Ltd.
'In A Sentimental Mood' (Ellington/Mills/Kurtz), Boosey & Hawkes Music Publishers Ltd. ©1935 by EMI Music Inc (publisher) and Warner Bros Publications US Inc (print). Sole agent for the British Commonwealth (excluding Canada), the continent of Europe including Scandinavian territories, and South Africa: Lafleur Music Ltd. ©1940 by Hawkes & Son (London) Ltd. Definitive corrected edition ©1987 by Hawkes & sons (london) Ltd. Permission also granted for reproduction in Canada (IMP) and the United States (Hal Leonard).
'Take Five' (Desmond) Valentine Music Group.

ILLUSTRATIONS

Unless specified here, the photographs used in the book come from the Balafon Image Bank and were taken by Miki Slingsby, Nigel Bradley, or Will Taylor. The following key identifies the two other picture sources – **LC** Lebrecht Collection or **RF** Redferns – with a page number and caption identifier followed by the credit. Some illustrations were made for the book by Rob McCaig, credited as **RM**.

6 Playing the harpsichord, Royal Academy of Music/**LC**. 12 Beethoven's piano, **LC**. 14 Clara Schumann, **LC**; Jules Massenet, **LC**. 17 Steinway celebration, **LC**. 24 Scott Joplin stamp, **LC**; Jelly Roll Morton, **LC**. 25 Artur Schnabel, **LC**. 26 Busoni, **LC**; Gilels, S. Lauterwasser/**LC**. 27 Gould, Don Hunstein (Sony), **LC**. 28 Lewis, **LC**. 29 Richard, **LC**. 30 Powell, **LC**; Evans, **LC**. 31 Hancock, **LC**; Zimerman, S. Lauterwasser/**LC**. 32 Brendel Mike Evans/**LC**. 33 Perahia, Jim Four/**LC**; MacGregor, **LC**. 45 Rubinstein, **LC**. 56 Henry VIII, **RM**. 58 Purcell, **RM**. 72 Mozart, **RM**. 99 Schenker, **RM**. 105 Morris dancer, **RM**. 116 J.S.Bach, **RM**. 132 Monk, **RM**. 140 Haydn, **RM**. 153 Satie, **RM**. 156 C.P.E.Bach, **RM**. 163 Hopkins, Fin Costello/**RF**. 176 Clementi, **RM**. 190 Brahms, **RM**. 192 Schubert, **RM**. 193 Chopin, **RM**. 209 Gershwin, **RM**. 219 Beethoven, **RM**. 232 Schoenberg, **RM**. 243 Palmeiri, Simon Ritter/**RF**. 255 Lewis, David Redfern/**RF**.

ON THE CD

You will find the accompanying CD for this book in the pocket opposite. The performances by Carl Humphries on a Steinway piano were recorded in July 2002 by John Taylor at Potton Hall, Dunwich, Suffolk, England.

The following list indicates track number, exercise number ("Ex") where relevant, and the page number(s) where the music for the exercise or piece appears in the book.

1. Ex 1.6. p46.
2. Ex 1.7. p47.
3. Ex 1.8. p48.
4. Ex 1.9. p48.
5. Ex 1.10. p49.
6. Ex 1.11. p49.
7. Ex 1.12. p50.
8. Ex 1.13. p50.
9. Ex 1.14. p51.
10. Ex 2.2, *Greensleeves*. p56.
11. Ex 2.3, Purcell *Minuet in Aminor*. p58.
12. Ex 2.4, J.S.Bach *Minuet in G*. p59.
13. Ex 2.6, *Song of the Lonely Beetle*. p60.
14. Ex 3.1, Purcell *Air in Dminor*. p69.
15. Ex 3.2, *Gnome Dance*. p70.
16. Ex 3.3, Mozart *Minuet*. p71.
17. Ex 3.4, Haydn *Allegretto*. p72.
18. Ex 3.5, *Somersaults*. p73.
19. Ex 4.1, Clementi *Un Poco Adagio*. p75.
20. Ex 4.2, Bach *Musette in D*. p76.
21. Ex 4.5, Schumann *Humming Song*. p78.
22. Ex 5.3, *Wheelbarrow Man*. p84.
23. Ex 5.4, Beethoven *Für Elise*. p86.
24. Ex 7.6, *Clowns*. p104.
25. Ex 7.7, *Country Gardens*. p105.
26. Ex 8.7, Bach *Prelude in C*. p114.
27. Ex 8.10, Burgmüller *Ballade*. p119.
28. Ex 10.1, Schumann *First Loss*. p135.
29. Ex 10.2, Heller *Avalanche*. p137.
30. Ex 10.3, repeated staccato note study. p139.
31. Ex 10.5, Haydn *Allegro in G*. p141.
32. Ex 11.3, Haydn theme *Sonata in A*. p152.
33. Ex 11.5, Satie *Gymnopédie No.1*. p154-5.
34. Ex 11.6, C.P.E.Bach *Solfeggio*. p157.
35/36. Rock ballad/rock shuffle. p165.
37. Country shuffle. p165.
38. Orleans. p166.
39. Cajun. p166.
40. Straight-eight boogie. p166.
41. Get down rock. p166.
42. Country. p166.
43. R&B. p166.
44. Gospel waltz. p167.
45. Straightahead gospel. p167.
46. Funk. p167.
47. *Lullaby* lead sheet. p170.
48. *Lullaby* embellished arrangement. p172.
49. Ex 13.1, Clementi. p177-9.
50. Ex 13.3, Mozart *Sonata in C*. p182-5.
51. Ex 14.1, Brahms *Waltz in Dminor*. p191.
52. Ex 14.2, Schubert *Impromptu in Aflat*. p192.
53. Ex 14.3, Chopin *Prelude in Eminor*. p194.
54. Ex 16.1, J.S.Bach *Invention in C*. p213-4.
55. Ex 16.2, *The Entertainer*. p216-7.
56. Ex 16.3, octave study Csharp minor. p218.
57. Ex 16.4, Beethoven *Scherzo in C*. p220.
58. Ex 16.5, *Pathétique* slow movt. p221-2.
59. Ex 16.6, Beethoven *Bagatelle in Bflat*. p223.
60. Ex 17.1, Debussy *The Little Negro*. p227-8.
61. Ex 17.2, Schoenberg Opus 19 No.6. p231.
62. Ex 17.3, Bartok *Change Of Time*. p234.
63. Ex 10.2, Heller *Avalanche*. p137.
64. Salsa montuno. p240.
65. *Sentimental Mood*, Ellington. p245.
66. *Sentimental Mood*, Evans. p245.
67. Desmond *Take Five*. p256-7.
68. Two-hand linear groove. p253.
69. Drum chart as piano dance groove. p254.

"To play this music, you have to love music. So if you love music, then it follows you love to listen to it – which makes the ear the most essential instrument in the world." Duke Ellington, 1973